Travel Discount Coupon

This coupon entitle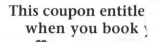
when you book y

D0447083

TRAVEL
RESERVA...

Hotels ♦ Airlines ♦ Car Rentals ♦ Cruises
All Your Travel Needs

Here's what you get: *

♦ A discount of $50 USD on a booking of $1,000** or more for two or more people!

♦ A discount of $25 USD on a booking of $500** or more for one person!

♦ Free membership for three years, and 1,000 free miles on enrollment in the unique Travel Network Miles-to-Go® frequent-traveler program. Earn one mile for every dollar spent through the program. Redeem miles for free hotel stays starting at 5,000 miles. Earn free roundtrip airline tickets starting at 25,000 miles.

♦ Personal help in planning your own, customized trip.

♦ Fast, confirmed reservations at any property recommended in this guide, subject to availability.***

♦ Special discounts on bookings in the U.S. and around the world.

♦ Low-cost visa and passport service.

♦ Reduced-rate cruise packages and special car rental programs worldwide.

> Visit our website at http://www.travelnetwork.com/Frommer or call us globally at 201-567-8500, ext. 55. In the U.S., call toll-free at 1-888-940-5000, or fax 201-567-1838. In Canada, call at 1-905-707-7222, or fax 905-707-8108. In Asia, call 60-3-7191044, or fax 60-3-7185415.

* To qualify for these travel discounts, at least a portion of your trip must include destinations covered in this guide. No more than one coupon discount may be used in any 12-month period, for destinations covered in this guide. Cannot be combined with any other discount or promotion.

**These are U.S. dollars spent on commissionable bookings.

***A $10 USD fee, plus fax and/or phone charges, will be added to the cost of bookings at each hotel not linked to the reservation service. Customers must approve these fees in advance. If only hotels of this kind are booked, the traveler(s) must also purchase roundtrip air tickets from Travel Network for the trip.

Valid until December 31, 1998. Terms and conditions of the Miles-to-Go® program are available on request by calling 201-567-8500, ext 55.

BPA234

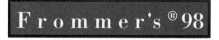

PARIS
FROM $70 A DAY

The Ultimate Guide to Comfortable Low-cost Travel

by Jeanne Oliver

Macmillan • USA

ABOUT THE AUTHOR

Jeanne Oliver practiced law for 10 years in New York City before her love of French culture and cuisine prompted her to relocate to Paris. She worked in the tourist industry for several years before becoming a freelance writer, specializing in France and Europe for various magazines and guidebooks.

MACMILLAN TRAVEL

A Simon & Schuster Macmillan Company
1633 Broadway
New York, NY 10019

Find us online at **www.frommers.com**
or on America Online at Keyword: **Frommers**

ISBN 0-02-861869-6
ISSN 1055-5315

Editor: Matt Hannafin
Production Editor: Carol Sheehan
Design by Michele Laseau
Digital Cartography by Jim Moore, Roberta Stockwell, and Ortelius Design

SPECIAL SALES

Bulk purchases (10+ copies) of Frommer's and selected Macmillan travel guides are available to corporations, organizations, mail-order catalogs, institutions, and charities at special discounts, and can be customized to suit individual needs. For more information write to: Special Sales, Macmillan General Reference, 1633 Broadway, New York, NY 10019.

Manufactured in the United States of America

Contents

List of Maps

ACKNOWLEDGMENTS

The author wishes to thank Alain Fortin and Mona Fritsche for their advice on food, wine, and politics in Paris and Philippe Touzet for his historical knowledge. She also wishes to thank Mona Ediers and Leslie Alan Horvitz for their invaluable support and encouragement during the course of this project.

INVITATION TO THE READERS

In researching this book, we discovered many wonderful places—hotels, restaurants, shops, and more. We're sure you'll find others. Please tell us about them, so we can share the information with your fellow travelers in upcoming editions. If you were disappointed with a recommendation, we'd love to know that, too. Please write to:

Frommer's Paris from $70 a Day '98
Macmillan Travel
1633 Broadway
New York, NY 10019

AN ADDITIONAL NOTE

Please be advised that travel information is subject to change at any time—and this is especially true of prices. We therefore suggest that you write or call ahead for confirmation when making your travel plans. The authors, editors, and publisher cannot be held responsible for the experiences of readers while traveling. Your safety is important to us, however, so we encourage you to stay alert and be aware of your surroundings. Keep a close eye on cameras, purses, and wallets, all favorite targets of thieves and pickpockets.

WHAT THE SYMBOLS MEAN

✪ Frommer's Favorites

Our favorite places and experiences—outstanding for quality, value, or both.

The following abbreviations are used for credit cards:

AE	American Express	EURO	Eurocard
CB	Carte Blanche	MC	MasterCard
DC	Diners Club	V	Visa
DISC	Discover		

FIND FROMMER'S ONLINE

Arthur Frommer's Outspoken Encyclopedia of Travel (www.frommers.com) offers more than 6,000 pages of up-to-the-minute travel information—including the latest bargains and candid, personal articles updated daily by Arthur Frommer himself. No other Web site offers such comprehensive and timely coverage of the world of travel.

Paris at a Glance

av. de Clichy

17e Arr.

Cimetière du
Montmartre

place de
Clichy

Parc
Monceau

MONTMARTRE

av de la
Grande Armée

Gare
St-Lazare

av Foch

Arc de
Triomphe

Grands Boulevards

av des Champs-Elysées

← Bois de
Boulogne

8e Arr.

av Victor Hugo

Grand
Palais

Petit
Palais

place
de la
Concorde

rue de Rivoli

place du
Trocadéro

Musée d'Art
Moderne

Jardin des
Tuileries

Kléber

Palais de
Chaillot

Musée
d'Orsay

Tour
Eiffel

PASSY

St-Germain-
des-Prés

16e Arr.

Champ de Mars
Ecole
Militaire

Hôtel
des
Invalides

bd.
St-Germain

Seine

ST-GERMAIN-
DES-PRES

pont de Grenelle

6e Arr.

Statue de Liberté

av. de Breteuil

7e Arr.

Jardin
du
Luxembourg

rue de la
Convention

15e Arr.

Gare
Montparnasse

place de
Breteuil

bd. Montparnasse

rue de Vaugirard

14e Arr.

MONTPARNASSE

bd. Raspail

Général
Leclerc

av. du
Maine

Cimetière
du Montparnasse

place
Denfert-
Rochereau

bd. Victor

rue d'Alesia

3-0160

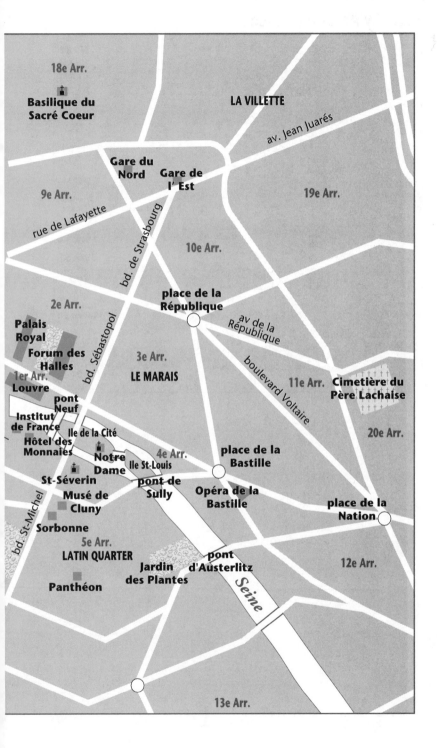

Paris by Arrondissement

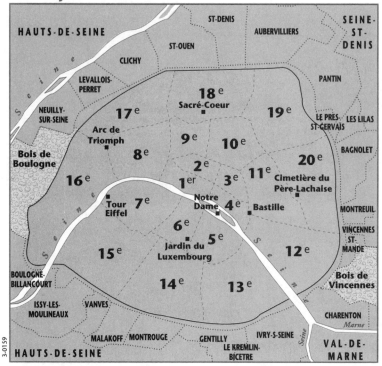

HAUTS-DE-SEINE

SEINE-
ST-
DENIS

ST-DENIS

AUBERVILLIERS

ST-OUEN

CLICHY

PANTIN

LEVALLOIS-
PERRET

NEUILLY-
SUR-SEINE

18e
Sacré-Coeur

17e

19e

LE PRES-
ST-GERVAIS

LES LILAS

Arc de
Triomph

9e

10e

BAGNOLET

Bois de
Boulogne

8e

20e

2e

16e

1er

3e

11e

Cimetière du
Père-Lachaise

MONTREUIL

Tour
Eiffel

7e

Notre
Dame

4e

Bastille

VINCENNES
ST-
MANDE

6e

5e

12e

15e

Jardin du
Luxembourg

Bois de
Vincennes

BOULOGNE-
BILLANCOURT

14e

13e

ISSY-LES-
MOULINEAUX

VANVES

CHARENTON

Marne

MALAKOFF

MONTROUGE

GENTILLY

LE KREMLIN-
BICETRE

IVRY-S-SEINE

VAL-DE-
MARNE

HAUTS-DE-SEINE

3-0159

Introducing Paris 1

To measure the importance of Paris, try to imagine a world where Paris did not exist. Imagine a world without the medieval Parisians that first built soaring Gothic cathedrals. Imagine a cultural life that did not include the wit of Voltaire, the novels of Victor Hugo, Sartre's existentialism, or the impressionists—Monet, Renoir, Manet, and Pissarro—who rubbed shoulders in the music halls of Montmartre. What other city would have nurtured such a diverse group of foreigners as Chopin, Picasso, Oscar Wilde, Josephine Baker, Ernest Hemingway, Bud Powell, and James Baldwin?

The splendor of Paris's intellectual and artistic traditions is echoed in a cityscape that celebrates greatness of spirit. There is glory in the towering monuments that recall the ages of kings and emperors, of battles and revolutions. A sense of grandeur infuses sweeping vistas such as the Eiffel Tower from Trocadéro, or the noble promenade that begins in the courtyard of the Louvre and marches up the Champs-Elysées through the Arc de Triomphe.

But the city's real originality is in the cunning attention to detail that balances the majestic proportions. The 19th-century boulevards that open the city to an expanse of light and sky are composed of beautifully crafted buildings and wrap around intimate neighborhoods of pleasing shapes and angles. Wander the Marais, for example, and your eye will be caught at every glance. A massive burnished door opens into an elegantly proportioned courtyard. You glance up at a frieze under a window and notice the intricate pattern of a wrought iron balcony. Each building is unique; each street has a personality.

The streets and boulevards and panoramas of Paris create a civilized urban environment within which daily life flourishes with grace and sensuality. Visit a local street market and catch the briny aroma of fresh mussels or the pungency of roasting chicken. Bring a fresh baguette and some cheese to a neatly manicured park. You'll notice flower beds arranged with an attention to color and harmony that recalls the paintings of Monet. Sample the creations of a fine bistro cook or local pastry maker and you'll see that Parisians bring as much creative genius to the art of living as they do any other lofty endeavor.

Paul Valéry called Paris the "most personal" of metropolises. For some visitors, Paris is the city of legendary museums and exquisitely prepared food. And it's true that the cuisine and artistic treasures of

Paris are unrivaled. Others seek the "gai Paree" of music halls and sumptuous art nouveau decor, the Paris captured in the songs of Edith Piaf and the paintings of Toulouse-Lautrec. And that Paris, too, is here.

For me, Paris is an inexhaustible source of discovery. Even a familiar walk yields surprises—an unexpected passage that veers off the main road, an unusual facade I'd never noticed before, a cluster of houses around a square that contains some half-forgotten history from centuries past. And sometimes I feel a glimmer of Victor Hugo's exaltation when he wrote: "Paris is a sum total; the ceiling of the human race. The prodigious city is an epitome of dead and living manners and customs. To observe Paris is to review the whole course of history; filling the gaps with sky and stars."

1 Frommer's Favorite Affordable Experiences

- **An Evening Cruise on the Seine.** Touristy? Yes, but it doesn't matter. "Cities, like cats, reveal themselves at night," said the British poet Rupert Brooke, and the city of light is no exception. The monuments that are impressive by day are lit with theatrical flair at night and Paris becomes a glittering light show. Gliding down the river under softly glowing bridges with the towers of Notre Dame set against a night sky and the Eiffel Tower transformed into a golden web of light is a purely Parisian and purely magical experience.

- **A Day at the Musée d'Orsay.** Is it heresy to place the Musée d'Orsay ahead of, you know, that *other* great museum? The Orsay museum is less overwhelming than the Louvre, so you probably won't leave feeling disoriented and winded, and it holds the world's most comprehensive collection of impressionist art, in addition to preimpressionists, postimpressionists, and neoimpressionists. See the sculptures on the ground floor and then head upstairs to have a look at a spectacular collection of Van Goghs, some little-known Gauguins, and a roomful of Toulouse-Lautrec pastels. (For more information, see chapter 6.)

- **A Weekend Afternoon in the Jardin du Luxembourg.** If you really want to observe the fine-grained bourgeois glory of Parisian life, station yourself in an iron chair or on a bench some sunny afternoon here. Neatly dressed and perfectly mannered Parisians of all ages enjoy a great range of activities from tennis to pony rides and even bee-keeping—the city of Paris offers bee-keeping classes in the southwest corner of the gardens. Don't miss the espaliered orchards, where fruit is carefully cultivated for the table of the French Senate and also for local charities. (For more information, see chapter 6.)

- **A Walk Through the Marais.** The old Marais combines sprawling manors built by 17th-century nobility with narrow streets of fairy-tale quaintness. The new Marais attracts artists, artisans, and arty types who are bringing their own unique and sometimes whimsical style to this historic district. Stroll down **rue des Rosiers** in the heart of the old Jewish quarter, browse the antiques shops at **Village St-Paul,** and take a break in the tranquil **place des Vosges.** The main streets are lively with bars and cafes at night while the side streets are so quiet you can hear your footsteps echo in the dark. (For more information, see chapter 6.)

- **Tomb-Hopping in Pére Lachaise.** From Abelard and Héloïse to Jim Morrison, this lush necropolis is a who's who of famous Parisians, and there's no wrong season or weather to visit. The bare trees of winter lend it a haunting quality; on rainy days the cemetery is brooding and melancholy; on a summer day it's the ideal place for a contemplative stroll. Best day to visit? All Saints' Day, of course, when the tombs are festooned with flowers. (For more information, see chapter 6.)

- **Food Shopping, Parisian Style.** Shopping in a neighborhood market is where you can observe the French indulging their passion for meat, fruit, fish, fowl, pâté, cheese, sausage, rabbit, and unusual animal parts: brains, kidneys, veal's head, tongue, and tripe. The merchants know their products and are happy to offer advice and even a few cooking tips to their clientele. The markets on **rue Mouffetard** and **rue de Buci** are the best known, but the market on **rue Montorgeuil** has an equally tempting array of produce and is less touristy.

- **Touring the Arcades.** Fortunately, not all of Paris's architectural treasures are outdoors. The iron- and glass-covered passages that weave through the 2e arrondissement were designed to shelter 19th-century shopaholics from nasty Parisian weather. Whether you're looking for stamps, old books, discount clothing, designer boutiques, or nothing in particular, exploring these picturesque passages is a delightful way to while away an afternoon. (For more information, see chapter 6.)

- **Bird-Watching on the quai de la Mégisserie.** Fat pheasants, fluffy white pigeons, mandarin ducks, and cackling hens are part of the feather brigade lined up in cages along the sidewalk. Inside the pet shops are more exotic birds keeping company with kittens, puppies, hamsters, turtles, and fish. The menagerie shares sidewalk space with tables of flowers and seeds while a screen of trees and giant potted plants blots out the traffic along the quai. Think of it as Amazon on the Seine.

- **Watching the Sunset from the Pont-des-Arts Bridge.** It's hard to go wrong with a sunset, but here you can ponder the meaning of it all from Paris's only footbridge across the Seine. Behind you are the spires of Notre-Dame and ahead is the river and its bridges stretching toward the setting sun. It just might be the most romantic sight in Paris.

- **Paris in August.** Shunned by tourists, abandoned by its residents, the city seems to heave a giant sigh of relief. The streets are miraculously free of traffic jams and the air begins to smell like air again. Nightlife withers but the parks and gardens are in full bloom. Although many restaurants close, enough remain open to give you a healthy sampling of the local diet. And there are always the museums. And the banks of the Seine. And old neighborhoods to explore. Without the bustle, what's left is beauty, art, and the realization that in this great metropolis not one bit of serious work is being done.

- **Dinner at Bofingers.** A landmark brasserie with a splendid belle epoque interior and excellent food could get away with being snooty and overpriced, but at Bofingers every night is opening night. Waiters in long white aprons go out of their way to make you feel at home—that is, how you'd feel if your home happened to include a gleaming brass and wood dining room under a stained-glass ceiling. In true brasserie style, the mood is festive and relaxed without losing one ounce of glamour. (For more information, see chapter 5.)

- **Strolling Along the Canal Saint-Martin.** Immortalized in the Marcel Carné film *Hôtel du Nord,* the canal runs through east Paris, an area rarely visited by tourists. Pity. Along the tree-lined promenades you'll find elderly men dozing in the sun as mothers watch their toddlers play in one of the little kiddie parks along the canal. Footbridges connect the promenades on either side of the water and every so often the quiet is interrupted by a boat passing through the locks on its way to or from the Seine. The whole scene evokes the low-key tranquility of prewar working-class Paris.

- **Dancing in the Streets.** Parisians can be an industrious lot, but on June 21, the day of the summer solstice, everyone pours into the streets to celebrate the Festival de la Musique. Whether banging, strumming, warbling, tinkling, wailing, or pounding, musicians are everywhere. Although the quality varies from don't-give-up-your-day-job to top-rung artists, it's exhilarating just to join the parties in progress in every park, garden, and square.

2 Paris Today

As the new millennium approaches, a huge panel on the Eiffel Tower counts down each day to the year 2000. The symbolism is perfect. The monument most closely identified with Paris is facing down a new age just as the city itself is poised between a glorious past and an uncertain future.

Of course, it is Paris of yesteryear that attracts 20 million tourists each year from all corners of the globe. The medieval labyrinth of streets winding through the Latin Quarter or Montmartre evokes an age when life was smaller, more intimate—more manageable, somehow. Spend a lazy afternoon at an outdoor cafe or watch old men play *boules* in a park and you are participating in rituals of public life that have remained unchanged for centuries.

But Paris is not, and never has been, content to rest on its laurels. Like a palimpsest in which each generation has written its story over that of the preceding generation, the face of Paris is continually changing. Monuments such as the Arab Institute in the Latin Quarter, the Pompidou Center in Beaubourg, the Opera at the Bastille, and the Bibliothèque National in southeast Paris have completely transformed old neighborhoods. The looming skyscrapers of La Defense have created a futuristic office world in the west of Paris while the complex of La Villette is a futuristic science world in the city's northeast corner. The boldness and imagination of these hugely expensive projects reflects the determination of French people to keep their capital in the forefront of the modern world.

Despite the grandiose projects, there is no concealing the fact that the center of the world's attention has shifted westward across the Atlantic. As Parisians read the latest American best-seller or watch the latest Hollywood blockbuster, there is naturally a fear that Paris's best days are past. Whether or not the city exerts its influence in the future as brilliantly as it did in the past remains to be seen. But a city that has survived war, revolution, occupation, and political disarray has demonstrated a strength and resiliency that should sustain it well into the 21st century.

3 History 101

Dateline

- **3rd century B.C.** The Parisii settle around the area that is now Paris.
- **53 B.C.** Julius Caesar mentions Paris in De Bello Gallico.
- **A.D. 250** Christianity introduced by St. Denis.
- **360** Julian the Apostate proclaimed emperor of Rome; Lutetia is renamed Paris and becomes the imperial capital.

continues

FROM ROMAN LUTETIA TO MEDIEVAL PARIS   In the beginning there was the river. And an island in the river.

Paris began on the Ile de la Cité, where Notre-Dame stands today and where you can locate Kilometer 0 of the French road and highway system in the place du Parvis Notre-Dame in front of the cathedral.

The first historical mention of what is now Paris appeared in 53 B.C. in Julius Caesar's *De Bello Gallico,* when it was the capital of the Parisii, a Celtic tribe that was conquered by the Romans. The Romans established a settlement at the site called Lutetia (Lutèce in the French version), a name meaning "habitation surrounded by water." The city's birth by the river is still commemorated in its coat of arms, a boat with the inscription *"Fluctuat Nec Mergitur"* ("It Floats and Does Not Sink"), which refers both to Paris's fluvial origins and to its less than tranquil history. The public baths at the Hôtel de Cluny and the Arènes de Lutèce are the best-preserved remnants of Roman Paris.

Christianity was introduced around A.D. 250 by St. Denis, the first bishop of Paris and the city's most famous martyr, who, after his beheading on the mont de Mercure, is reputed to have picked up his head and miraculously walked 4 miles. The mont was renamed mont des Martyrs and subsequently over the years became Montmartre. A century later, in another miracle, the city was spared a visit by Attila and his Huns thanks to the miraculous intervention of St. Geneviève; she later became Paris's patron saint.

In 508, Clovis, king of the Franks, chose Paris as his capital, but around 786, the Carolingian dynasty, whose roots were closer to the Rhine in the east, abandoned Paris in favor of Aix-la-Chapelle and left it unprotected against a series of Viking (Norman) attacks. In 885 and 886, Eudes, Comte de Paris, defended the city against the invaders, and his victory led to the rise of a new Capetian dynasty; his grand-nephew, Hugh Capet, was proclaimed king of France in 987, and the Capetians ruled over the Ile-de-France region until 1328.

Once again, Paris was turned into a capital city. And what a dynamic city it became! Two Gothic masterpieces, Notre-Dame and the Sainte-Chapelle, were built on the Ile de la Cité, and across the river on the Left Bank, one of Europe's first universities developed: the Sorbonne. The University of Paris was officially founded in 1215, and Thomas Aquinas was among its early professors. Scholars and students came from all over the continent to what was then the largest city in the Christian world—as they still do today. Latin was their *lingua franca,* hence the name Latin Quarter.

The city's reputation as a leading theological center was enhanced by the major role that France played in the Crusades, a role personified by St. Louis (Louis IX, 1226–70), who built the awesome Sainte-Chapelle to house such treasures from the Holy Land as the Crown of Thorns. His successors Philip III and Philip IV further strengthened the monarchy, but the rest of the 14th century was consumed by the Hundred Years' War, which

- 508 Clovis, king of the Franks, chooses Paris as his capital.
- 786 Carolingians move their capital to Aix-la-Chapelle.
- 800 Charlemagne crowned Holy Roman Emperor.
- 885–86 Viking invasions; Comte Eudes defends Paris.
- 987 Eudes's grand-nephew, Hugues Capet, proclaimed king.
- 1066 William the Conqueror invades England.
- 1140 St. Denis, the first Gothic cathedral, is built just north of Paris.
- 1163 Construction of Notre-Dame begins.
- 1215 The University of Paris is founded.
- 1357 Etienne Marcel's revolt.
- 1420 English occupy Paris.
- 1431 English burn Joan of Arc at the stake in Rouen.
- 1436 End of English occupation.
- 1515–47 Reign of François I.
- 1530 Foundation of the Collège de France.
- 1562 Start of the Wars of Religion.
- 1572 St. Bartholomew's Day Massacre.
- 1594 Henri IV converts to Catholicism.
- 1598 Edict of Nantes.
- 1604 The Pont Neuf completed.
- 1605 The place des Vosges built.
- 1610 Henri IV assassinated.
- 1635 Richelieu founds Académie Française.
- 1643–1715 Reign of Louis XIV.
- 1789 The storming of the Bastille and the beginning of the French Revolution.
- 1790 The Festival of the Federation.
- 1793 Louis XVI and Marie Antoinette guillotined. The Louvre becomes a public museum.

continues

- **1794** Robespierre guillotined.
- **1799** Napoléon enters Paris.
- **1804** Napoléon crowns himself emperor.
- **1815** Napoléon's defeat at Waterloo. The Bourbons are restored to the throne of France.
- **1830** Louis-Philippe replaces Charles X.
- **1832** A cholera epidemic kills 19,000 people.
- **1848** Revolution. Louis Napoléon elected "prince-president." The Second Republic proclaimed.
- **1852** Louis Napoléon proclaimed Emperor Napoléon III.
- **1863** The revolutionary impressionist exhibit at the Salon des Refusés.
- **1870–71** The Franco-Prussian War.
- **1870** The Third Republic proclaimed.
- **1871** The Paris Commune.
- **1875** Construction of the Opéra Garnier completed.
- **1885** Death of Victor Hugo.
- **1889** Exposition Universelle held in Paris; the Eiffel Tower erected.
- **1900** First Métro line opens.
- **1914–18** World War I.
- **1920** The Unknown Soldier is buried under the Arc de Triomphe.
- **1929** Construction of the Maginot line.
- **1940** Germany invades France and occupies Paris.
- **1944** Normandy landings; Paris liberated.
- **1946–54** War in Indochina.
- **1958** The Fifth Republic proclaimed; Charles de Gaulle elected president.
- **1960** Most of France's African colonies gain independence.

continues

lasted from 1337 to 1453. The English and their Burgundian allies occupied Paris from 1420 to 1436, and Henry had himself crowned in Notre-Dame as Henry VI, king of England and France. After liberating Orléans, Joan of Arc tried to free Paris and was wounded in the thigh (this was the only episode of her life connecting her with Paris). Not until 1453 were the English finally driven out of France. Also during this dark period, the city's first commune was declared by Merchant Provost Etienne Marcel in 1358.

PARIS IN THE 16TH CENTURY   After the chaos of the Hundred Years' War, the consolidation of the monarchy's power resumed most dramatically under François I. He established his official residence in Paris, tearing down the old medieval Louvre and replacing it with a magnificent palace. Under François, France's international prestige grew: Cartier and Verrazano explored the New World for the French king; the Collège de France, with its humanistic interest in diverse languages and the sciences, was founded in 1530 to rival the conservative Sorbonne. Politically, François I laid the foundation for the rise of an absolute monarchy, a concept that would reach its zenith with Louis XIV more than a century later.

The period of stability, though, did not last long. From 1562 to 1598 the Wars of Religion tore Paris asunder. The St. Bartholomew's Day Massacre in 1572 saw Paris awash in blood as thousands of Protestants were killed; on the Day of the Barricades in 1588, Henri III was forced to flee. Henri of Navarre, the legal heir of Henri III and a Protestant, laid siege to the city. He was opposed by the Catholic League, led by the Guise family, who terrorized the city. Henri defeated the league but was forced to convert to Catholicism before being allowed to enter Paris on March 22, 1594, when he was rumored to have said *"Paris bien vaut une messe"* ("Paris is well worth a mass").

One of France's most beloved kings, Henri IV succeeded in restoring France's prosperity and encouraging greater religious tolerance, and also bestowed many gifts upon Paris. Today, his statue can be seen standing beside the Pont Neuf, the city's oldest bridge, which was completed during his reign in 1604. He and his minister, the duc de Sully, were also responsible for building the place Royale (now the place des Vosges), which became the cornerstone of the later development of the Marais as an aristocratic quarter in the 17th century. He also laid out the place Dauphine, built the quai d'Horloge, and enlarged the Cour Carrée at the Louvre to four times its previous size, adding the Grande Galerie and the Pavillon Henri IV, which housed the Galerie d'Apollon. The Edict of Nantes, which he issued in 1598, protected the religious rights of the Protestants. For this act and others Henri IV was assassinated by a Catholic fanatic in 1610.

FROM LOUIS XIII TO LOUIS XVI   Louis XIII succeeded to the throne, and during his reign the expansion and beautification of Paris continued. He joined two islands in the river, fashioning them into the Ile St-Louis. Marie de Medici, Henri IV's widow queen, built the Luxembourg Palace, inspired by the architecture of her native Tuscany; also, to the west of the Tuileries Palace, she laid out the cours la Reine, a fashionable carriageway. Louis XIII's brilliant minister, Cardinal Richelieu, founded the Académie Française (still so influential in French cultural life even today) and built the Palais Cardinal (later Palais Royal) and the Jardin des Plantes. Richelieu was followed by the equally brilliant Jules Mazarin, who endowed the Collège Mazarin in the Hôtel de L'Institut, home today of the Académie Française. His own palace in the 2e arrondissement occupied the future site of the Bibliothèque Nationale.

Under Louis XIV, the Sun King who ruled for 72 years, the centralization of power under the monarchy reached its zenith. Although Louis XIV shunned Paris, establishing his court at Versailles, he contributed much to the city's splendor. He added the magnificent colonnade to the Louvre, completed the Tuileries Palace, and laid out the Grands Boulevards, the place Vendôme, and the place des Victoires. He also built the Hôtel des Invalides for sick soldiers, the Observatory, the Gobelins factory, and the pont Royal. His desertion of Paris, though, alienated the citizenry and prepared the ground for the ideas that kindled the French Revolution.

The many wars that Louis XIV fought weakened France's financial strength, and the trend continued during the reigns of Louis XV (1715–74) and Louis XVI (1774–92), although it was not always apparent. Louis XV laid out the grandiose place Louis XV (later place de la Concorde), created the rue Royale, and began the Madeleine church. He also erected such grand edifices as the Ecole Militaire (1751), the Champs-de-Mars, and the church of Ste-Geneviève (now the Panthéon). On the Right Bank, people flocked to the gardens of the Palais Royal and to its new galleries, which had been added in 1761 and housed all kinds of entertainments including cafes, shops, and a waxworks. In the 1780s, such theaters as the Comédie Italienne, the Odéon, and the Comédie Française thrived, and literary clubs and cafes were also popular. In these literary clubs and cafes, the revolutionary spirit grew.

During the two great reigns of Louis XIV and Louis XV, Paris dominated the Western world, nourishing some of Europe's greatest architects and intellectuals—the

- **1962** Algeria becomes independent.
- **1968** Strikes and student demonstrations. De Gaulle resigns.
- **1969** The old central markets at Les Halles transferred to Rungis.
- **1970** The RER (Réseau Express Régional) inaugurated.
- **1977** The Centre Pompidou inaugurated.
- **1981** François Mitterrand elected president.
- **1989** Bicentennial of the French Revolution. The Louvre pyramids and the Opéra Bastille inaugurated.
- **1991** Edith Cresson becomes France's first woman prime minister.
- **1992** Disneyland Paris opens in the suburbs.
- **1995** Jacques Chirac, former mayor of Paris, becomes president.
- **1996** Bibliothèque National de France opens in southeast Paris.
- **1997** Lionel Jospin takes office as prime minister.

Mansarts, Soufflot, Molière, Racine and Corneille, Gluck, Rameau, and Lully, Fragonard, Watteau and Boucher, Voltaire, and Montesquieu.

The financial strain of pomp, glamour, and military conquest, though, had drained the treasury, and eventually, in 1788, the king was forced to summon the Estates General—the old parliamentary assembly—for the first time since 1614.

FROM THE FRENCH REVOLUTION TO THE SECOND EMPIRE   The summoning of the Estates General set into motion the chain of events that led to the revolution. In many ways, Paris was its center. On July 14, 1789, a Paris mob stormed the Bastille, and 3 days later Louis XVI was forced at the Hôtel de Ville to kiss the new French tricolor. A year later, on July 14, 1790, the Festival of the Federation was celebrated on the Champs-de-Mars: About 300,000 people attended a mass at which the king swore an oath of loyalty to the constitution. Yet radical factions grew. On August 10, 1792, revolutionary troops and a Parisian mob stormed the Tuileries, taking the king prisoner, and in 1793 he and Queen Marie Antoinette were beheaded in the place de la Concorde. Robespierre presided over the Reign of Terror from 1793 until his arrest on July 27, 1794. A reaction ushered in the Directory (1795–99), which was ended by Napoléon's coup. In 1804, at Notre-Dame, Napoléon crowned himself emperor and his wife, Joséphine, empress; he then embarked on a series of campaigns until he was defeated at the Battle of Waterloo in 1815. During his reign, he gave Paris many of its most grandiose monuments, notably the Arc de Triomphe, the Arc de Triomphe du Carrousel, and the Bourse. His greatest gift, however, was the Louvre, which he set on its course to becoming an art museum. Here, he displayed the art he had "acquired" in his many military campaigns; it later became the core of the museum's collection.

Although today you can still see traces of Roman and medieval Paris, as well as the Paris of the 16th, 17th, and 18th centuries, the look that most of us associate with the city of light was created in the 19th century. It was Napoléon who landscaped the view from the Louvre, extending the perspective past the Tuileries and the place de la Concorde to the Champs-Elysées—then quite deserted—and the Arc de Triomphe. He also built fountains, cemeteries, and the arcades along the rue de Rivoli.

After Waterloo and the restoration of the Bourbons, the canals of St-Martin, St-Denis, and de l'Ourcq were opened in eastern and northeastern Paris. The city grew at an amazing rate, from 547,000 persons in 1801 to 2.3 million in 1881. This growth was fueled by industrialization and the arrival of the first railroad in 1837. In its wake, industrialization brought great social change and democratization, which certainly contributed to the two 19th-century revolutions, the first in 1830, which replaced Charles X with Louis-Philippe, and the second in 1848, which ushered in Louis Napoléon, first as president of the Second Republic and later, in 1852, as Emperor Napoléon III.

From 1852 to 1870, Napoléon III reshaped Paris with the aid of Baron Haussmann, who razed whole neighborhoods so that he could lay out the boulevards and avenues that we associate with Paris today. The grand railroad stations were linked by these broad streets, and great crossroads like the Etoile, the place de l'Opéra, and the place de la République were created where these streets met. Twenty-four parks were also established during the Second Empire, including the Bois de Boulogne and the Parc de Monceau; a new sewage system was begun; and the market pavilions at Les Halles were constructed. Much of what is still familiar in the cityscape today is due to the vision of Baron Haussmann.

In this Paris the artistic giants of the day lived and worked—Balzac, Baudelaire, Dumas, Hugo, Sand, Chopin, Berlioz, Delacroix, Ingres, Daumier, and Manet, to name only a few who frequented the new boulevards with their cafes, music halls, and theaters. Famous courtesans reveled in their social prominence, and one, La Paiva, amassed such a fortune that she was able to open a palace on the Champs-Elysées. Everyone came to Paris for pleasure; the French from the provinces came to shop, to go to the theater, and to occupy the plush red banquettes at cafes lit with gilt chandeliers. Even the English came to indulge their every pleasure before returning home to complain about French decadence and customs. The life that filled the boulevards then can most easily be seen in the paintings of Manet, Renoir, Degas, Toulouse-Lautrec, and the other impressionists. The city was the art capital of Europe, and its achievements were showcased in a series of International Exhibitions from 1855 to 1900. The Eiffel Tower, built for the 1889 expo as a temporary structure, caused a sensation, and despite much controversy it was allowed to remain standing, the tallest structure in the world at the time. The first Métro line opened in 1900, and both the Grand Palais and the Petit Palais were unveiled for the exposition of that year.

FROM THE PARIS COMMUNE TO WORLD WAR I   The empire had ended disastrously in the Franco-Prussian War (1870–71), during which Paris was again occupied and Napoléon III captured and ultimately exiled. A communist uprising occurred shortly after the Prussians withdrew in March 1871. In 2 short months it was quickly and bloodily suppressed, but not before the mob had torched the Tuileries, burning all but the Pavillon de Flore to the ground. The last of the communards were executed at Père-Lachaise, and a Third Republic was established, lasting 60 years.

Under the Third Republic, French painters and writers made France a world center of art and literature. The change from the romantic era to the modern era was clearly marked by the death of writer Victor Hugo in 1885. Hugo had been the great romantic symbol of France. His body lay in state at the Arc de Triomphe for 24 hours, and thousands came to pay him their last respects. But signs of artistic change were evidenced in the more realistic works of Manet, Courbet, and Zola. In particular, Manet's *Déjeuner sur l'herbe*, shown at the Salon des Refusés in 1863, had caused a scandal not only because of its subject matter but also because of its technique. Eleven years later, in 1874, Manet, Pissarro, Renoir, Cézanne, Monet, Morisot, Degas, Sisley, and 21 other artists, calling themselves the Société Anonyme, held their first exhibition in photographer Nadar's studio, at 35 bd. des Capucines. Their paintings were greeted with revulsion and were dismissed as mere muddy scrapings. They themselves were dubbed madmen, and a critic in *Charivari* referred to the show as the "exhibition of the impressionists"—a name that stuck. A second exhibition in 1876 was greeted with the same disgust, and one critic even suggested that someone should "try to explain to M. Renoir that a woman's torso is not a mass of decomposing flesh with those purplish green stains which denote a state of complete putrefaction in a corpse."

By the 1890s, though—in Paris, at least—impressionism had arrived. In 1895, Samuel Bing opened his shop L'art nouveau Bing, and its name (abstracted to "art nouveau") became synonymous with the fluid, sinuous style that dominated the first decade of this century and can still be seen in such grand restaurants as Maxim's (1890) on the rue Royale, Laperousse on the Quai des Grands Augustins, or out on the street at the one of the few remaining Métro entrances designed by Hector Guimard. The experimentation continued, giving birth to cubism (1907–14), dadaism (1915–22), surrealism, and art deco in the 1920s.

By the turn of the century, Paris had 27,000 cafes, about 150 cafe concerts, and thousands of restaurants—a phenomenal number when you consider that there were a mere 50 such places in 1800. The shop girls, milliners, barmaids, prostitutes, and other workers flocked to the cafes along the Grands Boulevards and in Montparnasse and Montmartre. Montmartre in particular became the favorite gathering place of artists such as Manet, Monet, and Renoir, who frequented the Café Gouerbois, the Nouvelle-Athènes in the place Pigalle, Le Chat Noir, and Aristide Bruant's Le Mirliton.

The cafe concert was a late 19th-century invention where people ate and drank while they watched the show, commented throughout, and often joined in the singing. Both Mistinguett and Maurice Chevalier started their careers in such places, the most famous of which were the Folies Bergères and the Moulin Rouge in Montmartre. We know the dancers and other characters who frequented the Moulin Rouge—Colette, La Goulue, and Jane Avril—from the posters, pastels, and oils of Toulouse-Lautrec.

The party ended, though, in August 1914, when the troops marched off singing the "Marseillaise." Paris was not occupied, but France bore the brunt of the war. The peace treaty was signed in the Hall of Mirrors at Versailles, where in 1871 William I, after defeating the French, had been proclaimed emperor of Germany. French premier Georges Clemenceau exacted heavy war reparations and insisted on imposing a tough treaty on the Germans, which some historians believe led directly to World War II.

FROM 1920 TO 1945   On November 11, 1920, the Unknown Soldier was buried under the Arc de Triomphe; the war had ended only 2 years before, and 8.4 million French soldiers had been killed. France regained Alsace and Lorraine, which it had lost to the Prussians in 1870.

Between the wars, Paris became a magnet for writers and artists from all over the world, in particular for Americans. In the United States, Prohibition laws had been passed in 1919, and nativism and isolationism dominated the political scene. Paris, by contrast, was fun and the art capital of the world—and very cheap to live in by American standards. Young Americans came in droves—F. Scott Fitzgerald, Henry Miller, Ernest Hemingway, Gertrude Stein, Natalie Barney, and so many more. They gathered on the Left Bank in the cafes of Montparnasse at Le Dôme, Le Select, and La Coupole, all still operating today. And Americans were not the only ones to come—James Joyce, Marc Chagall, and George Orwell came as well. In the 1940s and 1950s the bohemian focus moved to St-Germain, where intellectuals like Jean-Paul Sartre and Simone de Beauvoir frequented the Café des Deux- Magots, Café de Flore, and Brasserie Lipp, all still thriving on the boulevard St-Germain today.

In the 1930s, economic depression throughout Europe, German rearmament, and the appeasement of Hitler eventually led to the outbreak of World War II. In May 1940, Germany invaded the Netherlands, Luxembourg, and Belgium; broke through France's defensive Maginot Line; and occupied Paris on June 14, 1940, establishing their headquarters at the Hôtel Lutetia on the boulevard Raspail. The Vichy government, led by Marshal Pétain, in theory ran unoccupied France, but in fact collaborated with the Germans, while General Charles de Gaulle became leader of the Free-French and organized le Maquis (the Resistance) throughout the country, proclaiming in a famous radio broadcast from London that France had lost a battle but not the war. The Allies landed in Normandy in June 1944, and on August 24 General Leclerc entered Paris, followed two days later by General de Gaulle, who paraded down the Champs-Elysées. Joy broke out in the capital. By the end of the year the Germans had been expelled from France and de Gaulle was heading a provisional government before the official proclamation of the Fourth Republic.

THE POSTWAR YEARS   The Fourth Republic saw the violent end of colonial French rule around the world. In the late 1940s, some 80,000 soldiers lost their lives fighting the revolt in Madagascar. In the mid-1950s, Indochina was abandoned in the hope that the United States would defeat the Chinese-funded revolutionaries. In North Africa, Morocco and Tunisia won their independence, but France would not let go of Algeria, which was a *département,* technically a part of France. The Algerian war of liberation became a bloody conflict that led to the collapse of the Fourth Republic. The country was flooded with refugees from Algeria. Later in 1958, de Gaulle was recalled to head the Fifth Republic and to resolve another Algerian crisis created when a right-wing military coup there threatened France. In 1962, after a referendum in France proposed by de Gaulle himself, Algeria gained its independence.

André Malraux, the writer, was de Gaulle's minister of cultural affairs from 1958 to 1969. Caring deeply for Paris's legacy of great architecture and urban splendor, he protected and restored such districts as the Marais, which had fallen into disrepair. Elsewhere in the city, modern architecture took over. The Maison UNESCO, in the 7e arrondissement, and the Maison de la Radio, on the Seine in the 16e arrondissement, were built in 1958 and 1960, respectively.

The decade ended with still more turmoil. In 1968 workers were striking around the country; at the same time, in Paris, students took to the streets rebelling against France's antiquated educational system. Some political analysts date the more recent changes in the French attitudes toward modernization from 1968. De Gaulle was swept from power and in 1969 Georges Pompidou became president.

In 1970, the Réseau Express Régional (RER, express train through Paris) was inaugurated. Three years later, the Montparnasse Tower was completed; according to Saul Bellow, the skyscraper is "something that had strayed away from Chicago and had come to rest on a Parisian street corner." While the uniformly low lines of the Paris skyline were altered, this was only a preview of what was yet to come.

The 1980s saw the further transformation of Parisian architecture. In this age of futuristic *grands projets,* the Centre Pompidou and the Forum des Halles were completed, as well as the Musée d'Orsay, the Institute of the Arab World, the Opéra de la Bastille, the Arche de la Défense, I. M. Pei's controversial pyramids for the new Louvre, and the complex at La Villette. The most recent project is the glass-walled Bibliothèque National de France, part of a massive redevelopment scheme for southeastern Paris.

François Mitterrand, France's first socialist president, was elected in 1981 and reelected in 1988. In 1989, France celebrated two great birthdays: the bicentennial of the French Revolution and the centennial of the Eiffel Tower, both great gifts to the culture of the western world, both symbols of hope, progress, and change. Since then the political situation has declined. Although former Paris mayor Jacques Chirac won the presidency in 1995 upon a promise to jump-start the economy, today unemployment is more than 12% and the economy has stagnated. Confrontations with the unions have occurred, such as the transit-workers strike that paralyzed Paris at the end of 1995. Economic distress has helped fuel hostility to North African and other immigrant groups, while many of the second-generation immigrants are more angry than their parents at being treated as second-class citizens and shut out from economic advancement. Although the face of Paris is well maintained thanks to large government subsidies that also support cultural icons, French society is under stress, particularly as it struggles to meet the goal of a single European currency. Fiscal austerity measures mandated by the Maastricht Treaty are widely perceived as contributing to France's record level of unemployment. The climate of insecurity prompted a backlash among voters in the 1997 legislative elections. President Jacques Chirac's conservative party lost heavily, forcing Mr. Chirac to "cohabit" with Lionel Jospin, leader of the opposition Socialist Party. Cutting the deficit to 3% of the gross national product as required by the Maastricht Treaty while also creating jobs for the jobless remains a formidable challenge for President Chirac and Prime Minister Jospin.

4 Famous Parisians

Pierre Abélard (1079–1142) and **Héloïse** (1101–64) Abélard was a theologian and logician at the University of Paris who fell in love with his pupil, Héloïse, whom he later secretly married. Theirs was a tragic love story if there ever was one. Héloïse's uncle had Abélard castrated, and she entered a convent. They continued to communicate through love letters until Abélard's death. The lovers were finally reunited in Père-Lachaise cemetery.

Josephine Baker (1906–75) Born in St. Louis, Missouri, Josephine Baker was the star of the Revue nègre in Paris in the 1920s; her Charleston revolutionized the city. Her theme song, "J'ai deux Amours" ("I Have Two Loves"), refers to the United States and Paris.

Honoré de Balzac (1799–1850) A native of Tours, Balzac was the author of some 95 novels, collected under the title of *La comédie humaine* (*The Human Comedy*). His works provide a masterful tableau of French society in the first half of the 19th century.

Charles Baudelaire (1821–67) Paris-born poet Baudelaire was author of *Les fleurs du mal* (*Flowers of Evil*), a collection regarded as sinful by Second Empire moralists when it was published in 1857. He foreshadowed symbolist and surrealist poetry. He also translated Edgar Allan Poe into French. Though his influence extended into the 20th century, he died in poverty.

Simone de Beauvoir (1908–86) A novelist and essayist, she was Jean-Paul Sartre's lifelong companion. Her *Le deuxième sexe* (*The Second Sex*) is a classic feminist study. In *Mémoires d'une jeune fille rangée* (*Memoirs of a Dutiful Daughter*), she narrates the story of her youth in a bourgeois Parisian family.

Sarah Bernhardt (1844–1923) The greatest tragedian of her day, Bernhardt worked for the Comédie-Française before founding her own theater. She excelled in her roles in *Phèdre* and *La Dame aux camélias* (*Camille*).

Georges Bizet (1838–75) Bizet's name will forever be linked with the world's favorite opera, *Carmen*. Sadly, he died following the opera's disastrous premier, never realizing he had created a masterpiece.

Henri Cartier-Bresson (b. 1908) Cartier-Bresson's sober photographs are among the masterpieces of 20th-century art. A native Parisian, he has traveled around the world to capture decisive moments of human action on film.

Gabrielle "Coco" Chanel (1883–1971) Chanel's legendary fame as a fashion designer began at a shop in Deauville. In Paris she popularized costume jewelry and evening scarves, created the "little black dress," and introduced Chanel No. 5 perfume.

Maurice Chevalier (1888–1972) One of France's best-known popular singers—and, abroad, the archetypal Frenchman—Maurice Chevalier starred in such Hollywood films as *Folies Bergères* and *Gigi*.

Frédéric Chopin (1810–49) Very much a Polish composer, Chopin lived in Paris for many years and became the idol of the *salons*. He died of consumption at a house on the place Vendôme. His grave at Père-Lachaise is a pilgrimage site for Poles visiting Paris.

Colette (1873–1954)   Colette was a novelist of the sensual; her female characters are often trying to find a balance between that sensuality and common sense. Among her works are *La Vagabonde, Chéri,* and *Gigi.* Born in a small village in Burgundy, Colette made her last residence in Paris in an apartment at the Palais-Royal. She's buried at Père-Lachaise.

Marie Curie (1867–1934)   Polish-born Marie Curie, assisted by her husband, Pierre, discovered polonium and radium. She was the first woman to be named a professor at the Sorbonne; in 1903 she received the Nobel Prize for physics, and in 1911 the Nobel Prize for chemistry.

Christian Dior (1905–57)   After World War II, Dior established his couture house in Paris. His "New Look" of 1947 revolutionized the French fashion world.

Charles de Gaulle (1890–1970)   Uncompromising leader of the Free-French during World War II, de Gaulle went on to dominate French political life for 25 years. Elected first president of the Fifth Republic, de Gaulle pulled a demoralized France back together and ended the Algerian war for independence.

André Gide (1869–1951)   Gide was one of France's greatest 20th-century writers. His *L'Immoraliste* (*The Immoralist*) is an early apology for sensual pleasure, while *Les Faux monnayeurs* (*The Counterfeiters*) is a novel within a novel within a novel. In *Corydon* he defends homosexuality; in *Retour de l'U.R.S.S.* (*Return from the U.S.S.R.*) he views that communist society with skepticism. Gide received the Nobel Prize for Literature in 1947.

Georges Eugène, Baron Haussmann (1809–91)   If any one person transformed Paris, it was Haussmann. Hired by Napoléon III to lay the city's boulevards, Haussmann gave the city its present urban design.

Victor Hugo (1802–85)   In many ways, Hugo symbolizes the 19th century. His romantic genius led him to espouse liberal causes in both art and politics. A poet, playwright, and novelist, he was the author of *Hernani* and *Les Misérables.* You can visit his house at the place des Vosges.

Allan Kardec (1804–69)   Kardec (his real name was Hippolyte Rivail) popularized spiritism in France. His *Book of Spirits* went through 50 editions in the 50 years after it was published, and even today his grave at Père-Lachaise attracts many who believe in the world of spirits.

Edouard Manet (1832–83)   When Manet exhibited his *Déjeuner sur l'herbe* at the Salon des Refusés in 1863, he created a big scandal. The same happened a little later with his *Olympia.* But then again, impressionist painting itself, not only its subject matter, was not well viewed by the conservative artistic circles of the mid–19th century.

Molière (1622–73)   Born Jean-Baptiste Poquelin, Molière was France's greatest author of comedies: *Don Juan, Le Misanthrope,* and *Le Malade imaginaire* (*The Imaginary Invalid*) are only three. In his work, he presents the foibles of 17th-century society; many of his characters have become archetypes.

Claude Monet (1840–1926)   Monet's painting *Impression: soleil levant* inspired an art critic to invent the term *impressionist,* used at the time disrespectfully. With his *Nymphéas,* painted at Giverny, he fulfilled Proust's observation that Monet's goal was to cross "the magic mirror of reality."

Yves Montand (1921–92)   Born in Italy, Yves Montand was one of France's best-loved singers and actors. His performances, both at concerts and in movies, often exhibited a political dimension.

Edith Piaf (1915–63)   Considered by many as the best popular singer of all time, Piaf began singing in the streets of her native Pigalle. She rose to international stardom with such songs as *"La vie en rose"* and *"La foule."*

Marcel Proust (1871–1922)   Proust wrote *À la recherche du temps perdu* (*Remembrance of Things Past*), a seven-part masterpiece on life during the belle epoque. Perhaps no other writer has written as masterfully as Proust on the subtle process of memory. The madeleine scene in the first part, *Du côté de chez Swann* (*Swann's Way*), is a classic.

Auguste Rodin (1840–1917)   Rodin revolutionized sculpture in the 19th century. You can see his work—*The Kiss, The Thinker, The Gates of Hell*—at the Musée Rodin in the 7e arrondissement.

Marquis de Sade (1740–1814)   The man whose name provides the root for *sadism*, the Marquis de Sade wrote novels about sexual fantasy and perversion. His works include *La philosophie dans le boudoir* and *Justine.*

George Sand (1804–76)   Born Aurore Dupin, George Sand wrote deeply passionate novels as well as an autobiography. She surrounded herself with poets and artists and was Chopin's lover for 10 years.

Jean-Paul Sartre (1905–80)   Playwright, novelist, and essayist, Sartre is forever linked with existentialism. Interested in revolutionary change while at the same time remaining a pessimist, he expressed his view of the world in such works as *La Nausée* (*Nausea*) and *Les Mots* (*The Words*), a beautiful autobiography. He was Simone de Beauvoir's lifelong companion.

Madame de Sévigné (1626–96)   Few other people's correspondence is as wonderfully varied as that of this 17th-century aristocrat. Her letters, addressed to her Parisian friends and her daughter in Provence, vividly bring to life the sparkling society of the age of Louis XIV.

Gertrude Stein (1874–1946)   Born in Pennsylvania, Stein moved to Paris in 1903 and remained there until her death—even during the war, despite her Jewish origins. At her apartment at 27 rue de Fleurus, she welcomed contemporary artists, including Picasso, as well as many members of America's Lost Generation.

François Truffaut (1932–84)   First a critic for the prestigious Cahiers du cinéma and then a film director, Truffaut inaugurated a new era for French and foreign moviegoers. His films include *Les Quatre Cents Coups* (*The 400 Blows*), *Jules et Jim, L'Histoire d'Adèle H.* (*The Story of Adele H.*), and *Le Dernier Métro* (*The Last Train*). Truffaut is buried in Montmartre cemetery.

Eugène-Emmanuel Viollet-le-Duc (1814–79)   An architect, Viollet-le-Duc was responsible for the restoration of Notre-Dame and the Sainte-Chapelle in the mid–19th century. His ideas, presented in his *Dictionnaire raisonné de l'architecture française du XIe au XVIe siècle* and *Entretiens sur l'architecture,* influenced several generations of architects.

Voltaire (1694–1778)   The smiling skepticism of the 18th-century Enlightenment is embodied in Voltaire's satirical masterpiece, *Candide.* His fearless defense of freedom of thought profoundly influenced the leaders of the French Revolution.

5 Parisian Art

Art in Paris is not merely French art. Many French movements—impressionism is only one of them—began or developed here, but that's only part of the whole picture. Generations of artists from all parts of the world have thrived in Paris, and though the stereotype of the painter starving, *La Boheme*–style, in a Montmartre garret may be a thing of the past, the city's museums and galleries hold enough art to last a visitor several lifetimes of daily viewing. From Egyptian, Assyrian, and Greco-Roman art at the Louvre, through realism and impressionism and art nouveau at the Musée d'Orsay, to the modern international masters at the Centre Pompidou, Paris offers a vast wealth of art.

Don't bypass the small museums; often less crowded than their larger and more famous counterparts, they hold their own unique wonders. Also, consult newspapers and magazines for listings of special exhibitions such as those regularly held at the Louvre and the Grand Palais, as well as contemporary artists exhibiting at private galleries on both sides of the Seine.

The history of art in Paris is inseparable from that of art in France. From medieval times on, French artists have often found inspiration in Paris and the surrounding areas. In their famous devotional book *Les très riche heures* of the duc de Berry, the Limbourg brothers, 15th-century illuminators, represented the blue skies of the Ile de France region as well as some recognizable Parisian scenes.

From the Renaissance to the 19th century, numerous French artists created an astoundingly rich body of painting. In the 16th century, Jean Clouet and his son François combined the traditions of Gothic art with native French styles, producing paintings that are remarkable for their design. In the 17th century, Nicholas Poussin studied in Italy and, inspired by Italian painters as well as by the art of ancient Greece and Rome, became one of the foremost neoclassical artists. The delicate paintings of Antoine Watteau dominated the first half of the 18th century, while the second half belonged to Jean-Honoré Fragonard; with his soft palette, his works represent the pinnacle of rococo art in France. After the French Revolution, classicism reigned supreme, with such artists as Jacques-Louis David and Jean-Auguste-Dominique Ingres, while Eugène Delacroix later became the master of romantic painting. None of these artists, however, paid much attention to the artistic representation of Paris. The city became the center of world art as well as an important subject for the impressionists in the second half of the 19th century.

The critics and the public were at first scandalized by the art of those painters who were later described as impressionists, and their works were often rejected by the official Salon. Thus they were forced to create their own Salon des Refusés. It was precisely at the 1874 Salon de Refusés that Monet exhibited his *Impression: soleil levant* (*Impression: Rising Sun*); the term *impressionism* was derived from the painting's title by a disrespectful critic. Impressions, though, were what many of these painters had in mind—not simply to paint an object, but rather to capture the impression produced by it. The impressionists argued that every vision of the object occurs in a particular light, at a particular time, and what the eye really perceives is not simply the object, but its impression. Light and color were brought to the foreground, and even shadows were represented as areas of color. Artists such as Monet, Renoir, Pissarro, Sisley, Seurat, Gauguin, and van Gogh painted their own impressions of Paris, and thus we have a better artistic record of Paris in the late 19th century than we do of any of the preceding centuries.

From this period on, Montmartre is especially well represented in painting. At the turn of the century, Toulouse-Lautrec painted the Moulin Rouge and its cancan dancers, and in the first half of the 20th century, Maurice Utrillo devoted his art to capturing the modest streets of this district.

In the 20th century, the Parisian art scene is clearly marked by internationalization. Picasso, Chagall, Modigliani, and the Cuban painter Lam all worked here, and their works are exhibited in Paris's two world-class museums of modern art, Musee National d'Art Moderne and Musee d'Art Moderne de la Ville de Paris.

6 From Gothic Gargoyles to Pei & the Pompidou

Parisians in general have a passion for architecture. Few major projects are completed in the city without first being examined and debated—not only by the respective commissions in charge of approving them but also by the citizens of Paris. Controversy, of course, is often the result, and the merits and faults of individual projects are discussed with such gusto that it seems controversy is really the salt of construction.

Among the most debated projects of the last century? First, the Eiffel Tower. Its critics absolutely hated its shape and the iron with which it was built; the writer Huysmans described it as a "hollow candlestick." And in recent years similar protests (as well as apologies) were heard regarding I. M. Pei's pyramids for the Louvre. If the Centre Pompidou, scorned when it was first built, has now won a place in the hearts of most Parisians, almost no one has yet cozied up to Uruguayan-born architect Carlos Ott's Opéra Bastille, which is often described as looking like a piece of sanitary equipment.

But whether you are a lover of the classical or the avant-garde—or a combination thereof—Parisian architecture will probably fascinate you. Gothic or French baroque, art nouveau or international style, all major movements are represented along the city's streets and boulevards. Elegant proportions dominate the cityscape. Windows are just as long and as wide as they should be. Roofs are softly curved. And time, as Saul Bellow has observed, confers on all buildings a similar shade of gray: *la grisaille.* Probably no other metropolis can boast as much uniformity, and subtle variety, as Paris in its architecture.

Little remains of Paris's Roman architecture—only the Arènes de Lutèce and the baths at the Musée de Cluny, both on the Left Bank. Neither can rival the great Roman remains in the south of France. You'll have to let your imagination do some work. When you walk along rue St-Jacques, leading from the Seine almost parallel to the boulevard St-Michel, think about this: This is the old road from Lutèce to Rome.

The medieval period is an altogether different matter. Although the Romanesque style is not abundant (the best example being the church of St-Germain-des-Prés), Paris's Gothic architecture is among the richest in Europe. With its glorious stained glass and statuary, Notre-Dame Cathedral is one of the foremost examples of religious architecture anywhere. As the British writer John Russell put it, the cathedral was for many centuries "the center of gravitation for events great and small." The beauty of its design played no small role in this, as Russell pointed out: "It persuaded Gandhi that 'the men who made such things must have had the love of god in their hearts.'" Also on the Ile de la Cité is another not-to-be-missed jewel of Gothic architecture, the Sainte-Chapelle, with its remarkable stained glass.

Unlike elsewhere in Europe, Renaissance architecture in Paris is not abundant. But the château at Fontainebleau, an easy day trip from Paris, is a wonderful example of Italian influence on French architecture. King François I wanted to create an Italian-style court in France, and one way to achieve this was by imitating that country's artistic creations.

The 17th and 18th centuries gave us French baroque architecture, which is astoundingly well represented in Paris. Classical symmetry and a profusion of columns and statues abound. Architects adapted the baroque cupolas of Rome, and domes rose over the city in the Hôtel des Invalides, the church of St-Paul–St-Louis in the Marais, and the Panthéon. The mansions in the Marais and the Faubourg–St-Germain are to this day clear examples of the high level reached by domestic architecture in these centuries; with their majestic facades and courtyards, these *hôtels particuliers* are a remarkable addition to Paris's urban texture.

Neither the French Revolution nor Bonaparte's empire nor the first half of the 19th century really transformed the city's architecture. A few landmarks were added, such as the Arc de Triomphe and the church of the Madeleine. During the Second Empire, however, Paris was virtually transformed.

Baron Haussmann, urban planner under Napoléon III, razed entire neighborhoods and replaced the old labyrinthine streets with magnificent grand boulevards. Politics was at the heart of this decision: Revolutionary mobs were easier to control in large avenues than in tiny alleyways. Interestingly, the real revolution was Haussmann's, for Paris acquired a new style, even a trademark. Paris without its boulevards would not be Paris. Garnier's imposing Opéra, the Eiffel Tower, the pont Alexandre III, and the Grand Palais are all monuments from the last three decades of the 19th century, and they are emblematic of Paris's growth into a modern metropolis. The art nouveau gateways to the Métro are also representative of this period, in which technological advance and artistic flair went hand in hand.

For such a classical-looking city as Paris, the richness of its 20th-century architecture is remarkable. From the Palais de Chaillot, built in the 1930s, to the Montparnasse Tower, the Centre Pompidou, the Opéra Bastille, the Institut du Monde Arabe, and the Grande Arche de la Défense, all built in the last 20 years, Paris has embraced modern architecture with vigor, even if consensus has been lacking. In most instances, success has been achieved precisely by juxtaposing the classical and the avant-garde. The classical beauty of the Louvre's facade and the postmodern simplicity of Pei's pyramids complement and accentuate each other. And even more projects have been completed in the last few years: the square glass structures on the Seine that are the Centre International des Conférences, in the 7e arrondissement; the new Bibliothèque de France, in the 13e, with its four glass towers shaped like open books on a square as large as the place de la Concorde; the geometrical exuberance of Frank Gehry's new American Center in the 12e, across the Seine from the Bibliothèque. Far from resting on its glorious past, architecture in Paris is rushing head-on to meet the new millennium.

7 The Moveable Feast

One of the great pleasures of Parisian life is the food. Stroll through any street market and you'll be struck by the quality and variety of fresh produce ready to be transformed into mouthwatering meals. Although it can no longer be said that you can't get a bad meal in Paris, the general level of cooking skills is still high. At the top of the ladder are the gifted chefs behind some of the world's finest restaurants, concocting elaborate dishes with ingredients like foie gras and truffles. But even on a less exalted level you'll find competent bistro cooks producing excellent meals from old family recipes and young chefs making tasty and affordable dishes through the imaginative use of simple ingredients. Although there are plenty of overpriced mediocre restaurants, with a little planning you can eat very well at a reasonable price. (See chapter 5, "Great Deals on Dining," for more tips.)

DINING CUSTOMS   Breakfast is not a big deal in France. If you must have eggs, bacon, and toast, you'll pay dearly for it. Instead, save your appetite for lunch and enjoy a light breakfast of café au lait, buttery croissants, and a fresh baguette.

Lunch hour in Paris is often hectic. The traditional 2-hour wine-soaked lunch has not disappeared but is saved for special occasions—Mammon's visit from the country or impressing important clients. Whether eating pizza or a three-course meal, you'll find service at lunch brisk and efficient.

Dinner is the meal to be lingered over and is approached with the all the reverence of a religious ceremony. At finer restaurants a maître d' will cordially welcome you and the waiters will hasten to provide attentive service—in France, waiting tables is a serious professional career. Your part in the ceremony is also crucial. Dress for the occasion. Although jeans are increasingly accepted in all but the most sophisticated places, you'll be treated better if you dress up a little. Sneakers are frowned on everywhere other than McDonalds.

Never underestimate the importance of *la politesse*. Smooth your way with such essential phrases as *"Bonjour, monsieur"* and *"Merci, madame."* Never refer to the waiter as "Garçon"—that's only used in American movies. Use *"Monsieur, s'il vous plaît!"* or *"Madame, s'il vous plaît!"* French table manners require that all food be eaten with a knife and fork—even fruit.

Be aware of the traditional way of serving food. An *aperitif* precedes the meal but French people dislike numbing the palate with strong liquor. Instead you may wish to try a *kir*, which is a mixture of white wine and crème de cassis. You will always be served bread with your meal but not butter. Water is not placed on the table automatically—you must ask for it. Cheese follows the main course and is usually accompanied by red wine. Coffee is not drunk with dessert but follows it. Although a proper meal consists of three or sometimes four courses, portions are usually moderate. If you have food left on your plate, it is not the custom to ask for a doggie bag.

DINING ESTABLISHMENTS   Bistros, brasseries, and restaurants all serve food but offer different dining experiences. The typical bistro used to be a mom-and-pop operation with a zinc bar and pigeonholes for the regulars to store their napkins. The menu was scrawled on a blackboard and usually consisted of standbys like *l'oeuf mayonnaise, boeuf bourguignon,* and *tarte Tatin.* Today many bistros have expanded upon the old classics but retained the tradition of offering hearty, relatively low-priced dishes in a convivial atmosphere. Tradition is strong, though. Take the case of l'oeuf mayonnaise (basically a hard-boiled egg with mayonnaise): The old favorite is held in such regard that it has an organization dedicated to its "protection"—the Association de Sauvegarde de l'Oeuf Mayonnaise. They award prizes every year.

Brasserie means "brewery" in French and refers to the Alsatian menu specialties that are brasserie staples—beer, Reisling wine, and *choucroute* (sauerkraut, usually topped by various pork cuts). Most brasseries are large, cheerful, brightly lit places that open early and close late. You can usually get a meal any time of day, even in off-hours when restaurants and bistros are closed.

At their best, restaurants are where you come to savor French cuisine in all its glory. Classic dishes are expertly interpreted in their kitchens, and new taste sensations are invented. Dining is usually more formal than in bistros or brasseries, and service is slower. Like bistros, restaurants serve lunch between noon and 2:30pm and dinner between 7 and 10pm.

THE CUISINE   As economic uncertainty rattles daily life in France, people are turning to the comforts of the cooking they grew up with. The tiny portions and

Impression

How can you be expected to govern a country that has 246 kinds of cheese?
—Charles de Gaulle

steak-and-strawberry-sauce experiments of nouvelle cuisine are history. "Give me a good coq au vin," diners demanded—and chefs listened. The old-fashioned dishes that *tante Marie* used to make—*blanquette de veau, confit de canard, pot au feu*—are turning up on menus all over town, but with less butter and lighter sauces than the original recipes. When properly prepared, *bourgeoise cuisine* is as calorically correct as nouvelle cuisine and as satisfying as traditional cooking.

The real genius of French cuisine has always been the variety of its regional tables, and they are well represented in Paris. Regional restaurants provide a gastronomic tour of France—oysters and crepes from Brittany, fondue from Savoy, cassoulet from the Southwest and Provençal dishes based on tomatoes, herbs, and olive oil. The wine list will also showcase local wines, sometimes at excellent prices.

Every so often even French people need a break from French food. As Paris becomes a multiethnic community, the flavors and textures of a panoply of countries enliven the dining scene. The most popular ethnic dish is couscous from North Africa—steamed semolina garnished with a ladleful of broth, stewed vegetables, and whatever meat you've chosen. Chinese, Thai, Vietnamese, Indian, Tex-Mex, and Russian restaurants are also popular although not necessarily cheaper than French food.

DRINKS   France is, of course, a nation of wine drinkers, and French wine is, of course, excellent. Moreover, having wine with your meal is less expensive than having juice or a soda.

The *menu du jour* at many establishments often includes wine, either red or white. The standard measure is a $^1/_4$-liter carafe (*un quart*). If wine is not included, you can order *vin ordinaire* (house wine) or a Beaujolais or Côtes du Rhône, which are very reasonably priced.

If you want a free glass of water (as opposed to its bottled counterpart), ask for *une carafe d'eau.* Coffee is never drunk during a meal. *Café* means an espresso; *café au lait* is a larger cup of espresso and steamed milk. If you would like to dilute your espresso with a little milk, ask for *café noisette.* For decaffeinated coffee ask for *un deca;* decaffeinated herbal tea is *infusion.*

8 Recommended Books & Films

BOOKS

GENERAL   Janet Flanner's *Paris Was Yesterday* is a collection of articles written for *The New Yorker* on diverse aspects of the city's life in the 1920s and 1930s; it's full of themes you can still observe today. Dealing with the same period—and America's Lost Generation—is Ernest Hemingway's *A Moveable Feast.* For a French perspective on life in the first decades of the 20th century, read Simone de Beauvoir's *Memoirs of a Dutiful Daughter,* a critical account of the author's bourgeois upbringing. Julian Green's *Paris* (M. Boyars, 1993) is a wonderful evocation of life around the city.

History buffs will enjoy Simon Schama's *Citizens* (Knopf, 1989), an in-depth and entertaining account of the French Revolution. For a biography of Louis XIV, see Nancy Mitford's *The Sun King.* Madame de Sévigné's *Selected Letters* (Penguin, 1982) is a marvelous introduction to the 17th century.

For an intelligent vision of the city, beautifully illustrated with paintings and photographs, read John Russell's *Paris* (Abrams, 1983).

THE ARTS   Much of Paris's beauty is found in its art. Three excellent books discussing France from this perspective are *The History of Impressionism,* by John Rewald (Museum of Modern Art, 1973), a collection of documents on this valuable period in art history; *The French Through Their Films,* by Robin Buss (Ungar, 1988), an exploration of the history and themes of more than 100 films; and *The Studios of Paris: The Capital of Art in the Late Nineteenth Century,* by John Milner (Yale University Press, 1988), a study of the dynamic forces that made Paris one of the most complex art centers in the early modern era.

Modern architecture enthusiasts will want to see the bilingual *Guide to Modern Architecture in Paris,* by Hervé Martin. It includes very good photographs as well as maps.

FICTION, TRAVEL & BIOGRAPHY   Foreign writers have written many novels about Paris. Perhaps the best known is Charles Dickens's *A Tale of Two Cities,* set during the French Revolution. Henry James contrasted American innocence and French experience in such works as *The American* and *The Ambassadors.* Henry Miller's *Tropic of Cancer* will lead you to the heart of bohemia. Canadian Mavis Gallant often sets her short stories in Paris, where she lives. Argentinean writer Julio Cortázar's *Hopscotch* (Pantheon, 1987) is a highly experimental novel about literature, partially set along the city's streets and bridges and in its garrets. Carlos Fuentes's *Distant Relations* (Farrar, Straus and Giroux, 1982) also takes place partially in Paris—at the Automobile-Club de France on place de la Concorde and in houses near Parc Monceau and in the 7e arrondissement.

Of course, foreign writers don't have a monopoly on Paris observation. The city is often a primary character in the novels of such great classic French novelists as Victor Hugo and Honoré de Balzac, specifically in Balzac's *Père Goriot* and Hugo's well-known *Les Misérables* and *Notre-Dame de Paris* (*The Hunchback of Notre Dame*). Marcel Proust's long, rich *Remembrance of Things Past* examines the convergent paths of the aristocracy and the bourgeoisie during the belle epoque. Shorter and equally sensual, but in a different way, are Colette's romantic novels, like *Chéri* and *Gigi.*

France is a choice territory of travel writers. Henry James's *A Little Tour in France* is a classic view of several provincial cities in the 19th century, with meditations on the capital. Mark Twain stops by Paris for a while in his *Innocents Abroad.*

FILMS

As the city is so photogenic, it's no surprise that hundreds of films have Paris as their setting. From *An American in Paris* and *Moulin Rouge* to Truffaut's *The Last Metro* and Clement's *Is Paris Burning?,* the city has inspired moviemakers and audiences through much of the 20th century. Other favorites are *The Sun Also Rises,* based on Hemingway's novel; *Charade,* a dramatic dark comedy from the early 1960s with Cary Grant and Audrey Hepburn; *Last Tango in Paris,* with Marlon Brando and Maria Schneider; Roman Polanski's *Frantic,* in which a visiting American (Harrison Ford) searches for his vanished wife; and Woody Allen's *Everyone Says I Love You,* in which Allen plays a New York writer living in Paris.

Planning an Affordable Trip to Paris

2

Your trip to Paris will be much more enjoyable, and cost less, if you plan it properly. This chapter is designed to help you do just that, step by step. It answers the many questions you probably have concerning the what, when, where, and how of travel, from what documents you need to take with you to how to get to Paris easily and economically. It tells you what you can expect to pay for an accommodation, a meal, a theater ticket, or a roll of film, and provides tips for travelers with special needs (students, families, people with disabilities, gays and lesbians) as well as a calendar of special events.

1 The $70-a-Day Premise

Paris is expensive—more expensive than any American city, including New York—but you can still enjoy a marvelous, affordable vacation in this bewitching city without going into hock, and that's the raison d'être for this particular book. Affordable, though, does not mean poor-quality accommodations, unappetizing meals, and the feeling that you're being cheated out of the experience of Paris. Instead, affordable means taking the time to seek out the best possible value for every dollar and refusing to overpay for mediocrity. Visiting Paris on a budget means you'll be living more like Parisians, who also like to enjoy high standards without emptying their wallets.

Expect simple comforts in your **hotel.** The room will likely be small, the towels thin, and the decor basic—although it will probably contain a TV, a telephone, and a tiny bathroom with shower/bath and toilet. Although it's becoming harder and harder to find budget hotels that have rooms with private baths at affordable rates, they do exist, and that's what this book will help you find—good clean hotels at modest prices.

Food in Paris has always been exceptional, but good budget meals cannot be found automatically at every restaurant on the street. Some cheap restaurants get away with serving indifferently prepared meals. To be sure of getting a good meal at a good price, follow the restaurant suggestions in the dining chapter and supplement eating out with occasional picnics assembled from the array of pâtés, cheeses, *charcuterie,* and fruit available at street markets and boulangeries throughout the city.

As for **sightseeing,** the city is still a moveable feast, and wandering its streets is pleasure enough. The historic monuments commemorating the events that created Paris are free; the art and other museums are myriad and extraordinary and offer reduced entrance fees on certain days; the parks, filled with exquisite sculptures and pastimes like puppet shows, are free; and even a simple walk through the streets will expose you to buildings that resonate with literary and historical associations. Evenings, there's the whole of floodlit Paris to dream in, great jazz to enjoy, and cafes and wine bars for hanging out.

The cover of this book promises that two people traveling together can have a fine, affordable vacation for anywhere from $70 a day per person. That $70 is meant to cover the per person price of a double room and three meals a day, with the budget breaking down as follows: $35 for the room, $5 for breakfast, $8 for lunch, $17 for dinner, and $5 for sightseeing and transportation. This kind of a budget will provide you with more than adequate accommodations (sometimes with bath), continental breakfast, a fine picnic lunch or a decent pizza, and a fine evening repast. To save more and eat better, you can take advantage of the reasonable fixed-price lunches offered throughout Paris and save your light meal for dinner. And you can modify the budget by opting to do it for less or more.

2   Fifty-Five Money-Saving Tips

PLANNING & TRANSPORTATION

1. People read *Consumer Reports* and similar magazines because information gives consumers knowledge, and that can lead to savings. So **read as much as you can** about Paris before you go, ask advice of friends who have been there, and secure as much free information as possible from the tourist office.

2. **Plan well in advance.** Airlines, even car rentals and hotels, need to sell their inventory of seats, cars, and rooms and will reward the advance purchaser with a discount. A 21-day advance purchase airfare is a lot cheaper than a regular economy ticket. Remember, you pay for last-minute spontaneity.

3. Often the most expensive part of any trip is the cost of the airfare, so scour your newspaper for the latest information. Airlines want to fill every flight, so they adjust their pricing frequently, and you can often take advantage of **special airfare promotions.** Keep calling all the airlines that fly to Paris. And look for airlines that have just begun flying there, because they often launch the route with low fares.

4. **Fly during the week** rather than on weekends; it's cheaper. Also, travel off-season if you can—you'll save on airfares and accommodations.

5. Don't be afraid of using **consolidators** and **charters,** especially in the high season. They use scheduled airlines and offer great savings on fares. For example, in the summer of 1997 you'd pay $630 round-trip for an APEX ticket on Air France versus $440 on a charter from Jet Vacations.

6. **Consider going as a courier** if you have plenty of time and are not concerned about traveling with a companion.

7. Do-it-yourself always pays. In the travel arena this means **pack light.** That way you won't need a cart or a porter and you're less likely to succumb to the desire for a taxi.

8. **Take the cheapest way into the city** from the airport, unless you can't bear to ride the rails or take a bus at the end of a long flight. In Paris, you can save $30 by taking a train or bus instead of a cab from Roissy, and about $15 from Orly.

9. **Consider taking a package tour.** Sometimes you can secure a week or more in a destination that includes airfare, transfers, and hotel for very little over the cost of a traditional airfare. You don't have to sign up for the tour's features or join the group activities, but you can enjoy the price tag.

ACCOMMODATIONS

10. The best budget choices fill up fast; you'll have a wider and more affordable selection if you **book accommodations early.**

11. **Think about what you really need in a hotel room.** All rooms in Paris have a sink with hot and cold water. If a private bathroom is not crucial, then you can stay in lower-priced rooms with a bathroom down the hall. Ask yourself how important it is to have a television in the room if you don't understand the French programs.

12. **Negotiate the room price,** especially in low season. Ask for a discount if you're a student or over 60; ask for a discount if you stay a certain number of days. Don't be shy.

13. **Stay at a hotel that doesn't insist you take breakfast,** which can add another $5 to $10 a day to your bill.

14. If you're a sociable person and genuinely interested in experiencing the life of the country, **sign up for a homestay program** such as Servas.

15. If you're not shy and don't mind dorm accommodations, **consider staying at a youth hostel** or someplace similar.

16. A **home swap** or renting a **short-term apartment** in Paris is a good option if you don't need the services of a hotel.

17. **Don't call home from a hotel phone** unless you know that you can access USA Direct. If you do have to make a call, do so from a public phone booth to avoid hotel surcharges. Another way to save money is to call home and ask the person to call you back, as U.S. rates are much lower.

DINING

18. Scrumptious offerings are always on display in **patisseries, boulangeries, and street markets**—bring a Swiss-army knife with a corkscrew and you'll have all the implements you need to make a meal. Every boulangerie also sells sandwiches and individual quiches for about 20F ($3.45).

19. **Get in the habit of making lunch your main meal.** Many establishments offer fantastic deals on a fixed-price lunch. After two or three courses at midday you'll be happy to eat lightly at dinner.

20. **Seek out creperies** where you can enjoy savory *galettes* and dessert crepes in an upbeat atmosphere.

21. **Try the ethnic neighborhoods** east of central Paris for tasty and inexpensive Vietnamese, Thai, and North African cuisine.

22. Good **chain restaurants** such as Batifol, Hippopotamus, Leon de Bruxelles, or L'Ecluse also offer good-value meals. Pommes des Pains and Lina's are popular chains for sandwiches.

23. At budget restaurants, to save money, **opt for the *plat du jour*,** which will be the cheapest main dish on the menu. Or, if that's not enough food, then order the *formule* or *prix fixe* menus. Two-course menus will usually provide an appetizer and a main dish, or a main dish and a dessert. Three-course menus include a starter, main dish, and dessert. Wine is usually not included, although some menus do offer a *boisson,* which may be a glass (*verre du vin*) or small jug (*pot*) of wine. So read the posted menus carefully. Coffee is usually extra.

24. **Pay attention to the details of the menu.** On most menus the cheaper dishes are made of cheaper cuts of meat or the organs of animals, like brains, tripe, and so on. Andouillette is one such dish. It's not a "little" sausage as you might expect, but a delicacy made of chitterlings (hog intestines).

25. When it comes to beverages, note that **wine is cheaper than soda.** Also, some mineral waters are less expensive then others. Unless you can really taste the difference, ask for tap water (*une carafe d'eau*).

26. **Don't take breakfast at your hotel** unless you want to pay 30F to 50F ($5.20 to $8.70) for the privilege. Go to a cafe. And once there, you'll save as much as 40% if you take your coffee and croissant at the counter as opposed to a table.

27. **Know the tipping rules.** Service is usually included at restaurants, so don't double-tip by mistake.

SIGHTSEEING

28. **Use the Métro or walk.** Take advantage of the passes available that lower the cost of a single ticket—from $1.40 per ticket to 80¢ per ticket if you buy a *carnet* of 10.

29. **Check the calendar of events below.** Many of the festivals and fairs are free and provide a rare opportunity to participate in a uniquely Parisian event.

30. Instead of paying to look out over the **rooftops** of Paris, go to places that are free, such as the top floor of the department store La Samaritaine.

31. **Go to the parks.** They're like set pieces of everything that makes Paris the most civilized city in the world.

32. **Tour the historic monuments**—from the place de la Concorde to the place Vendôme and place des Vosges. This is where so much of Parisian history happened, and each one resonates.

33. **Enjoy public art in the streets and parks.** The statues can give you a quick history course in the great figures and personalities that have shaped Paris, or maybe just afford you a chance to appreciate the male and female nude, such as the Maillol sculptures in the Tuileries.

34. **Hang out in the food markets.** There's one in each arrondissement. Some favorites? Mouffetard, Montorgueil, and Rue de Buci. Go early.

35. **Churches are free.** Take the opportunity to sit and contemplate, or attend a service. A mass at Notre-Dame or St-Eustache is a memorable experience. Many churches also have dramatic interiors and famous art works—paintings by Delacroix at St-Sulpice, sculptures by Coysevox at St-Roch, and etchings by Rouault at St-Severin, to name only a few.

36. Consider purchasing the **carte intermusée,** but only if you are such a museum hound that you know for sure you'll be visiting two or three museums a day. It's 70F ($12.15) for 1 day, 140F ($24.35) for 3 days, and 200F ($34.80) for 5 days. Admission to the Louvre is 45F ($7.80) and entrance fees to most other museums are the same or less, so you do the math. The card gives you access to 65 museums and monuments, allowing you to proceed directly into the museums without waiting on line—a distinct benefit at the Louvre, for example.

37. **Visit the cemeteries.** There are several worth spending time exploring: Père-Lachaise, Montmartre, and also Montparnasse.

38. Take advantage of the **reduced tariff at museums,** which usually applies on Sunday or late in the day about 2 hours before closing—ideal if you can only stand an hour or so in a museum.

39. Pick up a copy of the *Gazette de l'Hôtel Drouot,* which comes out every Friday, and check to see if there are any **auctions** that interest you. There are five major auction houses—Drouot Montaigne, Drouot Nord, Drouot Richelieu, the Salle des Ventes Saint Honoré, and the Salle des Ventes du Particulier.

SHOPPING

40. **Know what the prices are at home** if you want to save money.

41. Paris is expensive and there are very few great buys even on products made in France. **Film and toiletries** are much more expensive in Paris than in, say, the United States or the United Kingdom. Bring enough to get you through your trip.

42. For discounts on **china and other table settings,** check out the stores on the rue Paradis.

43. If **jewelry** is a pet purchase, your best bet is to go to one of the jewelry stores featuring Tibetan or Afghan jewelry. They're good quality and relatively inexpensive.

44. Most **perfumes** are steeply discounted in the United States at discount stores, so note the price you pay for your favorite fragrance before you buy it in Paris. There are discounters like Freddy in Paris, but the greatest opportunity lies in finding fragrances that are not available in the United States at discount prices.

45. Go to Monoprix, Prixunic, and other discount stores like Tati. For **discounts on fashion,** try Reciproque on rue de la Pompe, Anne Lowe on rue faubourg St-Honoré, and the Mouton a Cinq Pattes on the rue St-Placide.

46. **Look for the sign "soldes,"** meaning sale, in store windows. There are also regular seasonal sales in January and July.

47. For **antique browsing,** go to one of the great centers like the Louvre des Antiquaires at 2 place du Palais Royal, in the 1er arrondissement, or Village St.-Paul in the 4e between rue St-Paul and rue Charlemagne. Otherwise, explore the streets in the 6e arrondissement—especially rue Jacob, rue des St-Pères, and the rues de Bac and Beaune, which contain beautiful stores and galleries.

48. For a more **contemporary art scene,** stroll through the 11e arrondissement around the Bastille or along rue Quincampoix near the Centre Pompidou.

49. **Go to the markets.** Even if you don't purchase anything, the whole experience is fun. The huge Marché aux Puces, with its thousands of stalls, is one possibility; or you can enjoy smaller markets like the Bird Market and the flower markets and the many different food markets, especially Mouffetard.

50. You can secure a **tax refund,** but only if you spend $348 or more in one store. It's a complicated process, but if you spend that much in one store it's worth applying for the refund.

PARIS AFTER DARK

51. **Nightlife here is expensive.** We'll share some tricks on saving money, but don't expect to save much. Allot some money in your budget to go out on the town.

52. For **half-price theater** and other performance tickets, go to one of the kiosks by the Madeleine, on the lower level of Châtelet Les Halles Métro, or at the gare Montparnasse.

53. **Free or low-cost concerts** (about $20 per person) are often given in churches. The weekly *Pariscope* magazine contains complete concert listings and can be found at every newsstand.

54. At **clubs** you can save money by sitting at the bar instead of at a table. Some clubs are cheaper than others (see listings) and some are also cheaper during the week. Avoid weekends if you want to save money (you'll also meet more Parisians this way).

55. Unless you really must go, avoid places like the **Crazy Horse Saloon** and the **Lido**—it's not really worth blowing your budget on them.

3   Visitor Information & Entry Requirements

VISITOR INFORMATION

IN THE UNITED STATES   Your best source of information—besides this guide, of course—is the **French Government Tourist Office,** 444 Madison Ave., 16th Floor, New York, NY 10022; 676 N. Michigan Ave., Suite 3360, Chicago, IL 60611-2819; or 9454 Wilshire Blvd., Suite 715, Beverly Hills, CA 90212-2967. To request information at any of these offices, call the **France on Call** hotline at ☎ **900/ 990-0040** (50¢ per minute). For the office's Web site, see below.

IN CANADA   Write or phone the **Maison de la France/French Government Tourist Office,** 1981 av. McGill College, Suite 490, Montréal, H3A 2W9 (☎ **514/ 288-4264**).

IN THE UNITED KINGDOM   Write or phone the **Maison de la France/ French Government Tourist Office,** 178 Piccadilly, London, W1V 0AL (☎ **0891/ 244-123;** fax 0171/493-6594).

IN IRELAND   Write or phone the **Maison de la France/French Government Tourist Office,** 35 Lower Abbey St., Dublin 1, Ireland (☎ **01/703-4046**).

IN AUSTRALIA   Write or phone the **French Tourist Bureau,** 25 Bligh St., Sydney, NSW 2000, Australia (☎ **02/9231-5244;** fax 02/9221-8682).

IN NEW ZEALAND   There's no representative in New Zealand, so citizens should contact the Australian representative.

IN PARIS   The prime source of tourist information is the **Office de Tourisme et des Congrès de Paris,** 127 av. des Champs-Elysées, 75008 Paris (☎ **01-49-52- 53-54;** Métro: Charles-de-Gaulle-Etoile or Georges-V).

ONLINE INFORMATION SOURCES

* **Office de Tourisme et des Congrès de Paris**
  http://www.paris-promotion.fr
* **French Government Tourist Office**
  http://www.fgtousa.org
* **Maison de la France**
  http://www.franceguide.com
* **Relais & Châteaux**
  http://www.integra.fr/relaischateaux
* **The Paris Pages**
  http://www.paris.org
* **FranceScape**
  http://www.france.com/francescape
* **WebMuseum**
  http://sunsite.unc.edu/wm

ENTRY REQUIREMENTS

DOCUMENTS

For visits of less than 3 months, all American and Canadian travelers need is a valid passport. For longer stays, American travelers must apply for a long-term visa. Applications and information are available from the **French Embassy,** 4101 Reservoir Rd. NW, Washington, D.C. 20007 (☎ **202/944-6000**), or from the **consulate** at 935 Fifth Ave., New York, NY 10021 (☎ **212/606-3653**).

Citizens of Britain and Ireland need only their national identity card. Citizens of New Zealand need only a valid passport, but Australians also need a visa.

CUSTOMS

Customs restrictions differ for citizens of the European Union (EU) and for citizens of non-EU countries. Non-EU nationals can bring in duty free 200 cigarettes or 100 cigarillos or 50 cigars or 250 grams of smoking tobacco. This amount is doubled if you live outside Europe. You can, as well, bring in 2 liters of wine and 1 liter of alcohol over 38.80 proof. In addition, you can bring in 50 grams of perfume, $^1/_4$ liter of toilet water, 500 grams of coffee, and 200 grams of tea. Those 15 and over can also bring in 300F ($52.15) in other goods; for those 14 and under, the limit is 150F ($26).

Visitors from EU countries can bring in 200 cigarettes or 100 cigarillos or 50 cigars or 250 grams of smoking tobacco. The limit for spirits is 5 liters of table wine, $1^1/_2$ liters of alcohol over 38.80 proof, and 3 liters of alcohol under 38.80 proof. In addition, visitors can bring in 75 grams of perfume, $^3/_8$ liter of toilet water, 1,000 grams of coffee, and 80 grams of tea. Visitors 15 and over can bring in other goods totaling 2,800F ($487); for those under 15, the limit is 700F ($121.75).

Items destined for personal use, including bicycles and sports equipment already in use, whether or not contained in personal luggage, are admitted without formality, providing the quantity or the type of goods imported does not indicate the owner's intention to carry out a commercial transaction. These items cannot be sold or given away in France and must be reexported.

A Note on Customs for British Citizens   British citizens traveling within the European Union can bring back to the United Kingdom virtually as much as they like provided items are purchased in ordinary French stores and not in the duty-free outlets. Customs and Excise does set theoretical limits: 10 liters of spirits, plus 110 liters of beer, 20 liters of fortified wine, 90 liters of ordinary wine (no more than 60 liters of this can be champagne), 800 cigarettes, 400 cigarillos, 200 cigars, and 1 kilo of tobacco. But remember, this only applies to goods bought in ordinary shops.

You cannot buy goods and take them with you for resale at home. This is a criminal offense in the United Kingdom, and customs officers claim to be looking out for those making repeated trips or those laden down with goods.

4 Money

The French **franc** (F) is divided into 100 **centimes.** There are coins of 5, 10, and 20 centimes, and $^1/_2$, 1, 2, 5, 10, and 20 francs. Sometimes there are two types of coins for one denomination (this became especially common after the bicentennial of the French Revolution). Bills come in denominations of 20, 50, 100, 200, and 500 francs.

The value of all national currencies fluctuates on the market. This guidebook has been written under the assumption that you can buy 5.75F for US$1 and 9.4F for £1. Call a commercial bank or look in the financial pages of your newspaper to find the current rate of exchange. You will get slightly less than this published rate when you exchange money.

For information on currency exchange, see "Fast Facts: Paris," in chapter 3.

CREDIT CARDS & ATM CARDS   Automatic-teller machines that accept **bank cards** associated with the Plus or Cirrus systems are increasingly widespread in Paris. The exchange rate is usually very good, and the convenience is unbeatable. In fact,

The French Franc, the U.S. Dollar & the British Pound

For American Readers   At this writing $1 = approximately 5.75 francs (or 1 franc = 17¢), and this was the rate of exchange used to calculate the dollar values in this book (rounded to the nearest nickel).

For British Readers   At this writing £1 = approximately 9.4 francs (or 1 franc = 11p), and this was the rate of exchange used to calculate the pound values in the table below.

Note: The rates given here fluctuate from time to time and may not be the same when you travel to France. Therefore, this table should be used only as a guide.

F	U.S.$	U.K.£	F	U.S.$	U.K.£
1	.17	.11	100	17.39	10.63
2	.35	.22	125	21.73	13.29
3	.52	.33	150	26.08	15.95
4	.69	.44	175	30.43	18.61
5	.87	.55	200	34.78	21.27
6	1.04	.66	225	39.13	29.25
7	1.22	.77	250	43.47	23.93
8	1.39	.88	275	47.82	29.25
9	1.56	.99	300	52.17	31.91
10	1.73	1.10	325	56.52	34.57
15	2.60	1.65	350	60.86	37.23
20	3.47	2.20	375	65.21	39.89
25	4.34	3.30	400	67.56	42.55
50	8.69	6.50	500	86.95	53.19

as long as the fees for such transactions remain low, obtaining cash this way is the best way to go.

Major credit cards are accepted throughout Paris, but their use, especially at budget restaurants and hotels, is not as widespread as it is in North America. Always check beforehand. Both **American Express** and **Diners Club** are widely recognized. The French equivalent for **Visa** is Carte Bleue. If you see the Eurocard sign on an establishment, they'll accept **MasterCard.** The exchange rate you get on a credit card purchase is based on the current rate when your bill is generated, not what the rate was when you actually made the purchase.

You can also use credit cards with a personal identification number (PIN) to withdraw francs from ATMs at many banks in France as long as your PIN has four digits. Check with your credit card company before leaving home.

TRAVELER'S CHECKS   You can easily exchange traveler's checks in U.S. dollars for French francs all over Paris, but don't expect to use them directly at many budget establishments; change them for francs at a bank and use cash instead. Most establishments also will not accept traveler's checks in French francs either. Even those places that do accept traveler's checks in U.S. dollars will probably give you a poor exchange rate. Before leaving home, purchase traveler's checks and some French currency—about 50 to 100 dollars' worth—unless you don't mind waiting at the exchange offices at the Paris airports.

American Express (☎ **800/221-7282** in the U.S. and Canada) is the most widely recognized traveler's check abroad; the agency imposes a 1% commission. Checks are free to members of AAA and to holders of certain types of American Express cards.

What Things Cost in Paris	U.S. $
Taxi from Charles-de-Gaulle Airport to the city center	38.00
Taxi from Orly Airport to the city center	25.00
Public transportation for an average trip within the city (from a Métro carnet of 10)	.80
Local telephone call	.40
Double room at the Hôtel des Grands Ecoles (moderate)	82.00
Double room at the Grand Hôtel Léveque (budget)	58.00
Lunch for one, without wine, at Hippopotamus (moderate)	13.00
Lunch for one, without wine, at Chez Max (budget)	13.00
Dinner for one, without wine, at Bofinger (moderate)	29.50
Dinner for one, without wine, at Le Petit Keller (budget)	14.00
Dinner for one, without wine, at Au Bon Accueil (moderate)	24.00
Glass of wine	3.50
Coca-Cola	4.00
Cup of coffee	2.50
Roll of ASA 100 color film, 36 exposures	9.00
Admission to the Louvre	8.00
Movie ticket	9.00
Concert ticket (at the Salle Pleyel)	13.00

You can also try **Bank of America** (☎ 415/622-3456), which charges a 1% commission everywhere but California, MasterCard-affiliated **Thomas Cook** (☎ 800/223-7373 in the U.S., or 212/974-5696, collect, in Canada), or **Citicorp** (☎ 800/645-6556 in the U.S., or 813/623-1709, collect, in Canada).

Each of these agencies will refund your checks if they are lost or stolen, provided that you can produce sufficient documentation (to be safe, keep these records separate from your checks). American Express and Bank of America have the most offices around the world. Purchase checks in a variety of denominations—$20, $50, and $100. Remember that you always get a better rate if you cash traveler's checks at the banks or agencies that issued them: Citicorp at Citibank, American Express at American Express, and so forth.

5 When to Go

Although April in Paris may at times be too cold for some travelers, spring and fall are generally the best times to experience the city. Temperatures are usually mild, and the performing arts and other cultural activities are in full swing. In winter, lack of sunshine and occasional bitter-cold winds can be disappointing, but then again, there is so much to see and to do that you won't miss the picnics in the parks.

Summer can be mild or extreme, depending on the year and your luck, and you'll have to deal with a deeper glut of tourists. Many Parisians, especially in August, head for the coast or the mountains. The city is transformed, and the banks of the Seine become a makeshift beach: Paris-Plage. Cultural life dwindles and many restaurants, cafes, and shops close for up to a month—what the French call the *fermeture annuelle* (annual closing). The long hours of daylight, though, will give you more time to explore the city and its street life. You may also be able to negotiate a better deal with your hotel in August, since you won't be competing with business travelers for hotel space.

Paris's Average Daytime Temperature and Rainfall

	Jan	Feb	Mar	Apr	May	June	July	Aug	Sept	Oct	Nov	Dec
Temp. °F	38	39	46	51	58	64	66	66	61	53	45	40
Rainfall (in.)	3.2	2.9	2.4	2.7	3.2	3.5	3.3	3.7	3.3	3.0	3.5	3.1

HOLIDAYS

France has lots of national holidays, most of them tied to the church calendar. On these days, shops, businesses, government offices, and most restaurants will be closed: New Year's Day (January 1); Easter Monday (late March or April); Labor Day (May 1); Liberation Day (May 8); Ascension Thursday (in May or June, 40 days after Easter); Whit Monday, also called Pentecost Monday (51st day after Easter, in May or June); Bastille Day (July 14); Assumption Day (August 15); All Saints' Day (November 1); Armistice Day (November 11); and Christmas Day (December 25).

In addition, schedules may be disrupted on Shrove Tuesday (the Tuesday before Ash Wednesday, in January or February) and Good Friday (late March or April).

PARIS CALENDAR OF EVENTS

When you arrive, check with the French Tourist Office and buy *Pariscope* (a weekly guide with an English-language insert) or *L'Officiel des Spectacles* for dates, places, and other up-to-date information.

January
- **La Grande Parade de Montmartre.** Instead of simply pulling the covers over their heads after New Year's Eve, many Parisians head up to the place Pigalle for a big, brassy parade that shows that even a city renowned for its elegance likes a little bit of Rose Bowl–style flash once a year. Elaborate floats represent everything from trade associations to the local firehouse, and there are majorettes and bands galore. The parade begins at 2pm in the place Pigalle in the 18e arrondissement and ends at the place Jules-Joffrin, also in the 18e. Great fun. Call ☎ 01-42-62-21-21 for information. January 1.
- **Epiphany (Fête des Rois).** If you're in Paris on January 6, you might wonder why you see people wearing gold-paper crowns. They're celebrating the Feast of the Three Kings. The main object of celebration—a flaky closed tart filled with almond paste and concealing a charm usually made of ceramic (watch your teeth)—is sold at all patisseries, and the crown comes with it. According to custom, whoever finds the charm becomes king or queen for the day, is entitled to wear a crown, and has free reign, as it were, in his or her choice of a consort. Now, of course, every pastry contains a charm. You work out the social implications. January 6.
- **La Mairie de Paris Vous Invite au Concert.** As a way of beating the winter doldrums and animating the city, the city government of Paris sponsors a two-for-the-price-of-one special on a variety of different jazz and classical concerts all over the city. The special promotion lasts 2 weeks. For information, call ☎ 01-42-78-44-72. Mid-January.
- **Commemorative Mass for Louis XVI.** One of the odder events on the Parisian annual calendar is this mass in honor of the beheaded king. It draws a full

turn-out of French aristocrats and royalists, along with a sampling of French far-right types. The event takes place at the Chapelle Expiatoire at 29 rue Pasquier in the 8e arrondissement. For information, call ☎ **01-42-65-35-80.** Sunday closest to January 21.

- **Chinese New Year Festival.** The traditional Chinese New Year's parade with fireworks and dragon dancers is a good time to discover Paris's thriving Chinatown. This neighborhood in the 13e arrondissement has little architectural charm—it's mostly high-rises—but it does have good street life and many excellent restaurants. For information, call ☎ **01-45-20-74-09.** Date varies.

- **18 Francs à 18 Heures.** Translating roughly as "$3.15 at 6pm," this extremely popular annual midwinter film promotion allows you admission to the 6pm showing (or the nearest thereabouts) of any film in town for 18F ($3.15). It's a great opportunity to catch up with the latest French and foreign films at bargain rates. Get to the theater early, though, since long lines form quickly. Date varies.

February

- **Foire à la Feraille de Paris.** Offering an opportunity to visit one of the lesser-known but most beautiful parks in Paris—attractive even in midwinter—this annual antique and secondhand fair is held in the Parc Floral de Paris, a garden in the Bois de Boulogne in the 12e arrondisement. Call the **Paris Tourist Office** for exact dates at ☎ **01-49-52-53-54.**

- **Salon de l'Agriculture.** This annual fair offers a fascinating glimpse of rural and agricultural France, which is where the country's heart really lies, as hundreds of farmers come to town to display their animals and produce. Different regional food stands offer a great taste of corners of the country you may never get to visit, and the atmosphere is friendly and quintessentially French. It's held at the Parc des Expositions de Paris, Porte de Versailles, in the 15e arrondissement. For more information, call ☎ **01-49-09-64-70.** Last week of February to first week of March.

March

- **Salon de Mars.** Even if you haven't any intention of buying, this high-caliber annual art and antiques fair is a fascinating place to visit. The majority of what's on display are 17th-, 18th-, and 19th-century antiques and paintings. The fair is held in a temporary exhibition space near the Eiffel Tower known as the Espace Eiffel Branley. A 50F ($8.70) admission fee is charged. For more information, call ☎ **01-44-94-86-80.** Late March.

- **Foire du Trone.** Not only does it offer great people watching, but this large and very popular annual carnival held at the Pelouse de Reuilly in the Bois de Vincennes might also offer an antidote to anyone who's overdosed on the city's rich cultural offerings. They have a huge Ferris wheel, lots of other rides and games, and sell all kinds of hokey souvenirs and high-calorie fairgrounds food. Call ☎ **01-46-27-52-29** for more information. Late March to end of May.

- **Prêt à Porter Fashion Shows.** Although these shows are not open to the general public, they're worth noting because hotels and restaurants are particularly booked up at this time. The same holds true for the autumn prêt à porter (ready-to-wear) shows, which are generally scheduled for early to mid-October. Mid-March.

- **La Passion à Menilmontant.** In a local tradition that's been observed since 1932, professional actors and residents of this Paris neighborhood have been performing the Passion Play for a month around Easter. The play is staged at the Theatre de Menilmontant in the 20e arrondissement. Call ☎ **01-46-36-98-60** for performance schedule and ticket prices. Mid-March to mid-April.

- **Le Chemin de la Croix.** A crowd of the faithful (which anyone can join, faithful or not) follows Cardinal Lustiger, the Archbishop of Paris, from the square Willette in Montmartre up the steps to the basilica of Sacré Coeur, and watch as he performs the 14 stations of the cross. 12:30pm on Good Friday.
- **Salon International du Livre.** The largest book fair in the Francophone world also has an important foreign-languages section and an interesting line up of visiting writers who read from their works. Call the **Paris Tourist Office** (☎ **01-41-90-47-40**) for exact dates, venue, and opening hours. Mid-March.

April

- **April Fool's Day.** Watch your back on April 1 if you're in Paris; local tradition is to stick a paper fish on the back of anyone unsuspecting, thereby awarding him or her a dunce cap. In French, this day is known as Poisson d'Avril. If you're reading a French newspaper and come upon an article about an elephant giving birth to a human baby girl, don't panic; phony articles are a tradition in French newspapers, too. April 1.
- **Paris Marathon.** This increasingly popular urban road race surely has some of the most magnificent scenery in the world, as the route takes in a variety of the city's most beautiful monuments. Held on a Sunday in mid-April, it attracts enthusiastic crowds. For more information, call ☎ **01-53-17-03-10.** Mid-April.
- **Foire de Paris.** A sprawling fair held at the Parc des Expositions at the Porte de Verailles, with hundreds of stands selling food and wine, often at excellent prices, as well as a variety of clothing and household goods. Very popular with Parisians, it's a great place to bargain hunt and people-watch. Call ☎ **01-49-09-60-00** for more information. Late April to early May.
- **La Marie de Paris Vous Invite au Theatre.** Perhaps you'll have to speak French to appreciate this annual theater promotion, wherein anyone buying one theater ticket gets a second one free. Check the theater listings in the weekly entertainment guide *Pariscope* to see what's on, though, since the odd English-language play is occasionally staged here. For information, call ☎ **01-42-78-44-72.** Late April to early May.

May

- **May Day.** On the French version of Labor Day, you'll see people selling corsages of lilies-of-the-valley all over the city. Banks, post offices, and most museums are closed, and although union membership has dwindled over the years, there's a lively workers' parade that terminates at the place de la Bastille. Call the **Paris Tourist Office** (☎ **01-49-52-53-54**) for more information. May 1.
- **TBB Jazz Festival.** Held at the Theatre Boulogne-Billancourt in the adjacent and Métro-accessible suburb of the same name, this is a lively jazz festival with a generally good program. Call ☎ **01-46-03-60-44** for more information. Early to mid-May.
- **Vintage Car Rally, Montmartre.** Held annually since 1924 on the Sunday closest to May 15, this is a wonderful sepia-toned event, as a splendid array of antique cars makes its way through the streets of Montmartre. The rally starts at 10am in the tiny rue Lepic and ends at the place du Terte. For more information, call ☎ **01-42-62-21-21.** Mid-May.
- **Les Cinq Jours Extraordinaire.** The title of this annual Left Bank antiques event translates as The Five Extraordinary Days, and that's what they always are. The shops in the rues du Bac, de Lille, de Beaune, des St-Pères, and de l'Université, and also on the quai Voltaire, hold a free week-long open house featuring some special object that's been chosen according to an annually different theme—one

year it might be the Great Castles of Europe, the next Voyages of Discovery. The whole quarter takes on a festive ambience as the streets are lined with red carpets and shop fronts are dressed up with plants and flowers. Call ☎ **01-42-61-82-06** for information. Third week of May.

- **D'Anvers aux Abbesses.** Continuing the artistic traditions of the Montmartre quarter, artists currently working the area open their studios to the general public for 3 days. This is a fascinating way to explore this neighborhood and maybe meet the next Lautrec or Utrillo. Call ☎ **01-42-52-79-78** for information. Third week in May.

- **Grandes Eaux Musicales et Grandes Fêtes de Nuite de Versailles.** Seeing the magnificent fountains in the gardens of the Château de Versailles come alive to the sounds of Baroque music is a truly unforgettable experience. There are performances at 11:15am and 3:30pm every Sunday from mid-May to early October. The Grandes Fêtes are a spectacular sound and light show with fireworks that are held two Saturdays in July and two Saturdays in September. Château de Versailles, Versailles. Call ☎ **01-39-50-36-22** for more information. Sundays, May to October.

- **French Tennis Open.** The French are mad for tennis, and the French Open is a big event on the city's annual calendar. It's held in the Stade Roland Garros on the western edge of the city during the last week in May and first week in June, and tickets are keenly sought after. Unsold tickets—many are taken by corporate sponsors—go on sale 2 weeks before the competition starts. The stadium is located at 2 av. Gordon Bennett in the 16e arrondissement. Call ☎ **01-47-43-48-00** for more information. May to June.

June

- **Fireworks at La Villette.** The Parc de la Villette was one of the most ambitious redevelopment schemes to have been undertaken in Paris in this century. Today, a science museum and a vast modern music center stand on the site of the former municipal slaughterhouses. Once a year, a famous architect or designer is invited to design this annual fireworks celebration, which takes place along the banks of the canal de l'Ourcq. Call ☎ **01-40-03-75-03** for more information. Mid-June.

- **Festival Chopin à Paris.** The Orangerie in the beautiful Bagatelle gardens on the edge of the Bois de Boulogne is the backdrop for this much loved annual series of piano recitals. Call ☎ **01-45-00-22-19** for details. Daily from mid-June to mid-July.

- **Festival de la Musique.** Culture takes to the streets every June 21 when the entire city becomes a concert venue in celebration of the summer solstice. Everything from jazz to the latest dance music is offered free in different locations around town. The program changes from year to year, but there's usually a big rock concert in the place de la Republique and a fine classical concert in the gardens of the Palais-Royal. For scheduling information, call ☎ **01-40-03-94-70.** June 21.

- **Festival du Marais.** A series of concerts, dance events, plays, and readings celebrates this historic neighborhood in the heart of the city. For information and tickets to various dates, stop by the festival office at 44 rue François-Miron in the 4e arrondissement, or call ☎ **01-48-87-60-08.** Second week of June to second week of July.

- **The Paris Air Show.** One of the most important aeronautical events in the world takes place in odd-numbered years at Le Bourget Airport just outside of Paris. It's a delight for plane buffs, as all of the latest technology is on display. Call the **Paris Tourist Office** for more information at ☎ **01-49-52-53-54.** June 15 to 27.

- **Fête des Tuileries.** You get a spectacular view of the city from the enormous Ferris wheel this carnival sets up on the rue de Rivoli side of the Tuileries Gardens from late June to late August. It's a great night out if you're traveling with children. June to August.
- **La Course des Garçons de Café.** The 5-mile race in which cafe waiters and waitresses dash along with fully loaded trays is surely one of the most original and amusing special events on the Paris calendar. The race starts and ends in the square in front of the Hôtel de Ville, or Paris's City Hall, in the 4e arrondissement. Call ☎ 01-46-33-89-89 for more information. Late June or early July, on a Sunday.
- **Fête du Cinema.** Another highlight on the calendar of local cinema-lovers, this is a 3-day event that begins on the last Sunday in June. After buying one full-price movie ticket, you get a pass which enables you to see as many other films as you like for 10F a show. Last Sunday to last Tuesday in June.
- **Grand Prix de Paris.** One of the most important and stylish racing events of the year in Paris is held at the Longchamp Racecourse in late June. The track is located in the Bois de Boulogne; call ☎ 01-49-10-20-30 for information. Late June.
- **Halle That Jazz.** One of liveliest and highest-caliber jazz festivals in Paris is held annually at the Grand Halle de la Villette in the Parc de la Villette, 211 av. Jean-Jaures, 19e (☎ 01-40-03-75-75). Big-name talent might include Wynton Marsalis or Herbie Hancock. Late June to early July.

July

- **New Morning All-Stars' Festival.** Every night in July at 8:30pm, this granddaddy of Paris jazz clubs hosts different world-class talent. The club's located at 7–9 rue des Petites Ecuries in the 10e arrondissement. Call ☎ 01-45-23-51-41 for information. Daily in July.
- **Bastille Day.** The 14th of July is the French national holiday that celebrates the storming of the Bastille. The celebrations begin on the evening of the 13th with *bals,* or dances, held in fire stations all over the city. Some of the best bals are in the fire station on the rue du Vieux-Colombier near the place St-Sulpice, 6e arrondissement; the rue Sevigne in the 4e arrondissement; and the rue Blanche, near the place Pigalle in the 9e arrondissement. The bals are free and are open to one and all. On the 14th, there's a big military parade starting at 10am on the Champs-Elysées; get there early if you hope to see anything. Capping it all off is the sound and light show with terrific fireworks at the Torcadéro; it's extremely crowded, so many people watch the fireworks from the Champs de Mars across the river. Call ☎ 01-49-52-53-54 for more information. July 14.
- **Paris, Quartier d'Eté.** The emphasis during this annual city-sponsored summer festival is on open-air cultural events held all over town, including contemporary dance, music, and film. The open-air cinema at the Parc de la Villette is a particularly popular part of this festival. Call ☎ 01-44-83-64-40 for more information. July 14 to August 15.
- **Tour de France.** Perhaps the most famous bicycle race in the world always ends in Paris on the Champs-Elysées. Depending upon the annually decided route, you can see the cyclists whir by elsewhere in the city as well. Call ☎ 01-41-33-15-00 for information. Third or fourth Sunday in July.
- **Musique en l'Ile.** A delightful series of mostly baroque concerts held at the handsome 17th-century church of St. Louis on the Ile Saint Louis. Call ☎ 01-44-62-70-90 for program information. Late July through the end of August.

August

- **Fête de l'Assomption.** The Feast of the Assumption is an important French holiday celebrated on August 15. The services at Notre-Dame are the most popular and colorful, and banners are draped from the church's towers to celebrate the day. Call ☎ 01-43-34-56-01 for the hours of scheduled masses. August 15.

September

- **Biennale des Antiquaires.** One of the largest and most prestigious antiques shows in the world is held in even-numbered years in the Cour Carré du Louvre, the underground exhibition space connected to the Louvre Museum. The show will probably return to the Grand Palais after it's been renovated, probably in the year 2000. Usually held at the beginning of September, the show is open to the public. Contact the **Paris Tourist Office** at ☎ 01-49-52-53-54 for more information. Early September.
- **Journées Portes Ouvertes.** You'll be lucky if you're in Paris on this mid-September Saturday and Sunday as hundreds of generally off-limits palaces, churches, and other official buildings are opened to the general public. Since lines can be enormous, you should plan what you want to see and show up early. A list and map of all the open buildings are available from the **Paris Tourist Office,** ☎ 01-49-52-53-54. Weekend closest to September 15.
- **Festival d'Automne.** This superb arts festival, held at venues all over town, is recognized throughout Europe for its innovative programming and for the high quality of its performers. Programs are available by mail so that you can plan and book ahead for events you don't want to miss. Write to the Festival at 56 rue de Rivoli, 75001, Paris, or call ☎ 01-42-96-12-27. September 15 to December 31.

October

- **Fêtes des Vendanges à Montmartre.** A high-times Bacchanalian party that celebrates the now almost completely bygone days when Montmartre was planted with vineyards. A single vineyard remains, and the wine that is produced, known as Clos Montmartre, is auctioned off at high prices to benefit local charities. (Word is that it's an act of charity to try and drink the stuff, too.) Held on the first or second Saturday of October, the party also sees locals dressed in old-fashioned costumes and the streets alive with music. For more information, call ☎ 01-42-62-21-21. Early October.
- **Prix de l'Arc de Triomphe.** The ultimate day at the races and the most prestigious equestrian event in France. The well-dressed crowd gets through a lot of champagne, and the atmosphere is festive. The race is held in early October at the Hippodrome de Longchamp in the Bois de Boulogne. Call ☎ 01-49-10-20-30. Early October.
- **FIAC (Foire Internationale d'Art Contemporain).** One of the largest and most contemporary art fairs in the world began in 1975 and now has stands from more than 150 galleries, half of them foreign. Photography was added to the event in 1994 and has since become very popular. As interesting for browsing as buying, the fair is currently held in the temporary exhibition space Espace Branley, near the Eiffel Tower; it will return to the Grand Palais once repairs are completed to this glass-domed space. For more information, call ☎ 01-41-90-47-47. Early October.
- **La Genie de la Bastille.** The Bastille District, formerly a working-class area with lots of furniture-making workshops, has become home to many artists within the past 20 years. This festival, which runs for 4 days in mid-October, allows you to visit about 100 different artists and view their work in their homes and studios. Call ☎ 01-43-42-52-22 for more information. Mid-October.
- **Paris Auto Show.** One of the premier car shows in the world, this one is held in even-numbered years in the exhibition halls at the Porte de Versailles. It's open to the general public, and though the offerings come from all over the world, it's an

especially great place to check out the latest in European chrome. For more information, call the **Paris Tourist Office** at ☎ **01-49-52-53-54.** Mid-October.

November

- **Mois de la Photo.** The month of November celebrates photography with shows in many of the city's major museums and galleries. Check listings in the weekly entertainment guide *Pariscope,* or call ☎ **01-43-53-41-78.** All November.
- **Armistice Day.** Every November 11, the French commemorate their dead from WWI and WWII with a wreath-laying ceremony at the Arc de Triomphe. November 11.
- **Beaujolais Nouveau.** The annual release of the year's first Beaujolais, a fruity red wine from the vineyards north of Lyon, makes for a lively night out in late November. Wine bars and cafes are packed, as are many bistros, so book ahead if you're out to dinner that night. Third Thursday in November.
- **Festival d'Art Sacré de la Ville de Paris.** An annual series of holiday concerts offered in the churches and monuments of Paris and sponsored by the city. For program information, call ☎ **01-44-70-64-10.** November 25 to December 25.
- **Lancement des Illuminations des Champs-Elysées.** The most glorious Christmas lights in Paris are the tour-de-force decorations hung in the trees lining this grand avenue. The annual inauguration of the lights is a festive evening in late November, with jazz concerts and an international star du jour who pushes the symbolic button that lights up the avenue. For more information, call the **Paris Tourist Office** at ☎ **01-49-52-53-54.** Late November.

December

- **La Crèche sur le Parvis.** At the invitation of the city of Paris, a different foreign city each year installs a life-sized Christmas manger scene in the plaza in front of the Hôtel de Ville. The crèche is open daily from 10am to 8pm. December 1 to January 3.

6 Health & Insurance

MEDICAL REQUIREMENTS & HEALTH CONCERNS

Unless you are arriving from an area known to be suffering from an epidemic, no inoculations or vaccinations are required to enter France. If you are currently on medication, carry a doctor's prescription (written in the drugs' generic names, not name brands) along with enough of your medication to last the entire trip.

Paris should not pose any major health hazards, although some travelers suffer from diarrhea caused by a change in your normal intestinal bacteria. It's usually nothing to worry about; just take along some antidiarrhea medicine. Although the water in France is considered safe, if you're prone to intestinal difficulties you may want to consume mineral water only.

Sometimes travelers find that a change of diet in France leads to constipation. If this occurs, eat a high-fiber diet and drink plenty of mineral water. Avoid large lunches and dinners with wine.

You can obtain a list of English-speaking doctors in France from the **International Association for Medical Assistance to Travelers (IAMAT),** in the United States at 417 Center St., Lewiston, NY 14092 (☎ **716/754-4883**); in Canada, at 40 Regal Rd., Guelph, ON, N1K 1B5 (☎ **519/836-0102**). Getting medical help in France is relatively easy, compared to what you must go through in many countries, so don't be unduly worried if you fall ill, even in rural areas. Competent doctors can be found in every part of the country.

If your medical condition is chronic, always talk to your doctor before taking an international trip. For such conditions as epilepsy, heart condition, diabetes, or some other affliction, wear a **Medic Alert Identification Tag,** which will immediately alert any doctor as to the nature of your trouble. It also provides the number of Medic Alert's 24-hour hotline so that a foreign doctor can obtain your medical records. For a lifetime membership, the cost is a well-spent $35, $50, or $75 (price depends on whether you choose a stainless steel, sterling silver, or gold tag). Contact the Medic Alert Foundation, 2323 Colorado Ave., Turlock, CA 95382-2018 (☎ **800/ 432-5378**).

Don't forget to carry all your vital medicine with you in your carry-on luggage, in the event your checked luggage is lost.

INSURANCE

Most American travelers are covered by their hometown policies in the event of an accident or sudden illness while away on vacation. Also, some credit card companies offer free, automatic travel-accident insurance, up to $100,000, when you purchase travel tickets on their cards. Before you purchase additional protection, check to see if you are already covered in foreign countries by your HMO or insurance carrier.

Many homeowners' insurance policies cover theft of luggage during foreign travel and loss of documents—Eurailpass, passport, or airline ticket, for example. Coverage is usually limited to about US$500. To submit a claim on your insurance, remember that you'll need police reports.

Comprehensive policies against lost or damaged baggage and trip cancellation or interruption costs can also be purchased from travel agents, credit card companies, and the following:

Tele-Trip Company, Mutual of Omaha Plaza, Omaha, NE 68175 (☎ **800/ 228-9792**). In addition to selling all types of travel-related insurance, the company offers foreign exchange services at most major airports or by mail.

Travel Guard International, 1100 Center Point Dr., Stevens Point, WI 54481 (☎ **800/826-1300;** 800/634-0644 in Wisconsin). A 7-day comprehensive insurance package costs $72. Some limitations apply.

Travelers Insurance Company, Travel Insurance Division, One Tower Sq., 10 NB, Hartford, CT 06183-5040 (☎ **800/243-3174**). Travel accident and illness coverage starts at $10 to $65 for 6 to 10 days; $500 worth of coverage for lost, damaged, or delayed baggage costs $20 for 6 to 10 days; and trip cancellation insurance costs $5.50 for each $100 worth of coverage.

7 Tips for Travelers with Special Needs

FOR TRAVELERS WITH DISABILITIES

If you have a disability you can still travel to France, as facilities are certainly above the world average and in general are superior to others in Europe. The French government does more and more every year to make the country's public facilities more accessible and easier to navigate.

If you're contemplating a trip to France, contact one of the French Government Tourist Offices abroad (see "Visitor Information," earlier in this chapter). You'll be sent a publication with an English glossary called *Touristes Quand Même.* It provides a province-by-province overview of the facilities for the disabled in the French transportation system and at monuments and museums.

Nearly all modern hotels in France now provide rooms specially modified for the needs of travelers with disabilities. Older hotels, unless they've been renovated, may not provide such important features as elevators, special toilet facilities, or ramps for wheelchair access. For a list of hotels in France providing such facilities, write to **Association des Paralysées de France,** 22 rue du Père-Guérin, 75013 Paris (☎ 01-44-16-83-83).

Another source of information is **Moss Rehabilitation Hospital,** 1200 W. Tabor Rd., Philadelphia, PA 19141 (☎ 215/456-9600), which provides info to telephone callers only. It not only will give you a general overview of facilities in Paris and other cities, but also will provide special toll-free airline numbers set up for the hard of hearing.

You may also want to consider joining a tour designed specifically for disabled visitors. Names and addresses of such tour operators can be obtained by writing to the **Society for the Advancement of Travel for the Handicapped,** 347 Fifth Ave., Suite 610, New York, NY 10016 (☎ 212/447-7284). Yearly membership dues in this society are $45, $25 for senior citizens and students. Send a self-addressed stamped envelope.

You might also contact the **Federation of the Handicapped,** 211 W. 14th St., New York, NY 10011 (☎ 212/727-4200), which offers summer tours for members (the annual membership fee is low).

In France, most high-speed trains are equipped for wheelchair access. Guide dogs ride free. Older trains have special compartments built for wheelchair boarding. On the Paris Métro, handicapped persons are able to sit in wider seats provided for their comfort. Some stations don't have escalators or elevators, however, and this obviously presents problems.

FOR SENIORS

Many discounts are available for seniors—that is, men and women who have reached, as the French say, "the third age." At any railway station in the country, senior citizens (men and women 60 years of age or older) can obtain a **Carte Vermeil** (silver-gilt card) for a cost of 143F ($24.85). This card entitles you to a 50% discount on train fares in both first- and second-class compartments, but not during peak periods. Additional discounts include a 10% reduction on all rail excursions. Carte Vermeil also delivers reduced prices on certain regional bus lines as well as on theater tickets in Paris and half-price admission to some museums. The Vermilion Card is valid for 1 year.

The French domestic airline, Air Inter, honors "third agers" by offering them 25% to 50% reductions on its regular, nonexcursion tariffs. Again, restrictions do apply. Reductions are available on about 20 Air France flights a week to Nice.

One of the most dynamic travel organizations for seniors is **Elderhostel,** 75 Federal St., Boston, MA 02110-1941 (☎ 617/426-8056), established in 1975. It operates an array of programs throughout Europe, including France. Most courses last around 3 weeks and represent good value, since they include airfare, accommodations in student dormitories or modest inns, all meals, and tuition. Courses involve no homework, are ungraded, and are often liberal arts oriented. They're not luxury vacations, but they are fun and fulfilling. Participants must be 60 years of age or older. However, if two members go as a couple, only one member needs to be of age. Write or call for their free newsletter and a list of upcoming courses and destinations.

SAGA International Holidays is also well known for its all-inclusive tours for seniors. They prefer that travelers be at least 60 years old. Insurance is included in the price of any of their tours, which encompass dozens of locations in Europe and usually last for an average of 17 nights. Contact SAGA International Holidays, 222 Berkeley St., Boston, MA 02116 (☎ 800/343-0273).

In the United States, the best organization to belong to is the **American Association of Retired Persons,** 601 E. St. NW, Washington, DC 20049 (☎ **202/434-2460**). Members are offered discounts on car rentals, hotels, airfares, and, in some cases, sightseeing via their Travel Experience program.

Information is also available from the **National Council of Senior Citizens,** 8403 Colesville Rd., Silver Spring, MD 20910 (☎ **301/578-8800**). A nonprofit organization, the council charges $12 per person to join (couples pay $16), for which you receive a monthly newsletter, part of which is devoted to travel tips. Discounts on hotels and auto rentals are previewed.

FOR SINGLES

The travel industry seems to be geared to people traveling in groups of two or more. This is especially true in Paris, where single rooms are hard to come by and are often outrageously expensive.

If you don't want to travel alone but can't talk any friends into the trip, there are companies that can help you. One such company that matches like-minded travelers is **Travel Companion Exchange,** P.O. Box 833-F, Amityville, NY 11701 (☎ **516/454-0880**). It provides listings of people interested in finding partners in travel. Matches are made by a computer, which groups travelers into categories by special interests, education, age, and location. The service costs $99 for 8 months and boasts more than 2,000 active participants.

Singleworld, P.O. Box 1999, Rye, NY 10580 (☎ **800/223-6490** or 914/967-3334), is a travel agency that operates tours geared to solo traveling. Two basic types of tours are available, either youth-oriented tours for people under 35 or else jaunts for all ages. Annual dues are $25.

Since single supplements on tours usually carry a hefty price tag, a way to get around that is to find a tour operator that allows you to share a room. One such company that offers a "guaranteed-share plan" is **Globus-Cosmos,** with offices at South Federal Plaza, Littleton, CO 80123 (☎ **800/221-0090**).

FOR FAMILIES

If you're planning to take your family abroad, you'll need to do some advance planning. If you have very small children, you may want to discuss your vacation plans with your family doctor and take along whatever the child will need, including such standard supplies as children's aspirin, a thermometer, Band-Aids, and the like.

On airlines, you must request a special menu for children at least 24 hours in advance. If baby food is required, however, bring your own and ask a flight attendant to warm it to the right temperature.

Arrange ahead of time for such necessities as a crib, bottle warmer, and car seat if you're driving. (*FYI:* In France, small children are prohibited from riding in the front seat.) Find out if the place you're staying stocks baby food, and, if not, take some with you and plan to buy some abroad in French supermarkets.

Most hotels can arrange baby-sitting, but you should always hold out as long as you can for one with at least a rudimentary knowledge of English.

Anyone under age 18 is admitted free to France's national museums.

If you have a child under age 16 and you plan to travel by train in France, you should explore the possibility of buying a **Carte KIWI** for the child. At 444F ($77.20) it's not cheap, but it may be a good idea in the long run. With this card, the child gets a 50% discount on trips that start in the *période blanche* or *période bleue* (white or blue period) of the train riders' calendar, some 300 days a year. In addition, everybody accompanying the child (up to four people who need not be relatives) also benefits from a 50% discount. For more information, get the brochure **"Votre enfant voyage en train"** (yes, it has an English section) from any train station.

FOR STUDENTS & PEOPLE UNDER AGE 26

The **International Student Identity Card (ISIC),** available for $16 from the Council on International Educational Exchange (CIEE), 205 E. 42nd St., New York, NY 10017 (☎ **800/GETANID** or 212/822-2600), enables students aged 12 and up to take advantage of discounts on transportation, lodging, admission to national museums, and even movie and theater tickets. It's the best international proof of your student status. Emergency medical coverage is also included among the benefits.

To get an ISIC card, you must be enrolled full or part time in a degree program. The application must include proof of student registration (transcript or bursar's receipt, for example), a $16 registration fee, and one passport-size photo. The 1998 card is valid from September 1997 through December 1998. It comes with a guide listing student travel offices worldwide. These offices are great contact points in any city, and they can tell you how to get the most mileage out of the card in their country.

For people under the age of 24 who are not students, CIEE issues the **GO 25 Card.** Applicants must send proof of age (a copy of your birth certificate, passport, or driver's license), a $16 fee, and one passport-size photo. The card, valid from September of one year through December of the next, comes with the Travel Handbook listing discounts for cardholders.

Both the ISIC and GO 25 cards carry basic accident and sickness insurance coverage, and cardholders have access to a worldwide hotline for help in medical, legal, and financial emergencies.

CIEE has offices in Paris at 66 Champs-Elysées (☎ **01-40-75-95-10**) and also at 16 rue de Vaugirard 75006 (☎ **01-44-41-89-88**), 22 rue des Pyramids 75001 (☎ **01-44-55-55-44**), and 1 place de l'Odéon (☎ **01-44-41-74-74**).

Paris, with its huge population of both native and foreign students, has all sorts of organizations providing information on student discounts:

AJF (Accueil des Jeunes en France), 112 rue Maubeuge 9e (☎ **01-42-85-36-13;** Métro: Poissoniére). AJF helps students and people under 30 find inexpensive lodgings, student cards, and discount train, bus, and plane tickets, as well as packages. This central booking office is open in summer Monday to Friday from 10am to 12:30pm and 1:30 to 6pm. There is also an office at the Gare du Nord (☎ **01-42-85-86-19;** Métro: Gare du Nord) that's normally open June to September daily from 7:30am to 10pm.

UCRIF (Union des Centres de Rencontres Internationales de France), 27 rue de Turbigo 75002 (☎ **01-40-26-57-64;** Métro: Etienne Marcel). This union operates 60 hostels throughout France, and though it caters to groups, it has an information and reservation service for individuals.

FOR GAY & LESBIAN TRAVELERS

"Gay Paree," with one of the world's largest homosexual populations, has dozens of gay clubs, restaurants, organizations, and services. Other than publications (see below), one of the best sources of information on gay and lesbian activities is **Centre Gai & Lesbien,** 3 rue Keller, 75011 (☎ **01-43-57-21-47;** Métro: Bastille). Well-equipped to dispense information and to coordinate the activities and meetings of gay people from virtually everywhere, it's open daily from 2 to 8pm. Sundays, they adopt a format known as *Le Café Positif* and feature music, cabaret, and information about AIDS, the care of people living with AIDS, and the prevention of sexually transmitted diseases.

SOS Écoute Gay (☎ 01-44-93-01-02) is a gay hot line, theoretically designed as a way to creatively counsel persons with gay-related problems. A phone counselor responds to calls Monday to Friday from 6 to 10pm. **SOS Homophobie** (☎ 01-48-06-42-41) is a separate hot line specifically intended for victims of homophobia or gay-related discrimination; calls are received by a panel of French-trained lawyers and legal experts who offer advice and counsel every Monday to Friday from 8am to 10pm. Although the counselors speak some English, neither hot line can provide in-depth counseling in English. For advice on HIV issues, call **F.A.C.T.S.** (☎ 01-44-93-16-69) Monday, Wednesday, and Friday 6 to 10pm. The acronym stands for Free Aids Counseling Treatment and Support and the English-speaking staff provides counseling, information, and doctor referrals.

Another helpful source is **La Maison des Femmes,** 8 Cité Prost, 11e (☎ 01-43-79-61-91; Métro: Charonne), which offers information about Paris for lesbians and bisexual women and sometimes sponsors informal dinners and get-togethers. Call any Monday, Wednesday, or Friday from 3 to 8pm for further information. The **Organisation Flora Tristan** (☎ 01-47-36-96-48) is a 24-hour women's hot line. For a superb collection of books on women, go to the **Librairie des Femmes,** 74 rue de Seine, 6e (☎ 01-43-29-50-75; Métro: Odéon).

A publication, Gai Pied's *Guide Gai* (revised annually) is the best source of information on gay and lesbian clubs, hotels, organizations, and services—even restaurants. Lesbian or bisexual women might also like to pick up a copy of *Lesbia,* if only to check out the ads. These publications and others are available at Paris's largest and best-stocked gay bookstore, **Les Mots à la Bouche,** 6 rue Ste-Croix-de-la-Bretonnerie, 4e (☎ 01-42-78-88-30). Hours are Monday through Saturday from 11am to 11pm, Sunday from 3 to 8pm. Both French- and English-language publications are available.

France is one of the world's most tolerant countries toward gays and lesbians, and there are no special laws that discriminate against them. Technically, sexual relations are legal for consenting partners age 16 and over. However, one doesn't come of legal age in France until 18, so there could still be legal problems with having sex with anyone under 18. Paris, of course, is the center of gay life in France, although gay and lesbian establishments exist throughout the provinces as well.

The following information may be helpful before you leave home.

PUBLICATIONS Before going to France, men can order *Spartacus,* the international gay guide ($32.95) or *How to Say Faaabulous in 8 Different Languages: A Foreign Phrase Book for Gay Men* ($9.95). Lesbians can look at the France section of *Women Going Places: A Women's Complete Guide to International Travel* ($14). Both lesbians and gay men can order *Guide Gai/Gay Guide* ($16), a bilingual guide to France published in Paris, or *Paris Scene* ($10.95), a thorough guide for lesbian and gay travelers that includes suggestions for where to go. These books and others are available from **Giovanni's Room,** 345 S. 12th Street, Philadelphia, PA 19107 (☎ 215/923-2960; fax 215/923-0813).

Our World, 1104 N. Nova Rd., Suite 251, Daytona Beach, FL 32117 (☎ 904/441-5367), is a magazine devoted to gay and lesbian travel worldwide. It costs $35 for 10 issues. *Out & About,* 8 W. 19th St., Suite 401, New York, NY 10011 (☎ 800/929-2268), has been hailed for its "straight" reporting about gay travel. It profiles the best gay or gay-friendly hotels, gyms, clubs, and other places, with coverage ranging from Key West to Paris. Its cost is $49 a year for 10 information-packed issues. It's aimed at the more upscale gay traveler and has been praised by everybody from *Travel & Leisure* to the *New York Times.*

ORGANIZATIONS **The International Gay Travel Association (IGTA),** P.O. Box 4974, Key West, FL 33041 (☎ **305/292-0217** or voice mailbox 800/ 448-8550), is an international network of travel industry businesses and professionals who encourage gay/lesbian travel worldwide. With around 1,000 members, it offers quarterly newsletters, marketing mailings, and a membership directory that's updated four times a year. Membership often includes gay or lesbian businesses but is open to individuals as well for $125 yearly, plus a $100 administration fee for new members. Members are kept informed of gay or gay-friendly hoteliers, tour operators, airline and cruise-line representatives, and also ancillary businesses such as the contacts at travel guide publishers and gay-related travel clubs.

TRAVEL AGENCIES **Our Family Abroad,** 40 W. 57th St., Suite 430, New York, NY 10019 (☎ **800/999-5500** or 212/459-1800), operates a range of escorted tours, including about a dozen itineraries through Europe. Tour guides serve on a volunteer basis, and are gay-sensitive.

In California, a leading gay-friendly option for travel arrangements is **Above and Beyond,** 300 Townsend St., Suite 107, San Francisco, CA 94107 (☎ **800/397-2681** or 415/284-1666).

Also in California, **Skylink Women's Travel,** 2953 Lincoln Blvd., Santa Monica, CA 90405 (☎ **800/225-5759** or 310/452-0506), runs about six international trips for lesbians yearly.

8 Learning Vacations & Homestays

EDUCATIONAL/STUDY TRAVEL

Studying in Paris will afford you a perspective on the city that travelers normally do not experience. Probably the easiest course you can enroll in is a language course at the **Alliance Française,** 101 bd. Raspail, 75270 Paris CEDEX 06 (☎ **01-45-44-38-28;** fax 01-45-44-89-42). This state-approved nonprofit organization has a network of more than 1,300 organizations in 130 countries, offering an education in French to some 400,000 students. Fees tend to be very reasonable, and the school also offers numerous activities and services. Write for information and forms at least 1 month before your departure to Paris.

A very good source of information on studying abroad, including France, is the **Council on International Educational Exchange,** 205 E. 42nd St., New York, NY 10017 (☎ **800/349-2433** or 212/661-1414). Ask for their *Work, Study, Travel Abroad: The Whole World Handbook* ($13.95 plus $1.50 postage) and a copy of their free *Student Travels* magazine.

HOMESTAYS

Homestays can provide a much deeper insight into the culture of the country you're visiting than staying at a hotel would. The following organizations make this experience possible.

The **Friendship Force,** 57 Forsyth St. NW, Suite 900, Atlanta, GA 30303 (☎ **404/522-9490**), is a nonprofit organization existing for the sole purpose of fostering and encouraging friendship among disparate people worldwide. Dozens of branch offices throughout North America arrange en masse visits, usually once a year. Because of group bookings, the airfare to the host country is usually less than you'd pay if you bought an individual APEX ticket. Each participant is required to spend 2 weeks in the host country, with 1 full week as a guest in the home of a family. Most volunteers spend the second week traveling.

Servas (from the Esperanto word meaning "to serve"), represented in the United States by the U.S. Servas Committee, 11 John St., Suite 407, New York, NY 10038

(☎ 212/267-0252), seeks to promote friendship and goodwill through homestays of a minimum 3 nights. Although it costs $55 per year to join, finding a family through Servas is one of the purest ways to experience local living, as hosts are not paid. After a screening process, you pay a refundable $25 deposit for a list that provides information on hosts' location, occupation, age, languages spoken, and interests. You then write the host and set up the visit. You may stay with several hosts in the same city and are not required to reciprocate by becoming a host yourself.

HOME EXCHANGES

The **Vacation Exchange Club,** 12006 111th Ave., Unit 12, Youngtown, AZ 85363 (☎ 602/972-2186), can help you set up a home swap—your house or apartment for a residence in France or in any other country. Whether you would like to place a listing in the directory or you would just like to buy a copy of the listings, the cost is $70.

You might also want to check out **FUSAC** (France USA Contacts), a Paris-based publication that contains listings of apartments in Paris available for rental or exchange. It is available in the U.S. for $10 an issue or $90 a year. Contact **France Contacts,** P.O. Box 115, Cooper Station, New York, NY (☎212/929-2929; fax 212/255-5555)

APARTMENT RENTAL

No matter how alluring your hotel, nothing beats living in Paris as a Parisian. In your own apartment you can conduct cooking experiments with French ingredients, taste fine wines that would be too expensive in a restaurant, and entertain newfound friends. Although the daily rate can be higher than a budget hotel, the room will be larger and you can save a considerable sum on meals.

The most practical way to rent an apartment is through an agency, most of which require a 7-day minimum stay. Some offer discounts for long stays. Naturally, the apartments vary considerably in size, location, and amenities. At the bottom end of about 500F ($87) per day, you'll find yourself in either a small, centrally located studio or a larger studio in an outlying arrondissement. The apartment will be equipped with a convertible couch, a few armchairs, a bathroom with either a tub or shower, and a tiny kitchenette equipped with a refrigerator, stove, coffeemaker, and sometimes a micro oven. Dishes, cutlery, pots and pans, telephone, television, iron, vacuum cleaner, linen, and sometimes washing machines are also provided. For about 700F to 800F ($122 to $139) per day, you can rent a small, centrally located one-bedroom apartment suitable for a couple with children. As with anything else, higher prices pay for larger, more luxurious spaces.

Watch for what is not included in the daily rate, since extras can add up. Some agencies tack on linen fees, cleaning fees, visitor's tax, telephone maintenance fees, and the cost of electricity (which is expensive in France). Often you will be asked to buy a "Welcome Kit" of salt, pepper, coffee, tea, sugar, and oil—at a substantial markup.

Generally, the smaller agencies provide more personal service and include more in the quoted rate. Rates at **Paris Connection,** 301 N. Pine Island Road, Suite 106, Ft. Lauderdale, FL 33324 (☎ 954/475-0615; fax 954/475-0630; e-mail: 100541.1266@compuserve.com), start at $135 a day but include all utilities, linen, cleaning, and taxes as well as free local telephone calls, a transport pass for the Métro and bus, and a kitchen stocked with all the necessities plus a bottle of wine. The owner, Jim Buongiorne, meets guests at the apartment for a 2-hour Paris orientation and remains on call throughout the stay. Apartments are primarily in the Left Bank and should be reserved some months in advance.

Another agency that provides all-inclusive rentals and excellent service is **RothRay,** 10 rue Nicolas Flamel, 75004 Paris (☎ **01-48-87-13-37;** fax 01-42-78-17-72). Rates start at 550F ($95.65) a day and also include all services, taxes, and fees except for telephone calls, which are metered. The apartments are in the 1st through 6th arrondissements. All apartments are well stocked with the necessities, including juice and wine, and many have stereo systems. Ray Lampard, one of the owners, meets guests at the apartment (saving you the hassle of picking up your keys in a distant office) and is available should problems arise.

Larger agencies may have vacancies when others are full. Try **Paris Appartements Services,** 69 rue d'Argout, 75002 Paris (☎ **01-40-28-01-28;** fax 01-40-28-92-01; Web site: http://www.pariserve.tm.fr/paris-apt). Their apartments are in the 1er through 4e arrondissements and start at 500F ($87) a night. Another option is **Paris Séjour Réservation,** 645 North Michigan Ave., Suite 638, Chicago, IL 60611 (☎**302/587-7707;** fax 312/587-9887; Web site: http://www.qconline.com/parispsr/ index.html). The agency has 600 apartments throughout Paris, beginning at 400F ($69.55) a night. Their Web site allows you to view apartments on-line.

9 Getting There

BY PLANE
FROM THE UNITED STATES & CANADA

Flying time to Paris from New York is about 7 hours; from Chicago, 9 hours; from Los Angeles, 11 hours; from Atlanta, 8 hours; from Miami, $8^1/_2$ hours; from Washington, D.C., $7^1/_2$ hours.

THE MAJOR AIRLINES/REGULAR FARES   In the past, you could fly to Paris only from New York, but now it's possible to fly from several major cities in North America. Flexibility, though, will guarantee you the best fares. Also consider flying into another European city and proceeding from there to Paris by train or bus.

The major American carriers offering regularly scheduled nonstop flights to Paris include: **American Airlines** (☎ **800/433-7300**) from Boston, Chicago, Dallas/ Ft. Worth, Los Angeles, Miami, and New York; **Continental** (☎ **800/231-0856**) from Houston and Newark; **Delta Airlines** (☎ **800/221-1212**) from Atlanta, Cincinnati, and New York; **Northwest Airlines** (☎ **800/225-2525**) from Detroit; **TWA** (☎ **800/892-4141**) from Boston and New York; **United Airlines** (☎ **800/ 241-6522**) from Chicago, Los Angeles, San Francisco, and Washington; and **US Airways** (☎ **800/428-4322**).

Among non-U.S. airlines, **Air France** (☎ **800/237-2747**) has the most frequent direct service to Paris, with flights from New York, Washington, Miami, Chicago, Houston, San Francisco, and Los Angeles.

Air Canada (☎ **800/776-3000** from the U.S. and Canada) runs flights to Paris from Toronto and Montréal. Nonstop flights from Montréal and Toronto depart every evening for Paris. Two of the nonstop flights from Toronto are shared with Air France and feature Air France aircraft.

Fares and conditions for the flights of these airlines are competitive in most cases. Most airlines divide their year roughly into seasonal slots, the least expensive fares being offered between November and mid-March. Shoulder season is only slightly more expensive and includes all of October, which many travelers consider the ideal time to visit France.

When purchasing your tickets, call the airline and ask for the lowest-priced fare available on the date you wish to fly. If you can be flexible about the date, say so, because you may be able to secure a cheaper fare by staying an extra day, flying during the middle of the week, or purchasing your ticket a certain number of days in advance. Most airlines won't volunteer this information. Keep shopping around and you'll probably find a flight for less.

One airline that has been offering cheaper flights to Europe for years is **Icelandair** (☎ **800/223-5500**). You can fly round-trip for about $460 in the off-season to Luxembourg and then take the short trip from there into Paris. Of course, you have to fly via Iceland to secure this bargain.

Most carriers offer a consistently popular **advanced-purchase excursion (APEX)** fare that requires a 21-day advance payment and an obligatory stay abroad of between 7 and 21 days. In most cases this ticket, although reasonably priced, is not completely refundable if you change flight dates or destinations.

A regular **"economy class"** ticket on these airlines is substantially more expensive. With this ticket you can catch any flight, as long as seats are available.

In mid-1997, you could obtain a round-trip, 21-day advance-purchase fare from New York for $501 and from Los Angeles for $593, depending on which airline you called. This compares, by the way, to $400 to $450 fares offered by charter companies. Still, airline competition is fierce, so always check newspapers for special promotions and always shop around to secure the least expensive fare.

BEST BUDGET FARES   Proceed with caution through the following suggestions. Prices and rules change constantly in the airline industry. It's hard to keep up, even if you're a travel agent. The airline industry is quite volatile.

Consolidators   These companies buy up blocks of unsold tickets from major transatlantic carriers and resell at a discount. The airlines typically request that the consolidator not reveal the name of the airline to their clients in advance. In effect, they function as clearinghouses for the airlines, especially during slow travel periods.

Tickets are discounted anywhere from 20% to 35% off the full fare. Terms of payment can vary—sometimes you have to pay 45 days before departure, and sometimes you can snag a last-minute sale as an airline makes a final attempt to fill a semiempty craft.

While consolidator fares are low, special airline promotions are sometimes even lower. Always compare prices before you buy. Note that tickets from a consolidator cannot be used on other airlines in the event a flight is canceled and that they also carry hefty cancellation penalties.

Nationally advertised consolidators are usually not as competitive as the smaller back-room operations, but they have toll-free telephone numbers and may be more reliable. The following are just a few of those operating.

TFI Tours International, 34 W. 32nd St., 12th floor, New York, NY 10001 (☎ **800/745-8000** or 212/736-1140 in New York State); **TMI (Travel Management International),** 39 JFK St. (Harvard Square), 3rd floor, Cambridge, MA 02138 (☎ **800/245-3672**); and **UniTravel,** 1177 N. Warson Rd., St. Louis, MO 63132 (☎ **800/325-2222**). Again, check their fares against those offered directly by the airlines.

Travac, 989 Sixth Ave., New York, NY 10018 (☎ **800/TRAV-800** or 212/563-3303), sells discounted seats on about 20 major carriers to European capitals, including Paris. Your own travel agent might use this company, or you can deal with it directly.

Charters   The second-cheapest way to cross the Atlantic is on a charter flight. Most charter operators advertise and sell their seats through travel agents, making these local professionals your best source of information for available flights. Two well-known operators that sell tickets directly to passengers include **Travac** (see above) and **Council Charters,** 205 E. 42nd St., New York, NY 10017 (☎ **800/223-7402** or

212/661-0311). Look for summer fares as low as $418 to $500 round-trip from New York; less in winter. Council can also arrange flights to such French cities as Lyon, Lille, Mulhouse, Strasbourg, and Nice for a supplement to the prices mentioned above.

Before deciding to take a charter flight, check the restrictions on the ticket. You may be asked to purchase a tour package, pay far in advance of the flight, be amenable if the day of departure or the destination is changed, pay a service charge or steep cancellation penalties, or fly on an airline with which you are not familiar or comfortable. Some charter companies have proved unreliable in the past. It may be preferable to deal with subsidiaries or affiliates of major international carriers. Some of these include the following:

Jet Vacations, 1775 Broadway, New York, NY 10019 (☎ **800/538-0999** or 212/247-0999), is a wholly owned subsidiary of Air France and an obvious charter airline choice for Paris. It offers both charter flights and discounted transatlantic tickets from many airlines, not just Air France.

If you're visiting other countries in Europe, there are additional options. For example, you might use **Balair Ltd.,** 608 Fifth Ave., Suite 803, New York, NY 10020 (☎ **800/322-5247** or 212/581-3411), the charter-airline subsidiary of Swissair. It runs charter flights from Miami and San Francisco to Zurich or Geneva, only a few hours away by train from Paris.

DER Tours, Inc., 380 NW Highway, Suite 220, Des Plaines, IL 60016 (☎ **800/717-4247**), sells seats on flights to Paris at discounted prices, from the unsold inventory of major airlines. All flights to Paris depart from Minneapolis, Boston, or Detroit.

Another possibility, useful for Midwesterners, is **Europa Travel Service,** 911 E. 185th St., Cleveland, OH 44119 (☎ **800/677-1313** or 216/481-3612), which offers discounted seats to Paris from Cleveland, Columbus, and Dayton.

Going as a Courier   Not for everybody, because you have to be fairly flexible. Companies transporting time-sensitive materials, such as film, blood, or documents for banks and insurance firms, regularly hire air couriers, who fly at a discounted price. It's not difficult, as the courier company handles the check-in and pickup of packages at each airport. All you have to do is give up your checked-baggage allowance and make do with carry-on. Expect to meet a courier-service representative at the airport before departure to get the manifest of the checked items; upon arrival, you deliver the baggage-claim tag to a waiting courier agent. Flights are often offered at the last minute, and you may have to arrange a pretrip interview to make sure you're right for the job.

One drawback, besides restricted baggage, is that you have to travel alone, since only one person can take advantage of any given flight, although if two of you are traveling you may be able to arrange departures on 2 consecutive days.

Two popular courier services are **Now Voyager, Inc.,** 74 Varick St., Suite 307, New York, NY 10013 (☎ **212/431-1616,** 10am to 5:30pm weekdays, noon to 5pm Saturday); and **Halbart Express,** 147–05 176th St., Jamaica, NY 11434 (☎ **718/656-8189,** 10am to 3pm).

Most flights depart from New York, so you may have to tack on the additional cost of getting to the gateway city. Prices change all the time, from low to very low. If a company needs emergency courier service and you can fly immediately, you could travel free or for next to nothing.

FROM THE UNITED KINGDOM

From London, **Air France (☎ 0181/742-6600)** and **British Airways (☎ 0345/222111,** accessible in U.K. only) fly frequently to Paris with a trip time of only one hour. Between the two of them, these airlines operate up to 17 flights daily from Heathrow. Many commercial travelers also use regular flights originating from the London City Airport in the Docklands. You can also fly direct to Paris from major cities such as Manchester, Edinburgh, and Southampton. Contact **Air France, British Airways, British Midland** (☎ 0181/754-7321) or **Air UK** (☎ 0345/666777) for details.

Flying from England to France is often quite expensive, even though the distance is short. That's why most Brits rely on a good travel agent to get them the lowest possible airfare. Good values are offered by a number of companies, including **Nouvelles Frontières,** 2–3 Woodstock St., London W1R 1HE (☎ **0171/ 629-7772**).

There are no hard-and-fast rules about getting the best deals for Paris flights. Daily papers often carry advertisements for companies offering cheap flights. Of these, a couple good choices are **Trailfinders** (☎ 0171/937-5400), which sells discounted fares, and **Avro Tours** (☎ 0181/715-0000), which operates charters.

In London, there are many ticket consolidators (who buy inventories of tickets from airlines and then resell them at a discounted price) in the neighborhood of Earl's Court and Victoria Station. For your own protection, make sure that the company you deal with is a member of the IATA, ABTA, or ATOL.

FROM AUSTRALIA & NEW ZEALAND

The fastest flight to Paris from Sydney is offered by the French airline AOM, which takes about 22^1/$_2$ hours with one refueling stop. The price is competitive with other major carriers and ranges from A$2,700 to A$3,000, depending on the season. Fares are highest in the summer. Just a little checking around however, will turn up a much better fare.

The *Sydney Morning Herald* and Melbourne's *The Age* have Saturday travel sections chock-full of discounted fares. The catch is that the airline may be obscure and the flight may entail a lengthy and exhausting series of layovers. A persistent travel agent who deals with consolidators should be able to produce a flight on a mainstream airline that costs between A$1,500 (low season) and A$2,500 (high season). Flights are a few hundred dollars cheaper from Perth. STA Travel and Flight Centres International are known for their discounted airfares and have offices throughout Australia and New Zealand.

GETTING DOWNTOWN FROM THE AIRPORTS

Paris has two airports handling international traffic: Charles-de-Gaulle and Orly.

AÉROPORT CHARLES-DE-GAULLE   The larger, busier, and more modern airport, commonly known as CDG and sometimes called Roissy-Charles-de-Gaulle, is 14^1/$_2$ miles northeast of downtown. Terminal 1 (*Aérogare 1*) is devoted to foreign airlines; Terminal 2 (*Aérogare 2*) is reserved for Air France and Air Inter, its affiliate, plus some foreign airlines, including Air Canada. A shuttle bus (*navette*) connects the two terminals.

There are several ways to get from the airport to downtown. If you've arrived at **Terminal 1,** a shuttle operates to the Roissy-Charles-de-Gaulle station of the RER suburban train line; if you've come into **Terminal 2,** there's a new RER station directly accessible from the terminal. From both stations, RER Line B3 trains depart about every 15 minutes for the half-hour trip into town, stopping at Gare du Nord; Châtelet-Les-Halles Métro interchange; and the RER stations of St-Michel, Luxembourg, Port-Royal, and Denfert-Rochereau, before heading southward out of the city again. A ticket into town on the RER costs 46F ($8).

Besides the RER, **Air France runs shuttle buses** from both terminals to the Porte-Maillot Métro station, next to Paris's huge convention center on the western end of the city, and to place Charles-de-Gaulle and the Arc de Triomphe, near some of the budget hotels listed in chapter 4. There are buses every 12 minutes, and the ticket costs 55F ($9.55) for the 40-minute trip. If you're headed for the Left Bank, there are also hourly buses to the Gare Montparnasse for 65F ($11.30). The RATP, or Paris Transit Authority, also runs a bus (the Roissybus) from both terminals to the rue Scribe in the heart of town, across the street from the Opéra Garnier; tickets cost 40F ($7), but there is no luggage service.

A **taxi** into town from Charles-de-Gaulle takes between 40 and 50 minutes and costs about 220F ($38.25) from 7am to 8pm, and about 40% more at other times.

AÉROPORT D'ORLY (ORLY)   Orly is $8^1/_2$ miles south of the city center and receives mostly charter and tour flights at its two terminals: Orly-Ouest for French domestic flights and Orly-Sud for European and intercontinental flights. Shuttle buses connect the two terminals, and other shuttles run between Orly and Charles-de-Gaulle airports every half hour or so.

To get downtown from Orly, take the **shuttle bus** (leaving every 15 minutes) to the RER station named Pont-de-Rungis-Aéroport d'Orly and catch a Line C2 train for 28.50F ($5) for the 25-minute trip into town. The train has several downtown stops; at Gare d'Austerlitz, St-Michel, and Invalides you can change to the Métro to reach your final destination.

You can also take **Orlyval,** a shuttle train that leaves about every 5 minutes, to the RER B line at Antony for the 30-minute trip into town, which costs 54F ($9.40). The train stops at Denfert-Rochereau and St-Michel–Notre-Dame in the Left Bank, and Chatelet and Gare de Nord on the right bank. From those stations you can change to the Métro. Try to avoid changing at Chatelet if possible; the station is enormous.

There's also an **Air France shuttle bus** for 40F ($7) from Orly to the Air France bus terminal, the Aérogare des Invalides, right at the Invalides Métro station just across the Seine from place de la Concorde. The bus runs about five times per hour and takes a half hour to reach the center. On the way, it makes a stop at Gare de Montparnasse just south of downtown.

A **taxi** from Orly into the city costs about 145F ($25.20) and takes 40 to 50 minutes.

BY TRAIN

If you're already in Europe, you may want to go to Paris by train, especially if you have a **Eurailpass.** If you don't, you'll pay—London to Paris, for example, is around $85 one way on the new under-the-English-Channel Eurostar train. Paris has six major train stations. For information, call **SNCF** (Société Nationale des Chemins de Fer) at ☎ **01-53-90-20-20** and ask for someone who speaks English, or go to a travel agent or one of the information booths at the stations.

Coming from northern Germany or Belgium, you'll probably arrive at **Gare du Nord** (some trains from London arrive here as well). Trains from Normandy come into **Gare St-Lazare,** in northwest Paris. Trains from the west (Brittany, Chartres, Versailles, Bordeaux) head to **Gare de Montparnasse;** those from the southwest (the Loire Valley, the Pyrénées, Spain) to **Gare d'Austerlitz;** those from the south and southeast (the Riviera, Lyon, Italy, Geneva) to **Gare de Lyon.** From Alsace and eastern France, Luxembourg, southern Germany, and Zurich, the arrival station is **Gare de l'Est.** All train stations are next to a Métro station bearing the same name.

BY BUS

Bus travel to Paris is available from most major cities in Europe. European Railways operates **Europabus** and **Eurolines.** These companies do not have American offices as yet and so travelers must make bus transportation arrangements after arrival in Europe. **In Great Britain,** contact Eurolines at the Victoria Coach station. Call ☎ **0582/40-45-11** for information. **In Paris,** the contact is Eurolines, 28 av. du General de Gaulle, 93541 Bagnolet (☎ **01-49-72-51-51**). If you're **in Germany,** contact Europabus at Mannheimerstrasse 4, 6000 Frankfurt (☎ **069/23-07-35**) or L'Agence Wasteels, Am Hauptbahnhof 18, 6000 Frankfurt (☎ **069/23-23-85**).

International buses pull into Paris's **Gare Routière Internationale (International Bus Terminal)** at av. Charles de Gaulle in the suburb of Bagnolet, just across the *périphérique* (ring road) from the Gallieni Métro station. To go downtown, you take Line 3 and change according to your final destination.

FROM THE UNITED KINGDOM BY FERRY & TUNNEL

About a dozen companies run hydrofoil, ferry, and hovercraft across "La Manche" (the sleeve), as the French call the channel. Services operate day and night. Most carry cars, but some hydrofoils carry passengers only. Hovercraft or hydrofoils make the trip in just 40 minutes, while the shortest ferry route between Dover and Calais takes about 1 1/2 hours.

The major routes are between Dover and Calais and Folkestone and Boulogne (about 12 trips a day). Depending on weather conditions, prices and timetables can vary. It's always important to make a reservation, as ferries are crowded.

For information stateside call **Britrail** (☎ 800/677-8585 or 212/575-2667) or **P&O** (☎ 201/768-1187). In Britain, call **Sealink** (☎ 233/64-70-22; fax 1233/64-60-21). For **Hoverspeed,** call ☎ **0304/21-62-05.** Special fares are offered, but they change frequently. It's better to contact a travel agent—say, in London—to book your ticket for you. A good travel agent will help you sort out the maze of ferry schedules and find a suitable option.

The **Channel Tunnel** (or "Chunnel") opened in 1994, and the popularity of its Eurostar train service has had the happy effect of driving down prices on all cross-Channel transport. This remarkable engineering feat means that you can travel by train between London and Paris, and if you take your car aboard Le Shuttle in Britain you can be driving in France an hour later. Tickets may be purchased in advance or at the tollbooth.

BY CAR

Driving a car in Paris is definitely not recommended. Parking is difficult, and traffic is dense and at times ruthless. If you do drive, remember that Paris is encircled by a ring road called the *périphérique*—and that exits are not numbered. Avoid rush hours!

Few hotels, except the luxury ones, have garages, but the staff will usually be able to direct you to one nearby. The major highways in Paris are the A1 from the north (Great Britain and Belgium); the A13 from Normandy and other points in northwest France; the A109 from Spain and the southwest; the A7 from the Alps, the Riviera, and Italy; and the A4 from eastern France.

PACKAGE TOURS

Some people prefer that a tour operator take care of all the travel arrangements. There are many companies operating tours to France, each offering transportation to and within the country, prearranged hotel space, and such extras as a bilingual tour guide and lectures geared more or less to your general interests.

Some operate special-interest tours, arranging meetings with local aristocracy, "famous" artists, or leaders of the Resistance. Many of these celebrities are legitimate and can contribute much to your tour. Others are not, so beware of any undue sales pressure from a tour operator trying to clinch the deal, especially if the list of guest lecturers reads like the "A-list" from a social event in the *ancien régime* of prerevolutionary France.

The French Experience, 171 Madison Ave., New York, NY 10016 (☎ **212/ 986-3800**), offers several different options for fly-drive programs through different regions of France. You can specify the type and price level of hotels you want. The agency arranges the car rental in advance, and the rest is up to you.

American Express Vacations, P.O. Box 1525, Fort Lauderdale, FL 33302 (☎ **800/241-1700**), is perhaps the most instantly recognizable tour operator in the world. Their offerings in Paris and the rest of Europe are probably more comprehensive than those of any other company and include packaged tours as well as independent stays.

Getting to Know the City of Light

I like to think of Paris as a collection of villages on either side of the river Seine, each with its own special character that reflects its role in the development of the city.

The heart of Paris and the place from which all distances in France are measured is Notre-Dame on Ile de la Cité. The monumental law courts and administrative buildings dominating the island are testament to its origins as a seat of power, first for the Romans and later for the nascent French monarchy. Vestiges of the ancient Gallo-Roman settlement can be found in the archaeological crypt next to Notre-Dame, while the Conciergerie and Sainte-Chapelle are the last reminders of the Capetian palace that once stood on the Ile.

As the city spread north from the right bank and south from the left bank, the two great poles of Parisian life took shape. The right bank became a place of merchants and markets and, later, the home of royalty. The grandeur of the Louvre palace and the ornate mansions in the Marais expressed the prestige of an increasingly wealthy and influential city. The kings abandoned the Marais in the 17th century, but the ancient Jewish community remained, although now the kosher shops and synagogue are in the midst of a newly trendy district of restaurants, boutiques, and bars. The magnificent vista that stretches from the pyramid of the Louvre through the Tuileries Gardens to become the Champs-Elysées and the Arc de Triomphe follows the inexorable movement westward of 18th and 19th century aristocracy. This area still contains some of the most expensive real estate and the most elegant shops in the city.

While the right bank was developing into a bastion of money and power, the left bank became known for loftier pursuits. A celebrated Benedictine abbey flourished at St-Germain-des-Prés in the Middle Ages, while the Sorbonne University was drawing scholars from all Europe to the Latin Quarter. The thriving intellectual life gave rise to bookstores and cafes where lively minds could congregate to discuss the issues of the day. In the 1920s and 1930s, artists and writers flocked to the cafes of Montparnasse and returned after World War II to the cafes along the boulevard St-Germain, where Sartre was expounding his existentialist philosophy. The presence of the University of Paris (the Sorbonne) in the Latin Quarter continues a certain young, bohemian tradition even as the neighborhood is becoming known more for shopping than intellectual pursuits.

Paris

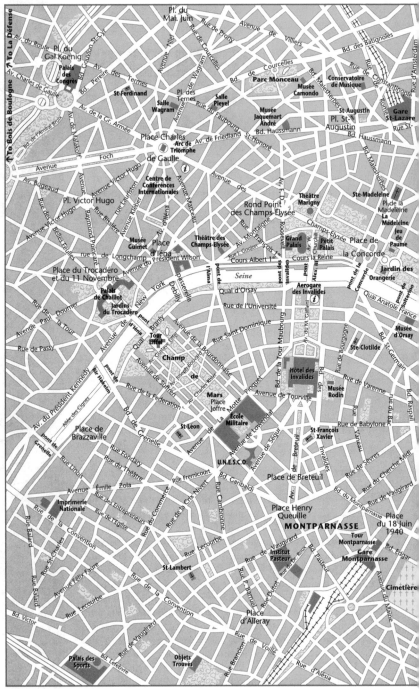

Also on the left bank is the Faubourg St-Germain, home of 18th-century aristocracy and now the site of embassies and official ministries.

In the 19th century, the city expanded beyond its core and gradually absorbed outlying villages. The village of Montmartre, in the north, replaced its vineyards and windmills with cabarets and music halls, luring a new generation of daring artists—Van Gogh, Renoir, Toulouse-Lautrec, and, later, Picasso, Braque, and Juan Gris. In the southwest, the fashionable villages of Passy and Auteuil were annexed to create a chic residential district. In the east, the cemetery of Pére-Lachaise was constructed where the villages Belleville, Menilmontant, and Charonne joined. Baron Hausmann designed Grands Boulevards to open up the old streets and the system of *arrondissements* was instituted.

The 20 arrondissements are municipal boroughs that start with number 1 at the Louvre and progress in a clockwise spiral to the outskirts of the city. Most Parisian addresses will bear the number of the arrondissement: For example, 1er (*premier*) is for the first arrondissement, 2e (*deuxième*) for the second, and so on. The arrondissement number is usually (but not always) the last three digits in the postal code. Thus the tourist office is in postal zone 75008—"75" for Paris and "008" for the 8e arrondissement.

The Métro stations make excellent orientation points when you're trying to find your way around. You can easily locate any station on a map and from there locate any hotel, restaurant, or museum, and figure out how to get there.

Paris streets change names as they make their way through the city. If you come to a corner and don't see the street name you expect, look on the opposite corner.

The 20 arrondissements are surrounded by Paris's vast *banlieue,* the suburbs. People often speak of *la région parisienne* (the Parisian region) to refer to the Greater Paris area.

1 Orientation

VISITOR INFORMATION

There are small information offices at the airports, and their staff will help you to make a hotel reservation but they only work with hotels that charge more than 350F ($61) a night. The prime source of information is the **Office de Tourisme et des Congrès de Paris,** 127 av. des Champs-Elysées, 75008 Paris (☎ **01-49-52-53-54;** Web site: **http://www.paris-promotion.fr**; Métro: Charles-de-Gaulle-Etoile or George-V), open daily from 9am to 8pm. For a fee, its staff will make a hotel reservation for you on the same day that you want a room; the service charge ranges from 20F ($1.70) for basic hotels to 50F ($10) for four-star luxury hotels. The office and its reservation service are often very busy in the summer season, and you will probably have to wait in line.

The Office de Tourisme has six auxiliary offices: at Gare du Nord (open May through October, Monday through Saturday from 8am to 9pm and on Sunday from 1 to 8pm; November through April, daily 1 to 8pm); at Gare de l'Est and Gare de Lyon (April through October, Monday through Saturday from 8am to 9pm; November through March, until 8pm); at Gare d'Austerlitz (year-round Monday through Friday from 8am to 3pm; Saturday from 8am to 1pm); at the Eiffel Tower (May through September, daily from 11am to 6pm); and at Gare Montparnasse (May through October, daily from 8am to 9pm; November through April, until 8pm).

CITY LAYOUT

To get an initial orientation to the way Paris is laid out, visit Notre Dame as soon as you can. This magnificent cathedral is visible from many parts of the city and will also help you understand that the Seine is actually Paris's most important "street." You'll quickly understand which direction you should be going in if you can ask people if you're walking towards or away from the river. It also helps to stand before the pyramid in the courtyard of the Louvre and look down the long unbroken axis that culminates in the Arc de Triomphe. Otherwise, the hideous Tour Montparnasse skyscraper is visible from almost anywhere on the Left Bank and is next to the Gare Montparnasse, while Sacré-Coeur on Montmartre is often glimpsed on the Right Bank; both will help you situate yourself on a map if you're lost. Finally, it's not only a pleasure but useful to look at Paris in one giant panorama from the top of the Eiffel Tower.

MAIN ARTERIES & STREETS   During the Second Empire, Baron Haussmann forever changed the look of Paris by creating the *grands boulevards.* Their names are legendary: St-Michel, St-Germain, Haussmann, Malesherbes, Sébastopol, Magenta, Voltaire, and Strasbourg. Haussmann also created the avenue de l'Opéra and the twelve avenues radiating starlike from the Arc de Triomphe.

The main streets on the Right Bank are the broad **avenue des Champs-Elysées,** beginning at the Arc de Triomphe and running to the place de la Concorde, and the narrower **rue de Rivoli,** which traces from the place de la Concorde to the place de la Bastille.

FINDING AN ADDRESS   Finding the neighborhood where an address is located in Paris is usually very easy. Most street addresses are accompanied by the arrondissement number. The last two digits in the postal code are also an indicator: 75005 means the 5e arrondissement; 75019 means the 19e, and so on. Addresses also often include the name of the nearest Métro station, in which case you simply need to hop on the train and go. At each Métro station are excellent *plans du quartier,* neighborhood maps that will help you locate your street. Addresses on streets that run parallel to the Seine generally follow the direction of the river (east to west). For perpendicular streets, the lowest numbers are closest to the Seine.

STREET MAPS   Maps printed by the *grands magasins* (department stores) are usually available free at hotels, and they're good for those travelers visiting Paris for only a few days and hitting only the major attractions. The best maps are those of the *Plan de Paris par Arrondissement,* smallish books with maps and a street index, available at most bookstores. They are extremely practical, and prices start around 40F ($8).

ARRONDISSEMENTS IN BRIEF

Each of Paris's 20 arrondissements possesses a unique style and flavor. You will want to decide which district appeals most to you and then find accommodations there. The accommodations and dining chapters are divided into "Right Bank" and "Left Bank," then by neighborhood, but to give you a good feel for each numbered district, I'll describe them in numerical order below.

1er Arr. (Right Bank, Musée du Louvre / Palais Royal / Les Halles)   "I never knew what a palace was until I had a glimpse of the Louvre," wrote Nathaniel Hawthorne. One of the world's greatest art museums (some say the greatest), **the Louvre,** a former royal residence, still lures all visitors to Paris to the 1er arrondissement. Here are many of the elegant addresses of Paris, along the rue de Rivoli, with the Jeu de Paume and Orangerie on raised terraces. Walk through its **Jardin des Tuileries,** the most formal garden of Paris (originally laid out by Le Nôtre, gardener to Louis XIV). Pause to take in the classic beauty of the **place Vendôme,** opulent, wealthy, and home of the Ritz Hotel. Zola's "the belly of Paris" (Les Halles) is no longer the food and meat market of Paris (traders moved to Rungis, a new and more accessible suburb), but is today **Forum des Halles,** a center of shopping and entertainment.

2e Arr. (Right Bank, La Bourse)   Home to **the Bourse** (stock exchange), this Right Bank district lies mainly between the Grands Boulevards and the rue Etienne Marcel. Often overlooked by tourists, this district nonetheless presents some interesting contrasts. From Monday through Friday, the shouts of brokers—*J'ai!* or *Je prends!*—echo across the place de la Bourse until it's time to break for lunch, at which time the movers and shakers of French capitalism bring their hysteria into the restaurants of the district. Much of the eastern end of the arrondissement (**Le Sentier**) is devoted to the wholesale outlets of the Paris garment district, while the center is honeycombed with meandering 19th-century arcades. "Everything that exists elsewhere exists in Paris," wrote Victor Hugo in *Les Misérables,* and if you take on this district, you'll find ample evidence to support his claim.

3e Arr. (Right Bank, Le Marais)   This district embraces much of **Le Marais** (the swamp), one of the best loved of the old Right Bank neighborhoods. Allowed to fall into decades of seedy decay, Le Marais has now made a comeback, although perhaps it will never again enjoy the grand opulence of its aristocratic heyday during the 17th century. Over the centuries, kings have called Le Marais home, and its salons have resounded with the witty, often devastating remarks of Racine, Voltaire, Molière, and Madame de Sévigné. One of the district's chief attractions today is **Musée Picasso,** stuffed with treasures that the Picasso estate had to turn over to the French government in lieu of astronomical inheritance taxes. Forced donation or not, it's one of the world's great repositories of 20th-century art.

4e Arr. (Right Bank, Ile de la Cité / Ile St-Louis / Centre Pompidou)   At times it seems as if the 4e has it all: Not only **Notre-Dame** on **Ile de la Cité,** but **Ile St-Louis,** with its aristocratic town houses, courtyards, and antique shops. Ile St-Louis, a former cow pasture and dueling ground, is home to dozens of 17th-century mansions and 6,000 lucky *louisiens,* its permanent residents. Voltaire found it "the second best" address in all the world, citing the straits of the Bosporus separating Europe from Asia as number one. Of course, the whole area is touristy and overrun. Forget the "I Love Paris" bumper stickers and seek out Ile de la Cité's two gems of Gothic architecture, **La Sainte-Chapelle** and **Notre-Dame,** a majestic and dignified structure that, according to the poet e. e. cummings, doesn't budge an inch for all the idiocies of this world.

The heart of medieval Paris, the 4e evokes memories of Danton, Robespierre, and even of Charlotte Corday, who stabbed Jean Paul Marat in his bath. Here you not only get France's finest bird and flower markets, but the nation's law courts, which have a long tradition of dispensing justice French style. It was here that Marie Antoinette was sentenced to death in 1793. If all this weren't enough, the 4e is also home to the **Centre Georges Pompidou.** It's one of the top three tourist attractions of France, partly because of its National Museum of Modern Art, but unfortunately it's closed for restoration until sometime in the year 2000. Finally, after all this pomp and glory, you can retreat to the **place des Vosges,** a square of perfect harmony and beauty where Victor Hugo lived from 1832 to 1848 and penned many of his famous masterpieces.

5e Arr. (Left Bank, Latin Quarter)   The **Quartier Latin** (Latin Quarter) is the intellectual heart and soul of Paris. Bookstores, schools, churches, smoky jazz clubs,

Paris by Arrondissement

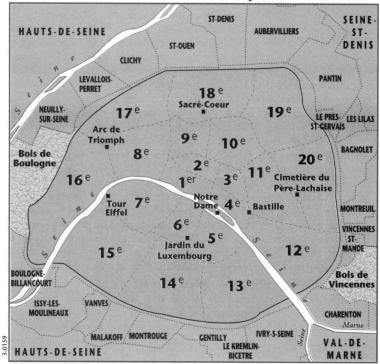

student dives, Roman ruins, publishing houses, and, yes, expensive and chic boutiques characterize the district. Discussions of Artaud or Molière over long, lingering cups of coffee are not just a cliché; they really happen here. Beginning with the founding of **the Sorbonne** in 1253, the *quartier* was called Latin because all students and professors spoke the scholarly language. As the traditional center of what was called "bohemian Paris," it formed the setting for Henri Murger's novel *Scènes de la vie de Bohème* (and later the Puccini opera *La Bohème*).

You'll follow in the footsteps of Descartes, Verlaine, Camus, Sartre, James Thurber, Elliot Paul, and Hemingway as you explore this historic district. For sure, the old Latin quarter is gone forever. Changing times have brought Greek, Moroccan, and Vietnamese immigrants, among others, hustling souvlaki, couscous, and fiery-hot spring rolls. The 5e also borders the Seine, and you'll want to stroll along **quai de Montebello,** inspecting the inventories of the *bouquinistes* who, in the shadow of Notre-Dame, sell everything from antique Daumier prints to yellowing copies of Balzac's *Père Goriot*. The 5e also stretches down to **the Panthéon,** which was constructed by a grateful Louis XV after he'd recovered from the gout and wanted to do something nice for Ste-Geneviève. It's the resting place of Rousseau, Gambetta, Emile Zola, Louis Braille, Victor Hugo, Voltaire, and Jean Moulin, the World War II Resistance leader who was tortured to death by the Gestapo.

6e Arr. (Left Bank, St-Germain / Luxembourg Gardens) This is the heartland of Paris publishing and, for some, the most colorful quartier of the Left Bank, where waves of earnest young artists still emerge from the famous **Ecole des Beaux-Arts.** Strolling the boulevards of the 6e, including St-Germain, has its own rewards, but the secret of the district lies in discovering its narrow streets and hidden squares.

Of course, to be really "authentic," you'll stroll these streets with an unwrapped loaf of country sourdough bread from the wood-fired ovens of **Poilâne,** the world's most famous baker, at 8 rue du Cherche-Midi. Everywhere you turn in the district, you encounter famous historical and literary associations, none more so than on rue Jacob. At 7 rue Jacob, Racine lived with his uncle as a teenager; Richard Wagner resided at 14 rue Jacob from 1841 to 1842; Jean Ingres once lived at 27 rue Jacob (now it's the offices of the French publishing house Editions du Seuil); and Hemingway once occupied a tiny upstairs room at no. 44. Today's "big name" is likely to be filmmaker Spike Lee checking into his favorite, La Villa Hôtel, at 29 rue Jacob.

Delacroix—whom Baudelaire called "a volcanic crater artistically concealed beneath bouquets of flowers"—kept his atelier in the 6e, and George Sand and her lover, Frédéric Chopin, used to visit him there to have their portraits done. His studio is now open to the public. **Rue Monsieur-le-Prince** has historically been a popular street for Paris's resident Americans, having been frequented by Martin Luther King Jr., Richard Wright, James McNeill Whistler, Henry Wadsworth Longfellow, and even Oliver Wendell Holmes. The 6e even takes in the **Luxembourg Gardens,** a 60-acre playground where Isadora Duncan went dancing in the predawn hours and a destitute writer, Ernest Hemingway, went looking for pigeons to cook for lunch while pushing a baby carriage full of his hunting trophies back to his humble flat.

7e Arr. (Left Bank, Eiffel Tower / Musée d'Orsay)   Paris's most famous symbol, the **Eiffel Tower,** dominates Paris and especially the 7e, a Left Bank district of respectable residences and government offices. Part of the **St-Germain neighborhood** is included here as well. The tower is now one of the most recognizable landmarks in the world, despite the fact that many Parisians (most notably some of its nearest neighbors) hated it when it was unveiled in 1889. Many of the most imposing monuments of Paris are in the 7e, including the **Hôtel des Invalides,** which contains both Napoléon's Tomb and the Musée de l'Armée. But there is much hidden charm here as well. Who has not walked these often narrow streets before you? Your predecessors include Picasso, Manet, Ingres, Baudelaire, Wagner, Simone de Beauvoir, Sartre, and even Truman Capote, Gore Vidal, and Tennessee Williams.

Rue du Bac was home to the swashbuckling heroes of Dumas's *The Three Musketeers* and to James McNeill Whistler, who, after selling *Whistler's Mother,* moved to 110 rue du Bac, where he entertained the likes of Degas, Henry James, Manet, and Toulouse-Lautrec. Auguste Rodin lived at what is now the **Musée Rodin,** at 77 rue de Varenne, until his death in 1917.

Even visitors with no time to thoroughly explore the 7e at least rush to its second major attraction (after the Eiffel Tower), the Musée d'Orsay, the world's premier showcase of 19th-century French art and culture. The museum is housed in the old Gare d'Orsay, which Orson Welles used in 1962 as a setting for his film *The Trial,* based on the book by Franz Kafka.

8e Arr. (Right Bank, Champs-Elysées / Madeleine)   The 8e is the heart of the Right Bank and its prime showcase is **the Champs-Elysées.** Here you'll find the fashion houses, the most elegant hotels, expensive restaurants and shops, and the most fashionably attired Parisians. Stretching grandly from the **Arc de Triomphe** to the delicate obelisk on **place de la Concorde,** the Champs-Elysées has long been cited as the perfect metaphor of the Parisian love of symmetry. However, by the 1980s, it had become a garish strip, with too much traffic, too many fast-food joints, and too many panhandlers. In the '90s, Mayor (and later President) Jacques Chirac launched a massive cleanup. The major change has been in broadened sidewalks, with new rows of trees planted. The old glory? Perhaps it's gone forever; what an improvement over the '80s, though.

Whatever it is you're looking for, in the 8e it will be the city's best, grandest, and most impressive. It has the best restaurant in Paris (Taillevent), the sexiest strip joint (Crazy Horse Saloon), the most splendid square in all of France (place de la Concorde), the best rooftop cafe (at La Samaritaine), the grandest hotel in France (The Crillon), the most impressive triumphal arch on the planet (L'Arc de Triomphe), the world's most expensive residential street (avenue Montaigne), the world's oldest Métro station (Franklin-D-Roosevelt), the most ancient monument in Paris (Obelisk of Luxor, 3,300 years old), and on and on.

9e Arr. (Right Bank, Opéra Garnier / Pigalle)   Everything from the **Quartier de l'Opéra** to the strip and clip joints of **Pigalle** (the infamous "Pig Alley" for the GIs of World War II) falls within the 9e. When Balzac was writing his novels, the author considered the most elitist address for his socially ambitious characters as the 9e's chaussée d'Antin. Radically altered by the 19th-century urban redevelopment projects of Baron Haussmann, the *grands boulevards* radiating through the district are among the most obvious of the baron's labors. Although the chaussée d'Antin is no longer particularly elegant, having been supplanted by some of Paris's largest department stores, the 9e endures, even if fickle fashion now prefers other addresses. Over the decades, the 9e has been celebrated in literature and song for the music halls that brought gaiety to the city. Marie Duplessis, known as Marguerite Gautier, heroine of *La Dame aux camélias* by Alexandre Dumas the younger (1824–95), died at 17 bd. de la Madeleine (and was resurrected as Greta Garbo in the film version of Dumas's novel, Hollywood-ized as *Camille*). Boulevard des Italiens is the site of the **Café de la Paix,** opened in 1856 and once the meeting place of the Romantic poets, including Théophile Gautier and Alfred de Musset. Later, Charles de Gaulle, Marlene Dietrich, and two million Americans started showing up.

At place Pigalle, gone is the Café La Nouvelle Athènes, where Degas, Pissarro, and Manet used to meet. Today, you're likely to encounter a few clubs where the action gets really down and dirty. Other major attractions include the **Folies Bergère,** where cancan dancers have been high-kicking it since 1868 and French entertainers such as Mistinguett, Edith Piaf, and Maurice Chevalier have appeared along with Josephine Baker, once hailed as "the toast of Paris." More than anything, it was the **Opéra Garnier** (Paris Opera House) that made the 9e the last hurrah of Second Empire opulence. Renoir hated it, but several generations later, Chagall did the ceilings. Pavlova danced *Swan Lake* here, and Nijinsky took the night off to go cruising.

10e Arr. (Right Bank, Gare du Nord / Gare de l'Est)   **Gare du Nord** and **Gare de l'Est,** along with movie theaters, porno houses, and dreary commercial zones, make the 10e one of the least desirable arrondissements for living, dining, and sightseeing in Paris. There are a few bright spots, though, particularly along the Canal St-Martin in the east. The **quai de Valmy** and **quai de Jemmapes** are scenic, tree-lined promenades along the canal, and two classic old restaurants provide more reasons to venture into the 10e: **Brasserie Flo** at 7 cour des Petites-Ecuries (go there for its *la formidable choucroute,* a heap of sauerkraut garnished with everything) and **Julien,** 16 rue du Faubourg St-Denis—called the poor man's Maxim's because of its belle epoque interiors and moderate prices.

11e Arr. (Right Bank, Opéra Bastille)   For many years, this quarter seemed to sink lower and lower into poverty and decay, overcrowded by working-class immigrants from the far reaches of the former French Empire. The opening of the **Opéra Bastille,** however, has given the 11e new hope and new life. The facility, called "the people's opera house," stands on the landmark **place de la Bastille,** where on July 14, 1789, 633 Parisians stormed the fortress and seized the ammunition depot as the French Revolution swept across the city. Over the years, the prison held Voltaire, the Marquis de Sade, and the mysterious "Man in the Iron Mask."

Even when the district wasn't fashionable, visitors flocked to **Bofinger,** at 5–7 rue de la Bastille, to sample its Alsatian *choucroute* (sauerkraut, usually topped by various pork cuts but here also available with seafood). Technically, Bofinger lies in the 4e arrondissement, although its fans have always associated it with the place de la Bastille. Established around 1864, it is perhaps the most famous brasserie in Paris.

The 11e has few landmarks or famous museums, but it's become a mecca for hordes of young Parisians looking for casual, inexpensive nightlife. Bargain hunters flock to *Le Marché* at place d'Aligre, for secondhand bric-a-brac: Everything is cheap, and although you must search hard for treasures, they often appear.

12e Arr. (Right Bank, Bois de Vincennes / Gare de Lyon)   The 12e's major attraction remains the **Bois de Vincennes,** a sprawling park on the eastern periphery of Paris. It's been a longtime favorite of French families who enjoy its zoos and museums, its royal château and boating lakes, and, most definitely, the Parc Floral de Paris, a celebrated flower garden whose springtime rhododendrons and autumn dahlias are among the major lures of the city. The dreary **Gare de Lyon** also lies in the 12e. This district, once a depressing urban wasteland, has been singled out for multimillion dollar resuscitation and will soon sport new housing, shops, gardens, and restaurants. The **Promenade Plantée,** a garden promenade that follows the former Reuilly railroad tracks, is the centerpiece of the new design.

13e Arr. (Left Bank, Gare Austerlitz)   Centered around the grimy **Gare d'Austerlitz,** the 13e has become a lively hub for Paris's Asian community. The Vietnamese restaurants along avenue de Ivry and avenue de Choisy are interspersed with stores selling every imaginable item from France's former Southeast Asian colonies. Although too much of the neighborhood has been given over to high-rises, a small section of village life has been preserved in a cozy network of streets and passages surrounding rue Butte-aux-Cailles. The opening of the new **Bibliotèque Nationale de France** is eventually expected to lure businesses and shops to the barren eastern end of the 13e, which is undergoing rapid reconstruction. Another good reason to visit the 13e is the **Manufacture des Gobelins** at 42 av. des Gobelins, the tapestry factory that made the word "Gobelins" internationally famous. Some 250 Flemish weavers, under the reign of Louis XIV, launched the industry to compete with the tapestries being produced in southern Belgium (Flanders), and in time they became the preferred suppliers of the French aristocracy—many of the walls of the Sun King's palace at Versailles were covered with Gobelins.

14e Arr. (Left Bank, Montparnasse)   The northern end of this large arrondissement is devoted to **Montparnasse,** former stomping ground of the "lost generation": Gertrude Stein, Alice B. Toklas, Hemingway, and other American expatriates who gathered here in the 1920s. After World War II, it ceased to be the center of intellectual life in Paris, but the memory lingers on in its cafes. One of its most visible monuments, one that helps set the tone of the neighborhood, is the Rodin statue of Balzac at the junction of boulevard Montparnasse and boulevard Raspail. At this corner are some of the world's most famous literary cafes, including La Rotonde, Le Select, La Dôme, and La Coupole. Though Gertrude Stein probably avoided this corner (she loathed cafes), all the other American expatriates, including

Hemingway and Scott Fitzgerald, had no qualms about enjoying a drink here (or quite a few of them, for that matter). Henry Miller, plotting *Tropic of Cancer* and his newest seduction of Anaïs Nin, came to La Coupole for his morning porridge. So did Roman Polanski, Josephine Baker (with a lion cub on a leash), James Joyce, Man Ray, Matisse, Ionesco (ordering *café liègeois*), Jean-Paul Sartre, and even the famous Kiki as she worked on her memoirs. The cafe-free Stein amused herself at home (27 rue de Fleurus) with Alice Toklas, collecting paintings (including those of Picasso) and entertaining the likes of Max Jacob, Apollinaire, T. S. Eliot, and Matisse.

At its southern end, the 14e arrondissement contains pleasant residential neighborhoods filled with well-designed apartment buildings, many of them built between 1910 and 1940.

15e Arr. (Left Bank, Gare Montparnasse / Institut Pasteur) A mostly residential district beginning at **Gare Montparnasse,** the 15e stretches all the way to the Seine. In size and population, it's the largest quartier of Paris, but it attracts few tourists—mostly because it has few attractions, aside from the **Parc des Expositions** and the **Institut Pasteur.** In the early 20th century, the artists Chagall, Leger, and Modigliani lived in this arrondissement in a shared atelier known as "The Beehive."

16e Arr. (Right Bank, Trocadéro / Bois de Boulogne) During most of his time in Paris, Benjamin Franklin lived in Passy, one of the 18th-century villages that make up this district. Highlights include the **Bois de Boulogne,** the **Jardin du Trocadéro,** the **Musée de Balzac,** the **Musée Guimet** (famous for its Asian collections), and the **Cimetière de Passy,** resting place of Manet, Talleyrand, Giraudoux, and Debussy. One of the largest of the city's arrondissements, the 16e is known today for its well-heeled bourgeoisie, its upscale rents, and some rather posh (and, according to its critics, rather smug) residential boulevards. Prosperous and suitably conservative addresses include the avenue d'Iéna and the avenue Victor Hugo. Also prestigious is the avenue Foch, the widest boulevard in Paris, with homes that at various periods were maintained by Aristotle Onassis, Shah Mohammad Reza Pahlavi of Iran, the composer Charles Debussy, Maria Callas, and Prince Rainier of Monaco. The arrondissement also includes what some visitors consider the best place in Paris from which to view the Eiffel Tower, the **place du Trocadéro.**

17e Arr. (Right Bank, Parc Monceau / Place Clichy) Flanking the northern periphery of Paris, the 17e incorporates neighborhoods of conservative bourgeois respectability (in its western end) and less affluent, more pedestrian neighborhoods in its eastern end. Regardless of its levels of prosperity, most of the arrondissement is residential, and most of it, at least to habitués of glamour and glitter, is rather dull. Highlights include the **Palais des Congrès,** which is of interest only if you're attending a convention or special exhibit, and the **Porte Maillot Air Terminal,** which has no grand distinction.

18e Arr. (Right Bank, Montmartre) The 18e is the most famous outer quarter of Paris, containing **Montmartre,** the **Moulin Rouge,** the **Basilica of Sacré-Coeur,** and the **place du Tertre.** Utrillo was its native son, Renoir lived here, and Toulouse-Lautrec adopted the area as his own. Picasso painted some of his most famous works at the Bateau-Lavoir (Boat Washhouse) on place Emile-Goudeau. Max Jacob, Matisse, and Braque were all frequent visitors. Today, place Blanche is known for its prostitutes, and place de Tertre is filled with honky-tonks, too many souvenir shops, and terrible restaurants. The quieter north, east, and west sides of the hill still retain traces of the old days and are well worth exploring. The city's most famous flea market, **Marché aux Puces de Clignancourt,** is another landmark.

19e Arr. (Right Bank, La Villette)   Today, visitors come to what was once the village of La Villette to see the angular, much-publicized **Cité des Sciences et de l'Industrie,** a spectacular science museum and park built on a site that for years was devoted to the city's slaughterhouses. Mostly residential, and not at all upscale, the district is one of the most ethnically diverse in Paris, the home of people from all parts of the former French Empire. A highlight is **Les Buttes–Chaumont,** a park where kids can enjoy puppet shows and donkey rides.

20e Arr. (Right Bank, Pére-Lachaise Cemetery)   The 20e's greatest landmark is **Père-Lachaise Cemetery,** the resting place of Edith Piaf, Marcel Proust, Oscar Wilde, Isadora Duncan, Sarah Bernhardt, Gertrude Stein, Colette, and many, many others. Otherwise, the 20e arrondissement is not likely to correspond to anyone's vision of legendary Paris—the new developments are too bland to be interesting and the old housing is too deteriorated to be attractive. Although nostalgia buffs sometimes head here to visit Piaf's former neighborhood, Ménilmontant-Belleville, it has been almost totally bulldozed and rebuilt since the bad old days when she grew up there. Now the district is a blend of cultures: On the streets of Belleville you'll find turbaned men selling dates in a scene directly out of northern Africa; numerous Chinese, Vietnamese, and Thai restaurants catering to the Asian community; and kosher couscous for the benefit of a Sephardic Jewish community transplanted from Algeria and Tunisia. Overlooking it all is the new **Parc de Belleville,** 11 acres of gardens and paths on a hill with a spectacular view of Paris.

2 Getting Around

BY PUBLIC TRANSPORTATION

SAVING MONEY   If you plan to use public transportation frequently, you should consider the **Carte Orange,** a weekly or monthly pass that's used by Parisians and is quite economical—72F ($13.40) for a week's unlimited travel (*coupon hebdomadaire*) or 243F ($46) for a month's pass (*coupon mensuel*). The only catch is that you must provide a little photo of yourself; many Monoprix stores, major Métro stations, department stores, and train stations have photo booths where you can get four blackand-white pictures for 20F ($4). The weekly Carte Orange can be bought any time from Monday through Wednesday morning, and it is valid through Sunday; get the monthly card on the first or second day of each month.

Otherwise, buying a 10-ticket *carnet* (booklet) for 46F ($8.80) is a good deal; a single ticket costs 8F ($1.50). *Carnets* are on sale at any Métro station as well as *tabacs* (cafes and kiosks that sell tobacco products).

BY METRO & RER   The best way to get around Paris is to walk, and entire neighborhoods—such as the Latin Quarter and the Marais—can be easily negotiated this way. For longer distances, the Métro (Paris's subway) is best. (See the "Paris Métro" map on the inside back cover of this book.)

Fast, quite safe, and easy to navigate, the Métro opened its first line in 1900. It is operated by the RATP (Régie Autonome des Transports Parisiens), as are city buses. The Métro has 13 lines and more than 360 stations, so there's bound to be one near your destination. It's connected to the Réseau Express Régional (RER), with four lines that stop at only a few stations, crisscrossing the city in minutes and connecting downtown Paris with its airports and suburbs. The trains run from 5:30am to past midnight, finishing up their final runs before 1am. The Métro and the RER operate on a zone system, at a different fare per zone, but it is unlikely that you will be traveling any farther than the first zone.

A single ticket (*un billet*) costs 8F ($1.50), but if you ask for *un carnet* (a booklet) you will get 10 (loose) tickets for 46F ($8.80), dropping the price per ticket to only 88¢. If you are going to be in Paris for a few days, it may be a better idea to get the weekly or monthly unlimited-ride Carte Orange (see above).

At the turnstile entrances to the station, insert your ticket in the turnstile and pass through. You must keep your ticket until you exit the train platform and pass the *limite de validité des billets.* An inspector may request to see your ticket at any time, and if you fail to produce it, fines must be paid on the spot. When you ride the RER, it is especially important that you keep your ticket since you will have to insert it in a turnstile once more when you exit the station.

Some of the older Métro stations are marked by elegant art nouveau gateways reading "Métropolitain"; others are marked by big yellow "M" signs. Every Métro stop has maps of the system, and these are also available at ticket booths. Once you decide which Métro line you need, make sure that you are going in the right direction: On Métro line 1, "Direction: Esplanade de la Defense" indicates a westbound train, while "Direction: Château de Vincennes" is just the opposite. To change train lines, look for the orange *correspondance* signs; blue signs reading *sortie* mark the exits.

Near the exits there is usually a *plan du quartier,* a pictorial and very detailed map of the streets and buildings surrounding each Métro station, with all exits marked. It's often a good idea to consult the *plan du quartier* before you climb the stairs, especially at very large stations; you may want to use a different exit stairway so as to be on the other side of a busy street or closer to your destination.

For more information on the city's public transportation, stop in at any of the two offices of the Services Touristiques de la RATP, at 53 bis, quai des Grands-Augustins, 6e (Métro: St-Michel), or at place de la Madeleine, 8e (Métro: Madeleine); or you can call ☎ **01-43-46-14-14** for information in French.

Pickpocket Warning: Most of the time the Métro is quite safe. Precautions are in order in the northern parts of the city and in deserted stations and in those long corridors between stations late at night. As a tourist, you are a special mark. You may feel safer riding in the first train car, where the engineer is. Watch out for pickpockets on the platforms and on the Métro trains. In Paris, bands of ragamuffins operate by quickly surrounding you, distracting you by waving something in your face, picking your pockets clean, and disappearing, all within seconds. *Don't let them near you.* Be rude if you have to.

BY BUS   The bus system in Paris is also convenient and can be an inexpensive way to sightsee without wearing out your feet. Each bus shelter has a route map, which should be checked carefully. Because of the number of one-way streets, the bus is likely to make different stops depending upon its direction. Métro tickets are also valid for bus travel or you can buy your ticket from the conductor. *Carnets* cannot be bought on board. Tickets must be punched in the machine and then retained until the end of the ride.

BY TAXI

Parisian taxis are fairly expensive, but you should know a few things just in case you need one. First, look for the blue "taxi" sign; although you can hail taxis in the street, most drivers will not pick you up if you are in the general vicinity of a taxi stand. Check the meter carefully, especially if you are coming in from an airport; rip-offs are distressingly commonplace. For one to three people, the drop rate in Paris proper is 13F ($2.60) plus 3.45F (65¢) for every kilometer from 7am to 7pm, after which rates rise to 5.70F ($1) for every kilometer. You will pay supplements from taxi ranks at train stations and at the Air France shuttle-bus terminals of 5F ($1.20), 6F ($1.20) for luggage, and, if the driver agrees to do so, 10F ($1) for transporting a fourth person or 4F (60¢) for a pet. It is common practice to tip your driver 2F to 3F (40¢ to 60¢), except on longer journeys when the fare exceeds 100F ($20); in these cases a 10F ($2) tip would be appropriate.

BY CAR

Don't even consider driving a car in Paris, because streets are narrow and parking is next to impossible. Besides, most visitors don't have the nerve, skill, and ruthlessness required.

If you insist on ignoring this advice, here are a few tips: Get an excellent street map and ride with a copilot because there's no time to think at intersections. "Zone Bleu" means that you can't park without a parking disk, obtainable from garages, police stations, and hotels. Parking is unlimited in these zones on Sunday and holidays. Attach the disk to your windshield, setting its clock to show the time of arrival. Between 9am and noon and from 2:30 to 5pm you may park for 1 hour; from noon to 2:30pm you can park for 2½ hours.

Drivers and all passengers (front and back) must wear seat belts. Children under 12 must ride in the back seat. Drivers are supposed to yield to the car on the right, except where signs indicate otherwise, as at traffic circles.

Watch for the gendarmes, who lack patience and who consistently countermand the lights. Horn blowing is absolutely forbidden except in emergencies. Flash your headlights instead.

BY BICYCLE

It's tough to negotiate the narrow, traffic-clogged streets filled with mean-spirited motorists who don't look kindly upon tourists on bikes. Save your cycling for the Bois de Boulogne or another park.

If you want to rent a bicycle, contact **Paris-Vélo,** 2 rue du Fer-à-Moulin, 5e (☎ **01-43-37-59-22;** Métro: St-Marcel). A steep deposit is required.

FAST FACTS: Paris

American Express   The grand Paris office of **American Express** at 11 rue Scribe, 9e (☎ **01-47-77-70-07;** Métro: Opéra Chaussée-d'Antin or Havre-Caumartin; RER: Auber), is open Monday through Friday from 9am to 6:30pm; the bank is also open on Saturday (same hours), but the mail pickup window is closed.

Baby-sitters   Call either of the following: **Allo Maman Poule** (☎ **01-47-48-01-01**) or **Kid Service,** 159 rue de Rome, 17e (☎ **01-47-66-00-52;** Métro: Gare St-Lazare).

Bookstores   See "Books," section of chapter 8.

Business Hours   The *grands magasins* (**department stores**) are generally open Monday through Saturday from 9:30am to 6:30pm; **smaller shops** close for lunch and reopen around 2pm, but this has become rarer than it used to be. Many stores stay open until 7pm in summer; others are closed on Monday, especially in the morning. Large **offices** remain open all day, but some also close for lunch. **Banks** are normally open Monday through Friday from 9am to noon and from 1 or 1:30 to 4:30pm. Some banks also have hours on Saturday morning. Some currency-exchange booths are open very long hours; see "Currency Exchange," below.

Climate See "When to Go," in chapter 2.

Currency Exchange Banks and *bureaux de change* (exchange offices) almost always offer better exchange rates than hotels, restaurants, and shops, which should be used only in emergencies. For very good rates, no fees or commissions, and quick service, try the **Comptoir de Change Opéra,** 9 rue Scribe, 9e (☎ **01-47-42-20-96;** Métro: Opéra; RER: Auber). It is open Monday through Friday from 9am to 5:15pm and Saturday from 9:30am to 4:15pm. The bureaux de change at all train stations (except Gare de Montparnasse) are open daily; those at 63 av. des Champs-Elysées, 8e (Métro: Franklin-D-Roosevelt), and 140 av. des Champs-Elysées, 8e (Métro: Charles-de-Gaulle-Etoile), keep long hours.

Despite disadvantageous exchange rates, long lines, and the counterterrorism security, many people prefer to exchange their money at **American Express** (see above).

Dentist You can call your consulate and ask the duty officer to recommend a dentist. For dental emergencies, call **SOS Dentaire** (☎ **01-43-37-51-00**) daily from 9am to midnight.

Doctor Call your consulate and ask the duty officer to recommend a doctor, or call **SOS Médecins** (☎ **01-47-07-77-77**), a 24-hour service.

Drugstores Paris has a number of all-night pharmacies, including the **Pharmacie Dhéry,** 84 av. des Champs-Elysées, 8e (☎ **01-45-62-02-41;** Métro: George-V), in the Galerie des Champs shopping center. Pharmacies are marked with a green cross. Incidentally, pharmacies in Paris are often upscale affairs, very proper and very expensive; it's cheaper to buy your toiletries elsewhere, such as a *supermarché* (supermarket).

Electricity The French electrical system runs on 220 volts. Adapters are needed to fit sockets, and are cheaper at home than they are in Paris. Many hotels have two-pin (in some cases, three-pin) sockets for electric razors. It's a good idea to ask at your hotel before plugging in any electrical appliance.

Embassies/Consulates If you have a passport, immigration, legal, or other problem, contact your consulate. Call before you go there, as they often keep strange hours and observe both French and home-country holidays. Here's where to find them: **Australia,** 4 rue Jean-Rey, 15e (☎ **01-40-59-33-00;** Métro: Bir-Hakeim); **Canada,** 35 av. Montaigne, 8e (☎ **01-44-43-29-00;** Métro: Franklin-D.-Roosevelt or Alma-Marceau); **New Zealand,** 7 ter, rue Léonard-de-Vinci, 16e (☎ **01-45-00-24-11,** ext. 280 from 9am to 1pm; Métro: Victor-Hugo); **United Kingdom,** 9 av. Hoche, 8e (☎ **01-42-66-38-10;** Métro: Madeleine); **United States,** 2 rue St-Florentin, 1er, (☎ **01-43-12-22-22;** Métro: Concorde).

Emergencies Call ☎ **17** for the **police.** To report a **fire,** dial ☎ **18**. For an **ambulance,** call ☎ **15** or **SAMU** (Service d'aide medicale d'urgence, or "emergency services") ☎ **01-45-67-50-50.** For help in English, call **SOS Help** at ☎ **01-47-23-80-80.** The main **police station,** at 9 bd. du Palais, 4e (☎ **01-53-71-53-71;** Métro: Cité) is open 24 hours a day.

Holidays See "When to Go," in chapter 2.

Hospitals Two hospitals with English-speaking staff are the **American Hospital of Paris,** 63 bd. Victor-Hugo, Neuilly-sur-Seine (☎ **01-46-41-25-25**), just west of Paris proper (Métro: Les Sablons or Levallois-Perret); and the **British Hospital of Paris,** 3 rue Barbes Levallois-Perret (☎ **01-46-39-22-22**), just north of Neuilly, over the city line northwest of Paris (Métro: Anatole-France). Note that the American Hospital charges about $600 a day for a room, not including doctor's fees. The emergency department will cost more than $60 for a visit, not including tests and X rays.

Hotlines   **SOS Help** (☎ **01-47-23-80-80**) is an English-language crisis line operating from 3 to 11pm. The Comité National pour la Réadaptation des Handicapes, 38 bd. Raspail, 7e (☎ **01-45-48-90-13;** Métro: Sèvres-Babylone), is an information service for disabled people; it's open Monday through Friday from 9:30am to noon and 2:30 to 8pm.

Information   See "Visitor Information & Entry Requirements," in chapter 2 and "Orientation," above.

Liquor Laws   Supermarkets, grocery stores, and cafes sell alcoholic beverages. The legal drinking age is 16. Persons under that age can be served an alcoholic drink in a bar or restaurant if accompanied by a parent or legal guardian. Wine and liquor are sold every day of the year. *Be warned:* The authorities are very strict about drunk-driving laws. If convicted, you faces a stiff fine and a possible prison term of 2 months to 2 years.

Lost Property   The central office is **Objets Trouvés,** 36 rue des Morillons, 15e (☎ **01-55-76-20-00;** Métro: Convention), at the corner of rue de Dantzig. The office is open Monday, Wednesday, and Friday from 8:30am to 5pm, with longer hours on Tuesday and Thursday (until 8pm) except July, August, and the last two weeks of December. For Lost and Found on the **Métro,** call ☎ **01-40-06-75-27.** If you lose your **Visa** or **MasterCard,** call ☎ **01-42-77-11-90.** To report lost **American Express** cards, call ☎ **01-47-77-72-00.**

Luggage Storage/Lockers   Most hotels will store luggage for you, and that's your best bet—especially if you plan to return to Paris after a tour of the provinces. Otherwise, try the *consignes* at railway stations or airports; luggage lockers are not recommended for more than brief storage.

Mail   Large **post offices** are normally open Monday through Friday from 8am to 7pm and Saturday from 8am to noon; small post offices may have shorter hours. There are many post offices (PTT) scattered around the city; ask anybody for the nearest one. Airmail letters and postcards to the United States cost 4.40F (88¢); within Europe, 3F (60¢); and to Australia or New Zealand, 5.20F ($1.04).

The city's **main post office** is at 52 rue du Louvre, 75001 Paris (☎ **01-40-28-20-00;** Métro: Louvre-Rivoli). It's open 24 hours a day for urgent mailings, telegrams, and telephone calls. This is where you should go to pick up Poste Restante mail, whereby mail can be sent to you c/o the post office and stored until you pick it up; be prepared to show your passport and pay a small fee for each letter you receive. If you don't want to use Poste Restante, you can receive mail c/o American Express. Holders of American Express cards or Amex traveler's checks get this service free; others have to pay a fee.

Maps   See "Street Maps," above in this chapter.

Money   See "Money," in chapter 2.

Newspapers/Magazines   Many newsstands carry the latest editions of the *International Herald-Tribune,* published Monday through Saturday, and usually the major London papers. *Time* and *Newsweek* are also readily available in Paris. The weekly entertainment guide *Pariscope,* which comes out on Wednesdays, also has an English-language insert that gives you up-to-the-minute information on the latest cultural events.

Police   Dial ☎ **17** in emergencies; otherwise call ☎ **01-53-71-53-71.**

Post Office   See "Mail," above.

Rest rooms   The good news is that public rest rooms are plentiful; the bad news is that you usually have to pay for them. Every cafe has a rest room but they are supposed to be for customers only. The best plan is to ask to use the telephone; it's usually next to the *toilette*. For 2F you can use the street-side toilets, which are automatically flushed out after every use. Some Métro stations have serviced rest rooms; you are expected to tip the attendant 2F.

Smoking   Although restaurants are required to provide nonsmoking sections, you may find yourself next to the kitchen or the rest rooms. Even there, your neighbor may light up and defy you to say something about it. Large brasseries, expensive restaurants, and places accustomed to dealing with foreigners are most likely to be accommodating.

Taxes   *Watch it:* You could get burned. As a member of the European Community, France routinely imposes a value-added tax (VAT) on many goods and services. This standard VAT on merchandise is 20.6% and is applied to clothing, appliances, liquor, leather goods, shoes, furs, jewelry, perfumes, cameras, and even caviar. Refunds on certain goods and merchandise are made—but not on services. The minimum purchase is 2,000F ($400) in the same store for nationals or residents of countries outside the European Union.

Telephone/Telex/Fax   Coin-operated **pay phones,** now found almost exclusively in bars, cafes and restaurants, take 1F, 2F, and 5F pieces; the minimum charge is 2F (40¢). Most public phone booths, though, take only telephone debit cards called *télécartes* that can be bought at post offices and at *tabacs* (cafes and kiosks that sell tobacco products). All you do is insert the card into the phone and make your call; the cost of the call is automatically deducted from the "value" of the card as recorded on its magnetized strip. The *télécarte* comes in 50- and 120-unit values, costing 40F ($8) and 96F ($19.20), respectively, and they're especially helpful if you're calling home from a phone booth. If you do not plan to make many phone calls, a *télécarte* may not be a very good idea, since you probably won't end up using its entire value, so seek out coin phones instead.

For placing **international calls from France,** dial 00, then the country code (for the United States and Canada, it's 1; for Britain, 44; for Ireland, 353; for Australia, 61; and for New Zealand, 64), then the area or city code, then the local number (for example, to call New York you'd dial 00 + 1 + 212 + 000-0000). **To place a collect call to North America,** dial 00/33-11 and an English-speaking operator will assist you. Dial 00/00-11 for an American AT&T operator.

For **calling from Paris to anywhere else in France** (called *province*), the country is divided into four zones with prefixes beginning 02-05; check a phone directory for the code of the city you're calling.

If you're calling France **from the United States,** dial the international prefix, 011; and then the country code for France, 33; followed by the number but leaving off the initial zero (for example, 011 + 33 + 1-00-00-00-00).

Avoid making any phone calls from your hotel room; many hotels charge at least 2F (40¢) for local calls and the mark-up on international calls can be staggering.

Telegrams may be sent from any Paris post office during the day (see "Mail," above), and anytime from the 24-hour central post office. In telegrams to the United States, the address is counted in the price; there are no special rates for a certain number of words, but night telegrams cost less. If you're in Paris and wish to send a **telegram in English,** call ☎ **01-05-33-44-11.** You can also send **telex** and **fax** messages at the main post office in each arrondissement of Paris, but it's often cheaper to use one of the commercial services.

Time   Paris is 6 hours ahead of eastern standard time; when it's noon in New York, it's 6pm in Paris.

Tipping   Service is supposedly included at your hotel, but it is still customary to tip the **bellhop** about 6F ($1.20) per bag, more in expensive splurge hotels. You might use 5% of the daily room rate as a guideline. If you have lots of luggage, tip a bit more. Though your *addition* (restaurant bill) or *fiche* (cafe check) will bear the words *"service compris"* (service charge included), it's customary to leave a small tip. Generally 5% is considered acceptable. Remember, service has supposedly already been paid for. **Taxi drivers** expect at least 5% of the fare as a tip. At the theater and cinema, tip 2F (40¢) if there is an usher who shows you to your seat. In **public toilets,** there is often a posted fee for using the facilities. If not, the maintenance person will expect a tip of about 2F (40¢), put it in the basket or on the plate at the entrance. **Porters** and **cloakroom attendants** are usually governed by set prices that are displayed. If not, give a porter 5F to 8F ($1 to $1.60) per suitcase, and a cloakroom attendant 2F to 4F (40¢ to 80¢) per coat.

Transit Info   Call ☎ **01-43-46-14-14.**

Water   Tap water in Paris is perfectly safe, but if you're prone to stomach problems, you may prefer to drink mineral water.

Weather   Call ☎ **01-36-68-00-75.**

Accommodations You Can Afford

Paris hotels perfectly mirror the diversity of the city. They run the full gamut from palaces fit for the sultan of Brunei to ramshackle hide-aways of oddly angled rooms and irregular plumbing. Between the two extremes is a large selection of comfortable and affordable hotels, many of them small, family run establishments. Partly because of competition from international chains, many budget hotels are holding the line on prices while adding elevators and sprucing up the interiors with paint and wallpaper, curtains, and bedspreads.

In general, you'll find that budget-priced French accommodations are reliably clean and comfortable. If you're used to the amenities offered for the same money in North American motels, however, you may be disappointed. Rooms tend to be smaller than you would expect, even in expensive hotels (unless you opt for a modern chain hotel). Rooms also vary greatly in size as well as furnishings. Ask to see a room before checking in, and if you don't like it, ask to see another. If you're reserving by phone and room size is an important factor, you would do better to reserve a triple in a modest hotel than a double in a higher-priced establishment. Most hotels sell their largest rooms as triples and they are generally much larger than a double at a comparable price. Also, if you're looking for a double room, keep in mind that a double bed is cheaper than two twin beds, but the two twin beds are likely to be in a larger room.

If you're a light sleeper, ask for a room in the rear or make sure the windows are double glazed—garbage is picked up early and loudly every morning in most places. Also, acoustics in old hotels can be unpredictable; your neighbors' noise may be as annoying as street noise. I'm a big believer in earplugs and wouldn't take a vacation without them.

You will often find a variety of plumbing arrangements as well, from rooms with "EC" (*eau courante,* or running water, meaning a sink) to those with private shower or bath. Note that a room with shower or bath does not necessarily mean that the room has a toilet as well. There are rooms with toilet and shower, rooms with toilet (WC) only, and rooms with shower only. Bathless rooms can be a real bargain, but many hotels charge for the use of the shower, which should be factored into the cost of your stay. The trend these days is to renovate small hotels and put a shower, toilet, and sink in each room, so those marvelously cheap bathless rooms are dwindling in number.

If you want to find the most attractive room at the best price, plan ahead. During the busiest times of year—late spring/early summer and early fall—rooms at the best budget hotels are reserved several months in advance. The dead of winter and August are lighter months and more space is available. Nevertheless, coming to Paris at any time without a reservation could mean paying a lot more than you expected.

If you do come to town without a reservation, try to arrive early in the day and head to one of the tourist offices in the airports, train stations, or on the Champs-Elysées. For a small fee they will book a room for you (see "Orientation," in chapter 3). It's also worth knowing that three-star hotels with unsold rooms often sell them through the tourist office at a steep discount. These can be great last-minute deals, but availability varies from day to day, so it's wise not to count on booking a room this way.

It's important to be flexible about what part of the city you stay in. Paris is relatively small and very well connected by public transportation. Even on the fringes of Paris you won't be more than a half hour from the center of town, where hotel rates are highest. The areas around the city's major train stations, especially the Gare du Nord, the Gare de Lyon, and the Gare de l'Est, have a large supply of reasonably priced accommodations that offer good value even if the neighborhoods are a bit bland. Less frequented residential quarters like the 9e, 11e, 13e and 15e arrondissements also have many small budget hotels. We've organized the hotels below by neighborhood, then within the neighborhoods, by price category: Doubles for Less than 350F ($61), Doubles for Less than 500F ($87), and Worth a Splurge.

The prices given below are for the high summer season and are correct as this book goes to press, but they may have changed by the time you arrive. Also, in high season you may be required to take breakfast with your room.

Note: France will be hosting the Soccer World Cup in 1998. From June 10 to July 12, a series of matches will be played in and around Paris. Hotel space will be extremely tight and some hotels may raise their rates.

1 Best Bets on a Budget

- **Best for Business Travelers:** Ideally situated near one of the city's main business districts, the **Hôtel Keppler,** 12 rue Keppler, 16e (☎ **01-47-20-65-05**), is a quiet, well-run hotel with a lot of amenities for the money. Its good address will favorably impress your French business associates as well and show them that you're *malin,* or shrewd.
- **Best for Historic Atmosphere:** With its rounded stone tower, the **Hôtel St. Merry,** 78 rue de la Verrerie, 4e (☎ **01-42-78-14-15**), oozes Parisian atmosphere. It occupies a former 17th-century presbytery, and the beamed ceilings, stone walls, and wrought iron light fixtures constantly evoke an aura of history. You might want to spend a little extra for a room with a view, since some of the rooms are a bit dark. Book well ahead of time.
- **Best for Families:** It's expensive to visit Paris as a family of four or more, but the four-person rooms at the **Hôtel Jardins des Plantes,** 5 rue Linné, 5e (☎ **01-47-07-06-20**), are a good buy, and the hotel has a variety of appealing extras like a roof terrace and a sidewalk cafe. The park and zoo of the nearby Jardins des Plantes are great if your kids want to let off a little steam.

    The Hôtel Marignan, 13 rue du Sommerard, 5e (☎ **01-43-54-63-81**), is also very family friendly, which means you'll have access to a washer-dryer and can even bring your own food into their dining room.

- **Best Overall Values:** On the Right Bank, the **Castex Hôtel,** 5 rue Castex, 4e (☎ **01-42-72-31-52**), has been owned by the same family for 70 years and is both well located and well kept. The **AM Hôtel Vertus,** 5 rue des Vertus, 3e (☎ **01-44-61-89-50**), also offers extraordinarily good value for the money, occupies a renovated 17th-century building, and has baths in every room. On the Left Bank, the **Familia Hôtel,** 11 rue des Ecoles, 5e (☎ **01-43-54-55-27**), is a charmer and even has CNN. Rooms at all of these hotels should be booked as far in advance as possible.
- **Best Location:** Bang in the middle of everything, the charmingly creaky **Hôtel Esmeralda,** 4 rue St-Julien-le-Pauvre, 5e (☎ **01-43-54-19-20**), has a lot of atmosphere and is just across the river from Notre-Dame and only 5 minutes from St-Germain-des-Près. The Louvre, Les Halles, and the Marais are all about a lovely 15-minute walk away.
- **Best for Romance:** If you're on a bare-bones budget, the **Hôtel du Lys,** 23 rue Serpente, 6e (☎ **01-43-26-97-57**), is the ideal setting for your Parisian romantic fantasy. Think floral wallpaper and exposed beams in a 17th-century turreted mansion on the Left Bank.

    If you can spend a bit more, the **Hôtel le Tourville,** 17 av. de Tourville, 7e (☎ **01-47-05-62-62**), is a delightful hotel in a quiet part of the fashionable, residential 7e arrondissement; it's not only air-conditioned but equipped with antique furniture and miniature Roget & Gallet toiletries in the baths.
- **Best Rooms with a View:** With a little advance planning, you can enjoy a view of the Eiffel Tower from your Paris digs at the **Hôtel Kensington,** 79 av. de la Bourdonnais, 7e (☎ **01-47-05-74-00**); book well in advance and request room 43 or 44. Or maybe you'd prefer to gaze over the city's rooftops while you have your morning croissants and coffee? If this sounds good, request a room with a view on the top floor of the **Ermitage Hôtel,** 24 rue Lamarck, 18e (☎ **01-42-64-79-22**). This Montmartre bed-and-breakfast has considerable charm and a lot of personality.
- **Best Splurge:** The **Hôtel de Fleurie,** 32–34 rue de Grégoire-de-Tours, 6e (☎ **01-43-29-59-81**), has it all: a great location in St-Germain, handsomely decorated rooms with air-conditioning, pink-marble baths, cable TV and hair dryers, peace and quiet, and a very friendly staff. It's popular with the French themselves when they come to the capital to enjoy a dose of metropolitan life.
- **Best Youth Hostel:** Located in a historic old mansion on a quiet side street in the Marais, **Foyer le Fauconnier,** 17 rue de Fauconnier, 4e (☎ **01-42-74-23-45**), has a lot of atmosphere with a pleasant courtyard and a beautiful main staircase, and all rooms have private showers. Reserve well in advance.
- **Best for Nightlife Lovers:** The clunky seventies decor at the **Pax Hôtel,** 12 rue de Charonne, 11e (☎ **01-47-00-40-98**), is practically chic again as a retro look. Better still, if you want to hit a lot of clubs and bars, this hotel is right in the heart of the Bastille, the busiest, youngest after-dark scene in Paris.
- **Best for a Taste of the Discrete Charm of the Bourgeoisie:** The **Hôtel Nicolo,** 3 rue Nicolo, 16e (☎ **01-42-88-83-40**), is located in the heart of one of Paris's most expensive residential districts, a neighborhood comparable to New York's swanky Upper East Side or Washington, D.C.'s embassy district. If you'd like to live in gilded surroundings, even on a budget, you might enjoy the slightly fusty, very traditional French charm of the Nicolo.
- **Best for Serious Shoppers:** The **Hôtel Alison,** 21 rue de Surène, 8e (☎ **01-42-65-54-00**), is conveniently located for window-shopping or real shopping on the rues Royal and St-Honoré and isn't far from the famous Avenue Montaigne or the department stores on the boulevard Haussman. Better still, by staying here you

might be able to apply your economies to an enticing new perfume, a scarf that will always make you think of Paris, or a bunch of French music CDs.

2 Right Bank

ILE DE LA CITÉ, LOUVRE & LES HALLES (1ER ARRONDISSEMENT)
DOUBLES FOR LESS THAN 350F ($61)

Hôtel de Lille. 8 rue du Pélican, 75001 Paris. ☎ **01-42-33-33-42.** 200F ($34.75) single without shower, 230F ($40) double without shower; 280F ($48.70) double with shower. Showers 30F ($5.20) extra. No credit cards. Métro: Palais-Royal or Louvre.

On a very quiet tiny street between Rousseau and Croix des Petits Champs, this hotel's excellent location near the Louvre makes it worth considering. Rooms are decent and functional, although a little faded. The proprietor doesn't speak English and there's no elevator.

Hôtel Henri IV. 25 place Dauphine, 75001 Paris. ☎ **01-43-54-44-53.** 21 rms (2 with shower). 120–155F ($20.85–$27) single; 180–200F ($31.30–$34.80) double; 255F ($44.30) double with shower. Showers 15F ($2.60) extra. Rates include continental breakfast. No credit cards. Métro: Pont-Neuf.

Located on a small, chestnut-lined square on the Ile de la Cité near Notre-Dame cathedral. Budget travelers have been returning to this old hotel year after year because it is so cheap. The building is several hundred years old and the hotel's rooms look it. They are average size but have high ceilings and large windows. The furnishings are, it seems, as old as the house. Each room contains a sink; a toilet and shower are down the hall on each floor. The rooms are located on five floors, but there is no elevator. The price and the location, though, are hard to beat.

Hôtel Richelieu-Mazarin. 51 rue de Richelieu, 75001 Paris. ☎ **01-42-97-46-20.** 13 rms (some with bath or shower). 300F ($52.15) single; 330F ($57.40) double. Continental breakfast 25F ($4.35) extra. DC, MC, V. Métro: Palais-Royal.

You'll be hard-pressed to find a Right Bank hotel with rates like these, and because of this the Hôtel Richelieu-Mazarin is usually booked many months in advance. Decor is not the priority here; cleanliness is. At your request, the management will serve breakfast in your room for an extra 5F (85¢). If you don't mind a little street noise and climbing the stairs to your room, this hotel can't be beat.

DOUBLES FOR LESS THAN 500F ($87)

Hôtel Agora. 7 rue de la Cossonerie, 75001 Paris. ☎ **01-42-33-46-02.** Fax 01-42-33-80-99. 29 rms all with bath or shower. TV TEL. 305–485F ($53–$84.30) single with shower; 585F ($101.75) single with bath; 495F ($86) double with shower; 630F ($109.50) double with bath. Breakfast 40F ($6.95) per person. AE, CB, MC, V. Métro: Châtelet.

This two-star hotel is one of the few budget hotels located on the Right Bank. It has a traditional French air and the rooms are furnished with old furniture pieces combined with prints of old Paris and old-fashioned wallpapers. The windows are double glazed, which helps muffle the traffic noise of this busy area.

Hôtel Montpensier. 12 rue Richelieu, 75001 Paris. ☎ **01-42-96-28-50.** Fax 01-42-86-02-70. 43 rms. TV TEL. 250–450F ($43.45–$78.25) single or double. 520F ($90.45) triple. Shower 25F ($4.35). Continental breakfast 35F ($6.10). AE, MC, V. Métro: Palais-Royal.

This sprawling hotel with a variety of different rooms, some without bath, was once the home of Mademoiselle de Montpensier, cousin of Louis XIV. Nice location in the center of the town, just a few steps from the beautiful Palais Royal.

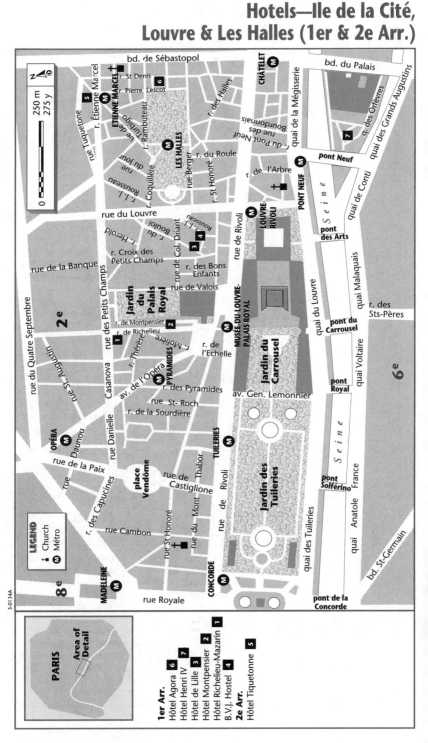

Hotels—Ile de la Cité, Louvre & Les Halles (1er & 2e Arr.)

bd. de Sébastopol

CHÂTELET

bd. du Palais

r. St-Denis

r. Pierre Lescot

r. Étienne Marcel

r. Tiquetone

r. de Turbigo

r. Rambuteau

r. des Halles

quai de la Mégisserie

q. des Orfèvres

quai des Grands Augustins

ÉTIENNE MARCEL

LES HALLES

r. du Jour

r. Coquillère

J.-J. Rousseau

r. Berger

r. du Roule

r. St-Honoré

r. du Pont Neuf

rue des Bourdonnais

pont Neuf

quai de Conti

rue du Louvre

r. Hérold

r. du Boulol

J.-J. Rousseau

r. du Col. Driant

r. de l'Arbre

PONT NEUF

LOUVRE-RIVOLI

Seine

pont des Arts

r. Croix des Petits Champs

r. des Bons Enfants

rue de Rivoli

quai Malaquais

rue de la Banque

rue des Petits Champs

rue de Col. Driant

rue de Valois

Jardin du Palais Royal

MUSÉE-DU-LOUVRE-PALAIS ROYAL

quai du Louvre

pont du Carrousel

r. des Sts-Pères

6e

2e

r. de Montpensier

r. de Richelieu

r. Thérèse

Molière

r. de l'Echelle

Jardin du Carrousel

pont Royal

quai Voltaire

rue du Quatre Septembre

rue St-Augustin

Casanova

av. de l'Opéra

PYRAMIDES

r. des Pyramides

rue St-Roch

r. de la Sourdière

av. Gén. Lemonnier

Seine

OPÉRA

rue Daunou

rue Danielle

TUILERIES

Jardin des Tuileries

pont Solférino

quai Anatole France

rue de la Paix

place Vendôme

rue de Castiglione

rue Thabor

rue de Rivoli

rue du Mont

quai des Tuileries

bd. St-Germain

r. des Capucines

r. St-Honoré

CONCORDE

8e

MADELEINE

rue Royale

CONCORDE

pont de la Concorde

LEGEND
✝ Church
Ⓜ Métro

N

250 m
275 y

0

PARIS

Area of Detail

3-0134A

Right Bank Accommodations

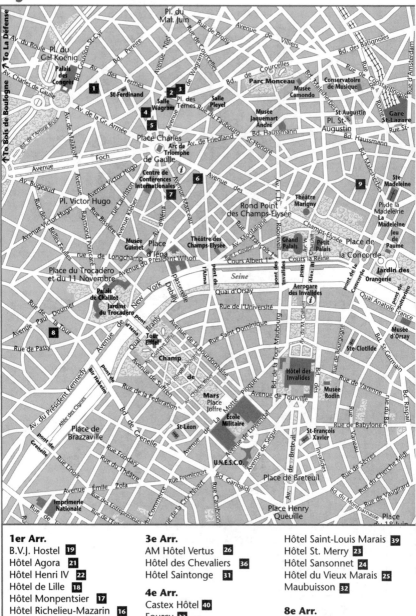

1er Arr.
B.V.J. Hostel 19
Hôtel Agora 21
Hôtel Henri IV 22
Hôtel de Lille 18
Hôtel Monpentsier 17
Hôtel Richelieu-Mazarin 16

2e Arr.
Hôtel Tiquetonne 20

3e Arr.
AM Hôtel Vertus 26
Hôtel des Chevaliers 36
Hôtel Saintonge 31

4e Arr.
Castex Hôtel 40
Fourcy 33
Grand Hôtel Jeanne d'Arc 35
Hôtel de la Herse d'Or 38
Hôtel de la Place des Vosges 37
Hôtel Pratic 34

Hôtel Saint-Louis Marais 39
Hôtel St. Merry 23
Hôtel Sansonnet 24
Hôtel du Vieux Marais 25
Maubuisson 32

8e Arr.
Hôtel Alison 9
Office de Tourisme et des
Congres de Paris 6

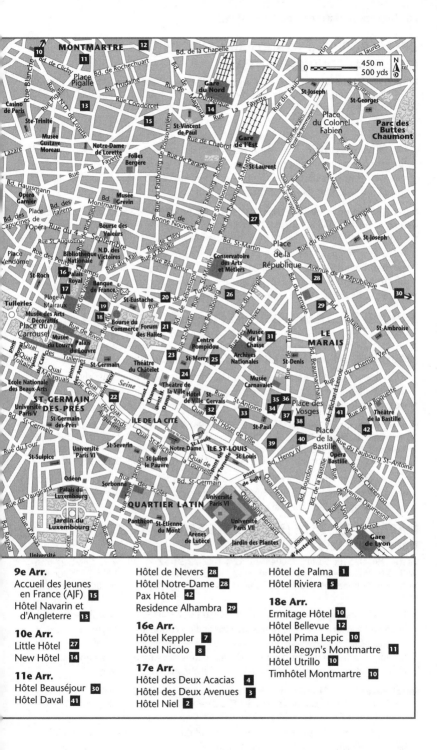

9e Arr.
Accueil des Jeunes
    en France (AJF) **15**
Hôtel Navarin et
    d'Angleterre **13**

10e Arr.
Little Hôtel **27**
New Hôtel **14**

11e Arr.
Hôtel Beauséjour **30**
Hôtel Daval **41**

Hôtel de Nevers **28**
Hôtel Notre-Dame **28**
Pax Hôtel **42**
Residence Alhambra **29**

16e Arr.
Hôtel Keppler **7**
Hôtel Nicolo **8**

17e Arr.
Hôtel des Deux Acacias **4**
Hôtel des Deux Avenues **3**
Hôtel Niel **2**

Hôtel de Palma **1**
Hôtel Riviera **5**

18e Arr.
Ermitage Hôtel **10**
Hôtel Bellevue **12**
Hôtel Prima Lepic **10**
Hôtel Regyn's Montmartre **11**
Hôtel Utrillo **10**
Timhôtel Montmartre **10**

75

OPÉRA, BOURSE & GRANDS BOULEVARDS (2E & 9E ARRONDISSEMENTS)

Hôtel Navarin et d'Angleterre. 8 rue Navarin, 75009 Paris. ☎ **01-48-78-31-80.** Fax 01-48-74-14-09. 26 rms (all with WC). TV TEL. 245F ($42.60) single with toilet only; 360F ($62.60) double with bath. Breakfast 30F ($5.20) extra. MC, V. Métro: St-Georges or Notre-Dame-de-Lorette.

The Maylin family, which has owned this hotel for more than 25 years, makes visitors feel extra welcome. The rooms, which have been renovated recently, are decently furnished, but the nicest aspect of staying here is the garden in the back, where you can take your breakfast seated by the fountain under the acacia trees. Rooms are spread out over four floors and there's no elevator.

Hôtel Tiquetonne. 6 rue Tiquetonne, 75002 Paris. ☎ **01-42-36-94-58.** 133F ($23.10) single without bath; 203F ($35.30) single with shower and WC; 236F ($41) double with shower and WC. MC, V. Métro: Etienne-Marcel or Réamur-Sébastopol.

Just a few steps off the rue St-Denis, this hotel is centrally located even if the neighborhood's a bit dull. What counts is that the rooms are clean and well priced (if a little worn) and that there's an elevator. Bathrooms are tiny with hardly enough space for the fixtures alone—sink, WC, shower, and bidet.

AROUND THE TRAIN STATIONS (10E ARRONDISSEMENT)

Little Hôtel. 3 rue Pierre-Chausson, 75010 Paris. ☎ **01-42-08-21-57.** Fax 01-42-08-33-80. 33 rms (all with bath or shower). TV TEL. 275F ($47.80) single with bath or shower; 350F ($60.85) double with bath or shower. AE, DC, MC, V. Métro: Jacques Bonsergent.

This pleasant hotel is located on a quiet side street between République and the Gare de L'Est. Most of the rooms have been refurbished recently and are modern and clean. The lobby contains a soda dispenser and an elevator is available.

New Hôtel. 40 rue St-Quentin, 75010 Paris. ☎ **01-48-78-04-83.** Fax 01-40-82-91-22. 41 rms (all with bath or shower). TV TEL. 345F ($60) single with shower and WC; 395F ($68.70) double with shower and WC; 480F ($83.45) double with bath and WC; 560–580F ($97.40–$100.85) triple. Rates include continental breakfast. AE, DC, EURO, MC, V. Métro: Gare du Nord.

This hotel, conveniently located in front of the Gare du Nord, is a good value. There are six floors of modern rooms equipped with hair dryers and cable TV. Some have air-conditioning. Elevator available.

MARAIS & BASTILLE (3E, 4E & 11E ARRONDISSEMENTS)
DOUBLES FOR LESS THAN 350F ($61)

Castex Hôtel. 5 rue Castex, 75004 Paris. ☎ **01-42-72-31-52.** Fax 01-42-72-57-91. 27 rms. 270F ($46.95) single with shower; 300F ($52.15) double without bath; 340F ($59.15) double with bath. Continental breakfast 25F ($4.35) extra. EURO, MC, V. Métro: Bastille or Sully-Morland.

Owned by the Bouchand family for almost 70 years, the Castex is a well-maintained hotel and a great value. The rooms are neat and exceptionally well kept, each with a writing table or a desk and chair; some have views over the courtyard. The staff is friendly and accommodating, and the son, who is carrying on the family tradition of hotel management, speaks English very well. Reserve well in advance.

Hôtel Beauséjour. 71 av. Parmentier, 75011 Paris. ☎ **01-47-00-38-16.** Fax 01-43-55-47-89. 32 rms (all with bath or shower). TV TEL. 270F ($46.95) single; 320F ($55.65) double. Breakfast 25F ($4.35) extra. AE, MC, V. Métro: Parmentier.

Situated between the place de la République and the Père-Lachaise cemetery, this hotel offers modern rooms decorated in pastels, with TVs and telephones as well as such

Hotels—Marais & Bastille (3e, 4e & 11e Arr.)

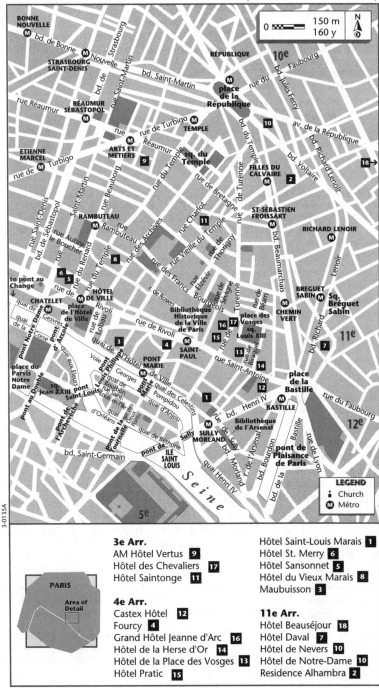

LEGEND
✝ Church
Ⓜ Métro

3e Arr.
AM Hôtel Vertus **9**
Hôtel des Chevaliers **17**
Hôtel Saintonge **11**

4e Arr.
Castex Hôtel **12**
Fourcy **4**
Grand Hôtel Jeanne d'Arc **16**
Hôtel de la Herse d'Or **14**
Hôtel de la Place des Vosges **13**
Hôtel Pratic **15**

Hôtel Saint-Louis Marais **1**
Hôtel St. Merry **6**
Hôtel Sansonnet **5**
Hôtel du Vieux Marais **8**
Maubuisson **3**

11e Arr.
Hôtel Beauséjour **18**
Hôtel Daval **7**
Hôtel de Nevers **10**
Hôtel de Notre-Dame **10**
Residence Alhambra **2**

PARIS
Area of Detail

3-0135A

77

extra features as safes and alarm clocks. An elevator is available, and there's a bar open daily for guests.

Hôtel de la Herse d'Or. 20 rue St-Antoine, 75004 Paris. ☎ **01-48-87-84-09.** Fax 01-48-87-94-01. 35 rms (some with shower). 160F ($27.80) single without shower; 200F ($34.80) double without shower; 260F ($45.20) double with shower. Showers 10F ($1.75). Continental breakfast 25F ($4.35) extra. No credit cards. Métro: St-Paul or Bastille.

Hôtel de la Herse d'Or is basic. In fact, if you look for the word *basic* in a dictionary, you'll probably find a picture of the Hôtel de la Herse d'Or. The furnishings are a bit faded; thankfully, really, for otherwise their palette would be too loud for you to rest peacefully at night. Things are clean, though, and the location is good, right on the busiest thoroughfare of the Marais and near all the action around place de la Bastille.

Hôtel de Nevers. 53 rue de Malte, 75011 Paris. ☎ **01-47-00-56-18.** Fax 01-43-57-77-39. 34 rms (7 with shower only, 11 with shower and WC). TEL. 170F ($29.55) single with sink; 220F ($38.25) single or double with shower; 245F ($42.60) single or double with shower and WC; 380F ($66.10) triple. Shower 20F ($3.45) extra. Breakfast 25F ($4.35) extra. MC, V. Métro: République.

The plant-filled lobby patrolled by two cats sets a friendly tone for a hotel that offers excellent value. You can take the elevator, but be sure to note the original gleaming brass railing along the staircase. The corridors are painted in light pastels that make them seem wider than they are. Although the rooms are not large, they are immaculately maintained and the owners have worked wonders with bright, flowery wallpaper and curtains. The spacious triples on the sixth floor have skylights, sloping ceilings, and views over the rooftops.

Hôtel Notre-Dame. 51 rue de Malte, 75011 Paris. ☎ **01-47-00-78-76.** Fax 01-43-55-32-31. 48 rms (13 with shower only, 31 with shower and WC). TV TEL. 190F ($33) single with sink and bidet; 280F ($48.70) single or double with shower; 330F ($57.40) double with shower and WC; 360F ($62.60) double with twin beds. Shower 20F ($3.45) extra. Breakfast 32F ($5.55) extra. MC, V. Métro: République.

Although this hotel lacks the folksy appeal of its next-door neighbor, the Hôtel de Nevers, it also represents excellent value for a slightly higher price. Both hotels are on a quiet side street only a short walk from the Marais, but the Hôtel Notre-Dame has double-glazed windows for extra tranquillity and the rooms are somewhat larger. Except for the sixth floor, the rooms have recently been renovated and are equipped with color TVs and alarm clocks.

Hôtel Pratic. 9 rue d'Ormesson, 75004 Paris. ☎ **01-48-87-80-47.** Fax 01-48-87-40-04. 23 rms. TEL. 180F ($31.30) single without bath; 250F ($43.45) single with bath; 245F ($42.60) double without bath; 340F ($59.15) double with bath. Continental breakfast 25F ($4.35). MC, V. Métro: St-Paul.

Near the pretty place du Marche Ste-Catherine, this hotel was recently renovated with a new breakfast room and freshly decorated halls. A particular curiosity is the oval-shaped bathroom between the first and second floors. The best, and priciest, rooms overlook the square and have WC, showers, and double-glazed windows.

Pax Hôtel. 12 rue de Charonne, 75011 Paris. ☎ **01-47-00-40-98.** Fax 01-43-38-57-81. 47 rooms (39 with shower, 36 with WC). TV TEL. Single with sink only 200F ($34.80); 250F ($43.45) single with shower; 286F ($49.75) double with shower. Continental breakfast 30F ($5.20). AE, MC, V. Métro: Bastille.

Though the lobby is an inadvertent shrine to dubious French taste during the 1970s (lots of brown plastic), this is a great spot for anyone who wants to be right in the thick of the trendy Bastille neighborhood, with all of its clubs, bars, and galleries.

Another advantage of staying here is that there are lots of good, cheap restaurants in the vicinity.

Résidence Alhambra. 11 bis and 13 rue de Malte, 75011 Paris. ☎ **01-47-00-35-52.** Fax 01-43-57-98-75. 58 rms (all with shower or bath and WC). TV TEL. 300F ($52.15) single; 320F ($55.65) double; 450F ($78.25) triple. Breakfast 28F ($4.85) extra. MC, V. Métro: Oberkampf or Filles du Calvaire.

The best feature of this attractive hotel is the backyard garden, which is perfect for breakfast or a snack *en plein air.* The simple rooms are clean and pleasant. Try to get one with a small balcony overlooking the garden—especially when the roses bloom. The lobby is large and comfortably furnished, and the hotel is only a short walk from the Marais and the Bastille.

DOUBLES FOR LESS THAN 500F ($87)

AM Hôtel Vertus. 5 rue des Vertus, 75003 Paris. ☎ **01-44-61-89-50.** Fax 01-48-04-33-72. 9 rms (all with bath or shower). MINIBAR TV TEL. 330F ($57.40) single; 480F ($83.45) double. Breakfast 35F ($6.10) extra. AE, DC, MC, V. Métro: Arts et Metiers.

This rather new and charming little hotel on the northern edge of the Marais occupies a completely renovated 17th-century building and offers a lot of comfort for the money. The lobby is air-conditioned, the hotel has an elevator, and all rooms have baths with hair dryers.

Grand Hôtel Jeanne d'Arc. 3 rue de Jarente, 75004 Paris. ☎ **01-48-87-62-11.** Fax 01-48-87-37-31. 36 rms (all with bath or shower). TV TEL. 300–460F ($52.15–$80) double; 530F ($92.15) triple; 590F ($102.60) quad. Breakfast 35F ($6.10) extra. MC, V. Métro: St-Paul or Bastille.

Located just off the center of the Marais, near the Musée Picasso, the Bastille, and the Opéra Bastille, the Grand Hôtel Jeanne d'Arc is a great budget bet. All the rooms are decorated with floral patterns and have desks and armoires as well as direct-dial telephones, cable television, and bedside tables. Most of the bathrooms are exceptionally large for a Parisian hotel. Breakfast is served in a common breakfast room and consists of coffee or tea, bread, brioches, and jam. There's also an elevator. Reserve well in advance.

Hôtel Daval. 21 rue Daval, 75011 Paris. ☎ **01-47-00-51-23.** Fax 01-40-21-80-26. 23 rms (all with shower or bath and WC). TV TEL. 350F ($60.85) single; 390–480F ($67.80–$83.45) double. Breakfast 45F ($7.80) extra. AE, MC, V. Métro: Bastille.

The action at the place de la Bastille is only a block away from this sleek, modern hotel. The style of the rooms is minimalist and the color scheme is strictly Blue Period, but everything is fresh and well tended. The best rooms overlook a large, picturesque courtyard. If you decide to forego the expensive hotel breakfast, there are a number of cafes and small grocery stores nearby.

Hôtel de la Place des Vosges. 12 rue de Birague, 75004 Paris. ☎ **01-42-72-60-46.** Fax 01-42-72-02-64. 16 rms (all with shower or bath). TV TEL. 330F ($57.40) single with shower and WC; 475–490F ($82.60–$85.20) double with bath and WC. Breakfast 30F ($5.20) extra. MC, V. Métro: Bastille.

This hotel has a terrific location on a side street just outside the place des Vosges. The rooms are small but clean. All have TVs suspended from the ceilings and desks. Beds are okay but covered with pink satinette bedspreads.

Hôtel du Vieux Marais. 8 rue du Plâtre, 75004 Paris. ☎ **01-42-78-47-22.** Fax 01-42-78-34-32. 30 rms (all with shower or bath and WC). TV TEL. 400–465F ($69.55–$80.85) single; 510–550F ($88.70–$95.65) double; 665F ($115.65) triple. Continental breakfast 35F ($6.10) extra. EURO, MC, V. Métro: Hôtel-de-Ville.

Located in an ancient building on a rather narrow street, Hôtel du Vieux Marais combines the charm of bygone days with all the comforts of the information age. A sober atmosphere has been preserved in the very pleasant rooms. The Centre Pompidou is a 2-minute walk away.

Hôtel Sansonnet. 48 rue de la Verrerie, 75004 Paris. ☎ **01-48-87-96-14.** Fax 01-48-87-30-46. TV TEL. 25 rms. 250F ($43.45) single without bath; 340F ($59.15) single with shower; 370–400F ($64.35–$69.55) doubles with bath. Continental breakfast 33F ($5.75). EURO, MC, V. Métro: Hôtel-de-Ville.

Occupying a historic old building in the heart of the Marais, this pleasant hotel offers good value in a very good location. Unfortunately, the lobby—with its striped wallpaper and old wrought iron stair railing—is prettier than most of the rooms, but accommodations here are quite comfortable. All rooms have satellite TV and all double rooms are equipped with hair dryers.

WORTH A SPLURGE

Hôtel des Chevaliers. 30 rue de Turenne, 75003 Paris. ☎ **01-42-72-73-47.** Fax 01-42-72-54-10. 24 rms (all with full bath). MINIBAR TV TEL. 725F ($126) single or double. 590F ($102.60) in winter. Continental breakfast 50F ($8.70) extra. AE, CB, DC, EURO, MC, V. Métro: St-Paul.

Hôtel des Chevaliers, as its name implies, is ready to welcome knights from another age—well-off knights, at least. It was built in the 17th century, like so much of the Marais, and you can still see the old wooden beams on some floors. But modern comforts are here as well: individual safety deposit boxes, direct-dial phones, automatic wake-up call, hair dryers, and cable TVs. Each newly renovated room has a full-length mirror, and every evening you'll find a bonbon on your pillow. The second floor, with its French windows, is especially attractive. Service is attentive and efficient. And the beautiful place des Vosges is just a step away around the corner.

Hôtel Saint-Louis Marais. 1 rue Charles-V, 75004 Paris. ☎ **01-48-87-87-04.** Fax 01-48-87-33-26. 15 rms (all with shower or bath). TEL. 350F ($60.85) single; 510–610F ($88.70) double; 710F ($123.50) double with two beds. Continental breakfast 40F ($6.95) extra. EC, MC, V. Métro: Sully-Morland.

The 300-year-old building that houses this appealing hotel was formerly a convent. Beamed ceilings and antique furniture give a lot of character to rooms that also have very modern bathrooms. Room nos. 19 and 20 are especially attractive, with slanted ceilings.

Hôtel St. Merry. 78 rue de la Verrerie, 75004 Paris. ☎ **01-42-78-14-15.** Fax 01-40-29-06-82. 11 rms (all with bath and shower). 400F ($69.55) single or double with shower only; 750–1100F ($130.45–$191.30) single or double with bath or shower and WC. Higher prices are for larger rooms with views. Breakfast 45F ($7.80) extra. No credit cards. Métro: Hôtel-de-Ville or Châtelet.

This atmospheric hotel stands beside the Church of St. Merri and occupies a 17th-century presbytery. Although the rooms are dark, they are filled with evocative Gothic-style elements—carved wood screens that serve as bed headboards, beamed ceilings, stone walls, and wrought iron chandeliers and sconces—which all contribute to the overall medieval effect. The attractive bathrooms are fully tiled. *Note:* There is no elevator.

Hôtel Saintonge. 16 rue Saintonge, 75003 Paris. ☎ **01-42-77-91-13.** Fax 01-48-87-76-41. 23 rms. MINIBAR TV TEL. 490F ($85.20) single; 560F ($97.40) double. Breakfast 39F ($6.80) extra. AE, MC, V. Métro: Filles du Calvaire or Républic.

Situated in the center of the Marais near the Musée Picasso, this hotel has very nice rooms with such additional features as alarm clocks. Beamed ceilings and touches of stone add warmth and an historic accent to the rooms, which are spacious enough to contain cane desks and chairs. An elevator is available.

CHAMPS ELYSÉES & ENVIRONS (8E & 17E ARRONDISSEMENTS)

Hôtel Alison. 21 rue de Surène, 75008 Paris. ☎ **01-42-65-54-00.** Fax 01-42-65-08-17. 35 rms (all with bath or shower). TV TEL. 456F ($79.30) single with shower and WC; 701F ($121.90) double with bath and WC. Breakfast 45F ($7.80) extra. AE, DC, EURO, MC, V. Métro: Madeleine or Concord.

Good location for shopping the rue St-Honoré and around the Madeleine. The rooms in this splurge hotel are furnished in modern style and include such additional features as safes and alarm clocks.

Hôtel de Palma. 46 rue Brunel, 75017 Paris. ☎ **01-45-74-74-51.** Fax 01-45-74-40-90. 37 rms (all with bath or shower and WC). TV TEL. 380F ($66.10) single or double with shower; 400F ($69.55) single or double with bath; 630F ($109.50) triple. Continental breakfast 35F ($6.10). MC, V. Métro: Argentine. RER: Neuilly–Porte-Maillot.

If you like comfort but don't want to pay top franc for it, head for the Hôtel de Palma. It may be a bit far from the center of things, but the nearest Métro line will take you rapidly and directly to the Champs-Elysées, place de la Concorde, the Louvre, and the Bastille, with easy connections to the Latin Quarter. In fact, since it's near the airport buses, it's rather convenient if you're only staying for a few days. The de Palma has a large lobby and well-kept rooms with modern tiled bathrooms and TV.

Hôtel des Deux Acacias. 28 rue de l'Arc de Triomphe, 75017 Paris. ☎ **01-43-80-01-85.** Fax 01-40-53-94-62. 32 rms (all with shower or bath). TV TEL. 310F ($53.90) single; 350–380F ($60.86–$66.10) double. Continental breakfast 25F ($4.35) extra. AE, EC, MC, V. Métro: Charles-de-Gaulle-Etoile.

On a quiet street just 2 blocks north of the Arc de Triomphe, this budget hotel offers clean, well-equipped rooms at a good price. Many of the rooms have been attractively redecorated with bright wallpaper and matching print bedspreads and curtains. The woman at the front desk is efficient and amiable. Take the avenue Carnot exit from the Métro.

Hôtel des Deux Avenues. 38 rue Poncelet, 75017 Paris. ☎ **01-42-27-44-35.** Fax 01-47-63-95-48. 32 rms (21 with bath or shower). 230F ($40) single without bath; 285F ($49.50) single with shower only; 355F ($61.70) single with bath; 265F ($46.10) double without shower; 315F ($54.80) double with shower only; 385F ($67) double with bath. Breakfast 30F ($5.20) extra. MC, V. Métro: Charles-de-Gaulle-Etoile.

Located on the quiet end of a lively market street near the Arc de Triomphe, this hotel offers a surprisingly good value. The lobby is bright and modern and the rooms are in good condition, although slightly frayed. The front rooms are cheerier than the back rooms, which are somewhat short of natural light. Nevertheless, everything is clean and correct, the owner is friendly, and an elevator is available.

Hôtel Niel. 11 rue Saussier-Leroy, 75017 Paris. ☎ **01-42-27-99-29.** Fax 01-42-27-16-96. 36 rms (25 with shower or bath). TEL. 215F ($37.40) single with sink only; 280F ($48.70) single with shower; 320F ($55.65) single with shower and WC; 270F ($46.95) double with sink, 335F ($58.25) double with shower, 375F ($65.20) double with shower and WC. Showers 25F ($4.35) extra, breakfast 25F ($4.35) extra. AE, MC, V. Métro: Ternes.

This large hotel has a feeling of simplicity, propriety, and tidiness. The helpful receptionist will tell you that each room is unique, but you will see that all are good and clean and have reading lamps over the beds—rare in Paris. The hotel is located on a quiet street half a block from a colorful street market.

Hôtel Riviera. 55 rue des Acacias, 75017 Paris. ☎ **01-43-80-45-31.** Fax 01-40-54-84-08. 26 rms (all with shower or bath). TV TEL. 270F ($46.95) single with shower only; 350F ($60.85) double with shower; 410F ($71.30) double with bath; 480F ($83.45) triple; 540F ($93.90) quad. Breakfast 27F ($4.70) extra. AE, MC, V. Métro: Ternes or Charles-de-Gaulle-Etoile.

The tiny reception area here is unimpressive, but the rooms are colorful and have oriental-style throw rugs. The modern bathrooms have hair dryers, and most rooms are equipped with new, firm beds. The rooms facing the street have double-glazed windows and some of the back rooms share a small patio with a table for an open-air breakfast. An elevator is available.

TROCADÉRO & LE SEIZIEME(16E ARRONDISSEMENT)

Hôtel Keppler. 12 rue Keppler, 75016 Paris. ☎ **01-47-20-65-05.** Fax 01-47-23-02-29. 49 rms. TV TEL. 460F ($80) single or double with bath; 520F ($90.45) triple. Continental breakfast 30F ($5.20) extra. AE, MC, V. Métro: Georges-V.

If you ditched your backpack years ago (or never deigned to use one in the first place), you'll love this chance to get a truly chic address in a very pretty neighborhood for a bargain price. The glory of this place is that you'll never be reminded that you're watching your pennies—rooms are spacious and furnished with character. An elevator, double-glazed windows, and hair dryers in the bath complete this happy picture.

Hôtel Nicolo. 3 rue Nicolo, 75016 Paris. ☎ **01-42-88-83-40.** Fax 01-42-24-45-41. 28 rms (all with shower or bath). TV TEL. 380F ($66.10) single; 420F ($73) double. Continental breakfast 35F ($6.10) extra. AE, CB, EURO, V. Métro: Passy or Muette.

Hôtel Nicolo is a proper establishment, located in one of Paris's blue-blooded residential districts. Past an unimpressive courtyard, you'll enter a lobby that resembles the *salon* of an elegant household, with tasteful furniture, plants, and flowers. All rooms are very quiet; some overlook the courtyard, some have large armoires, and still others feature pretty writing desks. On its business card, the hotel claims to be *"calme et confortable";* it is. Refreshments such as soda, beer, and mineral water are available. The only drawback here is the rather outlying location.

MONTMARTRE (18E ARRONDISSEMENT)
A DOUBLE FOR LESS THAN 350F ($61)

Hôtel Bellevue. 19 rue d'Orsel, 75018 Paris. ☎ **01-46-06-24-76.** Fax 01-46-06-15-94. 27 rms. 120F ($20.85) single without bath; 225F ($39.15) single with shower; 170F ($29.55) double without bath; 245F ($42.60) double with bath. Breakfast 20F ($3.45) extra. No credit cards. Métro: Anvers.

Basic but not unpleasant, this hotel offers spacious rooms to anyone who'd like to be in the Pigalle-Montmartre neighborhood near the basilica of Sacré-Coeur and the lively nightlife in and around Pigalle. Especially popular with students.

DOUBLES FOR LESS THAN 500F ($87)

Ermitage Hôtel. 24 rue Lamarck, 75018 Paris. ☎ **01-42-64-79-22.** 12 rms (all with shower or bath). TEL. 410F ($71.30) single with bath; 470F ($81.75) double with bath. Rates include breakfast. No credit cards. Métro: Lamarck-Caulaincourt.

Run by Madame Canipel, who speaks English, German, and Italian, this charming bed-and-breakfast is tucked away on a quiet residential street behind the Sacré-Coeur at the base of the Butte. The house has great atmosphere, created largely by the jade decor, the murals that adorn the walls, and the art displayed throughout. Each of the rooms is decorated differently with comfortable antiques. Guests may use the pleasant parlor. Best of all, breakfast is served in your room, and if you've managed to get one on the top floor, you can nibble your croissants while reveling in a superb view of Paris.

Hôtel Prima Lepic. 29 rue Lepic, 75018 Paris. ☎ **01-46-06-44-64.** Fax 01-46-06-66-11. 38 rms (all with bath or shower). TV TEL. 350F ($60.85) single with bath or shower and WC; 420F ($73) double with bath and WC. Breakfast 40F ($6.95) extra. MC, V. Métro: Abbesses or Blanche.

This hotel is very nicely decorated and maintained. All of the rooms are different, although no matter which you choose you'll likely find floral wallpaper and wicker furnishings. Rooms facing the street have double-glazed windows.

Hôtel Regyn's Montmartre. 18 place des Abbesses, 75018 Paris. ☎ **01-42-54-45-21.** Fax 01-42-23-76-69. 22 rms (all with shower or bath). TV TEL. 375F ($65.20) single with shower and WC, 385F ($67) with bath and WC; 425F ($73.90) double (one bed) with shower and WC; 445F ($77.40) double (one bed) with bath and WC. Breakfast 40F ($6.95) extra. AE, EURO, MC. Métro: Abbesses.

Some rooms are a little faded in this hotel, located on an attractive square at the bottom of the Butte, but the fourth floor has recently been renovated. Overall, the hotel represents good value. Front rooms on the fourth and fifth floor have a panoramic view over Paris, most rooms have desks, and there's also a pretty breakfast room.

Hôtel Utrillo. 7 rue Aristide Bruant, 75018 Paris. ☎ **01-42-58-13-44.** Fax 01-42-23-93-88. 30 rms (all with bath or shower). MINIBAR TV TEL. 305–360F ($53–$62.60) single; 385–455F ($67–$79.15) double. 525F ($91.30) triple. Breakfast 40F ($6.95) extra. AE, DC, V. Métro: Abbesses.

This hotel offers excellent value with its clean, modern rooms, all with TV and telephone, and hair dryers in the tiled bathrooms. Several sixth-floor rooms are large and offer a view of the Eiffel Tower. Facilities include a sauna, and breakfast is served buffet style. You can walk from the hotel to Sacré-Coeur and place du Tertre, although it's a bit of a climb.

WORTH A SPLURGE

Timhôtel Montmartre. 11 rue Ravignan (place Emile Goudeau), 75018 Paris. ☎ **01-42-55-74-79.** Fax 01-42-55-71-01. 61 rms (all with bath). TV TEL. 450F ($78.25) single; 550F ($95.65) double. Breakfast 49F ($8.50) extra. AE, MC, V. Métro: Abbesses.

This hotel is situated right next door to the Bâteau Lavoir, for those who want to imagine themselves rubbing shoulders with Picasso, Modigliani, and the other artists who once lived next door. The hotel is part of a reliable, well-run chain of hotels that feature clean, modern rooms. Everything is superclean, including the corridors. There's an elevator and the rooms are spacious—for Paris, at least—and are decorated primarily in blue florals. Bathrooms are tiled and showers have glass doors. Dogs are welcome.

3 Left Bank

LATIN QUARTER (5E & 6E ARRONDISSEMENTS)
DOUBLES FOR LESS THAN 350F ($61)

Delhy's Hôtel. 22 rue de l'Hirondelle, 75006 Paris. ☎ **01-43-26-58-25.** Fax 01-43-26-51-06. 21 rms (7 with shower, none with WC). TV TEL. 203F ($35.30) single with sink; 296F ($51.50) double with sink; 376F ($65.40) double with shower. Shower 25F ($4.35) extra. Continental breakfast 30F ($5.20) extra. AE, EURO, MC, V. Métro: St-Michel.

Left Bank Accommodations

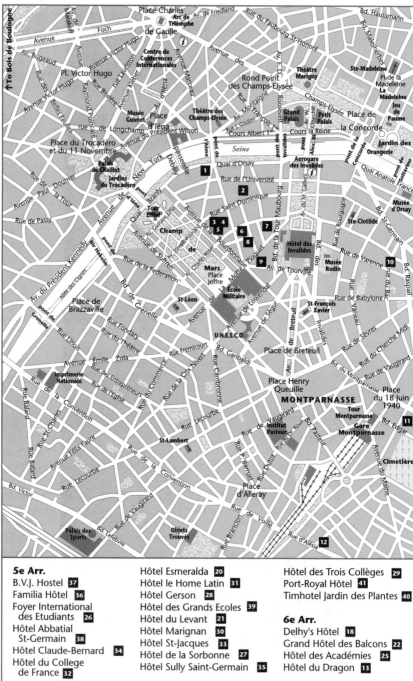

5e Arr.
B.V.J. Hostel **37**
Familia Hôtel **36**
Foyer International
  des Etudiants **26**
Hôtel Abbatial
  St-Germain **38**
Hôtel Claude-Bernard **34**
Hôtel du College
  de France **32**

Hôtel Esmeralda **20**
Hôtel le Home Latin **31**
Hôtel Gerson **28**
Hôtel des Grands Ecoles **39**
Hôtel du Levant **21**
Hôtel Marignan **30**
Hôtel St-Jacques **33**
Hôtel de la Sorbonne **27**
Hôtel Sully Saint-Germain **35**

Hôtel des Trois Collèges **29**
Port-Royal Hôtel **41**
Timhotel Jardin des Plantes **40**

6e Arr.
Delhy's Hôtel **18**
Grand Hôtel des Balcons **22**
Hôtel des Académies **25**
Hôtel du Dragon **13**

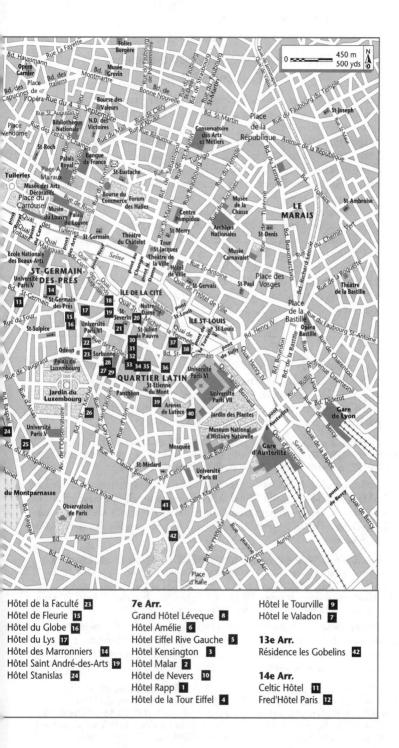

Hôtel de la Faculté	23	**7e Arr.**		Hôtel le Tourville	9
Hôtel de Fleurie	15	Grand Hôtel Léveque	8	Hôtel le Valadon	7
Hôtel du Globe	16	Hôtel Amélie	6		
Hôtel du Lys	17	Hôtel Eiffel Rive Gauche	5	**13e Arr.**	
Hôtel des Marronniers	14	Hôtel Kensington	3	Résidence les Gobelins	42
Hôtel Saint André-des-Arts	19	Hôtel Malar	2		
Hôtel Stanislas	24	Hôtel de Nevers	10	**14e Arr.**	
		Hôtel Rapp	1	Celtic Hôtel	11
		Hôtel de la Tour Eiffel	4	Fred'Hôtel Paris	12

85

Away in a Manger, Asleep on the Seine
(A Cautionary Tale)

The Quaker hostel was our refuge of last resort, but even they had rejected us. Stumbling, wretched, exhausted, we realized the enormity of our mistake: Paris. High season. No hotel reservations.

The night was dark and cool, and the lights of the night city twinkled around us. Silence and rolling water, broken by car, by call, by click of heel on pavement. We were on park bench beds, directly across from the high and locked gates of the Gare d'Austerlitz, with the Seine bubbling behind us and our luggage hid nervously beneath our legs, like a dog during fireworks. On paper, in planning, in imagination, our first night in Paris had not looked like this.

The old man approached us as we lay amidst our clutter. He was scruffy, and it was dark. He smelled of the city, was withered, dusty, clutched a newspaper in one hand and a cane in the other. On his head: an actual *beret*. He leaned toward us, paused, and before moving on, croaked, "Pockpickets! Watch out for pockpickets!"

We watched him move away, six inches to a step, and disappear into the night. Above the sewers of Paris, we drifted to sleep, dreaming of pillows, linens, and reservations.

—Edward Shannon & Matt Hannafin

If you can do without a toilet in the room, this no-frills hotel on a narrow pedestrian street offers a good deal. The tidy rooms are small but pleasantly decorated in subdued pastels. The narrow halls, winding staircase, and cozy breakfast room are well maintained and the location is great. If you don't take a room with a shower, however, you'll have to trudge down to the ground floor shower.

Hôtel Esmeralda. 4 rue St-Julien-le-Pauvre, 75005 Paris. ☎ **01-43-54-19-20.** Fax 01-40-51-00-68. TEL. 160F ($27.80) single with shower; 320–490F ($55.65–$85.20) doubles with bath. Shower 10F ($2). Breakfast 40F ($6.95). No credit cards. Métro: St-Michel.

This funky, ramshackle hotel in a very convenient but rather noisy location has diehard fans around the world. What they love is the unself-conscious charm—an old wooden staircase winding upstairs, dogs and cats dozing in the lobby, views of Notre-Dame. The notoriety of this place is such that you have to book many months in advance.

Hôtel Gerson. 14 rue de la Sorbonne, 75005 Paris. ☎ **01-43-54-28-40.** Fax 01-44-07-13-90. 24 rms (16 with shower only). 213F ($37) single without shower; 283F ($49.20) single with shower; 256F ($44.50) double without bath; 360F ($62.60) double with shower; 409F ($71.15) triple with shower. Showers 25F ($4.35). Continental breakfast 25F ($4.35) extra. MC, V. Métro: Cluny-La Sorbonne. RER: Luxembourg.

The one-star Gerson is in the heart of the Latin Quarter, just a few steps down the hill from place de la Sorbonne. It is the quintessential low-budget hotel, with soft beds and many nicks in the woodwork, but it has clean rooms, some with private baths that are newish and presentable.

Hôtel Marignan. 13 rue du Sommerard, 75005 Paris. ☎ **01-43-54-63-81.** 30 rms (9 with shower, 2 with bath, 24 with WC). 210F ($36.50) single with sink; 320F ($55.65) double with WC only; 400F ($69.55) double with shower and WC; 390–470F ($67.80–$81.75) triple; 480–590F ($83.45–$102.60) quad. Rates include a continental breakfast and showers. No credit cards. Métro: Maubert-Mutualité (a 2-minute walk) or St-Michel (a 6-minute walk).

Hotels—Latin Quarter (5e & 6e Arr.)

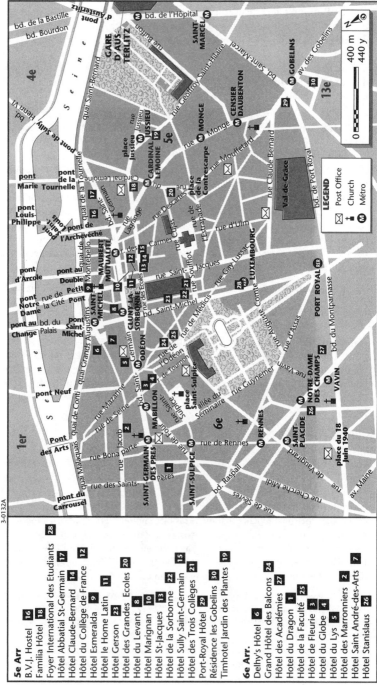

LEGEND
⊠ Post Office
⊕ Church
Ⓜ Métro

3-0132A

5e Arr

B.V.J. Hostel	**16**
Familia Hôtel	**18**
Foyer International des Etudiants	**17**
Hôtel Abbatial St-Germain	**14**
Hôtel Claude-Bernard	**12**
Hôtel du Collège de France	**9**
Hôtel Esmeralda	**11**
Hôtel le Home Latin	**23**
Hôtel Gerson	**20**
Hôtel des Grandes Ecoles	**8**
Hôtel du Levant	**10**
Hôtel Marignan	**13**
Hôtel St-Jacques	**22**
Hôtel de la Sorbonne	**21**
Hôtel Sully Saint-Germain	**15**
Hôtel des Trois Collèges	**29**
Port-Royal Hôtel	**30**
Résidence les Gobelins	**19**
Timhotel Jardin des Plantes	

6e Arr.

Delhy's Hôtel	**6**
Grand Hôtel des Balcons	**24**
Hôtel des Académies	**27**
Hôtel du Dragon	**1**
Hôtel de la Fleurie	**25**
Hotel du Globe	**3**
Hôtel du Lys	**4**
Hôtel des Marronniers	**5**
Hôtel Saint André-des-Arts	**2**
Hôtel Stanislaus	**26**
	7

87

Owners Paul and Linda Keniger have invested much time and energy in renovating their hotel. In the process they have retained much of the building's architectural detailing, such as the stucco ceiling moldings. Rooms have tiled bathrooms, wood dressers, and new carpets and beds. The Kenigers—Paul is French and Linda is American—welcome families, and you'll have a washer-dryer and iron at your disposal. They also don't mind if you bring your own food into the dining room; the kitchen is available, too, during the low season.

Port-Royal Hotel. 8 bd. Port-Royal, 75005 Paris. ☎ **01-43-31-70-06.** Fax 01-43-31-33-67. 45rms (14 with shower and WC, 6 with bath and WC). TEL. 168F ($29.20) single with sink only; 208F ($36.15) single or double with sink only; 310F ($53.90) double with bath or shower. Continental breakfast 27F ($4.70) extra. No credit cards. Métro: Gobelins.

When you enter the spacious air-conditioned lobby you'll wonder if you booked yourself into a three-star hotel by mistake. Rest assured: The Port-Royal has the rates of a superbudget hotel but the polished style of a much pricier establishment. The halls are freshly painted and all the rooms recently decorated with flowery pastel wallpaper. The front rooms have double-glazed windows and many rooms have (nonworking) fireplaces. The rooms are all of different sizes, of course, but tend to be larger than you would expect for this price. The hotel has recently been equipped with an elevator.

Résidence les Gobelins. 9 rue des Gobelins, 75013 Paris. ☎ **01-47-07-26-90.** Fax 01-43-31-44-05. 32 rms (14 with shower, 18 with bath, all with WC). TV TEL. 295F ($51.30) single with bath; 350–425F ($60.85–$73.90) double with shower or bath. Breakfast 36F ($6.25) extra. AE, MC, V. Métro: Gobelins.

Just a short walk from the Latin Quarter, this hotel offers good value at a reasonable price. The lobby and reception area are attractive and the rooms are furnished in a light, summery style with an accent on pastel colors and wicker furniture. Rooms facing the street tend to be smaller and less expensive. The inner courtyard has been turned into a delightful garden with a trellis, climbing vines, flowers, and potted plants.

DOUBLES FOR LESS THAN 500F ($87)

Familia Hôtel. 11 rue des Ecoles, 75005 Paris. ☎ **01-43-54-55-27.** Fax 01-43-29-61-77. 30 rms (all with bath or shower). TV TEL. 370F ($64.35) single; 370–520F ($64.35–$90.45) double. Breakfast 30F ($5.20). AE, DC, MC, V. Métro: Jussieu.

As the name implies, this is a hotel that has been family run for decades. It is currently in the hands of the dynamic young Eric Gaucheron, who is justifiably proud of the many personal touches that make his place unique. The walls of 14 rooms are graced with finely executed sepia drawings of Parisian scenes, eight rooms have restored stone walls, and seven rooms have balconies with delightful views over the Latin Quarter. All of the rooms have cable TV (including CNN), minibars, and hair dryers, making the hotel more comfortable than most in this price category.

Hôtel de la Sorbonne. 6 rue Victor-Cousin, 75005 Paris. ☎ **01-43-54-58-08.** Fax 01-40-51-05-18. 37 rms (all with shower or bath). TV TEL. 425F ($73.90) single or double with shower; 470F ($81.75) single or double with bath. Breakfast 35F ($6.10) extra. AE, EURO, MC, V. Métro: Cluny-Sorbonne or St-Michel.

The rooms here are well kept and modern and come equipped with hair dryers and clock radios. If you're traveling with your dog, you should know that he or she is welcome here too.

Hôtel des Grands Ecoles. 75 rue Cardinal Lemoine, 75005 Paris. ☎ **01-43-26-79-23.** Fax 01-43-25-28-15. 50 rms (all with bath or shower). TEL. 470F ($81.75) single or double with shower; 570F ($99.15) single or double with bath. Continental breakfast 40F ($6.95) extra. CB, MC, V. Métro: Cardinal Lemoine or Monge.

Housed in three adjoining buildings and tucked away from the street in a lovely garden, Hôtel des Grands Ecoles will make you feel as if you're in the French countryside. The owners have decorated and renovated these 18th-century bourgeois houses with floral wallpapers and pink and green accents. Breakfast is served in the main house at cafe tables with lace cloths.

Hôtel des Trois Collèges. 16 rue Cujas, 75005 Paris. ☎ **01-43-54-67-30.** Fax 01-46-34-02-99. 44 rms (all with shower or bath). TV TEL. 380–480F ($66.10–$83.45) single with shower; 540–600F ($93.90–$104.30) single with bath; 480F ($83.45) double with shower; 540–650F ($93.90–$113) double with bath. Breakfast is 42F ($7.30) extra. AE, MC, V. Métro: Odéon or St-Michel.

With its marble-floored and very modern lobby and tearoom, this hotel has a bit more personality than others in the same price range and neighborhood. The top floor has larger rooms with a view of the Sorbonne and the Panthéon. The staff is young and friendly, and there's a laundry room on the premises. Additional room amenities include hair dryers and double-glazed windows to ensure quiet.

Hôtel du Collège de France. 7 rue Thénard, 75005 Paris. ☎ **01-43-26-78-36.** Fax 01-46-34-58-29. 29 rms (all with shower or bath). TV TEL. 480F ($83.45) single or double with shower; 500–580F ($87–$100.85) double with bath. Continental breakfast (all you can eat) 33F ($5.75) extra. AE, EURO, MC, V. Métro: Maubert-Mutualité, St-Michel, or Cluny-Sorbonne.

Although some of the rooms have peeling paint, they are clean and comfortable. The bathrooms are tiled and contain hair dryers. The hotel has a fine location and overall is a decent value.

Hôtel du Levant. 18 rue de la Harpe, 75005 Paris. ☎ **01-46-34-11-00.** Fax 01-46-34-25-87. 46 rms (all with bath or shower and WC). 350F ($60.85) single with shower and WC; 460F ($80) double with shower and WC; 550F ($95.65) double (two beds) with shower and WC; 535F ($93) double with bath and WC; 585F ($101.75) double (two beds) with bath. No credit cards. Métro: St-Michel.

Great location on a street lined with budget restaurants. The comparatively large rooms sport modern beds, wall-to-wall carpet, desk, dresser, and chairs. The bathrooms are clean and contain hair dryers. Breakfast is served in a pretty room with a mural, art, and photographs portraying old Paris.

Hôtel Le Home Latin. 15–17 rue du Sommerard, 75005 Paris. ☎ **01-43-26-25-21.** Fax 01-43-29-87-04. 55 rms (all with bath or shower). TV TEL. 375F ($65.20) single; 445F ($77.40) double; 510F ($88.70) twin; 605F ($105.20) triple. Continental breakfast 39F ($6.80) extra. V. Métro: Maubert-Mutualité or St-Michel.

After extensive renovations, this hotel has earned a two-star rating. Decorated in coral shades, all the rooms have small bathrooms, full-length mirrors, and a table and chairs. The hotel is fairly large and quiet, but if you're worried about traffic noise, ask for a room at the back. A room here might be on the high end of your budget, but you won't be disappointed.

Hôtel St-Jacques. 35 rue des Ecoles, 75005 Paris. ☎ **01-44-07-45-45.** Fax 01-43-25-65-50. 35 rms (17 with shower, 15 with bath, 31 with WC). 190F ($33) single with sink only; 320F ($55.65) single with shower; 420F ($73) double with shower and WC; 480F ($83.45) double with bath; 560F ($97.40) triple with bath. Continental breakfast 30F ($5.20) extra. AE, EURO, MC, V. Métro: Maubert-Mutualité.

On busy rue des Ecoles, at the corner of rue Valette, the two-star Hôtel St-Jacques has attractive prices and generally spacious rooms. The furniture is rather basic, but there are some fine architectural details. Although the street is busy, all windows are double glazed to keep out at least some of the noise and 13 rooms have a view of the Panthéon and Notre-Dame.

WORTH A SPLURGE

Hôtel Abbatial St-Germain. 46 bd. St-Germain, 75005 Paris. ☎ **01-46-34-02-12.** Fax 01-43-25-47-73. 43 rms (all with bath or shower). TEL. 490–680F ($85.20–$118.25) single with shower or bath; 590F ($102.60) double with shower; 680F ($118.25) double with bath. A/C MINIBAR TV. Continental breakfast 50F ($8.70) extra. AE, EURO, MC, V. Métro: Maubert-Mutualité.

This three-star hotel has been totally refurbished. From the lobby on the ground floor, an elevator will take you to the rooms, which are decorated in cheerful shades and contain such amenities as safes. There are views of the Panthéon and Notre-Dame from the upper-floor rooms.

Hôtel Claude-Bernard. 43 rue des Ecoles, 75005 Paris. ☎ **01-43-26-32-52.** Fax 01-43-26-80-56. 34 rms (all with bath or shower). TV TEL. 480F ($83.45) single with shower; 620F ($107.80) double with shower; 710F ($123.50) double with bath; 830F ($144.35) triple. Continental breakfast 50F ($8.70) extra. AE, DC, MC, V. Métro: Maubert-Mutualité.

It's evident from the moment you enter the lobby that the three-star Hôtel Claude-Bernard keeps very high standards. Each congenial room has tasteful crimson wallpaper, a sleek bathroom, and often a charming piece of old-fashioned furniture such as a writing desk. There are also some particularly attractive suites available that feature couches and armchairs. A sauna is available for guests' use.

Hôtel Sully Saint-Germain. 31 rue des Ecoles, 75005 Paris. ☎ **01-43-26-56-02.** Fax 01-43-29-74-42. 56 rms (all with bath). TV TEL. 605F ($105.20) single; 700–750F ($121.75–$130.45) double or twin; 800–850F ($139.15–$147.80) triple; 950F ($165.20) quad. Buffet breakfast 50F ($8.70) extra. Métro: Maubert-Mutualité.

A medieval atmosphere prevails at this well-furnished three-star hotel, at least in the furnishings, where a splendid figure of a knight in armor graces the lounge. The room amenities, however, are up-to-the-minute and include such extras as minibars, safes, and hair dryers. Hotel extras include laundry service, a restaurant, a free exercise room, and a Jacuzzi, which can be used for a 100F ($19.25) charge.

Timhotel Jardin des Plantes. 5 rue Linné, 75005 Paris. ☎ **01-47-07-06-20.** Fax 01-47-07-62-74. 33 rms (all with shower or bath). MINIBAR TV TEL. 450F ($78.25) single with shower; 520F ($90.45) single with bath; 550F ($95.65) double with bath; 690F ($120) triple. Continental breakfast 49F ($8.50) extra. DC, MC, V. Métro: Jussieu.

This great two-star hotel owes its name to its location across from the fascinating Jardin des Plantes, the botanical gardens created on the order of Louis XIII's doctors in 1626 and called, at the time, the Jardin Royal des Plantes Médicinales. There are still some 15,000 medicinal herbs at the gardens and some regal comforts at the nearby hotel: a roof terrace, a sauna, a vaulted cellar with a fireplace, and a glass-fronted sidewalk cafe adjoining the lobby. All rooms have tiled bathrooms with hair dryers. Additional amenities include minibars. The color of the rooms on each floor is taken from a flower—iris, geranium, mimosa, and so on—and each room has a pretty floral decor in that color. The more expensive rooms on the fifth floor open onto a sunny terrace.

ST-GERMAIN (6E ARRONDISSEMENT)
DOUBLES FOR LESS THAN 350F ($61)

Hôtel de la Faculté. 1 rue Racine, 75006 Paris. ☎ **01-43-26-87-13.** Fax 01-46-34-73-88. 19 rms (all with shower). TEL. 345F ($60) single or double. Continental breakfast 29F ($5) extra. MC, V. Métro: Odéon, St-Michel, or Cluny–Sorbonne.

In a prime Latin Quarter location just steps off the busy boulevard St-Michel, this modest two-star hotel holds some surprises. The tiny lobby leads to a minuscule elevator and to a winding staircase. Down the narrow hallways, there are freshly renovated rooms with antique-style furnishings. All rooms face the street and the first and fourth floor rooms have balconies with a view of Notre-Dame. Everything may seem a bit cramped, but the prices won't dent your budget.

Hôtel des Académies. 15 rue de la Grande-Chaumière, 75006 Paris. ☎ **01-43-26-66-44.** 21 rms (17 with shower or bath). TEL. 210F ($36.50) single with sink and toilet; 275F ($47.80) single or double with shower; 315–340F ($54.80–$59.15) single or double with shower and WC. Continental breakfast 30F ($5.20) extra. No credit cards. Métro: Vavin.

This exceptional hotel is several blocks from the southwest corner of the Jardin du Luxembourg in a neighborhood just minutes from Odéon or St-Michel via the Métro.

Hôtel des Académies is proper and comfortable, with hearteningly low prices. Decor in the lobby and guest rooms is faded at worst, kitschy at best, but perfectly serviceable. There's no elevator, but rooms on the fourth and fifth floors are cheaper, so the climb pays for itself.

Hôtel du Globe. 15 rue des Quatre Vents, 75006 Paris. ☎ **01-46-33-62-69.** 15 rms (most with bath). 315–425F ($54.80–$73.90) single or double. Continental breakfast 35F ($6.10) extra. No credit cards. Métro: St-Sulpice.

It doesn't look like much from the outside, but as soon as you enter you'll know that great care has been taken in decorating the interior of this charming old building. Every room has the basic necessities, but each is decorated uniquely—most with a floral pattern and lace accents. One of the best is salmon-colored room no. 7. There's no elevator, but you probably won't mind climbing the wonderful narrow staircase. Prices vary according to room size and amenities.

Hôtel Stanislas. 5 rue du Montparnasse, 75006 Paris. ☎ **01-45-48-37-05.** Fax 01-45-44-54-43. 18 rms (all with shower or bath). TV TEL. 305F ($53) single with shower; 340F ($59.15) double with shower; 360F ($62.60) double with bath; 425F ($73.90) triple. Continental breakfast 30F ($5.20) extra. AE, EURO, MC, V. Métro: Notre-Dame-des-Champs.

A family hotel located on a quiet street on which many a famous artist has lived. Rooms are basically furnished but the price is right. There's a bar-cafe off the lobby where you can get breakfast, and light meals are served here until midnight.

DOUBLES FOR LESS THAN 500F ($87)

Grand Hôtel des Balcons. 3 Casimir Delavigne, 75006 Paris. ☎ **01-46-34-78-50.** Fax 01-46-34-06-27. 55 rms (all with bath or shower). TEL. 350–500F ($60.85–$87) single or double with bath or shower. Buffet breakfast 50F ($8.70) extra. EURO, MC, V. Métro: Odéon.

A gracious art nouveau–style entrance leads into the hotel, which has good, clean rooms with modern light oak furnishings and renovated facilities throughout. The breakfast room is attractive with etched-glass windows. An elevator is available.

Hôtel du Dragon. 36 rue du Dragon, 75006 Paris. ☎ **01-45-48-51-05.** Fax 01-42-22-51-62. 28 rms (18 with bath and WC, 10 with shower only). TV. 301F ($52.35) single with shower; 352F ($61.20) single with shower and WC; 392F ($68.15) double (one bed) with shower or bath and WC; 452F ($78.60) double (twin beds) with bath and WC. Continental breakfast 30F ($5.20) extra. AE, EURO, MC, V. Métro: St-Germain-des-Prés or Sèvres-Babylone.

Directly across from the Académie Julien, this hotel is a very good value. The rooms are done in a Laura Ashley style and the bathrooms are handsomely tiled. The Church of Saint-Germain-des-Prés is just up the street.

Hôtel du Lys. 23 rue Serpente, 6e, 75006 Paris. ☎ **01-43-26-97-57.** Fax 01-44-07-34-90. 22 rms (all with bath or shower). TV TEL. 380–450F ($66.10–$78.25) single; 480F ($83.45) double; 560F ($97.40) triple. Rates include breakfast. No credit cards. Métro: St-Michel or Odéon.

Housed in a 17th-century turreted Renaissance mansion, Hôtel du Lys rates two stars and has all the amenities of such an establishment, including direct-dial telephones, TVs, and hair dryers in the bathrooms. All the rooms, which vary in size, are very homey, with floral wallpapers and exposed-beam ceilings. Rooms 19 and 22 have balconies. If you're looking for a romantic but relatively inexpensive place to sleep in one of the world's most romantic cities, this hotel is exactly what you're after.

Hôtel Saint-André-des-Arts. 66 rue St-André-des-Arts, 75006 Paris. ☎ **01-43-26-96-16.** Fax 01-43-29-73-34. 32 rms (all with shower or bath and WC). TEL. 320–360F ($46.60–$62.60) single with shower or bath; 460F ($80) double with shower; 500F ($87) double with bath; 570F ($99.15) triple; 620F ($107.80) quad. Rates include continental breakfast. EURO, MC, V. Métro: Odéon.

Hôtel Saint-André is the stereotype of the romantic Latin Quarter hotel: on a crooked street of art galleries and cafes, in a half-timbered 17th-century building constructed of rough stone. The hotel has tiny rooms, high ceilings, and good prices, and the front-desk clerk speaks English. Aside from the small rooms, the one drawback here is the noise level. To find the place, take the Métro to the Odéon station, cross boulevard St-Germain, and walk down rue de l'Ancienne Comédie to rue St-André-des-Arts, on the right.

WORTH A SPLURGE

Hôtel de Fleurie. 32–34 rue de Grégoire-de-Tours, 75006 Paris. ☎ **01-53-73-70-00.** Fax 01-53-73-70-20. 29 rms (all with bath). MINIBAR TV TEL. 680–880F ($118.25–$153). Breakfast 50F ($8.70) extra. AE, DC, MC, V. Métro: Odéon.

Okay, if you really want to splurge, this is the place to do it—a charming Left Bank hotel with all the comforts, including air-conditioning, hair dryers, pink-marble baths, and fresh flowers all over the place. The staff is charming, and this is a superb location within shouting distance of everything you want to do on the Left Bank. The Odéon is just up the street.

Hôtel des Marronniers. 21 rue Jacob, 75006 Paris. ☎ **01-43-25-30-60.** Fax 01-40-46-83-56. 37 rms (all with bath or shower). TV TEL. 520F ($90.45) single with shower; 715F ($124.35) double with shower; 815F ($141.75) double with bath. Breakfast 45F ($7.80) extra. EURO, MC, V. Métro: St-Germain-des-Prés.

You'll find the entrance to this hotel tucked at the back of a courtyard entryway in the heart of St-Germain on antique-store–lined rue Jacob. Among the most appealing features of the hotel are the bright breakfast room and the garden that extends out back. In the rooms, the walls are covered with fabric in rich reds or blues, making for a lavish effect. They also contain hair dryers.

EIFFEL TOWER & INVALIDES (7E ARRONDISSEMENT)
DOUBLES FOR LESS THAN 350F ($61)

Grand Hôtel Léveque. 29 rue Cler, 75007 Paris. ☎ **01-47-05-49-15.** Fax 01-45-50-49-36. 50 rms (5 with sink only, 45 with shower and WC). 220F ($38.25) single with sink only; 335F ($58.25) single or double with shower and WC; 365F ($63.50) double (twin beds) with shower and WC. Continental breakfast 30F ($5.20) extra. EURO, MC, V. Métro: Ecole-Militaire or Latour-Maubourg.

Grand Hôtel Léveque is a large establishment on a colorful pedestrian street with a marketplace that's busy during the day. Many of the rooms have been entirely renovated to include a shower and toilet, satellite TV, hair dryers, and safes. An elevator has recently been added. The staff is very friendly and helpful, and, if you ask, they

Hotels—Eiffel Tower & Invalides (7e Arr.)

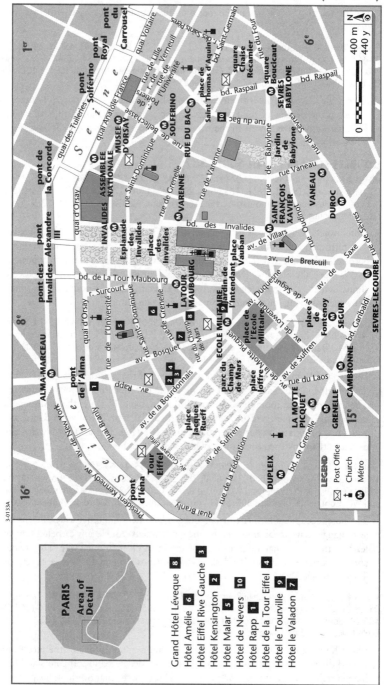

PARIS
Area of Detail

Grand Hôtel Léveque **8**
Hôtel Amélie **6**
Hôtel Eiffel Rive Gauche **3**
Hôtel Kensington **2**
Hôtel Malar **5**
Hôtel de Nevers **10**
Hôtel Rapp **1**
Hôtel de la Tour Eiffel **4**
Hôtel le Tourville **9**
Hôtel le Valadon **7**

LEGEND
⌧ Post Office
✝ Church
Ⓜ Métro

0   400 m
      440 y

3-0133A

may be able to give you one of the rooms on the fifth floor that have partial yet wonderful views of the Eiffel Tower.

Hôtel Eiffel Rive Gauche. 6 rue du Gros-Caillou, 75007 Paris. ☎ **01-45-51-24-56.** Fax 01-45-51-11-77. 30 rms (all with shower or bath). TV TEL. 260–335F ($45.20–$58.25) single; 280–420F ($48.70–$73) double; 490F ($85.20) triple. Continental breakfast 35F ($6.10) extra. AE, EURO, MC, V. Métro: Ecole-Militaire or Alma-Marceau.

Hôtel Eiffel Rive Gauche is an efficient establishment located on a peaceful side street almost in the shadow of the Eiffel Tower. The rooms are tranquil, all have satellite TVs, and some have flowers in the windows. There is also a patio. A 15% discount is offered to guests who stay at least 2 weeks.

DOUBLES FOR LESS THAN 500F ($87)

Hôtel Amélie. 5 rue Amélie, 75007 Paris. ☎ **01-45-51-74-75.** Fax 01-45-56-93-55. 16 rms (all with shower). TV TEL. 365F ($63.50) single; 430–470F ($74.80–$81.75) double; 540F ($93.90) triple. Continental breakfast 35F ($6.10) extra. AE, CB, DC, EURO, MC, V. Métro: Latour-Maubourg.

Hôtel Amélie is as pretty as its name suggests. The rooms, though smallish, are very well furnished and some have French windows. All are very clean, and many have been recently renovated. The second floor (known as the first floor in European hotels) is especially pleasing. Despite the central location, the atmosphere is peaceful, almost serene. The management is efficient and correct. Depending on the time of year, guests staying for several days may receive a discount.

Hôtel de la Tour Eiffel. 17 rue de l'Exposition, 75007 Paris. ☎ **01-47-05-14-75.** Fax 01-47-53-99-46. 22 rms (all with shower or bath). TV TEL. 320F ($55.65) single with shower; 370F ($64.35) double with shower; 400F ($69.55) double with bath. Continental breakfast 30F ($5.20) extra. AE, MC, V. Métro: Ecole-Militaire.

Next to the Romanian embassy and with a view of the statues in its garden, Hôtel de la Tour Eiffel is neither quaint nor romantic but modern and very comfortable. The well-appointed rooms have pleasant furnishings and TVs, and the bathrooms are up-to-date. The management is efficient and cordial, and, if you wish, they'll serve you a fine breakfast in your room for an extra 10F ($2). The *oeufs au plat* are more delicious than any fried eggs you may have eaten back home.

Hôtel de Nevers. 83 rue du Bac, 75007 Paris. ☎ **01-45-44-61-30.** Fax 01-42-22-29-47. 11 rms (all with shower or bath). MINIBAR TEL. 390F ($67.80) single with shower and WC; 420F ($73) twin with shower and WC; 410–450F ($71.30–$78.25) double with shower or bath and WC. Continental breakfast 30F ($5.20) extra. No credit cards. Métro: Rue-du-Bac.

The hotel occupies a former convent and is a landmark building, which means that any changes have to be approved by the government. An elegant carpeted staircase leads to the rooms that are primly decorated in an old-fashioned way. They're cozy and comfortable, with writing desks. Note that nos. 10 and 11 have large terraces. There is no elevator.

Hôtel Kensington. 79 av. de la Bourdonnais, 75007 Paris. ☎ **01-47-05-74-00.** Fax 01-47-05-25-81. 26 rms (all with shower or bath). TV TEL. 305F ($53) single; 390–490F ($67.80–$85.20) double. Continental breakfast 28F ($4.85) extra. AE, CB, DC, EURO, MC, V. Métro: Ecole-Militaire or Alma-Marceau.

Hôtel Kensington is located on one of the main avenues in one of the nicest residential districts near the Eiffel Tower. Rooms are decorated in soft colors and have long curtained windows and long mirrors. Those rooms that overlook busy avenue de la Bourdonnais are not as noisy as you may think (windows are double glazed). In summer you may have to keep the windows open, but then you'll enjoy the lush green of the leaves. From room nos. 43 and 44 there is a view of the Eiffel Tower rising over the neighboring roofs. All in all, this is a very pleasant place to stay.

Hôtel le Valadon. 16 rue Valadon, 75007 Paris. ☎ **01-47-53-89-85.** 13 rms (all with shower or bath). TV TEL. 375–440F ($65.20–$76.50) single; 435–485F ($75.65–$84.35) double. Continental breakfast 36F ($6.25) extra. AE, CB, DISC, EURO, MC, V. Métro: Ecole-Militaire.

Recently refurbished, Hôtel Le Valadon is very comfortable, with all kinds of special treats, such as hair dryers and full-length mirrors in every room and TVs with remote control. The navy-blue halls are quiet. Downstairs, in the back, there's a dining room with a skylight; refreshments are available at different times of the day. The location is excellent, on a quiet side street.

Hôtel Malar. 29 rue Malar, 75007 Paris. ☎ **01-45-51-38-46.** Fax 01-45-55-20-19. 17 rms (all with shower or bath). TV TEL. 300–380F ($52.15–$66) single with shower or bath; 360–460F ($62.60–$80) double with shower or bath; 520F ($90.45) triple with shower. Continental breakfast 30F ($5.20) extra. CB, EURO, MC, V. Métro: Latour-Maubourg. RER: Pont de l'Alma.

When you enter the smallish lobby of Hôtel Malar, you'll be pleasantly surprised by the modest yet attractive staircase and by the kind, gentle disposition of the English-speaking management. There's lots of light in the rooms, since they boast long French windows and (a luxury for Paris, really) lamps over the beds so that you can read after tucking yourself in. The rooms also are well kept and have modern furnishings. The neighborhood is quite pleasant; it's perhaps not the prettiest street of the 7e arrondissement, but is well located not far from both the Eiffel Tower and the Hôtel des Invalides.

Hôtel Rapp. 8 av. Rapp, 75007 Paris. ☎ **01-45-51-42-28.** Fax 01-43-59-50-70. 16 rms (all with shower or bath). TEL. 265F ($46.10) single; 350–370F ($60.85–$64.35) double. Continental breakfast 25F ($4.35) extra. MC, V. Métro: Alma-Marceau. RER: Pont de l'Alma.

Virtually in the shadow of the Eiffel Tower and very near the Seine (in fact, the nearest Métro is across the river on the Right Bank), Hôtel Rapp is small, quiet, and modern. The manager, who speaks English, extols the convenience and security of being located near several embassies. The rooms are well appointed, with fine dark furniture and yellow drapes, and everything is very clean. Parking is easy on this street, and you pay less with a card from the hotel.

WORTH A SPLURGE

Hôtel le Tourville. 17 av. de Tourville, 75007 Paris. ☎ **01-47-05-62-62.** Fax 01-47-05-43-90. 30 rms (all with bath). MINIBAR TV TEL. 690–1,090F ($120–$189.50). AE, DC, MC, V. Métro: St-Francois-Xavier.

What a difference a little more money can make—this place is splendid. Located just behind Les Invalides, you get almost all of the amenities you'd find in a considerably pricier hotel—Roger & Gallet toiletries, air-conditioning, chic decor with antique furniture—for prices that are still manageable. This place is a real charmer, and if you're coming to Paris to celebrate some special occasion, you'd do well to book here.

MONTPARNASSE (14E ARRONDISSEMENT)

Celtic Hôtel. 15 rue d'Odessa, 75014 Paris. ☎ **01-43-20-93-53.** Fax 01-43-20-83-91. 200F ($34.80) single; 230F ($40) double; 270F ($46.95) single or double with shower and WC; 290F ($50.45) single or double with bath and WC. Breakfast 20F ($3.45) extra. V. Métro: Montparnasse or Edgar Quinet.

This hotel will do in a pinch. The rooms are a little faded, but they're passable and dirt cheap.

Fred'Hotel Paris. 11 av. Villemain, 75014 Paris. ☎ **01-45-43-24-18.** Fax 01-45-43-27-26. 25 rms (23 with shower). TV TEL. 225F ($39.15) single with sink only; 295F ($51.30) single with bath and WC; 330–430F ($57.40–$74.80) double with bath and WC; 456F ($79.30) triple. Breakfast 30F ($5.20) extra. AE, DC, EURO, MC, V. Métro: Plaisance.

Although a little out of the way, the hotel is on a quiet street near a number of shops and restaurants. The rooms are clean and bright but rather blandly furnished. Most have good amenities such as radio-TVs and hair dryers. The more expensive rooms are fairly large and have recently been renovated.

4 Hostels & Dorms

Paris has plenty of youth hostels (*auberges de jeunesse*) and *foyers* (literally "homes") to accommodate the hordes of young travelers who descend on the city every summer. Quality varies from place to place, but the superior hostels offer excellent value for your money. While some are huge and impersonal and occupy similarly huge and impersonal buildings, other hostels are friendly, warm places where you can meet people from all over the world. Some of these hostels are housed in historical buildings that are both comfortable and handsome. Many of them welcome travelers regardless of their age.

Hostels in Paris are an especially good deal for solo travelers. As single rooms in hotels become scarce in summer and during the big international fairs (see "Paris Calendar of Events," in chapter 2), you may have to choose between paying for a double room or paying for a bed at a hostel. The latter option can be especially attractive, and not only from a financial point of view. Hostels are a great place to hook up with other travelers, exchange stories, and simply have pleasant company. The major drawback for some people, whether traveling alone or not, is the day lockout and the night curfew. If having a place to take an afternoon nap is essential to you, or late nightlife is what you came to Paris for, then staying at a hostel may not be your best choice.

Many hostels do not accept reservations from individual travelers. In that case, the best strategy is to show up at the hostel where you want to stay as early as possible in the morning—8am or earlier. You can also call ahead to find out what your chances are for getting a bed. For some hostels, like those run by the **Maisons Internationales de la Jeunesse et des Etudiants,** all this trouble is really worth it. Once you're "accepted," make sure you tell your host how many nights you plan to stay (five is the maximum at some places).

If you arrive late in the day and don't want to start calling up or going to hostels that may already be full, it's a good idea simply to head for one of the offices of the **Accueil des Jeunes en France (AJF).** This organization (which operates under the umbrella of Maisons Internationales) exists to find inexpensive beds for young people, and they will book you a bed for that night. If you want to stay at one of their own hostels (they're all great), tell them so. Their main office is at 112 rue Maubeuge, 9e (☎ **01-42-85-36-13;** Métro: Poissoniére).

The **Office de Tourisme et des Congrès de Paris,** 127 av. des Champs-Elysées, 75008 Paris (☎ **01-49-52-53-54;** Métro: Charles-de-Gaulle Etoile or Georges-V), will also book you a bed in a hostel for an 8F ($1.40) fee. There are other organizations that also specialize in providing young people with information on budget accommodations (see also "For Students & People Under Age 26," in "Tips for Travelers with Special Needs," in chapter 2).

B.V.J. Louvre. 20 rue Jean-Jacques-Rousseau 75001 Paris. ☎ **01-53-00-90-90.** 68 beds. 120F ($21.85) per person per night. Lunch or dinner 60F ($10.45) extra. Rates include continental breakfast. No credit cards. Open July–Oct 15. Métro: Palais-Royal-Musée-du-Louvre.

Run by the UCRIF (Union des Centres de Rencontres Internationales de France), this small hostel is clean and friendly and its location is excellent. There are anywhere from three to eight beds in each room; showers and toilets are down the hall on each floor.

UCRIF also runs **B.V.J. Quartier Latin,** 44 rue des Bernardins, 5e (☎ **01-43-29-34-80;** Métro: Maubert-Mutualité), in the Latin Quarter.

Foyer International des Etudiants. 93 bd. St-Michel, 75005 Paris. ☎ **01-43-54-49-63.** 160 beds. 145F ($25.20) single; 190F ($33) double. Rates include showers. No credit cards. Open June–Sept. Métro: Luxembourg.

Open to traveling students in the summer, this university residence has an excellent location and is quite comfortable.

Foyer le Fauconnier. 11 rue du Fauconnier, 75004 Paris. ☎ **01-42-74-23-45.** Fax 01-42-71-61-02. 118 beds. 125F ($21.75) per person per night in a multibedded room; 152F ($26.45) twin, 170F ($29.55) single. Rates include continental breakfast. No credit cards. Métro: St-Paul or Pont-Marie.

Run by the Maisons Internationales de la Jeunesse et des Etudiants (MIJE), this hostel is located in a historic *hôtel particulier* on a quiet street in the Marais, not far from the Seine. Despite the groups that sometimes overrun it, Le Fauconnier has a touch of elegance, with a pleasant courtyard and a beautiful staircase. All the rooms have private showers, and some rooms are singles or doubles—unusual for youth hostel accommodations.

Other MIJE hostels are located nearby: **Maubuisson,** at 11 rue des Barres, 4e (☎ **01-42-74-23-45**), with 114 beds; and **Fourcy,** at 6 rue de Fourcy, 4e (☎ **01-42-74-23-45**), with 206 beds.

5 | Great Deals on Dining

The culinary attractions of Paris match anything else the city has to offer, and you don't have to spend a fortune to enjoy them. Street markets are in every neighborhood and contain as fine a selection of cheese and *charcuterie* as any high-priced restaurant. Gleaming pastry shops beckon you with croissants, tarts, éclairs, and elaborate cakes. Even a humble sandwich becomes a Parisian specialty when it's made with a crusty baguette or the dense, chewy Pain Pôilaine.

Of course, you will also want to sample the offerings of the local chefs, and here I have good news as well: With a little planning, it is finally possible to be a gourmet without breaking the bank. The recent economic recession gripping France has forced Parisians to scrutinize prices as carefully as they scrutinize the wine list. In response to increasing price resistance, many famous Parisian chefs have opened lower-priced annexes, "baby-bistros," that offer excellent value, and a new generation of young chefs is taking pride in offering inventive bistro cooking for very low prices. Both established chefs and talented newcomers are offering fixed-price lunch menus that offer superb dining at moderate prices.

The key to fine dining on a modest budget is to eat where Parisians eat and stay away from restaurants surrounding major tourist attractions. You'll find few bargains around the Eiffel Tower or along the Champs-Elysées. Leave the mediocre cafes on the place de Tertre to the milling crowds and let others wander into the interchangeable Greek restaurants along the rue de la Huchette. Opt instead for restaurants in neighborhoods where people live and work, which are forced to keep their prices and quality competitive in order to keep a stable of regular customers.

Parisians start the day with a light breakfast, usually consisting of a café au lait and a croissant or a buttered baguette called a *tartine*. Unless breakfast is included in the price of your hotel room, go to a sidewalk cafe and stand at the counter. The experience is inimitably Parisian. You'll rub shoulders with workers throwing down shots of Calvados brandy with their *espresso* and hurried executives perusing the morning *Figaro* before work. Also, the price will be about 40% to 50% lower at the counter than if you sit down and have a waiter serve you.

Lunch is an important meal in Paris and you may wish to make it the main meal of the day. You'll notice that the majority of restaurants, bistros, and cafes offer a fixed-price lunch on weekdays called a *menu du jour* or *formule*, which is a two- or three-course meal that sometimes includes wine. The fixed-price meal can be a terrific bargain, allowing you to eat at otherwise unaffordable restaurants. A few establishments offer the same fixed-price menu at dinner, but in most places the dinner menu is more expensive, although still cheaper than ordering à la carte.

An alternative to a multicourse meal is the *plat du jour* or *plat garni,* a main-course platter garnished with vegetables and little extras that easily constitute a filling meal. It's usually made with the freshest and most seasonal ingredients and is cheaper than a full-course *menu du jour.*

For a simple meal, head for a cafe and order an omelet, sandwich, soup, or salad. Omelettes come plain with just a sprinkling of herbs or filled with cheese, ham, or other hearty additions. Onion soup is a traditional Parisian dish and you may see *soupe de poisson* (fish soup) on the menu. Another cafe favorite is the *croque monsieur,* a grilled ham sandwich covered with melted cheese, or a *croque madame,* which is the same dish topped with an egg. Or try a *salade Niçoise,* a huge bowl filled with lettuce, boiled potato, tuna, hard-boiled egg, capers, tomatoes, olives, and anchovies. These dishes make a light, pleasant meal for 35F to 65F ($6 to $11.30).

Ethnic spots offer a popular alternative to French cuisine and can be inexpensive, depending on the neighborhood. Most bargains are found in the ethnic communities outside central Paris, which can also be fascinating places to explore. Some of the best Chinese, Vietnamese, and Thai cooking is found along the streets radiating out from the Métro station **Belleville** in the 11e and **avenue d'Ivry** and **avenue de Choisy** in the 13e. Not far from Pére Lachaise cemetery, on the **boulevard de Belleville,** many restaurants serve hearty North African couscous dishes, in portions large enough to feed two people.

Small enclaves in central Paris also offer inexpensive ethnic dishes. Pita bread sandwiches stuffed with falafel and all the trimmings found on **rue des Rosiers** in the Marais are a meal in themselves. Spanish tapas are the latest food fad. Casual hangouts serving these small dishes of spicy meat, seafood, and rice are popping up everywhere in the Marais and also on **rue de Lappe** and **rue de Charonne** in the 11e.

By the way, Paris has a full complement of American-style fast-food eateries such as McDonald's and Pizza Hut. Parisians, too, respond to the appeal of uniform quality and (relatively) quick service, but you'll discover that fast-food prices are higher than in the United States. For inexpensive Parisian chains and cafeterias, see "The Best of the Budget Chains," later in this chapter.

One of the best ways to save money and also to participate in Parisian life is to picnic. Go to a *fromagerie* and purchase some cheese, to a *boulangerie* for a baguette, and to a *charcuterie* for some pâté, sausage, or salads. Add a friendly bottle of Cotes du Rhone—it usually goes well with picnics—and you'll have the makings of a delightful and typically French meal.

1 Best Bets

- **Best Spot for a Romantic Dinner:** With its big wooden beams, stone floor, and candlelit tables, the tiny **Le Maraicher,** 5 rue Beautreillis, 4e (☎ **01-42-71-42-49**), in the Marais is ideal for a meal to fall in love over. The food is delicious, too, and when the weather is cold, there's a fire in the big stone chimney at the back of the room.
- **Best Meals with a View:** To peer at Paris from a high-rise table is expensive, and even when money's not an issue, many of the city's tables-with-a-view are mediocre. Staying earthbound, though, you can still savor a wonderful view of

Notre-Dame from **Le Ver-Meer Café,** 19 quai de Montebello, 5e (☎ **01-40-46-94-50**), which is located just across the Seine from Notre-Dame.

In good weather, one of the loveliest views in Paris is to be had from an outdoor table at the **Restaurant du Palais-Royal,** 43 rue Valois, 1er (☎ **01-40-20-00-27**). This restaurant is located within the Palais-Royal, so you'll overlook its beautiful, peaceful gardens while dining on fine dishes like grilled sole with a garnish of carrots, parsley, red pepper, and baby squid.

- **Best Places for a Celebration:** If you want a glamorous night on the town with friends, try **Brasserie Flo,** 7 cour des Petites-Ecuries, 10e (☎ **01-47-70-13-59**). The handsome turn-of-the-century dining room is unfailingly convivial, which is why you'll likely see the waiters gathered around a table singing "Happy Birthday" at least once during a meal here.

  For something more decorous, **Le Cercle Ledoyen,** 1 av. Dutuit, 8e (☎ **01-47-42-76-02**), is a delightful place located in an elegant Belle Époque pavilion in the gardens of the Champs-Elysées. It's popular with stylish Parisians not only for the setting but because it offers the opportunity to sample the excellent cuisine of chef Ghislaine Arabian, Paris's premier female chef, at very reasonable prices.

- **Best Bistro:** Every Parisian has his or her pick for this title, but almost everyone agrees that **Chardenoux,** 1 rue Jules-Valles, 11e (☎ **01-43-71-49-52**), belongs in the top 10. It's a small place in an out-of-the-way location, but the food is excellent and the setting gloriously, eternally Parisian.

- **Best Modern Bistro:** You'll have to book the minute you get to town if you want to sample the wonderful food at the almost hopelessly popular **L'Epi Dupin,** 11 rue Dupin, 6e (☎ **01-42-22-64-56**). Beyond the excellence of dishes like a skirt steak of lamb with stewed eggplant, this place pulls them in because it's so modestly priced—the fixed-price lunch menu is 97F ($16.85) for two courses.

- **Best Brasserie:** The famous **Bofinger,** 5–7 rue de la Bastille, 4e (☎ **01-42-72-87-82**), opened its doors in 1864 and is one of the prettiest restaurants in Paris, with a gorgeous domed stained-glass ceiling over the main dining room. It recently became part of the Brasserie Flo chain of restaurants and the food has never been better.

- **Best Place for a Late-Night Meal:** You can always wander into one of the all-night brasseries along the rue Coquillière on the northern edge of Les Halles without a reservation, but if you're looking for an intensely Parisian experience, you'll find it at **La Tour Montlhéry,** 5 rue des Prouvaires, 1er (☎ **01-42-36-21-82**). This bustling, bawdy place is open nonstop from 7am on Monday to 7am on Saturday and is known for its gargantuan cuts of excellent meat, along with good house wines. Reservations are always required.

- **Best for Mingling with the Locals:** Parisians are avid bargain hunters themselves, which explains the huge popularity of new bistros offering moderate prices. Two of their recent favorites are **Chez Jean,** 52 rue Lamartine, 9e (☎ **01-48-78-62-73**) and **Chez Michel,** 10 rue de Belzunce, 10e (☎ **01-44-53-06-20**). Both restaurants, in off-the-beaten-track locations, are run by young chefs who pride themselves on their modern bistro cooking and fixed-price menus.

- **Best Breakfast:** Since this meal can mean mealy croissants and watery coffee in budget accommodations, if you make the effort to come here some morning, you'll wish that **Ladurée,** 16 rue Royale, 8e (☎ **01-42-60-21-79**), was next door to your hotel. This elegant tea salon with basalt-topped tables and painted cherubs squirming overhead is a great way of getting a dose of Parisian luxury on a small budget. Both the coffee and the croissants are excellent.

- **Best Afternoon Tea:** For a delightful time-out during an ambitious day of sight-seeing, head to **Mariage Frères,** 30–32 rue du Bourg-Tibourg, 4e (☎ **01-42-72-28-11**). The Mariage family first entered the tea trade in 1660, when Nicolas Mariage began importing tea from Persia for King Louis XIV. Take your pick from more than 350 different teas in the attractive, colonial-style salon at the back of the shop.
- **Best Sandwiches:** Italy is the inspiration for the *foccacia*-style bread and scrumptious fillings at **Cosi,** 54 rue de Seine, 6e (☎ 01-46-33-35-36). To accompany the freshly baked bread you can choose from an assortment of specialties, including arugula, mozzarella, and Parmesan cheese, Italian ham, roast tomatoes, and tapenade.
- **Best Places to Shop for Picnic Fare:** Two excellent places to do one-stop picnic shopping are **La Grande Epicerie,** Bon Mârché, 38 rue de Sèvres, 7e (☎ **01-44-39-81-00**), and **Lafayette Gourmet,** 52 bd. Haussmann, 9e (☎ **01-48-74-46-06**). The quiche sold at the Alsatian deli counter at the Grande Epicerie is a special treat. (For full descriptions of both stores, see the "Food" section in chapter 8, "Shopping.")
- **Best Spot for a Family Meal:** The **Batifol** chain of bistros, located all over Paris, including branches at 78 av. des Champs-Elysées, 8e (☎ **01-45-62-64-93**), and 1 bd. St-Germain, 5e (☎ **01-43-54-49-05**), offer good quality bistro cooking in attractive surroundings at very reasonable prices—the fixed-price menu is only 79F ($13.75) and the children's menu runs 37F ($6.45). (See "The Best of the Budget Chains," later in this chapter.)
- **Best Wine Bar:** For excellent Rhone Valley wines and generous plates of cold-cuts and cheese in a very lively little dining room, visit **A la Cloche des Halles,** 28 rue Coquillière, 1er (☎ **01-42-36-93-89**). *Cloche* means "bell" in French, and the name refers to the bell that used to toll the opening and closing of the main market of Paris when it was still nearby. Some of the old-market atmosphere still survives here, including an interesting mix of people and a high level of conviviality. It's a great place for a light and very French lunch.
- **Best Cafe Food:** Though you can get salads and omelettes in cafes all over town, they make an extra effort at the **Chaise au Plafond,** 10 rue Trésor, 4e (☎ 01-42-76-03-22), on a side street in the heart of the Marais. An off-beat decor of park benches and a ceiling painted black and white to resemble the markings on a cow attracts a young crowd who delight in the big, fresh, generous salads and cold plates served here.
- **Best Foreign Meal:** Paris is filled with excellent North African and Vietnamese restaurants, but **Le Manguier,** 67 av. Parmentier, 11e (☎ 01-48-07-03-27), may be the only chance you'll ever have to try West African cooking. Among the better dishes are the chicken yassa, with lemons and onions, or maybe the requin fume—or smoked shark, if you're feeling adventurous. This lively place also serves potent, mostly rum-based cocktails and plays African music.
- **Best Student Hangout:** For almost 100 years, generations of students from all over the world have been making a beeline for **Chartier,** 7 rue du Faubourg-Montmartre, 9e (☎ **01-47-70-86-29**). For an average of about 80F ($13.90) you can still get a decent meal here, and the fly-in-amber, turn-of-the-century decor and bustling international crowd are a wonderful backdrop. Don't come expecting a gourmet feast, but rather good, simple food.
- **Best French Regional Restaurant:** French regional cooking has been enjoying a new vogue in Paris. Three of the best places to dine in the provinces without leaving town are **Campagne et Provence,** 25 quai de la Tournelle,

5e (☎ **01-43-54-05-17**), for the sunny cooking of Provence; **Chantairelle,** 17 rue Laplace, 5e (☎ **01-46-33-18-59**), to sample the sturdy fare of the south-central Auvergne region; and **Au Bascou,** 38 rue Réaumur, 3e (☎ **01-42-72-69-25**), for a taste of the Basque country and southwestern kitchens.

- **Best Deals:** The 97F ($16.85) lunch menu at the hugely popular modern bistro **L'Epi Dupin,** 11 rue Dupin, 6e (☎ **01-42-22-64-56**), is probably the best noon-time bargain in town, while the 120F ($20.85) dinner menu at **Au Bon Acceuil,** 14 rue de Monttessuy, 7e (☎ **01-47-05-46-11**), offers a stunningly good meal for the money. Reserve as far in advance as possible for both restaurants.

2 Restaurants by Cuisine

AFRICAN/SENEGALESE
Le Manguier, 11e

ALSATIAN
Bofinger, 4e
L'Alsaco, 9e

AUVERGNAT
Chantairelle, 5e

BASQUE
Au Bascou, 3e

BELGIAN
Bouillon Racine, 6e

BRETON
A La Bonne Crêpe, 6e
Chez Michel, 10e

CAFES
Café Beaubourg, 4e
Café Cluny, 5e
Café de Flore, 6e
Café des Deux—Magots, 6e
Café Marly, 1er
Café Mouffetard, 5e
Fouquet's, 8e
La Chaise au Plafond, 4e
La Chope, 5e
La Coupole, 14e
La Palette, 6e
L'Eté en Pente Douce, 18e

CHINESE
La Dinette, 6e

CORSICAN
Vivario, 5e

DELI
Feri's Restaurant à Emporter, 8e

DUTCH-FRENCH
Le Ver-Meer Café, 5e

FRENCH
A La Bonne Crêpe, 6e
A Priori Thé, 2e
Amadeo, 4e
Auberge de Jarente, 4e
Auberge de la Reine Blanche, 4e
Au Bascou, 3e
Au Bon Accueil, 7e
Au Pied du Fouet, 7e
Au Clair de la Lune, 18e
Au Petit Prince, 6e
Au Pied de Cochon, 1er
Au Vieux Casque, 6e
Aux Charpentiers, 6e
La Bastide Odéon, 6e
Le Batifol, 1er
Bistrot le Beaubourg, 4e
Bistrot du Dome, 14e
Bistro de la Université, 6e
Bofinger, 4e
Brasserie Flo, 10e
Cercle Ledoyen, 8e
Champs-Elysées, 8e
Chantairelle, 5e
Chardenoux, 11e
Chartier, 9e
Chez Germaine, 7e
Chez Ginette, 18e
Chez Jean, 9e
Chez Madame de . . . , 4e
Chez Michel, 10e
Chez Pento, 5e

Feri's Restaurant à Emporter, 8e
Hippopotamus, 1er
Julien, 10e
La Boutique à Sandwiches, 8e
La Fontaine de Mars, 7e
L'Apostrophe, 5e
La Petite Chaise, 7e
La Petite Hostellerie, 5e
La Poule au Pot, 1er
La Truffe, 4e
La Tour de Montlhéry, 1er
La Café du Commerce, 15e
Le Cochon à l'Oreille, 1er
Le Coq Heron, 1er
Le Croque au Sel, 7e
Le Grenier de Notre-Dame, 5e
Le Gros Minet, 1er
Le Maraicher, 4e
Le Muniche, 6e
Le Petit Gavroche, 4e
Le Petit Keller, 11e
Le Petit Machon, 1er
Le Petit Plat, 15e
Le Petit St-Benoît, 6e
Le Petit Vatel, 6e
Le Trumilou, 4e
Les Banquettes Rouges, 6e
Les Temps des Cerises, 4e
L'Epi Dupin, 6e
Mamie Suzette, 8e
Ma Normandie, 2e
Marais Plus, 3e
Oh! Poivrier!, 15e
Rendez-Vous des Camionneurs, 14e
Rendez-Vous des Chauffeurs, 18e
Restaurant Chez Marius, 5e
Restaurant des Beaux Arts, 6e
Restaurant Lou Cantou, 9e
Restaurant du Palais-Royal, 1er
Restaurant L'Imprimerie, 3e
Restaurant L'Incroyable, 1er
Restaurant Perraudin, 5e

FRENCH BISTROS

Au Bascou, 3e
Au Bon Accueil, 7e
Au Pied du Fouet, 7e
Au Virage Lepic, 18e
Aux Trois Bourriques, 5e
La Bastide Odéon, 6e
Bistro de la Gare, 14e

Bistrot de Beaubourg, 4e
Brasserie Balzar, 5e
Chardenoux, 11e
Chez Jean, 9e
Chez Germaine, 7e
Chez Madame de . . . 4e
Chez Max, 1er
Chez Michel, 10e
Chez Pento, 5e
L'Epi Dupin, 6e
La Friterie, 5e
Le Gros Minet, 1er
Le Grizzli, 4e
Le Petit Keller, 11e
Le Polidor, 6e
L'Excuse Mogador, 9e
Rendez-Vous des Camionneurs, 14e
Rendez-Vous des Chauffeurs, 18e
Vagenende, 6e

FRENCH CAFETERIAS

Flunch—Rue de Berri, 8e
Universal Restaurant, 1er

FRENCH COUNTRY

Chez Maître Paul, 6e

GREEK

Restaurant Orestias, 6e

HUNGARIAN

Restaurant Beautreillis, 4e

INDIAN

Good Times, 11e

JEWISH

Jo Goldenberg, 4e
Sacha Finkelstein, 4e

NORTH AFRICAN

Le 404, 3e

PIZZA

Chicago Pizza Pie Factory, 8e

PROVENÇAL

La Bastide Odéon, 6e
Campagne et Provence, 5e
Chez Toutonne, 5e

RUSSIAN

La Datcha, 6e

SANDWICHES

Cosi, 6e

SEAFOOD

Bistrot du Dome, 14
Leon de Bruxelles, 6e

SOUTHWEST

Au Bascou, 3e
La Fermette de Soud-Ouest, 1er
Le Vieil Ecu, 1er
Relais de Soud-Ouest, 1er

TAPAS

Juveniles, 1er
Tapas de Montmartre, 18e

TEAROOMS

A La Cour de Rohan, 6e
A Priori Thé, 2e
Ladurée, 8e

Marais Plus, 3e
Mariage Frères, 4e
Salon de Thé de la Mosquée de Paris, 5e
Tea Caddy, 5e

VEGETARIAN

Le Grenier de Notre-Dame, 5e
La Truffe, 4e

WEST INDIAN

Chez Lucie, 7e

WINE BARS

Bistro du Peintre, 11e
A la Cloche des Halles, 1er
Clown Bar, 11e
Le Rubis, 1e.
L'Ecluse Saint-Michel, 6e
Le Sancerre, 7e
Taverne Henri IV, 1er

3 The Best of the Budget Chains

Paris has several good restaurant chains, the best of which is the **Batifol** group of bistros, which are located all over town and often occupy pretty, renovated old-fashioned bistros. They serve generally good food at very fair prices, too—their standard fixed-price menu is only 79F ($13.75). There's one on the Right Bank at 78 av. des Champs-Elysées, 8e (☎ **01-45-62-64-93**), and one on the Left Bank at 1 bd. St-Germain, 5e (☎ **01-43-54-49-05**).

You'll see the red awnings of **Hippopotamus** all over town, too. These places do decent red-meat dishes accompanied by fries and salad and served in a pleasant atmosphere. Parisians hold this popular chain in high regard for its uniform quality and moderate prices. Its extended hours are a convenience as well—you can get a hot meal here when most other places are closed.

Despite its remarkably stupid name, **Oh! Poivrier!** (Oh! The Pepper Mill!) features high standards in food, moderate prices, and long hours. Their salads make a pleasant light lunch or supper. **Lina's Sandwiches** packs an assortment of tasty fillings onto whole-meal bread and rolls. Add a soup or salad and finish with a brownie for a quick, filling meal. This popular chain also offers muffins, croissants, and coffee for breakfast.

If you like mussels, you might also want to keep your eyes peeled for a branch of **Leon de Bruxelles.** This Belgian chain serves up thirteen different styles of the crustacean, all accompanied with good frites. They also have a fine selection of Belgian abbey beers.

Though they are a bit dreary looking, some cafeterias also offer good food at moderate prices. Try **Flunch–Rue de Berri,** at 5 rue de Berri, 8e (☎ **01-42-25-09-98**), part of a large chain, where you will find an elaborate self-service restaurant with a dozen nicely decorated small dining rooms. **Universal Restaurant** 99 rue de Rivoli, 1er (entrance rue de Rivoli or from the Louvre Museum; ☎ **01-47-03-96-58**), is in the Carrousel de Louvre and offers a diverse grab bag of French and ethnic food.

4 Right Bank

LOUVRE, PALAIS-ROYAL & LES HALLES (1ER ARRONDISSEMENT)
MEALS FOR LESS THAN 85F ($15)

Juveniles. 47 rue de Richelieu, 1er. ☎ **01-42-97-46-49.** Reservations not necessary. Tapas 28–36F ($4.85–$6.25); main dishes 54–64F ($9.40–$11.15). MC, V. Mon–Sat noon–11pm. Métro: Palais-Royal. TAPAS.

One of Paris's best spots for tapas is Juveniles, located not far from the Palais-Royal. The restaurant is small but attractive, and you can choose from the à la carte menu, which features sandwiches, salads, and various daily specials like a brandade of haddock or a steak with dauphinoise potatoes. Or you can pick several dishes off the tapas menu. You might be interested in trying the tartine of goat cheese and black olives, the grilled sardines, or a Spanish tortilla with salsa verde. Juveniles specializes in French, Australian, and Spanish wines, so try something you've never heard of—you may be pleasantly surprised.

Universal Restaurant. 99 rue de Rivoli, 1er (entrance rue de Rivoli or from the Louvre Museum). ☎ **01-47-03-96-58.** Main dishes from 25F ($4.35); three courses à la carte 45–50F ($7.80–$8.70) V. Mon, Wed, Thurs, Sat 8am–11pm; Tues, Fri, Sun 8am–10pm. Metro: Palais-Royal–Museé-du-Louvre. FRENCH CAFETERIA/INTERNATIONAL.

Right next to the inverted pyramid in the Galerie Carrousel du Louvre, this busy cafeteria offers a rich assortment of ethnic and French specialties at unbeatable prices. Lunch is a madhouse as hungry hordes load up their trays from stands that offer Spanish tapas, Chinese lo mein, pasta salad, Mexican burritos, or all-American hamburger and fries. Other counters display Lebanese food, roast chicken, salads, muffins, ice cream, cheese, and crepes. The pick-and-choose style allows you to design your own meal—perfect for vegetarians or people on special diets. Spring rolls followed by crepes washed down with Sangria? No problem. Although the ambience is hardly relaxing (signs ask you not to "install yourself" at the tables), it's a quick place to fortify yourself between bouts with the Louvre.

MEALS FOR LESS THAN 120F ($21)

✪ **Chez Max.** 47 rue St-Honoré, 1er. ☎ **01-45-08-80-13.** Three-course lunch menu 65F ($11.30); fixed-price dinner menus 85F ($14.80) and 135F ($23.45). AE, MC, V. Mon–Sat noon–2pm and 7:30–11:45pm. Closed Aug. Métro: Chatelet. BISTRO.

Max himself is a friendly proprietor who is so proud of the high-quality home-cooked food served here that he will feign umbrage if you don't clean your plate. You will, though, once you've tasted his homemade soups, delicious *confit de canard,* and fruit tarts.

Le Coq-Héron. 3 rue Coq-Héron, 1er. ☎ **01-40-26-88-68.** Two-course lunch with glass of wine and coffee 68F ($11.80); à la carte 45–60F ($7.80–$10.45). MC, V. Mon–Fri noon–2pm; until 7:30pm on Friday. Métro: Louvre-Rivoli. FRENCH.

You'll really have to look for this gem. It's tucked away down a spiral staircase in front of the library de accueil and there is no sign to indicate that you're on the right track. Downstairs, you'll discover a restaurant with a couple of cavelike rooms serving some of the best budget food in Paris. Tables are well spaced, the service is good, and the pace leisurely. You might find such dishes as *confit cuisse de canard* (duck leg confit), osso bucco Milanese, or *crottin de Chavignol* (goat cheese).

Right Bank Dining

1er Arr.
A la Cloche des Halles ◆26
Au Pied de Cochon ◆28
Cafe Marly ◆30
Chez Max ◆34
Le Coq-Héron ◆27
La Fermette de Sud-Ouest ◆25
Le Gros Minet ◆33
Juveniles ◆23
Le Petit Machon ◆31
Le Poule au Pot ◆32
Restaurant du Palais-Royal ◆24
Le Rubis ◆20
Taverne Henri IV ◆36
La Tour de Montlhery ◆35

Universal Restaurant ◆29
Le Vieil Ecu ◆9

2e Arr.
A Priori The ◆22
Ma Normandie ◆21

3e Arr.
Le 404 ◆39
Au Bascou ◆40
Marais Plus ◆49

4e Arr.
Amadeo ◆47
Auberge de Jarente ◆52
Auberge de la
  Reine Blanche ◆54

Bistrot de Beaubourg ◆38
Bofinger ◆58
Cafe Beaubourg ◆42
La Chaise au Plafond ◆46
Jo Goldenberg ◆51
Chez Madame de . . . ◆53
Le Grizzli ◆37
Le Maraicher ◆55
Mariage Frères ◆44
Le Petit Gavroche ◆43
Restaurant Beautreillis ◆56
Sacha Finkelstein ◆50
Le Temps des Cerises ◆57
La Truffe ◆45
Le Trumilou ◆48

8e Arr.
La Boutique a Sandwiches
Cercle Ledoyen
Chicago Pizza Pie Factory
Feri's Restaurant a Emporter
Fouquet's
French-Rue de Berri
Laduree
Mamie Suzette

9e Arr.
L'Alsaco
Chartier
Chez Jean
L'Excuse Mogador
Restaurant Lou Cantou

10e Arr.
Brasserie Flo
Chez Michel
Julien

11e Arr.
Bistrot de Peintre
Chardenoux
Clown Bar
Le Maguier
Le Petit Keller

18e Arr.
Au Clair de la Lune
Au Virage Lepic
Chez Ginette

L'Eté en Pente Douce
Rendez-Vous des Chauffeurs
Tapas de Montmartre

Le Gros Minet. 1 rue des Prouvaires, 1er. ☎ **01-42-33-02-62.** Lunch menu 78F ($13.55); three-course fixed-price dinner menu 95F ($16.50). AE, DC, MC, V. Tues–Fri 11am–2pm and 7pm–midnight; Mon, Sat 7pm–midnight. Métro: Chatelet. FRENCH.

One of the most pleasing things about this very cozy and popular place is that even on a budget you get to eat some interesting food. The menu changes regularly but might offer red mullet with basil or a delicious blanquette de veau. Don't miss the chocolate mousse for dessert.

Le Petit Machon. 158 rue St-Honoré, 1er. ☎ **01-42-60-08-06.** Main courses 58–98F ($10–$17). Three-course fixed-price dinner menu 98F ($17) AE, V. Tues–Sun noon–2:45pm and 7–11pm. Métro: Louvre. FRENCH.

Sleek and modern with its polished wood bar and mirrored ceiling, this restaurant serves good Lyonnais cuisine. Start with the *saucisson chaud pommes à l'huile* (warm sausage with potatoes in oil) or salad with Roquefort and walnuts. Follow with a noisette d'agneau in an asparagus cream sauce, ham with lentils, or merlu (a white-fish similar to hake) in a delicate cream sauce.

Le Vieil Ecu. 16 Faubourg St-Honoré, 1er. ☎ **01-42-60-20-14.** Three-course lunch menus 65F ($11.30) and 85F ($14.80); à la carte main courses 69–99F ($12–$17.20). MC, V. Mon–Sat 11:30am–3pm and 6:30–11pm. Métro: Palais-Royal. SOUTHWEST.

Red-check tablecloths and fringed lampshades add color to this country-style restaurant. Classic dishes like confit of duck or a steak with shallot sauce are available.

WORTH A SPLURGE

Au Pied de Cochon. 6 rue Coquillière, 1er. ☎ **01-40-13-77-00.** Three-course menus 123F, 198F ($21.40, $34.45); main courses 85–132F ($14.80–$23) AE, DC, V. Open 24 hours. Métro: Châtelet-Les-Halles. FRENCH.

Once a fashionable hangout, this dramatic Parisian landmark boasts an excess of marble, murals, elaborate sconces, and chandeliers, and a surfeit of tourists. Still, it's fun, and you can have a fine plate of half a dozen oysters or onion soup to start. Follow with a grilled salmon or an entrecôte maître d'hôtel (in a rich red wine sauce) and finish with profiteroles. The à la carte menu features such classics as carre d'agneau and steak au poivre.

La Fermette de Sud-Ouest. 31 rue Coquillière, 1er. ☎ **01-42-36-73-55.** Grills 70–95F ($12.15–$16.50). MC, V. Mon–Sat noon–2:30pm and 7:30–10:30pm. Métro: Châtelet-Les-Halles. SOUTHWEST.

Stone and stucco walls, tile floor, and lace curtains hung across the French doors provide a typical French country look. Among the southwestern specialties are sausages from Toulouse, boudin paysan, and entrecôte perigourdin, as well as grilled steaks. To start, try the *terrine laperau a l'estragon* (a tarragon-flavored pâté).

La Poule au Pot. 9 rue Vauvilliers, 1er. ☎ **01-42-36-32-96.** Menu 160F ($27.80); main courses 100–150F ($17.40–26). AE, MC, V. Tues–Sun 7pm to dawn. Métro: Les Halles or Louvre-Rivoli. FRENCH.

The 160F menu will provide a choice of hot or cold *oeufs cocotte à la crème* (eggs baked in the oven with cream) and a chicken in the pot or poached eggs Basquaise (with onions, peppers, and tomatoes) or a breast of chicken en gêlée. Main dishes might be confit of duck, filet mignon au poivre, skate with capers (which is just great), or trout with champagne. Brass candlesticks grace the tables.

La Tour de Montlhéry. 5 rue des Prouvaires, 1er. ☎ **01-42-36-21-82.** Main courses 110–130F ($19.15–$22.60). MC, V. Mon–Fri 24 hours. Métro: Châtelet-Les-Halles. FRENCH.

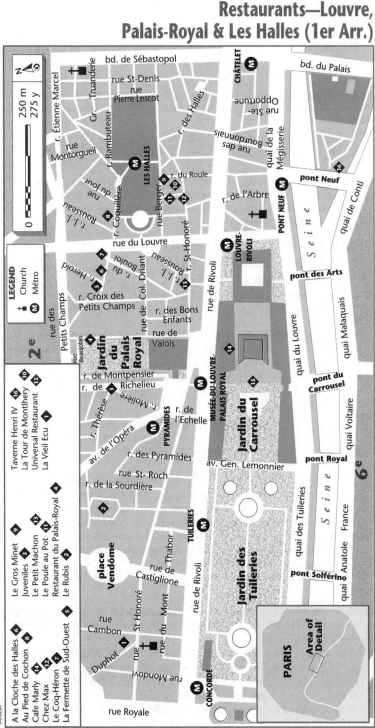

Restaurants—Louvre, Palais-Royal & Les Halles (1er Arr.)

250 m
275 y

bd. de Sébastopol
rue St-Denis
rue Pierre Lescot
Gr. Truanderie
r. Étienne Marcel
r. des Halles
rue Montorgueil
rue du Jour
r. Rambuteau
r. Coquillère
r. J.J. Rousseau
LES HALLES
r. du Roule
rue Berger
CHÂTELET
rue Ste-Opportune
rue des Bourdonnais
quai de la Mégisserie
pont Neuf
bd. du Palais
PONT NEUF
r. de l'Arbre
LOUVRE-RIVOLI
rue du Louvre
r. St-Honoré
rue de Rivoli
r. du Col. Driant
r. du Bouloi
r. Hérold
r. Croix des Petits Champs
r. des Bons Enfants
rue de Valois
rue des Petits Champs
2ᵉ
Jardin du Palais Royal
r. Beaujolais
r. de Montpensier
r. de Richelieu
r. de l'Echelle
r. Molière
r. Thérèse
av. de l'Opéra
r. des Pyramides
rue St-Roch
r. de la Sourdière
place Vendôme
rue de Castiglione
rue St Honoré
rue du Mont Thabor
rue de Rivoli
rue Cambon
rue Duphot
rue Mondovi
rue Royale
CONCORDE
TUILERIES
PYRAMIDES
MUSÉE-DU-LOUVRE-PALAIS ROYAL
Jardin du Carrousel
av. Gen. Lemonnier
Jardin des Tuileries
quai du Louvre
quai des Tuileries
quai Voltaire
quai Malaquais
quai de Conti
Seine
Seine
pont des Arts
pont du Carrousel
pont Royal
pont Solférino
quai Anatole France
6ᵉ

A la Cloche des Halles ❻
Au Pied de Cochon ❽
Cafe Marly ⓬
Chez Max ⓮
Le Coq-Héron ❼
La Fermette de Sud-Ouest ❺

Le Gros Minet ❾
Juveniles ❸
Le Petit Machon ⓭
Le Poule au Pot ⓫
Restaurant du Palais-Royal ❷
Le Rubis ❶

Taverne Henri IV ⓰
La Tour de Montlhery ❿
Universal Restaurant ⓯
La Vieil Ecu ❹

PARIS
Area of Detail

3-030SA

109

Beyond the zinc bar there's an attractive dining room with hams and sausages dangling from the beams. The less expensive items on the menu tend to be dishes like tripe Calvados or stuffed cabbage. Other typical dishes are grilled lamb chops and cod braised in Brouilly. It's Old Paris par excellence with a hearty atmosphere.

Restaurant du Palais-Royal. 43 rue Valois, 1er. ☎ **01-40-20-00-27.** Main courses 92F–146F ($16–$25.40). AE, MC. V. Mon–Fri 12:30–2:30pm and 7:30–10:30pm. Métro: Palais-Royal. FRENCH.

Tucked away in one of the most romantic locations in Paris—the elegant arcade that encircles the gardens inside the Palais-Royal—this charming restaurant serves excellent modern bistro cooking in very pleasant surroundings. Starters run to marinated leeks in a beet-juice vinaigrette or scallop salad, while main dishes vary with season but might be grilled tuna steak with a Basque relish or roast baby lamb. The desserts are delicious and the house red, served Lyonnais style in thick-bottomed bottles, is inexpensive and very good.

OPERA, BOURSE & GRANDS BOULEVARDS (2E, 9E & 10E ARRONDISSEMENTS)
MEALS FOR LESS THAN 85F ($15)

✪ **L'Alsaco.** 10 rue Condorcet, 9e. ☎ **01-45-26-44-31.** Three-course menu 79F ($13.75) lunch, 87F ($15.15) dinner. AE, V. Mon–Fri noon–2pm and 7:30–11pm; Sat 7:30–11pm. Métro: Anvers. ALSATIAN.

When the winter chill (which can last through spring) seeps into your bones, the best way to thaw out is to dig into a plate of steaming *choucroute* topped with sausage and cuts of ham. The sauerkraut served in the back room of this wine bar comes from the Alsatian village of Krautergersheim and is as aromatic as any you'll find in Paris. For only 46F ($8) you get a platter topped with three different sausages that goes well with a stein of Alsatian beer.

L'Excuse Mogador. 21 rue Joubert, 9e. ☎ **01-42-81-98-19.** Three-course lunch menu 75F ($13) and 95F ($16.50). Two-course menu of salad and dessert 65F ($11.30). Main courses 54–72F ($9.40–$12.50). No credit cards. Tues–Fri noon–2pm and 7–9pm; Mon noon–2pm. Métro: Trinité or Chausée-d-Antin. FRENCH.

So many restaurants crowd the area around the Grands Boulevards, but trying to find a decent meal at a good price is enough to ruin your appetite. This tiny bistro is jammed at lunch with local nine-to-fivers, relieved that their culinary quest is over. The menu includes specialties from several French regions as well as bistro standbys such as herring with warm potatoes, lentil salad, and grilled chicken breast topped with a light cream sauce. Bistro salads are often bland and monotonous but here you can try a salad made with *magret de canard* (sliced duck breast). There is an excellent selection of wines by the glass and the desserts are concocted on the premises.

✪ **Ma Normandie.** 11 rue Rameau, 2e. ☎ **01-42-96-87-17.** Menus 65F or 100F ($11.30 or $17.40). AE, EURO, MC, V. Mon–Sat 11:30am–2:30pm. Métro: Pyramides, 4 Septembre, or Bourse. FRENCH.

Located near the small square in front of the old Bibliothèque Nationale, Ma Normandie serves well-prepared food in homey surroundings. Cheerful waiters will greet you when you come in and show you to a table in the ground-floor dining room or upstairs. This is a good place to order such French staples as *terrine de saumon* (salmon pâté) and rump steak au poivre, as well as more elaborate dishes, and there's lots of delicious bread. The higher-priced fixed-price meal includes ¹/₂ liter of wine and coffee.

Restaurant Lou Cantou. 35 Cité d'Antin, 9e. ☎ **01-48-74-75-15.** Three-course menu, wine included, 59.50F ($10.35); plat du jour 41F ($7.15). No credit cards. Mon–Sat 11:30am–3pm. Métro: Chausée-d'Antin. FRENCH.

If you'd like to fuel up quickly, cheaply, and in pleasant surroundings, this homey bistro will do the job. Lace curtains, flowers, plants, and copper pots on the wall create an inviting space that attracts a middle-management crowd for lunch. The fixed-price menu includes a large choice of entrees and *plats*. None are culinary miracles, but they do provide a simple and satisfying meal. To find Cite d'Antin, look for the passage at 61 rue de Provence.

MEALS FOR LESS THAN 120F ($21)

Chartier. 7 rue du Faubourg-Montmartre, 9e. ☎ **01-47-70-86-29.** Three-course menu, wine included, 79F ($13.75); à la carte 30–45F ($6–$7.80). V. Daily 11:30am–3pm and 6–10pm. Métro: Rue-Montmartre. FRENCH.

At the turn of the century, Chartier was a "bouillon" or cantine for workers. Workers have been replaced by tourists from all parts of the globe who come more for the ambience than the food. The dark wood, mirrors, and hazy lighting in the spacious hall create a wonderful sense of intrigue that has been captured in several French films. The food is, as the French say, "correct"—nothing more, nothing less. There are about 100 items on the menu, including 16 main courses like poulet rôti, a variety of steaks and frites, and turkey in a cream sauce. Prices are low enough that a three-course repast is easy on the budget, even if you don't choose the fixed-price meal.

WORTH A SPLURGE

Brasserie Flo. 7 cour des Petites Ecuries, 10e. ☎ **01-47-70-13-59.** Three-course lunch menu 123F ($21.40), dinner menu 169F ($29.40); main courses 90–200F ($15.65–$34.80). AE, MC, V. Daily 7pm–2am. Métro: Château d'Eau. ALSATIAN.

Built in 1886, this is one of the city's oldest restaurants and it has a lovely turn-of-the-century ambience. People come for the prodigious sauerkraut, which will arrive accompanied by sausages, ham, and bacon. It's also well known for seafood, but that will certainly break the bank.

Chez Jean. 52 rue de Lamartine, 9e. ☎ **01-48-78-62-73.** Fixed-price menu 165F ($28.70). MC, V. Mon–Fri noon–2:30pm and 7:30–10:30pm. Closed Aug. Métro: Notre-Dame-de-Lorette. MODERN BISTRO.

Though the setting is a simple, crowded old-fashioned bistro, the food is of nearly haute cuisine quality. The daily menu features wonderful contemporary French dishes such as leeks with smoked salmon stuffed with salmon mousse to start and monkfish in lobster-cream sauce as a main course. The wine list offers several bargains, too, and you'll come away amazed to have eaten so well for so little money.

Chez Michel. 10 rue Belzunce, 10e. ☎ **01-44-53-06-20.** Fixed-price menu 160F ($27.80). MC, V. Tues–Sat noon–2pm and 7–11pm. Métro: Gare du Nord. BISTRO/BRETON.

Ever since it opened a 2 years ago, this bistro's been mobbed by a diverse crowd of Parisians coming for excellent and unusual food at a very fair price. Chef Thierry Breton is from Brittany and occasionally puts a few old-fashioned Breton dishes on his menu—look for his scallops with artichoke puree and *kig ha farz,* a sort of Breton pot-au-feu. Unusually, they serve good wines by the glass here, making it easier to keep the bill down.

Julien. 16 rue du Faubourg-St-Denis, 10e. ☎ **01-47-70-12-06.** Lunch menu 123F ($21.40); main courses 180–220F ($31.30–$38.25). Daily noon–3pm and 7pm–1:30am. Métro: Strasbourg-St-Denis. FRENCH.

The stunning art nouveau interior here is a national historic landmark. Start your meal with a classic smoked salmon with blinis and crème fraîche and follow with the cassoulet, the châteaubriand with a béarnaise sauce, or sole with sorrel sauce. Finish with the dark rich chocolate gâteau with a coffee crème anglaise.

BEAUBOURG, MARAIS & BASTILLE (3E, 4E & 11E ARRONDISSEMENTS)
MEALS FOR LESS THAN 85F ($15)

Amadeo. 19 rue François Miron, 4e. ☎ **01-48-87-01-02.** Three-course lunch menu 85F ($14.80), dinner menu 165F ($28.70), Tuesday dinner menu with aperitif 100F ($17.40). Mon–Fri noon–2:30pm and 8–11pm; Sat 7–11pm. MC, V. Métro: Hôtel-de-Ville. MODERN BISTRO.

The cuisine here is light, modern, full of surprises, and a delightful change from standard bistro fare. A marinated salmon appetizer is an unusual treat on a budget lunch menu, as are crisp wedges of onion tart topped with fried bacon bits. Also on the lunch menu is a fresh fish of the day in a delicate herbed sauce and an artfully confected fruit dessert. The more elaborate "gastronomic" menu offers such imaginative dishes as duck filet in a red fruit sauce. The classical music in the background and the tasteful decor soothe the nerves, and the wine list begins at a very reasonable 60F ($10.45) a bottle.

Bistrot de Beaubourg. 25 rue Quincampoix, 4e. ☎ **01-42-77-48-02.** Main courses 50–68F ($8.70–$11.80). MC, V. Daily noon–2am. Métro: Hôtel-de-Ville. BISTRO.

A lively young crowd fills this place, just a few steps away from the Centre Pompidou. The cooking is hearty, filling, and very reasonably priced. You can try dishes like *boeuf en daube* (braised beef), which comes with noodles, for 36F ($6.25), and wash it all down with a carafe of the house wine.

Chez Madame de . . . 5 rue de Sevigne, 4e. ☎ **01-42-74-75-90.** Three-course menus 67F ($11.65) or 93F ($16.15). No credit cards. Mon–Sat noon–2pm and 8–11:30pm. Métro: St-Paul. BISTRO.

This charming little place attracts an arty crowd of local regulars who come to feast on simple but appealing meals like *crudités* or assorted raw-vegetable salads, steak with frites, and fruit tart for dessert. If you want to come for lunch, get here early, since it fills up very quickly.

Le Petit Gavroche. 15 rue Ste-Croix-de-la-Bretonnerie, 4e. ☎ **01-48-87-74-26.** Lunch menu 45 ($7.80); three-course fixed-price menu 48F ($8.35). AE, DC, MC, V. Mon–Fri noon–3pm and 7–11:30pm, Sat 7–11:30pm. Métro: Hôtel-de-Ville. FRENCH.

This easygoing place is a fine spot to pop into for a sturdy feed. But get here early for lunch if you want a table, since it's very popular with a diverse crowd of friendly, funky locals. The food is better than average; try the steamed mussels with fries or goulash with noodles, followed by lemon tart.

Le Petit Keller. 13 rue Keller, 11e. ☎ **01-47-00-12-97.** Three-course fixed-price menu 70F ($12.15). MC, V. Mon–Sat noon–2:30pm and 7–11:30pm. Métro: Ledru-Rollin. FRENCH.

You won't be bowled over by the looks of this place when you arrive, but once you're settled in over a glass of their perfectly drinkable red wine—a small carafe of which comes with the 70F menu—you'll see why this place is so popular with trendy types from this hip part of town. The food's good, simple, and copious, running to dishes like sliced tomato salad, duck roasted with honey, and rice pudding.

Les Temps des Cerises. 31 rue de la Cerisaie, 4e. ☎ **01-42-72-08-63.** Reservations not accepted. Lunch menu 68F ($11.80). No credit cards. Mon–Fri 7:45am–8pm with lunch served 11:30am–2:30pm. Closed Aug. Métro: Bastille or Sully-Morland. FRENCH.

Restaurants—Beaubourg, Marais & Bastille (3e, 4e & 11e Arr.)

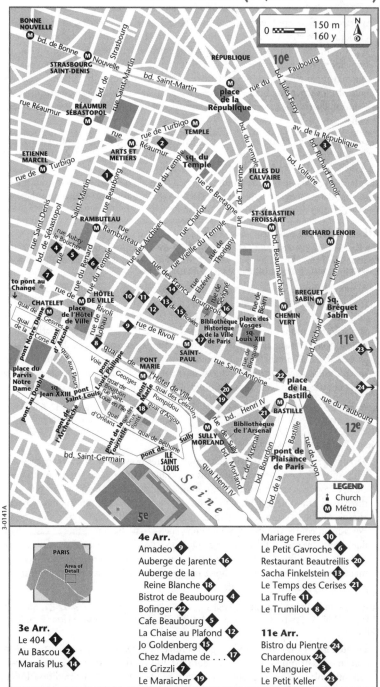

3e Arr.
Le 404 ①
Au Bascou ②
Marais Plus ⑭

4e Arr.
Amadeo ⑨
Auberge de Jarente ⑯
Auberge de la
  Reine Blanche ⑱
Bistrot de Beaubourg ④
Bofinger ㉒
Cafe Beaubourg ⑤
La Chaise au Plafond ⑫
Jo Goldenberg ⑮
Chez Madame de . . . ⑰
Le Grizzli ⑦
Le Maraicher ⑲

Mariage Freres ⑩
Le Petit Gavroche ⑥
Restaurant Beautreillis ⑳
Sacha Finkelstein ⑬
Le Temps des Cerises ㉑
La Truffe ⑪
Le Trumilou ⑧

11e Arr.
Bistro du Pientre ㉔
Chardenoux ㉔
Le Manguier ③
Le Petit Keller ㉓

113

This bistro is charged with history, for it's been in business since 1900 in an 18th-century building that once served as a convent. It's a classic French bar-bistro, with mosaic tile floor, pewter bar, and posters and other art covering the walls. Locals gather here to chat and hang out over a glass of wine or coffee. It's always packed at lunch, but it's a bargain and worth a little crowding. There's a choice of menus (which don't include a beverage) that might tempt you with anything from pâté and egg mayonnaise to start and paupiette of salmon with a citron-butter sauce or a steak with shallot sauce and braised endive to follow. The wines here can be expensive, but you can always select one of the blackboard wine specials or the inexpensive house wine.

Sacha Finkelstein. 27 rue des Rosiers, 4e. ☎ **01-42-72-78-91.** Most pastries 13F ($2.25) each, sandwiches 30–40F ($5.20–$7). No credit cards. Wed–Sun 10am–2pm and 3–7pm. Métro: St-Paul. CENTRAL EUROPEAN/JEWISH.

A famous pastry shop. The window is filled with all kinds of sweets—from brownies and date squares to apple strudel (105F/$18.25 a kilo) and strawberry charlotte. The deli also dishes out extralarge sandwiches.

MEALS FOR LESS THAN 120F ($21)

Au Bascou. 38 rue Réaumur, 3e. ☎ **01-42-72-69-25.** Lunch menu 90F ($15.65); main courses 75–115F ($13–$20). AE, MC, V. Mon–Fri noon–2:30pm and 8–10:30pm; Sat 8–10:30pm. Métro: Arts et Metiers. BASQUE/SOUTHWEST.

A popular and lively restaurant with excellent southwestern cooking, especially dishes from the Basque country, the corner of southwestern France on the Atlantic ocean and the Spanish border. Start with *piperade,* a delicious concoction of sautéed peppers and onions on salad leaves topped with ham; then try some superb seasonal fish or *agneau de lait des Pyrénées rôti* (roasted milk-fed lamb). Finish up with some gâteaux Basque, a cake made of ground almonds and jam, or a slice of the tangy sheep's milk cheese (*brebis*) produced in the region. To drink regionally as well, go with a bottle of Irouleguy, a smooth red.

Auberge de Jarente. 7 rue de Jarente, 4e. ☎ **01-42-77-49-35.** Appetizers 30–60F ($5.20–$10.45); main courses 60–85F ($10.45–$14.80); lunch menu 77F ($13.40); dinner menus 117F ($20.35), 132F ($23), 185F ($32.15). AE, MC, V. Tues–Sat noon–2:30pm and 7:30–10:30pm. Métro: Bastille or St-Paul. SOUTHWEST.

Serving specialties from the Basque region in southwestern France, where they cook with olive oil, tomatoes, and all kinds of peppers, Auberge de Jarente offers a nice change from the cream sauces that prevail elsewhere. You might opt for one of the three fixed-price menus (although if you choose carefully, you can still dine relatively cheaply off the à la carte menu), which might include a fish soup or frogs' legs to start. For a main course you can choose among such classic Basque dishes as cassoulet or duck confit, as well as the escalope de saumon a l'oseille (with a sorrel sauce) and the *cailles* (two quail) *à la façon du chef,* which is excellent. When you've finished your main course you'll be given a choice of cheese or salad. Don't skip dessert; try the gâteau Basque or the crème caramel.

Auberge de la Reine Blanche. 30 rue St-Louis-en-l'Ile, 4e. ☎ **01-46-33-07-87.** Menu 89F ($15.50). MC, V. Fri–Tues noon–midnight; Wed–Thurs 6pm–midnight. Métro: Pont-Marie. FRENCH.

Located in a 17th-century building, this restaurant has a very pleasant atmosphere. Tiny models of antique furnishings adorn the walls, and the tables are prettily set with salmon-pink napkins and tablecloths, with candles at night. The traditional menu offers coq au vin and duck à l'orange.

Chardenoux. 1 rue Jules-Valles, 11e. ☎ **01-43-71-49-52.** Main courses 85–140F ($14.80–$24.35). AE, MC, V. Mon–Fri noon–2pm and 8–10pm; Sat 8–10pm. Métro: Charonne. BISTRO.

Ask a Parisian for a list of his or her favorite bistros, and this small, charming place will invariably be mentioned. From the etched plate glass windows to the swirling stucco decorations on the walls and ceiling, the turn-of-the-century decor here is the very essence of old Paris. Service is friendly and English-speaking, too. A variety of French regional dishes appears on the menu—try the *oeufs en meurette*, a Burgundian dish of poached eggs in a sauce of red wine and bacon, and the *boeuf en daube*, braised beef as it's done in Provence. Desserts are homey and delicious, especially the fruit tarts and warm raspberries in cream sauce.

Jo Goldenberg. 7 rue des Rosiers, 4e. ☎ **01-48-87-20-16.** 70–80F ($12.15–$13.90). AE, DC, MC, V. Daily noon–1am. Métro: St-Paul. JEWISH/CENTRAL EUROPEAN.

In the heart of the Jewish Marais, this restaurant was bombed in 1982 and has been a place of pilgrimage ever since. In the long, narrow room you can secure good if somewhat pricey Eastern European fare—poulet paprika, goulash, stuffed pepper with either meat or rice, lamb shish kebab, and Wiener schnitzel. Gypsy musicians begin playing around 9pm.

La Truffe. 31 rue Vieille-du-Temple, 4e. ☎ **01-42-71-08-39.** Lunch menu 59F ($10.25); Plat du jour 85F ($14.80). MC, V. Daily noon–3pm and 6:30–11pm. Métro: Hôtel-de-Ville. VEGETARIAN.

Though vegetarians are often up against it in a country as carnivorous as France, this pleasant new place on one of the liveliest streets in the Marais offers delicious dishes, including their specialty of wild mushrooms served with brown rice and beans. The setting's attractive, too, and the dining room is totally nonsmoking.

Le 404. 69 rue des Gravilliers, 3e. ☎ **01-42-74-57-81.** Lunch menu 89F ($15.50); main dishes 60–120F ($10.45–$20.85). AE, DC, MC, V. Mon–Sat noon–3pm and 8–midnight; Sun noon–4pm. Métro: Arts et Métiers. NORTH AFRICAN.

It would be hard to find better *couscous* than the version served in this restaurant, owned by the popular French comedian Smain. The semolina is rolled by hand, making the pasta unusually light and fluffy. The steaming broth has a hint of sweet spices that enhances the flavor of the fresh vegetables. Portions are enormous; my two-course lunch filled me up for 1½ days. The wood-screened windows, dim lighting, and soft North African music make you feel as though you've entered a harem.

Le Manguier. 67 av. Parmentier, 11e. ☎ **01-48-07-03-27.** Appetizers 25–35F ($4.35–$6); main courses 65–88F ($11.30–$15.30). AE, CB, EURO, MC, V. Daily 11am–3pm and 7pm–2am. Métro: Parmentier. AFRICAN/SENEGALESE.

With a huge fish net hanging from a blue ceiling, Le Manguier is a wonderful, lively restaurant specializing in West African cuisine. At African restaurants, you don't just eat; you stay a long time enjoying the music and the festive atmosphere. The cocktails, such as the potent Le Dakar with rum and spices, are delicious. Not all that is available is listed on the menu, so ask your waiter for suggestions. Fish dishes, like the *requin fumé* (smoked shark), are very good.

Le Trumilou. 84 quai de l'Hôtel de Ville, 4e. ☎ **01-42-77-63-98.** Menus 65F and 80F ($11.30 and $13.90); main dishes 55–102F ($9.55–$17.75). MC, V. Daily noon–3pm and 7–11pm. Métro: Pont-Marie. AUVERGNE.

This typical bistro, with its leatherette banquettes and copper pots, serves traditional dishes like fillet de boeuf au poivre, steak and fries, and some specialty dishes from the Auvergne like stuffed cabbage or *canard aux pruneaux* (duck with prunes). The 65F ($11.30) menu might offer pâté or crudités followed by mutton stew, while the

80F ($13.90) menu might supply hors d'oeuvres followed by roast pork or chicken Provençal.

Restaurant Beautreillis. 18 rue Beautreillis, 4e. ☎ **01-42-72-36-04.** Lunch menu 65F ($11.30); main dishes 60–90F ($10.45–$15.65). AE, MC, V. Daily noon–11pm. Métro: Bastille. HUNGARIAN/CENTRAL EUROPEAN.

Fans of Jim Morrison will want to visit this restaurant, which contains much memorabilia. The food is almost incidental at this small cozy restaurant serving Hungarian cuisine—goulash, shashlik, cevapicci, and more.

WORTH A SPLURGE

Bofinger. 5–7 rue de la Bastille, 4e. ☎ **01-42-72-87-82.** Three-course menu including $^1/_2$ bottle of wine, 169F ($29.40). AE, MC, V. Mon–Fri noon–3pm and 6:30pm–1am, Sat–Sun noon–1am. Métro: Bastille. ALSATIAN.

Bofinger opened in 1864 as a brasserie specializing in the cuisine of France's German-influenced Alsace region, and it is now one of the best-loved French restaurants in the city. Its belle epoque decor—dark wood, gleaming brass, bright lights, glass ceiling, and waiters with long white aprons—will transport you back to the 19th century. The menu features many Alsatian specialties such as *choucroute* (sauerkraut), and is also famous for oysters and foie gras. And the prices are actually quite moderate for Paris.

Le Grizzli. 7 rue St-Martin, 4e. ☎ **01-48-87-77-56.** Lunch menu 115F ($20); dinner menu 155F ($27); main dishes 69–98F ($12–$17). AE, MC, V. Tues–Sat 12:30–2:30pm and 7:30–11pm; Mon 7:30–11pm. Métro: Châtelet-les-Halles. BISTRO.

On the dinner fixed-price menu you might find a choice of cold ratatouille with poached egg, a duck terrine, or hot sausage with pistachio to start. For the main course, the half dozen selections might include a *lapin aux raisins sec* (rabbit with raisins), a fricassee of chicken in cider, or a *daube de canard* (a richly flavored stew of duck). Cheeses (try the Saint Nectaire) and such desserts as nougat glace à la pistache or tarte au chocolat noir (made with rich dark chocolate) might close the meal. White lace curtains, mirrors, and candles create a romantic atmosphere.

✪ **Le Maraicher.** 5 rue Beautreillis, 4e. ☎ **01-42-71-42-49.** Lunch menu 100F ($17.40); main dishes 87–115F ($15.15–$20). MC, V. Tues–Sat noon–2:15pm and 8–11pm; Mon 8–11pm. Métro: Sully-Morland. FRENCH.

This atmospheric spot has stone and stucco walls, beamed ceilings, and a fireplace at the back of the room. You might start with a carpaccio of salmon and follow with the fish of the day or a ragout of beef braised in cassis.

CHAMPS ELYSÉES & ENVIRONS (8E ARRONDISSEMENT)
MEALS FOR LESS THAN 85F ($15)

Feri's Restaurant à Emporter. 8 rue de Ponthieu, 8e. ☎ **01-42-56-10-56.** Main courses 29–40F ($5–$7); less for salads and sandwiches. No credit cards. Daily 8am–6am. Métro: Franklin-D-Roosevelt. DELI.

Feri's is a little storefront deli and takeout that serves good food at fair prices. After 11am a line begins to form for lunch pickup, and it stays busy until after supper. Main courses might be roast chicken, *pot-au-feu* (a hearty stew), or spaghetti. You can drop in anytime for croissants, *pain au chocolat* (croissant with chocolate filling), and other snacks; from dinnertime right through until 6am they serve fresh pizzas.

✪ **La Boutique à Sandwiches.** 12 rue du Colisée, 8e. ☎ **01-43-59-56-69.** Sandwiches and light meals 20–70F ($3.45–$12.15). V. Mon–Sat noon–12:30am. Métro: St-Philippe-du-Roule or Franklin-D-Roosevelt. FRENCH/LIGHT MEALS.

In case you want to see the world.

At American Express, we're here to make your journey a
smooth one. So we have over 1,700 travel service locations in
over 120 countries ready to help. What else would you expect
from the world's largest travel agency?

do more

AMERICAN
EXPRESS

Travel

http://www.americanexpress.com/travel

In case you want to be welcomed there.

We're here to see that you're always welcomed at establishments everywhere. That's why millions of people carry the American Express® Card – for peace of mind, confidence, and security, around the world or just around the corner.

do more

AMERICAN EXPRESS

Cards

In case you're running low.

We're here to help with more than 118,000 Express Cash locations around the world. In order to enroll, just call American Express before you start your vacation.

do more

AMERICAN
EXPRESS

Express
Cash

And just in case.

We're here with American Express® Travelers Cheques and Cheques *for Two*.® They're the safest way to carry money on your vacation and the surest way to get a refund, practically anywhere, anytime.

Another way we help you...

do more

AMERICAN EXPRESS

Travelers Cheques

Restaurants—Champs Elysées & Environs (8e Arr.)

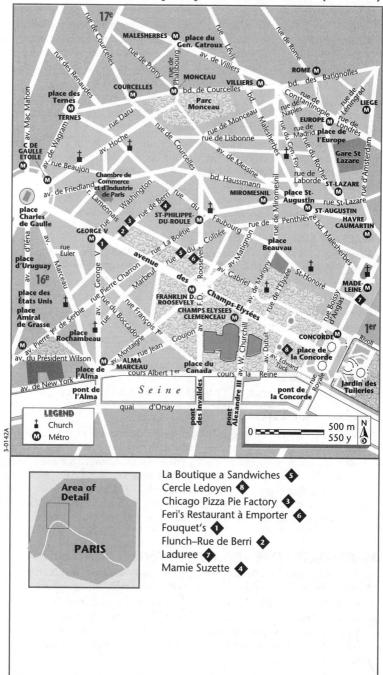

LEGEND
✝ Church
Ⓜ Métro

0 ━━━ 500 m
550 y

3-0142A

Area of Detail

PARIS

La Boutique a Sandwiches ◆5
Cercle Ledoyen ◆8
Chicago Pizza Pie Factory ◆3
Feri's Restaurant à Emporter ◆6
Fouquet's ◆1
Flunch–Rue de Berri ◆2
Laduree ◆7
Mamie Suzette ◆4

The stools are inviting, the owners are friendly, and on the counter you'll find ketchup and Tabasco sauce. La Boutique à Sandwiches is only one block from the Champs-Elysées, and it's a much better choice than the fast-food palaces littering that avenue. The daily specials are excellent. The *crêpe fourrée à l'indienne*, a delicious crêpe with ham, cheese, rice, mushrooms, and other vegetables (served on Mondays), costs 41F ($7.15). The onion soup, for 30F ($5.20), is very good as well.

Mamie Suzette. 45 rue de Berri, 8e. ☎ **01-45-62-43-64.** Two-course crepe meal, cider included, 45F ($7.80). EURO, MC, V. Mon–Sat 11:30am–3pm and 6:30–10pm. Métro: St-Philippe-du-Roule or Georges-V. BRETON/CREPES.

Mamie Suzette is an attractive little place with mesh curtains, lots of wood, and paintings on the wall. Like A la Bonne Crêpe on the Left Bank, this is a Breton crepe shop. The main course is usually a crepe with meat, seafood, or vegetable filling, garnished with portions of salad or *crudités* (sliced or grated raw vegetables), followed by a sweet dessert crepe, all washed down with a bowl of cider. By the way, *crêpes de froment* are wheat-flour crepes; *galettes de sarrasin* are buckwheat griddlecakes.

Meals for Less than 120F ($21)

Chicago Pizza Pie Factory. 5 rue de Berri, 8e. ☎ **01-45-62-50-23.** Depending on pizza size and toppings, 84–195F ($14.60–$33.90). AE, V. Daily 11:45am–1am. Métro: Georges-V. PIZZA.

If you're a little homesick, this restaurant, decorated with Chicago memorabilia, will take you home and drive the blues away—at least for the length of your meal. Here you can get deep-dish pizzas dripping with mozzarella cheese and tomato sauce and whatever topping you desire. If there are two of you and you can't decide on one combination, you can get individual pizzas. Better to arrive early in the evening, as it becomes crowded later.

Worth a Splurge

Cercle Ledoyen. 1 av. Dutuit, 8e. ☎ **01-53-05-10-02.** Main courses 100–110F ($17.40–$19.15). AE, DC, MC, V. Mon–Sat noon–2:30pm and 7:30–10:30pm. Métro: Champs-Elysées Clemenceau. NORTHERN FRENCH.

Chef Ghislaine Arabian, originally from the northern French city of Lille, is the most successful female chef in Paris and a really brilliant cook. Though her main restaurant, Ledoyen, is quite expensive, this very pleasant annex is a wonderful opportunity to sample her cooking at reasonable prices. The menu varies, but she does dishes like grilled swordfish with fennel and endives and *blanquette de veau* (veal in lemon-cream sauce). Desserts are wonderful, too, such as a raspberry and rhubarb tart. Though a meal for two here will run about $80, this place is well worth the splurge.

MONTMARTRE (18E ARRONDISSEMENT)

Au Clair de la Lune. 9 rue Poulbot, 18e. ☎ **01-42-58-97-03.** Menu 165F ($28.70). Tues–Sat noon–2:30pm; Mon–Sat 7–10:30pm. Métro: Abbesses. FRENCH.

Delve into your wallet for this atmospheric place, and start with pheasant terrine or *mackerel au muscadet* and follow with duck in a raspberry sauce, salmon in a champagne sauce, or a fricassee of chicken flavored with Indian spices. Finish with a chocolate or raspberry charlotte or the profiteroles. All this for 165F ($28.70).

Au Rendez-Vous des Chauffeurs. 11 rue des Portes-Blanches, 18e. ☎ **01-42-64-04-17.** Three-course fixed-price menu including a drink 63F ($11). MC, V. Mon, Tues, Thurs, Fri noon–2:30pm and 7–10:30pm; Sat, Sun noon–3pm and 7–10:30pm. Closed Aug. Métro: Marcardet-Poissonniers. FRENCH.

Cheap family-style restaurants are a dying breed in Paris, which is one reason this friendly place with its blue-checked tablecloths is so popular with locals. The 63F menu offers excellent value at noon and in the evening if you arrive before 8:30pm; afterwards, you'll have to order à la carte. The kitchen turns out solid basics like a delicious country terrine to start, followed by roast chicken or lamb stew and old-fashioned desserts like apricot tart. Although a little out of the way, this would be a good stop if you're hitting the flea market at Clignancourt.

Au Virage Lepic. 61 rue Lepic, 18e. ☎ **01-42-52-46-79.** Plats 65F ($11.30); main courses 55–68F ($9.55–$11.80). No credit cards. Daily 6:30pm–2am. Métro: Blanche. BISTRO.

This tiny place serves good traditional dishes like steak au poivre and roast chicken. There's also a variety of cheeses and boudins available.

Chez Ginette. 101 rue Caulaincourt, 18e. ☎ **01-46-06-01-49.** Lunch menu, including wine, 65F ($11.30); daily specials 62F ($10.80); main dishes 58–65F ($10–$11.30). V. Mon–Sat noon–3pm and 6:45–11pm. Métro: Lamarck Caulaincourt. FRENCH.

A typical French bistro. You might find such daily specials as *gigot d'agneau flageolets* (leg of lamb with white beans) or a *côte de veau normande* (veal with apples). Couscous is always available. The main courses might include *bavette échalotte* (beef in a shallot sauce) or *foie Provençale* (liver in a Provençale style with tomatoes). At night a pianist or guitarist adds to the seductive atmosphere.

Tapas de Montmartre. 6 rue des Abbesses, 18e. ☎ **01-42-55-36-36.** Tapas 12–20F ($2.40–$3.45); plats 55–60F ($9.55–$10.45) MC, V. Tues–Sun noon–2pm and 7pm–1:30am. Métro: Abbesses. TAPAS.

At this Spanish-inspired restaurant, where guitars wait to be taken down from the walls and plucked, you'll find a range of dishes such as red- and green-pepper salad, chorizo with peppers, chicken with tomato and peppers, and best of all, garlic-flavored prawns. The Spanish omelet and empanadas are also excellent.

5 Left Bank

LATIN QUARTER (5E ARRONDISSEMENT)
MEALS FOR LESS THAN 85F ($15)

Café Mouffetard. 116 rue Mouffetard, 5e. ☎ **01-43-31-42-50.** Eggs/sandwiches 18–23F ($3.15–$4); main dishes 42–48F ($7.30–$8.35). No credit cards. Tues–Sat 7am–9pm, Sun 7am–4pm. Métro: Censier-Daubenton. CAFE.

This is a small bustling cafe in the middle of the famous food market. In the early morning, market vendors and assorted others stop in for breakfast. Here you can secure an assiette of smoked salmon, as well as eggs and omelettes and such dishes as roast chicken or ham with braised endives.

La Petite Hostellerie. 35 rue de la Harpe, 5e. ☎ **01-43-54-47-12.** Three-course menu 59F ($10.25) and 89F ($15.50); wine 16F ($2.80). AE, DC, MC, V. Tues–Sat noon–2pm; Mon–Sat 6:30–10:30pm. Métro: St-Michel or Cluny-Sorbonne. FRENCH.

This little place, with its tables and chairs pretty tightly packed in the single dining room, is a typical Latin Quarter bistro. People come here for the small-restaurant ambience and decor, decent French country cooking, polite service, and excellent prices. Upstairs, there's a larger dining room with attractive boiserie. The lower-priced fixed-price menu might offer such staple country dishes as poulet roti, boeuf bourguignon, grilled brochette, or steak au poivre. And the location is great. (Rue de la Harpe is a side street running north of boulevard St-Germain just east of boulevard St-Michel.)

Left Bank Dining

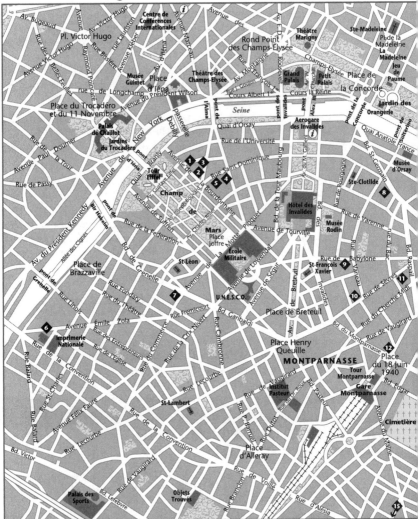

5e Arr.

L'Apostrophe 53
Aux Trois Bourriques 39
Brasserie Balzar 50
Café Mouffetard 56
Campagne et Provence 42
Chantairelle 54
Chez Pento 51
Chez Toutonne 40
La Chope 55
La Friterie 37
Le Grenier de Notre-Dame 38

Le Petit Hostellerie 34
Restaurant Perraudin 52
Salon de Thé la
   Mosquée de Paris 57
Tea Caddy 35
Le Ver-Meer Café 36
Vivario 41

6e Arr.

A la Bonne Crêpe 28
Aux Charpentiers 23
Au Petit Prince 44

Aux Vieux Casque 16
Les Banquettes Rouges 45
La Bastide Odéon 46
Boullion Racine 49
Café Cluny 43
Cafe des Deux Magots 21
Cafe de Flore 20
Chez Maître Paul 47
Cosi 25
A la Cour de Rohan 31
La Datcha 32
La Dinette 30

L'Ecluse-Saint-Michel ⟨33⟩
L'Epi Dupin ⟨11⟩
Le Muniche ⟨19⟩
La Palette ⟨17⟩
Le Petit St-Benoît ⟨18⟩
Le Petit Vatel ⟨27⟩
Le Polidor ⟨48⟩
Restaurant des Beaux Arts ⟨24⟩
Restaurant Orestias ⟨29⟩
Vagenende ⟨26⟩

7e Arr.
Au Bon Acceuil ⟨1⟩
Au Pied de Fouet ⟨9⟩
Chez Germaine ⟨10⟩
Chez Lucie ⟨3⟩
Le Croque Au Sel ⟨5⟩
La Fontaine de Mars ⟨4⟩
La Petite Chaise ⟨22⟩
Le Rivaldiere ⟨8⟩
Le Sancerre ⟨2⟩

14e Arr.
Au Rendez-Vous
  des Cammioneurs ⟨15⟩
Le Bistrot du Dome ⟨14⟩
Bistro de la Gare ⟨12⟩
La Coupole ⟨13⟩

15e Arr.
Le Café du Commerce ⟨7⟩
Le Petit Plat ⟨6⟩

121

L'Apostrophe. 34 rue de la Montagne-Ste-Geneviève, 5e. ☎ **01-43-54-10-93.** Two-course menu 65F ($11.30) until 8pm; three-course 85F ($14.80). MC, V. Daily 6pm–2am. Métro: Maubert-Mutualité. FRENCH.

L'Apostrophe is a romantic spot with low ceilings, candlelight, and red-check tablecloths. On the 65F ($11.30) menu there might be steak pizzaiola, a mixed brochette, and poulet gascoyne, while the more expensive menu might feature *pavé au roquefort* (beef with Roquefort butter), steak au poivre vert, or simply grilled steak with herbs.

Le Ver-Meer Café. 19 quai de Montebello, 5e. ☎ **01-40-46-94-50.** Main courses 50–70F ($8.70–$12.15). AE, MC, V. Métro: St-Michel. DUTCH-FRENCH.

A rare and welcome addition to the roster of budget restaurants in Paris, this place is friendly, tidy, and English-speaking, thanks to its Dutch staff. They make a real effort with the food here, such as an excellent starter of mixed green salad with imported Dutch cold cuts. Follow this with very tasty lamb chops served with creamed potatoes and green beans or boeuf bourguignon. The splendid view of Notre-Dame costs nothing.

MEALS FOR LESS THAN 120F ($21)

Aux Trois Bourriques. 5 rue des Grands Degrés, 5e. ☎ **01-43-54-61-72.** Main dishes 65–90F ($11.30–$15.65); menus 125F, 160F ($21.75, $27.80). V. Tues–Sat noon–2:30 and 7–10pm; Sun 7–10pm. Métro: St-Michel. FRENCH/REGIONAL NORMANDY.

With its red tablecloths, stone walls, and beamed ceilings, this is a very appealing restaurant and it also serves some fine Normandy-inspired food. For example, on the lower-priced menu you might find pintade à la Normande (flavored with apples or Calvados) along with a beef en daube (rich flavorful stew), while on the 160F ($27.80) menu there might be tournedos à la Normande as well as au poivre. Banana flambé or crepe flambé makes a fine finish to any meal.

Chez Pento. 9 rue Cujas, 5e. ☎ **01-43-26-81-54.** Lunch menu 83F ($14.45); two-course fixed-price dinner menu 104F ($18). AE, MC, V. Mon–Fri noon–2:30pm and 7–11pm; Sat, 7–11pm. Métro: Cluny-Sorbonne. BISTRO.

A funky Latin Quarter bistro that's enormously popular as much for its very reasonable prices as for the gastronomic accomplishments of the kitchen. The food's generally good, though, and if you don't mind paying a supplement for both, the escargots or the house foie gras are both delicious. The best bet here is the confit de canard, which teams nicely with the house Bordeaux.

La Friterie. 77 rue Galande, 5e. ☎ **01-43-25-95-93.** Main course 55–60F ($9.55–$10.45). No credit cards. Daily noon–midnight in summer; noon–9pm Thurs–Tues in winter. Métro: St-Michel. BISTRO.

A tiny place with a couple of tables outside, where you can savor great frites along with steak or a pot au feu or beef bourguignon. Good view of Notre-Dame.

Le Grenier de Notre-Dame. 18 rue de la Bûcherie, 5e. ☎ **01-43-29-98-29.** Three-course menu 75F ($13); three-course menu with coffee 105F ($18.25); main courses 45–125F ($7.80–$21.75). AE, DC, MC, V. Wed–Mon noon–2:30pm and 7–11:30pm. Métro: Maubert-Mutualité. VEGETARIAN.

Located near Notre-Dame and the boulevard St-Michel, Le Grenier is a well-established vegetarian restaurant. There are green tablecloths, fresh flowers, and small lamps on every table, and the food is outstanding. Especially recommended is the *cassoulet végétarien*, with white beans, onions, tomatoes, and soy sausage; the couscous and the cauliflower au gratin are also delicious. And don't forget the desserts, such as tarte de tofu, for which Le Grenier has a well-deserved reputation. The wine list here even includes a variety of organic wines.

Restaurants—
Latin Quarter & St-Germain (5e & 6e Arr.)

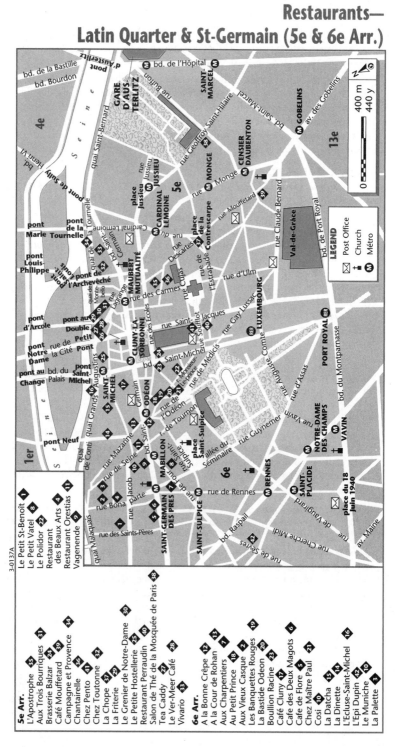

3-0137A

LEGEND
⊠ Post Office
✝ ➕ Church
Ⓜ Métro

400 m
440 y

5e Arr.
Le Petit St-Benoît ◆ 1
Le Petit Vatel ◆ 8
Le Polidor ◆ 22
Restaurant
  des Beaux Arts ◆ 4
Restaurant Orestias ◆ 11
Vagenende ◆ 9

5e Arr.
L'Apostrophe ◆ 35
Aux Trois Bourriques ◆ 31
Brasserie Balzar ◆ 24
Café Mouffetard ◆ 39
Campagne et Provence ◆ 34
Chantairelle ◆ 37
Chez Pento ◆ 36
Chez Toutonne ◆ 32
La Chope ◆ 30
La Friterie ◆ 29
Le Grenier de Notre-Dame ◆ 26
Le Petite Hostellerie ◆ 25
Restaurant Perraudin ◆ 40
Salon de Thé de la Mosquée de Paris ◆ 38
Tea Caddy ◆ 27
Le Ver-Meer Café ◆ 28
Vivario ◆ 33

6e Arr.
A la Bonne Crêpe ◆ 42
A la Cour de Rohan ◆ 13
Aux Charpentiers ◆ 7
Au Petit Prince ◆ 18
Aux Vieux Casque ◆ 2
Les Banquettes Rouges ◆ 19
La Bastide Odeon ◆ 20
Boullion Racine ◆ 23
Café Cluny ◆ 17
Café des Deux Magots ◆ 6
Cafe de Flore ◆ 5
Chez Maître Paul ◆ 21
Cosi ◆ 3
La Datcha ◆ 15
La Dinette ◆ 14
L'Ecluse-Saint-Michel ◆ 12
L'Epi Dupin ◆ 42
Le Muniche ◆ 10
La Palette ◆ 3

123

○ **Restaurant Perraudin.** 157 rue St-Jacques, 5e. ☎ **01-46-33-15-75.** Plats 59F ($10.25); three-course lunch 63F ($11); à la carte 120F ($20.85). No credit cards. Tues–Fri noon–2:15pm; Mon–Sat 7:30–10:15pm. Métro: Luxembourg. BISTRO.

This ever-popular restaurant with its red-check tablecloths and lace lampshades has been the haunt of students, professors, and editors for years. Classic dishes like salmon with a sorrel sauce, duck confit, steak au poivre vert, and gigot d'agneau with a gratin Dauphinois are served. Daily specials like guinea fowl stew are also available. To start, there's an artichoke heart and onion tart, and to follow there's a variety of ice creams and tarts such as apple or raspberry. Go early or you'll have to wait.

WORTH A SPLURGE

Brasserie Balzar. 49 rue des Ecoles, 5e. ☎ **01-43-54-13-67.** Main courses 73–119F ($12.70–$20.70). AE, DC, MC, V. Daily 8am–1am. Métro: Cluny-Sorbonne. BISTRO.

Located right in the heart of the Latin Quarter, Brasserie Balzar is a lively, fashionable place with very good food. It has hosted many of France's most famous intellectuals, including the likes of Jean-Paul Sartre, and it's always full, even in off hours. People stop here for coffee and pastry between lunch and dinner, and drop in for drinks after dinner. The wood tables are close together, but not uncomfortably so, and the staff is friendly and perfectly willing to accommodate your every need (including explaining the menu in English as best they can). Many of the regulars go for the *poulet rôti avec frites* (roast chicken with french fries) or the *choucroute garni*, but you can also get steak au poivre and any number of fresh fish dishes. There's always a soup of the day as well. For dessert, try the *tarte au citron* (lemon tart) or the *gâteau au chocolate amère* (bittersweet chocolate cake).

○ **Campagne et Provence.** 25 quai de la Tournelle, 5e. ☎ **01-43-54-05-17.** Lunch menu 120F ($20.85); main dishes 115F ($20). MC, V. Mon–Sat noon–2pm; Mon–Thurs 8–11pm, Fri–Sat 8pm–1am. Métro: Maubert-Mutualité. PROVENÇAL.

Sconce lighting and blue rush-seated chairs at white-clothed tables make for an intimate Provençal atmosphere at the Campagne et Provence, and the food is well prepared and innovative. Start with a mussel soup or grilled peppers with anchovies. For main courses you might find cod in a sauce flavored with thyme, rabbit stuffed with hazelnuts and almonds, or a bouillabaisse of red snapper with fennel. For dessert, try the pears in plum sauce with spiced bread.

Chantairelle. 17 rue Laplace, 5e. ☎ **01-46-33-18-59.** Lunch menus 75F and 89F ($13 and $15.50); main courses 67–99F ($11.65–$17.20). MC, V. Sun–Fri 11:30am–2pm and 7–10:30pm; Sat 7–10:30pm. Métro: Maubert-Mutualité. AUVERGNAT.

This charming little place offers you a quick visit to the Auvergne, the rugged south-central region of France. An old church door and a tiny fountain have been incorporated into the decor, a soundtrack plays such indigenous sounds as bird songs and church bells, and there are even tiny bottles of essential oils made from native plants so you can administer some aromatherapy while waiting for your food to arrive. This is sturdy and delicious peasant food, and portions are enormous. Order a first-course, maybe some of their famous charcuterie, only if you're ravenous, as main courses like the wonderful stuffed cabbage or *potee* (a tureen filled with pork, cabbage, potatoes, turnips, and leeks in broth) are substantial. The best Auvergnat wine is the Chateaugay, a fine fruity red.

○ **Chez Toutoune.** 5 rue de Pontoise, 5e. ☎ **01-43-26-56-81.** Lunch menu 118F ($20.50); lunch and dinner menu 168F ($29.20) except Sun. AE, V. Lunch Tues–Sun noon–2:30pm; Dinner daily 7:45–10:45pm. Métro: Maubert-Mutualité. PROVENÇAL.

Red walls, floral drapes, and tables set with bright cloths and place mats create a warm atmosphere for some excellent Provençal food. The more expensive menu contains four courses, beginning with a huge tureen of soup. Eat a lot of it because the courses that follow are relatively light. The entrees include a tasty *saumon juste marine aux herbes fine* (salmon marinated in fine herbs) and a mild eggplant purée topped with ham and a poached egg. Follow with one of the five or six main courses of meat or fish, imaginatively prepared with the savory herbs of Provence. Close with the chocolate tart with pistachio sauce or the crème brûlée flavored with a hint of orange.

Vivario. 6 rue Cochin, 5e. ☎ **01-43-25-08-19.** Main dishes 55–125F ($9.55–$21.75). AE, V. Tues–Fri noon–2pm; Mon–Sat 7–10pm. Métro: Maubert-Mutualité. CORSICAN.

To start, opt for the moules au Sicilienne, bathed in a flavorsome tomato sauce, or the saucisson sec, and follow with one of the goat dishes like *cabri rôti à la Corse* (roast goat) or the calamari in a spicy sauce. Finish with oranges poached in syrup.

ST-GERMAIN & LATIN QUARTER (6E ARRONDISSEMENT)
MEALS FOR LESS THAN 85F ($15)

A la Bonne Crêpe. 11 rue Grégoire-de-Tours, 6e. ☎ **01-43-54-60-74.** Three-course lunch with crepe as main course 50F ($8.70); crepes à la carte 14–50F ($2.30–$8.70); cider 22F ($3.80). Mon–Sat 12–3pm and 7–11pm. No credit cards. Métro: Odéon. BRETON/CREPES.

Brittany is known for its crepes and its ciders, which make a fine and typically French meal. Savory crepes filled with cheese, meat, seafood, or other hearty ingredients make the main course, and sweet crepes filled with jam or chocolate are a wonderful dessert. The cider is hard, Brittany's answer to beer. Rue Grégoire-de-Tours is a tiny street that begins between nos. 140 and 142 boulevard St-Germain and runs north toward the Seine.

Cosi. 54 rue de Seine, 6e. ☎ **01-46-33-35-36.** Sandwiches 32–48F ($5.55–$8.35). Daily noon–midnight. No credit cards. Métro: Odéon. SANDWICHES.

The New Zealand owner of Cosi is passionate about opera and Italian bread. While you decide whether to stuff your sandwich with baked salmon, roasted eggplant, smothered onions, roast beef, or mozzarella and tomatoes, *focaccia*-style bread is baking in the oven and opera melodies drift through the two-story shop. With moist, chewy bread and tasty fillings the sandwiches make a fine light meal. Add soup, a glass of wine, and a slice of the sinful chocolate cake and you'll have a small but perfect feast. You can take your food out or eat upstairs surrounded by photos of opera singers.

La Datcha. 56 rue St-Andrés-des-Arts, 6e. ☎ **01-46-23-29-25.** Main courses 32–115F ($5.55–$20). No credit cards. Daily noon–midnight. Métro: Odéon or St-Michel. RUSSIAN.

Russian dolls catch your eye at the front of this very Russian restaurant. You'll dine at wooden tables on such dishes as borscht, pirogi, or herring. One of the most reasonably priced Russian restaurants in the city.

La Dinette. 59 rue Dauphine, 6e. ☎ **01-43-54-35-15.** Three-course meal 45F ($7.80), drinks 12–16F ($2–$2.80). No credit cards. Daily 10:30am–11pm. Métro: Odéon. CHINESE.

La Dinette is a very attractive Chinese takeout that also has tables. The menu du jour offers soup, pâté, or salad, then shrimp dumplings or a main dish made with beef, pork, or chicken, plus Cantonese rice—all for one low price.

Le Petit Vatel. 5 rue Lobineau, 6e. ☎ **01-43-54-28-49.** Menu 61F ($10.60), main courses from 55F ($9.55). Tues–Sat noon–3pm and 7pm–midnight; Métro: Mabillon or Odéon. FRENCH.

Tiny and crowded and with good reason, because you can secure a decent two-course meal here for around $11. You might enjoy a fillet of hake or beef stew with either an appetizer or dessert. Even less expensive is the daily vegetarian plate for 45F ($7.80).

Restaurant Orestias. 4 rue Grégoire-de-Tours, 6e. ☎ **01-43-54-62-01.** Three-course menu 44F ($7.65) lunch and dinner except Fri and Sat night after 8pm. Mon–Sat noon–2:30pm and 5:30–11:30pm. MC, V. Métro: Odéon. GREEK/FRENCH.

The waiters in this folksy restaurant welcome you as though you were their long-lost relatives from Greece. Seated at long, wooden tables underneath beamed ceilings, you can satisfy the most ravenous hunger with heaping portions of food. The kitchen turns out basic Greek dishes such as stuffed grape leaves with salad, souvlaki, and baklava as well as roast chicken, lamb chops, and steak with potatoes, peas, and rice. You can't expect frills and thrills at these prices, but the ingredients are fresh and the dishes are cooked correctly.

MEALS FOR LESS THAN 120F ($21)

Au Petit Prince. 3 rue Monsieur-le-Prince, 6e. ☎ **01-43-29-74-92.** Appetizers 36–62F ($6.25–$10.80); main courses 70–99F ($12.15–$17.20); three-course menu 135F ($23.45). MC, V. Tues–Sat noon–2pm; Mon–Sat 7:15–11pm. Métro: Odéon. FRENCH.

Decorated with posters from St-Exupéry's novel of the same name, Au Petit Prince is small and casual. The menu changes almost daily, but some recent items on the fixed-price menu include a house terrine of chicken liver in a port jelly, delice of Roquefort with pears and nuts, a lukewarm salad of leeks with a poached egg, and poached chicken with a supreme sauce. Appetizers from the à la carte menu include smoked salmon and cold duck salad. Main courses run the gamut from sole meunière to breast of roast duck with fresh figs.

Au Vieux Casque. 19 rue Bonaparte, 6e. ☎ **01-43-54-99-46.** Menu, wine included, 98F ($17); plats du jour 50–60F ($8.70–$10.45); à la carte 40–70F ($7–$12.15). V. Mon–Sat 7–11:15pm. Métro: St-Germain-des-Prés or Mabillon. FRENCH.

Au Vieux Casque has lots of atmosphere, with a wood-and-stucco ground-floor dining room, a stone-vaulted cellar, and an upstairs room with rough-hewn beams. You can see the chef at work on the ground floor, preparing meals that are a cut above the rest. Try the delicate tomato salad to start, then veal cutlet in cream sauce with rice, followed by Camembert or fruit. Among the 14 or so main courses there might be a fish fillet Maître d'Hotel, lamb chop with herbs and green beans, or pork chop with spinach. With its updated classic French dishes and great atmosphere, this is definitely a superior choice.

Aux Charpentiers. 10 rue Mabillon, 6e. ☎ **01-43-26-30-05.** Plats du jour 75–95F ($13–$16.50); lunch menu 120F ($20.85); dinner menu 153F ($26.60), including $1/4$ liter wine; à la carte 70–120F ($12.15–$20.85). AE, DC, MC, V. Daily noon–11:30pm. Métro: Mabillon. FRENCH.

During the Middle Ages and the Renaissance, the carpenter's guild hall was located right next door to this restaurant, and it is from this that Aux Charpentiers takes its name. If you ask Parisians for a good budget restaurant, 9 out of 10 times they'll name this bistro, which has been operating for 130 years. The walls are decorated with photographs and plans of master carpentry, including models of wooden vaults and roof structures. The clientele is mostly local, and the prices are reasonable for traditional and hearty dishes such as steak with shallots or duckling with olives and port.

Bouillon Racine. 3 rue Racine, 6e. ☎ **01-44-32-15-60.** Appetizers 36–79F ($6.25–$13.75); main courses 65–119F ($11.30–$20.70); lunch menu 88F ($15.30); dinner menu 159F ($27.65); children's menu 59F ($10.25). EURO, MC, V. Mon–Sat 11:30am–12:30am. Métro: Cluny-Sorbonne, Odéon. BELGIAN.

Although Belgians are the butt of countless French jokes, their cuisine is no laughing matter and this is a good place to explore it. Belgian beer is used imaginatively in the preparation of marinated salmon, pork ribs, scallops, and *waterzooi* (fish stew). At the turn of the century the restaurant was a "bouillon" (a soup kitchen) and its new owners have restored it in an updated belle epoque style. The bright, airy interior sparkles with lights and mirrors, and the tables are spaced at a comfortable enough distance to ensure that you're not smelling your neighbor's aftershave. The downstairs bar offers a fine selection of Belgian beer.

Le Petit St-Benoît. 4 rue St-Benoît, 6e. ☎ **01-42-60-27-92.** Main dishes 48–65F ($8.35–$11.30). No credit cards. Daily noon–2:30pm and 7–10pm. Métro: St-Germain-des-Prés. FRENCH.

In summer the doors are flung open on this crowded dining room with tile floors and tables set with red tablecloths. The food is well priced and well prepared but not original. You might start with coquilles St-Jacques and follow with *pavé de rumpsteak aux chanterelles* (rump steak garnished with chanterelles) or *canard aux navets* (duck with turnips). Finish with an apple tart or the delicious lemon tart.

L'Epi Dupin. 11 rue Dupin, 6e. ☎ **01-42-22-64-56.** Lunch menu 97F ($16.85); dinner menu 153F ($26.60). MC, V. Mon–Fri noon–2:30pm and 8–11:30pm. Closed first 3 weeks of Aug. Métro: Sèvres-Babylone. BISTRO.

To eat here within budget, you'll have to come at noon, but even if you decide to splurge and come for dinner, make your reservation the moment you get to town— this new bistro is extremely popular, and with good reason. The food is outstanding, especially at such reasonable prices. The lunch menu changes daily and includes a glass of wine, but you might find such dishes as skirt steak of lamb with black olive sauce or guinea hen roasted with lemon and fennel. Desserts here are superb and the wine list is well chosen.

Le Polidor. 41 rue Monsieur-le-Prince, 6e. ☎ **01-3-26-95-34.** Lunch menu 55F ($9.55); dinner menu 100F ($17.40). No credit cards. Mon–Sat noon–2:30pm and 7pm–12:30am; Sun 7–11pm. Métro: Odéon. BISTRO.

An institution in Paris for more than a century, this bistro is always crowded with people sitting elbow to elbow in a frenzy-tinged atmosphere. The food is good— rabbit in mustard sauce, trout, beef bourguignon—the ambience historic, and the prices are right.

Les Banquettes Rouges. 28 rue Monsieur-le-Prince, 6e. ☎ **01-43-54-75-71.** Appetizers 36–58F ($6.25–$10); main courses 68–108F ($11.80–$18.80); menu 130F ($22.60). V. Mon–Sat noon–2:15pm and 7–11:15pm. Métro: Odéon. FRENCH.

Located just off rue Monsieur-le-Prince in a charming little courtyard, Les Banquettes Rouges attracts a young crowd and features an inventive menu. You can relax in attractive surroundings and listen to blues while you dine on the cassoulet, *lapin à la moutarde* (rabbit in a mustard sauce), or *mousse de foie gras*. There's always a fish of the day, and you shouldn't pass up dessert here; try the *charlotte du chocolat crème anglaise*.

Restaurant des Beaux Arts. 11 rue Bonaparte, 6e. ☎ **01-43-26-92-64.** Three-course menu, wine included, 85F ($14.80); à la carte 100–150F ($17.40–$26). No credit cards. Daily noon–2:30pm and 7–10:45pm. Métro: St-Germain-des-Prés. FRENCH.

When most people picture a typical Parisian artists' eatery, it usually looks like the Restaurant des Beaux Arts. Located across the street from Paris's famous Ecole Nationale Supérieure des Beaux Arts (School of Fine Arts), its decor features bentwood furniture, long tables covered in white paper, and wood-paneled walls. The menu du jour offers such traditional dishes as roast chicken, *boeuf bourguignon,* a vegetarian plate, and a fish dish—and the portions are large. If the downstairs dining room is full, try upstairs.

WORTH A SPLURGE

✪ **Chez Maître Paul.** 12 rue Monsieur-le-Prince, 6e. ☎ **01-43-54-74-59.** Reservations recommended. Appetizers 35–95F ($6–$16.50); main courses 80–145F ($13.90–$25.20); three-course meal including ¹/₂ bottle of wine 190F ($33). AE, DC, MC, V. Daily noon–2:30pm; 5pm–10:30pm. Métro: Odéon. FRENCH.

Small but comfortable, Chez Maître Paul serves specialties from the Franche-Comté region of eastern France. Start with the *saucisson chaude avec pommes a l'huile* (hot sausage with potatoes in oil) and follow with *poulet sauté au vin blanc* (chicken sautéed in white wine with mushrooms and tomatoes). I would also recommend *champignons à la grecque* (cold mushroom salad) and *filet de veau* (fillet of veal). The fixed-price menu includes wine, and you can have your choice of a plate of cheese or dessert. Chez Maître Paul is a little pricey, but it's well worth the extra money.

La Bastide Odéon. 7 rue Corneille, 6e. ☎ **01-43-26-03-65.** Fixed-price menus 139F ($24.15) and 180F ($31.30). MC, V. Tues–Sat 12:30am–2:30pm and 7:30–11pm. Closed Aug. Métro: Odéon. PROVENÇAL.

Young chef Gilles Ajuelos serves up delicious Provençal cooking—it's very fashionable in Paris right now—in this simple but attractive dining room just across the street from the Luxembourg Gardens. His menu changes regularly but typical of his creative approach are rabbit stuffed with eggplant as a starter and *gniocchi* with snails and garlic or grilled tuna steak with ratatouille as main courses. The red Coteaux du Tricastin is a particularly good choice from a wine list with many interesting bottles from southern France.

✪ **Le Muniche.** 22 rue Guillaume Appollinaire, 6e. ☎ **01-42-61-12-70.** Menu 149F ($25.90); main dishes 80–145F ($13.90–$25.20). AE, CB, DC, MC, V. Daily noon–2am. Métro: St-Germain-des-Prés. FRENCH.

At this large, lively brasserie, budget travelers will want to stick to the fixed-price menu, but that will surely provide a fine meal starting with six oysters or asparagus salad with ham. This might be followed by a choice of *Poêlée de thon aux confit de poireaux* (tuna in leek sauce) or beef with red peppers with seasonal vegetables. For the more adventuresome, the specialties of the house are *choucroute* (sauerkraut) garnished with veal knuckle and pig's ears. Finish with a strawberry charlotte or the apple and rhubarb tart.

Vagenende. 142 bd. St-Germain, 6e. ☎ **01-43-26-68-18.** Menu 138F ($23.60), main courses 70–135F ($12.15–$23.45). AE, MC, V. Daily noon–1am. Métro: Odéon. BISTRO.

If you're seeking a belle epoque experience in Paris, this is one place to find it. The art nouveau decor is authentic—mirrors, frescoes, and floral patterns abound. Lace curtains, globe lights, and spacious booths further create a very French atmosphere. The dishes are equally classic—confit de canard, sole meunière, or *pavé de morue sauce vierge* (cod with a lemon-flavored sauce). Start traditionally with fresh shellfish or smoked salmon.

EIFFEL TOWER & INVALIDES (7E ARRONDISSEMENT)
MEALS FOR LESS THAN 85F ($15)

Au Pied du Fouet. 45 rue de Babylone, 7e. ☎ **01-47-05-12-27.** Average meal 75F ($13). No credit cards. Mon–Fri noon–2:30pm and 7–9:45pm; Sat noon–2:30pm. Closed Aug. No credit cards. Métro: Vaneau. BISTRO.

This minuscule place in one of the most expensive parts of Paris is extremely popular with people who could pay much more. The cooking's homey and appetizing, if never surprising. Start with a salad of hot shredded cabbage with bacon, followed by chicken livers and then a slice of runny Camembert or maybe an apple tart. Coffee's taken at the bar to make way for the next round of hungry, penny-wise diners.

Chez Germaine. 30 rue Pierre-Leroux, 7e. ☎ **01-42-73-28-34.** Three-course fixed-price menu 65F ($11.30). No credit cards. Mon–Fri noon–2:30pm and 7–9:30pm; Sat noon–2:30pm. Closed Aug. Métro: Duroc. FRENCH.

Tucked away in one of the most bourgeois neighborhoods in Paris, Chez Germaine's crowd of discerning regulars is a good tip-off that you'll get a quality meal here, and at a great price. The menu changes regularly but runs to marinated leeks, calf's liver, and rice pudding. Note that this is one of the rare restaurants in Paris that's non-smoking.

Le Croque Au Sel. 131 rue St-Dominique, 7e. ☎ **01-47-05-23-53.** Two-course fixed-price menu until 8pm 59F ($10.25). Three-course fixed-price menu 98F ($17). MC, V. Mon–Fri noon–2:30pm and 7–10pm; Sat 7–10pm. Métro: Ecole-Militaire. FRENCH.

When the *grisaille* (grayness) blankets Paris, the splashy tropical decor here—flowers, plants, a palm tree—is the perfect retreat. Service is friendly and the food has a lot of flair for the price. The two-course menu changes daily and usually offers a main dish of either fish or meat served with rice. You might start off with a cool, fresh *terrine de poisson* or a chicken liver salad. Portions are not huge; if you come with a big appetite you might want to spring for the three-course menu. The pot-au-feu is also hearty and well prepared.

MEALS FOR LESS THAN 120F ($21)

Au Bon Accueil. 14 rue de Monttessuy, 7e. ☎ **01-47-05-46-11.** Three-course fixed-price lunch menu 120F ($20.85); dinner 145F ($25.20). V. Mon–Fri noon–2:30pm and 7:30–10pm; Sat 7:30–10pm. Métro: Alma-Marceau. BISTRO.

Book here as soon as your plane lands, since their 120F menu is one of the best-value meals you'll find in Paris. The menu changes daily according to what the chef finds in the markets, but you might start off with a slice of chicken-liver pâté or an artichoke vinaigrette and then go on to pot-au-feu or a veal steak with seasonal vegetables. Desserts are fantastic, too, including strawberry tart and a pastry cup filled with homemade pistachio ice cream.

Chez Lucie. 15 rue Augereau, 7e. ☎ **01-45-55-08-74.** Fixed-Price menus 98F ($17) and 130F ($22.60). Main courses 50–85F ($8.70–$14.80). CB, MC, V. Mon 7:30–11:30pm; Tues–Sat noon–1:30pm and 7:30–11:30pm. Métro: Ecole-Militaire. WEST INDIAN.

There is room for fewer than 20 people at this tiny restaurant—make sure you're one of them. This is one of France's best restaurants, specializing in *cuisine antillaise*, cooking from the Caribbean with a French touch. There are delicious fish dishes, exotic vegetables prepared au gratin, and delicate desserts. Cooking like this makes you wonder why Joséphine ever left her native Martinique.

Restaurants—Eiffel Tower & Invalides (7e Arr.)

LEGEND
⊠ Post Office
✝ Church
Ⓜ Métro

Au Bon Acceuil ◆ 1
Au Pied du Fouet ◆ 6
Le Café du Commerce ◆ 10
Chez Germain ◆ 7
Chez Lucie ◆ 3
Le Croque au Sel ◆ 5
La Fontaine de Mars ◆ 4
La Petite Chaise ◆ 9
Le Rivaldiere ◆ 8
Le Sancerre ◆ 2

PARIS
Area of
Detail

130

La Fontaine de Mars. 129 rue St-Dominique, 7e. ☎ **01-47-05-46-44.** Full meal 150–250F ($26–$43.45); lunch menu 85F ($14.80). EURO, V. Mon–Sat noon–2:30pm and 7:30–11pm. Métro: Ecole-Militaire. FRENCH.

On a small square with a fountain, La Fontaine de Mars is a wonderfully friendly restaurant. And that's only the beginning. The specialty is French country cuisine—the food is delicious, hearty, and abundant. The wine flows and the desserts beckon. In the summer, there is outside eating on the square. If your budget is tight, come for lunch, when La Fontaine de Mars offers a menu.

La Rivaldiere. 1 rue St-Simon, 7e. ☎ **01-45-48-53-96.** Three-course fixed-price menu 100F ($17.40). MC, V. Mon–Fri 12:15–2:30pm and 7:15–10:30pm; Sat 7:15–10:30pm. Métro: Solferino. BISTRO.

With a pretty grape border along its high ceiling, wooden floors, and yellow walls, this friendly place has an appealingly old-fashioned air. Come here for simple, home-style cooking from a menu that changes daily but always offers excellent eating at a very fair price. You might start with a salad garnished with sautéed wild mushrooms and then have scallops with lentils or lamb stew. The prunes marinated in wine are excellent for dessert. This is a great spot for lunch before a visit to the Musée d'Orsay, but you'll have to book ahead since it's very popular with people who work in the area's many government ministries.

WORTH A SPLURGE

La Petite Chaise. 36 rue de Grenelle, 7e. ☎ **01-42-22-13-35.** Plat and drink 110F ($19.15); two-course menu 150F ($26); three-course menu plus drink 180F ($31.30). MC, V. Daily noon–2pm and 7– 11pm. Métro: Severés-Babylone. FRENCH.

There's a small bar up front and a cozy dining room downstairs. Students and publishers gather here to dine on such typical dishes as escargots bourguignon to start followed by duck with a pear sauce, veal escalope with camembert, or seasonal fish in saffron sauce.

14E ARRONDISSEMENT (MONTPARNASSE)

Au Rendez-Vous des Camionneurs. 34 rue des Plantes, 14e. ☎ **01-45-40-43-36.** Three-course fixed-price meal 69F ($12). No credit cards. Mon–Fri noon–2:30pm and 7:30–9:30pm. Closed Aug. Métro: Alesia. BISTRO.

Though the name of this restaurant roughly translates to "The Meeting Place of the Truck Drivers," the reference is more to the convivial atmosphere than the actual clientele. This place has a steady crowd of local regulars who are spoiled by the friendly *patronne,* Monique. Her husband, Claude, runs the kitchen and sends out simple appetizing dishes like roast chicken, lamb stew, and pork chops, all of which are generously garnished, usually with mashed potatoes and a vegetable.

Bistro de la Gare. 59 bd. Montparnasse, 14e. ☎ **01-42-22-22-55.** Menus 60F ($10.45) and 78F ($13.55); main dishes 60–100F ($10.45–$17.40). MC, V. Daily 11:30am–1am. Métro: Montparnasse-Bienvenue. BISTRO.

One of the ultimate art nouveau Paris experiences. Dine in a room with tile-mosaics, a mirrored ceiling, and curvaceous boiserie, lit by large globe lights. The 78F ($13.55) menu offers such well-prepared dishes as roast pork au citron, breast of duck with cassis or green pepper sauce, and salmon with sorrel sauce. The less expensive prix fixe features such modest items as half a roast chicken with herbs.

Le Bistrot du Dome. 1 rue Delambre, 14e. ☎ **01-43-35-32-00.** Main courses 90–110F ($15.65–$19.15). AE, MC, V. Métro: Vavin. FRENCH/SEAFOOD.

Though fish is often expensive in Paris, the quality is generally excellent. This bistro annex of one of the most famous seafood restaurants in the city is a great place to get a first-rate catch of the day without doing nearly as much damage to your pocketbook. The daily specials appear on a blackboard and vary with the season. Signature first courses include baby clams with thyme and grilled baby squid, while grilled salmon is generally available. Surprisingly, desserts are quite good as well, including caramel-glazed cream puffs.

15E ARRONDISSEMENT (NEAR THE EIFFEL TOWER)

Le Café du Commerce. 51 rue du Commerce, 15e. ☎ **01-45-75-03-27.** Two-course meal, 85F ($14.80); three-course meal, wine included, 115F ($20). AE, DC, MC, V. Daily noon–11:30pm. Métro: Emile-Zola or Commerce. FRENCH.

Located not very far from the Eiffel Tower, Le Café du Commerce is one of the best dining bargains in this area. The list of dishes is astounding: about 15 appetizers, 5 fish dishes, 16 main courses, 7 vegetable side dishes, 4 cheeses, and more than a dozen desserts. The lowest-priced fixed-price menu will offer such items as l'oeuf mayonnaise (a hard-boiled egg with mayonnaise) to start, followed by a chicken with tarragon sauce and fruit compote.

Le Petit Plat. 49 Av. Emile Zola, 15e. ☎ **01-42-78-24-20.** Lunch menu 130F ($22.60); main dishes 45–85F ($7.80–$14.80). MC, V. Wed–Sun noon–2:30pm; Tues–Sun 7–10pm. Métro: Maubert-Mutualité. FRENCH.

This small, plain restaurant offers well-prepared dishes like breast of duck in cassis sauce and *poule au pot* (chicken in a pot). Start with a salmon pâté or plate of charcuterie and finish with any one of the sorbets or the chocolate gâteau. A good selection of country wines is also available.

6 Cafes

To a Parisian, a cafe is a combination club, tavern, and snack bar. You can read your newspaper, meet a friend, do your homework, or write your memoirs in a cafe. Often people meet at cafes to relax and talk before going to a show.

Cafes aren't restaurants, although the larger ones may serve complete and excellent meals. They aren't bars, either, although they do offer a variety of alcoholic drinks. And they aren't coffee shops in the American sense, because you can order a bottle of champagne just as readily as a hot chocolate.

Contrary to general belief, the coffee house is not a French invention. It began in 17th-century Vienna and flourished in London long before taking root in France. Parisians transformed it into the symbol of their inimitable talent for leisure. Cafes are plentiful; a single block in one of the centrally located arrondissements may hold three or four.

You'll find cafes on every street, but keep in mind that a cafe on a main street or boulevard is going to be more expensive than one on a side street. The cafes listed here that have rich literary or historical associations factor that into the price of their drinks, often with astonishing results. You'll be amazed to see how much you can pay for three tablespoons of coffee. Then again, you can nurse your drink until closing time and no impatient waiter will try to hustle you out the door.

ON THE RIGHT BANK

Café Beaubourg. 43 rue St-Merri, 4e. ☎ **01-48-87-63-96.** Métro: Hôtel-de-Ville.

This striking bilevel modern cafe just across the street from the Centre Pompidou is a fantastic place to linger over a coffee or tuck into a good salad and watch the world go by. An interesting international crowd frequents the place.

Café Marly. 93 rue de Rivoli, Cour Napoléon du Louvre, 1er. ☎ **01-49-26-06-60.** Métro: Palais-Royal.

This stunning new cafe at the Louvre has a gorgeous view of the glass pyramid that is the museum's main entrance, and is an especially lovely place to linger on a warm night when they serve outside and you can enjoy the exquisite lighting on the surrounding 18th-century facades. It pulls a very stylish crowd of Parisians, as well as tourists.

Fouquet's. 99 av. des Champs-Elysées, 8e. ☎ **01-47-23-70-60.** Métro: Georges-V.

Not far from the Arc de Triomphe, the turn-of-the-century Fouquet's is a Champs-Elysées institution whose guests have included James Joyce, Charlie Chaplin, Marlene Dietrich, Winston Churchill, Franklin D. Roosevelt, and Victoria Ocampo. You may still see an occasional celebrity, but again, you're paying for the glitzy associations and nostalgic fantasies.

La Chaise au Plafond. 10 rue Tresor, 4e. ☎ **01-42-76-03-22.** Métro: Hôtel-de-Ville.

Tucked away on a pedestrians-only side street in the heart of the Marais, this friendly, stylish place is a perfect time-out after visiting the Picasso Museum. They do good and copious salads and imaginative sandwiches.

L'Eté en Pente Douce. 23 rue Muller, 18e. ☎ **01-42-64-02-67.** Métro: Chateau-Rouge.

To escape the shoulder-to-shoulder tourists on Place du Tertre, head down the eastern steps under the Sacré-Coeur and you'll find yourself on a leafy square, popular with a local crowd. The terrace of L'Eté en Pente Douce is underneath two giant trees and faces the stairs and iron lamps painted by Utrillo. The interior is brightly decorated with mosaics, unusual objets d'art, and a lovely painted ceiling. Between the lunch and dinner meals, the restaurant serves a tempting array of pastries and sandwiches.

ON THE LEFT BANK

Café de Cluny. 102 bd. St-Germain, 6e. ☎ **01-43-26-98-40.** Métro: Cluny-Sorbonne.

Worried intellectuals have been gathering upstairs at the Café de Cluny for decades. What are they worried about? The state of the French language is the subject of the day for the academics of the French Academy who regularly hold breakfast debates here. Everyone else is content to enjoy the scene from the cafe terrace, ideally located on the corner of boulevard Saint-Germain and boulevard St-Michel.

Café de Flore. 173 bd. St-Germain, 6e. ☎ **01-45-48-55-26.** Métro: St-Germain-des-Prés.

Sartre is said to have written his trilogy *Les Chemins de la Liberté* at his table here. Other regulars included André Malraux and Guillaume Apollinaire. Located in the heart of the very pleasant St-Germain-des-Prés neighborhood, the cafe is still going strong, even if the famous writers have moved on and now you pay high prices for the opportunity to indulge in nostalgia.

Café des Deux-Magots. 6 place St-Germain-des-Prés, 6e. ☎ **01-45-48-55-25.** Métro: St-Germain-des-Prés.

Like its neighbor the Café de Flore, Deux-Magots was a hangout for Sartre and Beauvoir. The intellectuals met here in the 1950s, and Sartre wrote at his table every morning. It's an expensive place for literary-intellectual pilgrims but a great spot to watch the nightly promenade on the boulevard St-Germain.

La Chope. 2/4 place de la Contrescarpe, 5e. ☎ **01-43-26-57-26.** Métro: Cardinal Lemoine.

Hemingway didn't drink here, and Sartre didn't write here, but the cafe is worth a stop for its location on top of rue Mouffetard, right on pretty place de la

Contrescarpe. The square centers on four lilac trees and a fountain and is small enough that you can enjoy a peaceful espresso without cars whizzing by.

La Coupole. 102 bd. Montparnasse, 14e. ☎ **01-43-20-14-20.** Métro: Vavin.

This Parisian institution has been packing them in ever since Henry Miller used to come here for his morning porridge. The cavernous interior is always jammed and bristling with energy. Japanese businessmen, French yuppies, models, tourists, Eurotrash, and neighborhood regulars keep the frenzied waiters running until 2am. You won't know which is more interesting, the scene on the street or the parade that passes through the revolving doors.

La Palette. 43 rue de Seine, 6e. ☎ **01-43-26-68-15.** Mon–Sat 8am–2am. Métro: Mabillon.

As the name suggests, this is an artists' hangout and it's a great place to linger and watch the life of the Left Bank flow by. The interior is decorated with colorful murals and a palette hangs over the bar. The fare is cafe style—open-face ham sandwiches and the like, at reasonable prices.

7 Tea Salons (Salons de Thés)

A good cup of tea is hard to find in Paris. Unlike their neighbors across the Channel, the French have never placed a lot of emphasis on the stuff, preferring to fortify themselves with powerful little blasts of coffee. Tea lovers who are disappointed in the watery brews served up in most cafes and restaurants will find in tea salons a wide range of teas blended and steeped to perfection. In contrast to the smoke and bustle that characterize most cafes, tea salons are refined and often elegant establishments. The pastry selection is usually excellent, but full meals tend to be expensive.

ON THE RIGHT BANK

A Priori Thé. 35–37 Galerie Vivienne (entrances at 6 rue Vivienne, 4 rue des Petits-Champs, and 5 rue de la Banque), 2e. ☎ **01-42-97-48-75.** Continental breakfast 50F ($8.70); light lunch or supper 75–95F ($13–$16.50); Sat brunch 135F ($23.45); Sun brunch 146F ($25.40). MC, V. Mon–Fri 9am–6pm; Sat 9am–6:30pm; Sun 12:30–6:30pm. Métro: Bourse, Palais-Royal–Musée-du-Louvre, or Pyramides.

You can enjoy both the beautiful Galerie Vivienne and a good repast at A Priori Thé, a cleverly named tearoom that serves coffee, a large assortment of teas, light meals, tarts, salads, and desserts. Management is American and has created a harmonious and appealing blend of Parisian and New World styles. The emphasis is on light sauces and fresh ingredients. At teatime there are a variety of tarts available—chocolate, lemon cheese, and orange—as well as scones, muffins, cookies, and brownies.

Ladurée. 16 rue Royale, 8e. ☎ **01-42-60-21-79.** Beverages 20–30F ($3.50–$5.20); light meals from 50F ($8.20). MC, V. Mon–Sat 8:30am–7pm. Métro: Concorde.

Founded during the belle epoque, this is the most refined tearoom in Paris. Enter through the store selling the famous macaroons, marron glacée, and chocolate and you'll find yourself in a richly paneled and gilded room with rows of tiny black marble tables and antique chairs. Here you can join the important and wealthy and take tea under a ceiling bedecked with frolicking cupids. Prices are surprisingly reasonable for the deluxe ambience.

Marais Plus. 20 rue des Francs-Bourgeois, 3e. ☎ **01-48-87-01-40.** Breakfast, brunch, light lunch, or dinner 48–95F ($8.35–$16.50). AE, MC, V. Daily 10am–7:30pm. Métro: St-Paul.

The Marais has a number of restaurants but only one tea shop like Marais Plus. Here you can buy postcards, toys, guidebooks, and globes or head for one of the small cafe tables in the back and upstairs, where food and drinks are served. There are salads, sandwiches, and simple light meals, plus croissants and other delicious baked goodies. The crowd is often young, sophisticated, and good-natured.

Mariage Frères. 30–32 rue de Bourg-Tibourg, 4e. ☎ **01-42-72-28-11.** Pot of tea 36–59F ($6.25–$10.25). Lunch 75–100F ($13–$17.40). Daily noon–7:30pm. Métro: Hôtel-de-Ville.

The Mariage family has been importing teas since the 17th century and here they carry more than 450 varieties. The store sells all kinds of tea-making accoutrements while the adjacent tearoom serves tea and pastries in a heady atmosphere of orchids. They have even fashioned a cocktail that combines tea and champagne.

ON THE LEFT BANK

A la Cour de Rohan. 59–61, rue St-André-des-Arts, 6e. ☎ **01-43-25-79-67.** Pot of tea 27F ($4.70); pastry 37F ($6.45); lunch menu 95F ($16.50); weekend brunch 110F ($19.15) Daily noon–7:30pm. Métro: Odéon.

As soon as you open the tiny door, the warm, enticing aromas of freshly baked pastries surround you. *Voilà.* You're in the cozy salon of an 18th-century country house. Wicker chairs, flowery wallpaper, and chintz curtains under the beamed ceilings lend the two rooms an irresistible homespun charm. The upstairs room is the perfect place to end a love affair, since it would be inconceivable to make a scene amidst the soft music, the plants, and the quaintly mismatched china. From the downstairs salon, you can watch the passersby on the historic passage, Cour de Rohan, which was a hotbed of revolutionary activity in the 18th century. The house specialty is their own version of scones and the teas are superb.

Salon de Thé de la Mosquée de Paris. 39 rue Geoffroy-St-Hilaire, 5e. ☎ **01-43-31-18-14.** Glass of tea 10F ($1.75); pastries 10F ($1.75). Daily 10am–10pm. Métro: Monge.

Adjoining Paris's largest and most beautiful mosque, this tea salon is as popular for its Arabian Nights decor as for its delicious baklava and mint tea. Fountains, North-African music, plush banquettes, and colorful mosaics create an exotic but casual hangout for the local student population. The service is friendly and the salon is just a stone's throw from the Jardin des Plantes.

Tea Caddy. 14 St-Julien-le-Pauvre, 5e. ☎ **01-43-54-15-56.** Pastries and light main courses 20–50F ($4.70–$8.70). Thurs–Tues noon–7pm. Métro: St-Michel.

With its beamed ceiling, comfortable atmosphere, and tables perhaps just slightly too close together, this tearoom is a cozy spot. A variety of teas and coffees are served along with such items as scones and toast and more substantial dishes like omelettes and *croque monsieur.*

8 Wine Bars

ON THE RIGHT BANK

A la Cloche des Halles. 28 rue Coquillière, 1er. ☎ **01-42-36-93-89.** Wine from 14F ($2.45) a glass. Plat du jour 25–60F ($4.35–$10.45). No credit cards. Mon–Fri 8am–10pm; Sat 10am–5pm. Métro: Les Halles.

If you look closely on the exterior you can see the bell that used to toll the opening and closing of the vast food market that was once in this neighborhood. Today this tiny bar-cafe is crowded at lunchtime with people dining on plates of ham and terrine de campagne or quiche accompanied by a bottle of wine. Convivial and fun but very noisy and crowded. If you can't find a seat, you can usually stand at the bar and eat.

Bistro du Peintre. 116 av. Ledru-Rollin, 11e. ☎ **01-47-00-34-39.** Wine from 12F ($2) a glass. Light meals 30–45F ($5.20–$7.80). No credit cards. Daily 7pm–2am. Métro: Ledru-Rollin.

The zinc bar, wood paneling, and superb belle epoque style would make this wine bar a highlight even if the wine selection was not as reasonably priced as it is. A motley collection of Bastille types—painters, actors, nightcrawlers—gathers nightly at the bar or the tables on the large terrace.

✪ **Clown Bar.** 114 rue Amelot, 11e. ☎ **01-43-55-87-35.** Wine from 18F ($3.15) a glass. Plat du jour 48–62F ($8.35–$10.80) at lunch; 75F ($13) at dinner. No credit cards. Mon–Sat noon–2:30pm and 7pm–1am. Métro: Filles du Calvaire.

Aptly named and aptly decorated with a mélange of circus posters and circus-themed ceramic tiles. The food is passable but not as original as the decor. The wine list features an extensive selection of French wines.

L'Ecluse-Saint-Michel. 15 quai des Grands-Augustins, 6e. ☎ **01-46-33-58-74.** Wine from 12F ($2) a glass. Menu 89F ($15.50). MC, V. Daily noon–1:30am. Métro: St-Michel.

A small chain of wine bars bearing the name L'Ecluse has grown from this original. Casually chic and authentic, there are about 20 or so wines available by the glass, along with snacks like carpaccio. Good for late-night dining, too.

Le Rubis. 10 rue du Marché-St-Honoré, 1er. ☎ **01-42-61-03-34.** Wine from 6F ($1) a half glass. Plat du jour 48F ($8.35); sandwiches 14F ($2.45). No credit cards. Mon–Fri 7am–10pm; Sat 9am–4pm. Metro: Tuileries.

The Formica tables and hand-lettered signs provide an unpretentious decor to sample decent wines at unbeatable prices. The clientele runs the gamut from executives to laborers in blue overalls, and the jovial owner, Albert Prat, makes everyone feel at home. The atmosphere is relaxed and friendly and the daily bistro dishes are expertly prepared.

Le Sancerre. 22 av. Rapp, 7e. ☎ **01-45-51-75-91.** Wine from 15F ($2.60) a glass. Omelettes and quiches from 46F ($8). MC, V. Mon–Fri 8am–9:30pm; Sat 8:30am–4pm. Métro: Alma-Marceau.

Located across the street from one of the city's most beautiful examples of art nouveau architecture (designed by the architect Jules Lavirotte in 1901) is Le Sancerre, a popular wine bar and equally popular bistro. Once you settle yourself at one of the cozy tables, you'll find some typically French items on the menu, such as omelettes of all varieties with a side of fried potatoes. And, of course, there's the ubiquitous *andouillette*, a tripe sausage that is decidedly an acquired taste. You also have a choice of Loire wines—including, of course, Sancerre.

✪ **Taverne Henri IV.** 13 place du Pont Neuf, 1er. ☎ **01-43-54-27-90.** Wine from 20F ($3.45) a glass. Sandwiches 25F ($4.35). No credit cards. Mon–Fri noon–10pm; Sat noon–4pm. Métro: Pont-Neuf.

An authentic, old-fashioned bar frequented by men reading the newspaper, discussing the news of the day, and smoking vehemently. A variety of wines are available by the glass and can be accompanied by a variety of open-face sandwiches such as warm goat cheese, pâtés, and such cheeses as Cantal and Auvergne blue. Although on the expensive side, both the wine and the food are excellent.

Seeing the Sights 6

Paris is such a smorgasbord of delights that you'll be excused if you feel a little overwhelmed at first. With its museums crammed with masterpieces, its serene parks, legendary cafes, awe-inspiring churches, resplendent boulevards, and lofty monuments, it's hard to know where to start.

Like any great city, Paris reveals itself slowly and over time. On a first, second, or even third visit, you will get only a smattering of everything that you could want to see. The city's many delicacies are meant to be savored, not gobbled. Pick out a few highlights and take your time with them. It's infinitely better to see just a few things than to run from museum to museum without stopping to reflect on what you're seeing.

As you plan your touring, keep in mind that most museums close on either Monday or Tuesday and that at many of them admission is either free or reduced one day each week. Check the listings below for details.

The key that will unlock the pleasures of Paris is flexibility. Rather than sticking to a rigid schedule, allow yourself to drift and wander. Take the weather into account; Parisian weather is famously changeable. Spend that vibrant spring morning in a park and let the museum visit wait for the gray, rainy day that's sure to follow. Also, don't be afraid to get lost—in Paris, it's an adventure. In nearly every neighborhood you'll stumble across alleys, passages, and unusual buildings, neighborhood cafes redolent of smoke and strong coffee, and old streets that run off and wander a while before joining a boulevard.

Venture off the beaten track and experience the contrasts that make the city vital. The upscale stuffiness of the avenues de la Bourdonnais, Rapp, and Bosquet is offset by the funky young crowd that swarms through the streets around the Bastille. North African fashions and food are on display in the northeastern arrondissements while noodle shops feed the Asian clientele in "Little Chinatown" near the place d'Italie.

People-watch from a sidewalk cafe, select a scrumptious pastry from a *patisserie* and picnic in a park. Enter into the city's life, for this experience is as much a part of Paris as Notre-Dame's rose windows and the view from the Eiffel Tower.

Paris Attractions

Musée des Arts d'Afrique et d'Oceanie 48

Musée des Arts Décoratifs 27

Musée d'Orsay 13

Musée National des Arts Asiatiques—Guimet 4

Musée Jacquemart André 2

Musée Marmottan 7

Musée Picasso 42

Musée Rodin 12

Notre-Dame 35

Opéra Garnier 23

Palais Bourbon 14

Palais de l'Elysée 16

Palais du Luxembourg 30

Palais Royal 26

Panthéon 32

Parc du Champ-de-Mars 9

Parc Monceau 1

Place de la Concorde 18

Place des Vosges 46

Place Vendôme 24

Sacré-Cœur 22

Sainte-Chapelle 36

St-Germain-des-Prés 29

Sorbonne 33

139

Paris's Top Attractions for Free—or Almost

- The **rooftops of Paris,** which can be seen from many vantage points—including several that are free, like La Samaritaine, the Institut du Monde Arabe, and Sacré-Coeur.
- The **neighborhood markets,** such as the Latin Quarter's **rue Mouffetard, rue de Buci** in Saint-Germain, **rue Lepic** in Montmartre, **rue Montorgueil** near the Bourse, and **rue Daguerre** in Montparnasse.
- The **bird and flower markets** on the Ile de la Cité and quai de Mégisserie, and of course the **Marché aux Puces** (flea market).
- The **churches** of Paris, which have been so central to the life of the city. In addition to Notre-Dame and the Sacré-Coeur, visit St-Eustache in the heart of Les Halles, St-Séverin, St-Germain-des-Prés, and St-Sulpice for its Delacroix.
- The **cemeteries** of Paris—especially the granddaddy of them all: the evocative, melancholic **Pére-Lachaise.** The **Cimetiére de Montmartre** and the **Cimetiére de Montparnasse** also contain the tombs of famous writers, artists, and composers.
- **The Louvre on Sunday,** when it's half price, or if you're lucky, the first Sunday of every month when it's free.
- The **Opéra Garnier** and **place de la Madeleine,** where you can spend hours browsing in Fauchon.
- The **historic buildings** like the Hôtel de Sully, the Hôtel de Ville, and the Palais-Royal, all of which can be viewed for nothing.
- The city's spectacular gardens and parks. The most famous is the **Jardin des Tuileries. Bois de Boulogne** is the largest, and the **Jardin du Luxembourg** the most beloved.
- The museums that relate the stories of industries or crafts peculiar to France, such as the **Musée Baccarat** and **Musée du Parfum,** which are free.
- The **Seine and its bridges.** Take a day to stroll along the quays—it's one of the world's most romantic walks.
- The **antique stores** and **art galleries** that line the rue de Beaune, rue Jacob, rue de Seine, rue Bonaparte, and other streets in the Saint-Germain area.
- The **arcades** that wind through the 2e and 9e arrondissements. These intricate 19th-century iron-and-glass-covered passages are ideal for rainy day shopping.
- The **squares** of Paris, which are many and various. The **place de la Contrescarpe** in the Latin Quarter and **place des Vosges** in the Marais are great places to sit and watch Parisian life pass by, while the **Square Vert-Galant** on Ile de la Cité is ideal for a picnic by the water.

SUGGESTED ITINERARIES

Consider the following itineraries for at least the first few days. To augment the suggestions below, seven walking tours that will take you to different parts of Paris are to be found in chapter 7.

If You Have 1 Day

Start early by having coffee and croissants at a cafe. Then begin at Kilometer 0: All distances in France are measured from the square in front of **Notre-Dame,** on the

Ile de la Cité. The cathedral, with its glorious stained-glass windows, stands right in the center of Paris, and it's a great starting point for any tour. From here, cross the **River Seine** to the **Louvre.** Select a few rooms in a particular collection for your first visit, for this is one of the world's largest and finest museums, and it would take months to see it in its entirety.

From the museum, stroll through the beautiful **Jardin des Tuileries** to the **place de la Concorde,** with its Egyptian obelisk. Walk up the **Champs-Elysées** to the **Arc de Triomphe;** there are several budget restaurants near the Champs-Elysées where you can lunch. Note that Métro Line 1 runs in a straight line from the Louvre to the Arc de Triomphe (Métro: Charles-de-Gaulle-Etoile), or you can climb aboard bus 73 at the Concorde and ride up the Champs-Elysées to the Arc de Triomphe.

From the Arc de Triomphe, walk down avenue Kléber to place du Trocadéro for some splendid views of the **Eiffel Tower** (buses 22 and 30 also go to Trocadéro as well as the Métro Line 6). Visit the tower and then head for the Left Bank. You can catch the Réseau Express Régional (RER) at Champ-de-Mars, southwest of the Eiffel Tower on the Seine (a long walk), to the St-Michel station in the heart of the Latin Quarter. Bus 63 from Trocadéro runs along the Seine and then drops you off at the St-Germain-des-Prés church, right next to the famous Café des Deux-Magots and Café de Flore. Stroll down the lively boulevard St-Germain-des-Prés to place St-Michel and soak up the atmosphere along the boulevard and its maze of colorful side streets. This is an excellent area for dinner.

If You Have 2 Days

On the first day, follow the above itinerary from Notre-Dame to the Arc de Triomphe but take a little more time in the Louvre. From the Arc de Triomphe, either walk south on Avenue Marceau or take bus 92 to Alma-Marceau and board the Bateaux-Mouches for a **Seine boat ride.** Afterward, walk up posh Avenue Montaigne to the Champs-Elysées and take Métro Line 1 to St-Paul, in the heart of **the Marais;** walk east on rue St-Antoine and turn left on rue de Brague to see Paris's oldest square, the aristocratic **place des Vosges,** bordered by 17th century townhouses. After refreshment at one of the many bars and bistros in the neighborhood, wander the quiet lamp-lit streets built just wide enough for a horse and carriage.

Explore the Left Bank on your second day. Start at the Eiffel Tower and follow the Seine past the domed **Invalides** (which contains the Tomb of Napoléon) to the **Musée d'Orsay.** Spend a few hours with the impressionist masters before heading to St-Germain-des-Prés and the Latin Quarter. On the way, you'll pass through the **Faubourg St-Germain,** a district of stately 18th-century mansions, many of which have been converted to government offices and embassies. The **Musée Rodin** is also in this neighborhood.

If You Have 3 Days

Combine the above itineraries with visits to **Père-Lachaise** cemetery and **Montmartre** and **Sacré-Coeur.** You will also have time to explore a park: either the **Jardin du Luxembourg** on the Left Bank or **Parc Monceau** on the Right Bank.

If You Have 5 Days

Five days is a sensible amount of time to stay in Paris, and if you have a week or 10 days, so much the better. You will probably have time to see the **Sainte-Chapelle** and the **Conciergerie** on the Ile de la Cité; explore more museums; and visit **Versailles, Fontainebleau,** or **Chartres** outside the city.

1 Attractions by Type

MUSEUMS

ARCHITECTURAL HIGHLIGHTS, HISTORIC BUILDINGS & MONUMENTS

2 The Top 10 Sights to See

You may not want to see all of them, but the following sights are the most celebrated in Paris. The city is certainly much more than the sum of 10 famous highlights, but these are the attractions that have been so often photographed, painted, talked about and written about that they seem to have entered into our collective subconscious. Yet no photograph, movie, or guidebook can prepare you for the majesty of Notre-Dame, the grand sweep of the Eiffel Tower, or the boundless treasures of the Louvre. Fads come and go, styles change, empires and hemlines rise and fall, but some pleasures really are here to stay.

✪ **Musée du Louvre.** Rue de Rivoli, 1er. ☎ **01-40-20-53-17,** or 01-40-20-51-51 for recorded information. Web site: http://www.louvre.fr. Admission 45F ($7.80) adults; 26F ($4.50) after 3pm and all day Sun, free the first Sunday of the month and for children 17 and under. Mon (certain rooms only) and Wed 9am–9:45pm; Thurs–Sun 9am–6pm. Call ☎ 01-40-20-52-09 for hours of tours in English for 33F ($5.75) adults, 22F ($3.80) students. Métro: Palais-Royal–Musée-du-Louvre.

Even 63 years ago, the Louvre made it to "the top" of Cole Porter's song of superlatives. The overall excellence of the collection, the enormous quantity of works on display, and the abundance of recognizable masterpieces make the Louvre one of the top museums in the world. It can also be exhausting as well as exhaustive. The sheer immensity of the place can be intimidating, as galleries stretch onto halls that open onto more galleries.

Loving the Louvre means limiting your focus. The 90-minute guided tour will cover the most popular works and give you a quick orientation to the museum's layout. The audioguide system is also practical. The "audiotour" is designed to last four hours and has the virtue of allowing you to set your own pace.

If you choose to go it alone, try to zero in on a particular department, collection, or wing. The museum is divided into seven departments: Egyptian antiquities; Oriental antiquities; Greek, Etruscan, and Roman antiquities; sculptures; paintings; graphics and the graphic arts; and art objects. The departments are spread across three wings: Sully, Denon, and the recently renovated Richelieu Wing.

First timers usually head to the three most famous works: *Mona Lisa, Winged Victory of Samothrace,* and *Venus de Milo.* Finding your way is easy; the route is clearly marked by signs and the great flow of other tourists carries you along like a cork on a wave. In the Denon wing, the *Winged Victory of Samothrace,* dating from the 2nd century B.C., is a masterpiece of Hellenic art. Before you climb the staircase topped by this magnificent sculpture, follow the sign that directs you to *Venus de Milo* (in the Sully wing), sculpted in the 1st century B.C. as the quintessence of feminine grace and sensuality. Don't miss the nearby fragments from the 5th-century B.C. Parthenon. Also in the Sully wing are the *Seated Scribe* and the crypt of Osiris, the 18th-century rococo paintings of Fragonard and Boucher, and Ingres's *Turkish Bath.*

On the route from *Winged Victory* to *Mona Lisa* you will pass David's vast *Coronation of Napoléon* opposite his languid *Portrait of Madame Récamier.* Stop and admire Ingres's *Grand Odalisque.* In the Salle des Etats, Leonardo da Vinci's *La Gioconda (Mona Lisa)* is the center of attention. As camera clickers crowd around the portrait like crazed paparazzi, the famous Florentine gazes out at the throng with bemused implacability. The secret of her tantalizing smile is a technique known as *sfumato,* which blends the borders of the subject into the background. The artist blurred the outlines of her features so as to make the corners of her mouth and eyes fade away, making her expression ever changeable and eternally mysterious.

Da Vinci became so enamored of the painting that he carted it around with him on all his travels. In 1516, François I invited the painter and his beloved portrait to his château in the Loire valley and eventually bought *Mona Lisa.* The priceless painting was stolen from the Louvre in 1911 and finally discovered in Florence in 1913. Now, a guard and bulletproof glass protect the lady from further adventures.

No such security paraphernalia mars enjoyment of the other great paintings in the room, which contains a superb display of Italian Renaissance art. Da Vinci's *Virgin with the Infant Jesus and St. Anne* and *The Virgin of the Rocks* are as enchanting as the *Mona Lisa.* Notice Titian's *Open Air Concert,* Raphael's *La Belle Jardiniére,* and Veronese's massive *Marriage at Cana* among the many masterpieces. Other highlights of the Denon wing include Velasquez's infantas, Ribera's *Club Footed Boy,* Botticelli's frescoes, Michelangelo's powerful *Slaves,* Canova's *Psyche Revived by the Kiss of Cupid,* and works by Murillo, El Greco, and Goya.

The inauguration of the Richelieu wing in 1993 opened several acres of new exhibition space, allowing display of some 12,000 works of art in 165 airy, well-lit rooms. Before heading into the galleries, look in at the adjoining Cour Marly, the glass-roofed courtyard that houses the rearing *Marly Horses* by Coustou. The *Code of Hammurabi* in the Babylonian collection, Rubens' Medici cycle, Rembrandt's self-portraits, Holbein's *Portrait of Erasmus,* and Van Dyck's portrait of Charles I of England are among the profusion of legendary works in this new wing. For a change of pace, see the apartments of Napoléon III, decorated and furnished in over-the-top Second Empire style (open mornings only).

While you tour the Louvre, you will no doubt be impressed by its architecture. Before becoming a museum, it was a royal palace and, before that, a fortress-castle. Abandoned by the French monarchs in the 15th century in favor of their châteaux on the Loire, the Louvre became a royal residence again with François I in 1528; his

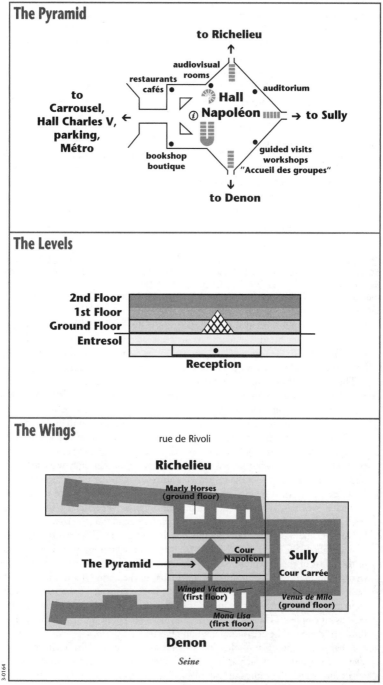

The Louvre

The Pyramid

to Richelieu

audiovisual rooms

restaurants cafés

Hall Napoléon

auditorium

to Carrousel, Hall Charles V, parking, Métro

(i)

→ to Sully

bookshop boutique

guided visits workshops "Accueil des groupes"

to Denon

The Levels

2nd Floor
1st Floor
Ground Floor
Entresol

Reception

The Wings

rue de Rivoli

Richelieu

Marly Horses (ground floor)

Cour Napoléon

The Pyramid →

Sully

Cour Carrée

Winged Victory (first floor)

Venus de Milo (ground floor)

Mona Lisa (first floor)

Denon

Seine

3-0164

collection of Italian art was the start of the future museum. The king also commissioned the building's transformation into a Renaissance palace. The Louvre's Cour Carrée ("square courtyard," the easternmost courtyard) is in fact one of the highest achievements of French Renaissance architecture.

But in the 17th century, with the construction of Versailles, the Louvre's regal connection was again eclipsed. Not until the French Revolution would the palace find its true calling. In 1791, the National Assembly decreed that a public museum be created in the Louvre.

Since then, the collections have increased and they continue to grow today. The enormous glass pyramid that serves as the museum's new entrance was a controversial undertaking supported by President Mitterrand during the last decade. While many admired the audacious design, others feared that its modernism would clash with the palace's classical lines. Like other monuments that initially faced strong opposition, the pyramid has gradually won over most critics. Whether by day when the pyramid gathers and reflects the sunlight or by night when the courtyard sparkles with artificial light, the monument has taken its place among the beauties of Paris.

✪ **Cathédrale de Notre-Dame.** 6 Parvis Notre-Dame, Ile de la Cité, 4e. ☎ **01-42-34-56-10.** Cathedral, free. Crypt, 32F ($5.50) adults, 21F ($3.65) ages 12–25. Cathedral open daily 8am–6:45pm (closed Sat 12:30–2pm); Crypt, Apr–Sept daily 10am–6pm, Oct–Mar 10am–5pm; museum, Wed and Sat–Sun 2:30–6pm; treasury, Mon–Sat 9:30am–5:30pm. Six masses are celebrated on Sun, four on weekdays and one on Sat. Métro: Cité or St-Michel. RER: St-Michel.

In 1768, geographers decided that all distances in France would be measured from Notre-Dame. One hundred and seventy-six years later, when Paris was liberated during World War II, General de Gaulle rushed to the cathedral after his return, to pray in thanksgiving. In many ways, Notre-Dame was and still is the center of France.

The Gothic loftiness of Notre-Dame dominates the Seine and the Ile de la Cité as well as the history of Paris. On the spot where this majestic cathedral now stands, the Romans had built a temple, which was followed by a Christian basilica and then a Romanesque church. Maurice de Sully, bishop of Paris, decided to build a new cathedral for the expanding population, and construction started in 1163. The building was completed in the 14th century, but that's just the beginning of Notre-Dame's eventful history. Crusaders prayed here before leaving on their holy wars, and polyphonic music developed in the cathedral. Parisians, like other urban dwellers in the Middle Ages, learned religious history by looking at the statuary and the glorious stained-glass windows of their cathedral. Built in an age of illiteracy, the cathedral retells the stories of the Bible in its portals, paintings, and stained glass.

Notre-Dame was pillaged during the French Revolution: Citizens mistook statues of saints above the portals on the west front for representations of their kings, and, in the midst of their revolutionary fervor, took them down. Some of these statues were found in the 1970s, almost 200 years later, in the Latin Quarter. It was in the cathedral that Napoléon, wishing to emphasize the primacy of the state over the church, crowned himself emperor, and then crowned Joséphine, his Martinique-born wife, as his empress. (The job would normally have been done by an archbishop. Pope Pius VII, there for the occasion, raised no objections.)

A happier chapter was Viollet-le-Duc's restoration in the 19th century. Writer Victor Hugo and artists such as Ingres called attention to the dangerous state of disrepair into which the cathedral had fallen, thus raising a new awareness of its artistic value. Whereas 18th-century neoclassicists had virtually ignored the creations of the Middle Ages—and had even replaced the stained glass at Notre-Dame with normal glass—19th-century romantics saw that remote period with new eyes and greater appreciation. Besides bringing new life to the rose windows and the statues, Viollet-le-Duc combined scientific research with his own very personal creative ideas and designed Notre-Dame's spire, a new feature of the building. Also in the 19th century, Baron Haussmann (Napoléon III's urban planner) evicted those Parisians whose houses cluttered the cathedral's vicinity. The houses were torn down to permit better views of the edifice.

Excavations under the parvis have revealed traces of Notre-Dame's history from Gallo-Roman times to the 19th century. Vestiges of Roman ramparts, rooms heated by hypocaust (an ancient system with underground furnaces and tile flues), medieval cellars, and the foundations of a foundling hospital are displayed, as are several fascinating photographs of the surrounding neighborhood before Baron Haussmann's renovations.

Yet it is the art of Notre-Dame, rather than its history, that still awes. The west front contains 28 statues representing the monarchs of Judea and Israel. The three portals depict, from left to right, the Last Judgment; the Madonna and Child; St. Anne, the Virgin's mother; and Mary's youth until the birth of Jesus. The interior, with its slender, graceful columns, is impressive—there is room for as many as 6,000 worshipers. The three rose windows—to the west, north, and south—are masterful, their colors a glory to behold on a sunny day.

For a look at the upper parts of the church, the river, and much of Paris, climb the 387 steps up to the top of one of the towers. The south tower holds Notre-Dame's 13-ton bell, which is rung on special occasions

✪ **Musée d'Orsay.** 1 rue Bellechasse, 7e. ☎ **01-40-49-48-14,** or 01-40-49-48-48 for information desk. Web site: http://www.musee-orsay.fr. Admission 39F ($6.80) adults, 27F ($4.70) ages 18–24, free for ages 17 and under. Reduced admission on Sun, Tues–Wed and Fri–Sat 10am–6pm, Thurs 10am–9:45pm, Sun 9am–6pm. From June 20–Sept 20 the museum opens at 9am. Métro: Solférino. RER: Musée-d'Orsay.

More than a decade ago, a brilliantly renovated train station and the best art of the 19th century were combined to create one of the world's great museums.

The Gare d'Orsay, a fabulous turn-of-the-century building, was one of Paris's main train stations, a wonderful iron-and-glass monument to the industrial age. It was constructed by the Compagnie des Chemins de Fer d'Orléans, which serviced France's southwest. By 1939, though, the Gare d'Orsay was virtually abandoned. Years later it was featured in Orson Welles's film version of Franz Kafka's *The Trial.* In the 1970s, it was classified as a historical monument.

For years, Paris's collections of 19th-century art were distributed among the Louvre, the Musée d'Art Moderne, and the very crowded rooms of the small Musée du Jeu de Paume, with its unsurpassed impressionist masterpieces. In 1986, these collections were transferred to the Orsay. Thousands of paintings, sculptures, objets d'art, items of furniture, architectural displays, even photographs and movies, illustrate the diversity and richness of 19th-century art, including not only impressionism but also realism, postimpressionism, and art nouveau.

There are three floors of exhibits. On the ground floor you will find Ingres's *La Source,* Millet's *L'Angelus,* the Barbizon school, Manet's *Olympia,* and other works of early impressionism. Impressionism continues on the upper level, with Renoir's *Le Moulin de la Galette,* Manet's *Déjeuner sur l'herbe,* Degas's *Racing at Longchamps,* Monet's "Cathedrals," van Gogh's *Self-Portrait,* and *Whistler's Mother;* there are also works by Gauguin and the Pont-Aven school, Toulouse-Lautrec, Pissarro, Cézanne, and Seurat. Symbolism, naturalism, and art nouveau are represented on the middle level; the international art nouveau exhibit includes fabulous furniture and objets d'art as well as Koloman Moser's *Paradise,* an enticing design for stained glass.

Besides exhibiting astounding art, the Musée d'Orsay is a great place in which to spend an entire afternoon. Its restaurant and cafe are quite pleasant, and the bookstore and gift shop have an excellent selection.

✪ The Eiffel Tower (Tour Eiffel). Parc du Champ-de-Mars, 7e. ☎ **01-44-11-23-23.** Web site: http://www.tour-eiffel.fr. Admission 20F ($3.50) for the elevator to the 1st level (188 feet), 42F ($7.30) to the 2nd level (380 feet), 57F ($9.90) to the highest level (1,060 feet). Reduced admission for children under 12. Walking up the stairs to the 1st and 2nd levels costs 14F ($2.40). Sept to mid-June, daily 9:30am–11pm; late June–Aug, daily 9am–midnight. Note that in fall and winter the stairs are open only until 6:30pm. Métro: Trocadéro, Bir-Hakeim, or Ecole-Militaire. RER: Champs-de-Mars.

The Eiffel Tower was built as a temporary structure to add flair to the Exposition Universelle (World's Fair) of 1889, but it remained standing and eventually became one of the best known symbols of Paris. Praised by some and damned by others, the tower created as much controversy in its time as Pei's pyramid at the Louvre did in the 1980s.

The tower symbolizes the age of steel construction. At first many thought that it simply couldn't be built, and it took more than 2 years, but upon its completion the Eiffel Tower was the tallest human-built structure in the world. The Prince of Wales (later Edward VII) and his family were the first to ascend the tower. It was decried by artists and writers such as Maupassant, Verlaine, and Huysmans (who called it a "hollow candlestick"), and nature lovers thought that it would interfere with the flight of birds over Paris. Charles Garnier, architect of the Opéra, was among those who signed a protest. But the Eiffel Tower *was* admired by Rousseau, Utrillo, Chagall, and Delaunay, and in the 1960s it was the subject of a wonderful study by semiologist Roland Barthes.

People have hated it and loved it, but the Eiffel Tower has never been boring. In fact, it always seems to have triggered the whimsical side of human nature. In 1923, for instance, Pierre Labric, who was later to become mayor of Montmartre, went down the tower's steps on his bicycle.

Politics has also played a role in its life. During the war, the Germans hung a sign on it that read: *"Deutschland Siegt Auf Allen Fronten"* ("Germany is victorious on all fronts"). In 1958, a few months before Fidel Castro's rise to power, Cuban revolutionaries hung their red-and-black flag from the first level, and, in 1979, an American from Greenpeace hung one that read: "Save the Seals." In 1989, the Tower celebrated its centennial with music and fireworks (the show lasted 89 minutes).

Probably the best approach to the tower is to take the Métro to the Trocadéro station and walk from the Palais de Chaillot to the Seine. Besides fabulous views, especially when the Trocadéro fountains are in full force, you get a free show from the dancers and acrobats who perform around the Palais de Chaillot.

The best view is, of course, from the top level, where historians have recreated the office of engineer Gustave Eiffel. On a clear day, you can see the entire city from here but face an epistemological problem: What is a view of Paris worth that doesn't take in the Eiffel Tower?

The vast green esplanade beneath the tower is the Parc du Champs-de-Mars, which extends all the way to the 18th-century Ecole Militaire (Military Academy), at its southeast end. This formal lawn was once a parade ground for French troops.

The Eiffel Tower at night is one of the great sights of Paris and shouldn't be missed. The gold lighting highlights the delicacy of the steelwork in a way that is missed in daylight. Skip the tour buses and pickpockets on Trocadéro and head to the Ecole Militaire for a more tranquil view.

☺ Arc de Triomphe. Place Charles-de-Gaulle, 8e. ☎ **01-43-80-31-31.** Admission 35F ($6) adults, 23F ($4) ages 12–25 , free for children under 12. Apr 1–Sept 30 Tues–Sat 9:30am–10:30pm; Sun–Mon 9:30am–6pm. Oct 1–Mar 31 Tues–Sat 10am–10:30pm; Sun–Mon 10am–5:30pm. Closed major holidays. Métro: Charles-de-Gaulle-Etoile.

The imposing Arc de Triomphe is the largest triumphal arch in the world, commissioned by Napoléon in honor of his Grande Armée and its 128 victorious battles, whose names are inscribed here. "A monument dedicated to the Grande Armée must be large, simple, majestic and borrow nothing from antiquity," he instructed the architect, Chalgrin. Working within the neo-classical style, the architect nonetheless transcended it by dispensing with columns. Ironically, the arch was far from complete by the time France's imperial army had been swept from the field at the Battle of Waterloo in 1814 and in fact it was not completed until 1836. Although it has come to symbolize France and her greatness, it has also witnessed some singular defeats, as in 1871 and 1940, when victorious German armies marched through the arch and down the Champs-Elysées.

In August 1944, General de Gaulle came here after the liberation of Paris; those black-and-white pictures taken then are powerful symbols of the end of fascism and war. Napoléon's funeral cortege passed below the arch in 1840, but Victor Hugo is still the only person ever to lie in state beneath it.

Beneath the arch, under a gigantic tricolor flag, burns the eternal flame for France's Unknown Soldier, a flame which is re-lit every evening at 6:30. The inscription reads: *"Ici repose un soldat français mort pour la patrie, 1914–1918"* ("Here rests a French soldier who died for his country"). There is a special remembrance ceremony here on Armistice Day, November 11, as well as on other national holidays.

Several outstanding 19th-century sculptures cover the arch. The most famous of these is Rude's *La Marseillaise,* seen on the bottom right on the Champs-Elysées side. It represents the departure for the front of volunteer soldiers in 1792.

To reach the stairs and elevators that climb the arch, take the underpass via the white Métro entrances. Twelve avenues radiate from the place Charles-de-Gaulle, formerly place de l'Etoile, one of the busiest traffic hubs in Paris. Watch in amazement as cars careen around the arch yet somehow manage not to collide. From the top, 162 feet high, you can see in a straight line the Champs-Elysées, the obelisk in the place de la Concorde, and the Louvre. On the opposite side is the Grande Arche de la Défense, a multipurpose cube-shaped structure so large that Notre-Dame could fit beneath it. Also from the top you can see the elegant parklike avenue Foch, leading to the vast Bois de Boulogne.

☺ Basilique du Sacré-Coeur. 25 rue du Chevalier-de-la-Barre, 18e. ☎ **01-53-41-89-00.** Basilica, free; dome 15F ($2.60) adult, 8F ($1.60) students 6–25 and over 60; crypt 15F ($2.60) and 8F ($1.40) respectively. Dome and crypt, 30F ($5.20). Basilica, daily 7am–11pm. Dome and crypt, Apr–Sept, daily 9am–7pm; Oct–Mar, daily 9am–6pm. Métro: Anvers. Follow signs to the funiculaire, which takes you to the church for one Métro ticket.

Made famous by Utrillo and 100 lesser artists who lived in Montmartre, Sacré-Coeur is a vaguely Byzantine-Romanesque church built from 1876 to 1919. Its sensual white dome is almost as familiar as the Arc de Triomphe and the Eiffel Tower, and it, too, is a romantic symbol of Paris. Its construction was begun after France's defeat in the Franco-Prussian War; Catholics raised money to build this monument to the Sacred Heart of Jesus. Be sure to visit the dome. You must climb lots of stairs (that's why it's a good idea to take the elevator up from the Métro and ride the *funiculaire*), but the view is fabulous: 30 miles across the rooftops of Paris on a clear day.

On the other side of Sacré-Coeur is the place du Tertre, which has been totally swamped by tourists and an army of quick-sketch artists. Following any street downhill from the place du Tertre leads you to the quiet side of Montmartre and a glimpse of what Paris must have looked like before busy Baron Haussmann got to work building boulevards.

✪ **Cimetière du Père-Lachaise.** Bd. de Ménilmontant, 20e. Free admission. Mar 16–Nov 5, Mon–Fri 8am–6pm, Sat 8:30am–6pm, Sun 9am–6pm; Nov 6–Mar 15, Mon–Fri 8am–5:30pm, Sat 8:30am–5:30pm, Sun 9am–5:30pm. Métro: Père-Lachaise.

The Cimetière du Père-Lachaise may well be the world's most romantic cemetery. With its shady paths and profusion of flowers and sculpture, the dearly departed are resting in exquisite beauty as well as peace. See map on page 152.

What attracts most visitors, though, are the many famous people who are buried here—artists, writers, musicians, and dramatists: Molière, La Fontaine, Beaumarchais, Delacroix, Ingres, Balzac, Chopin, Corot, Bizet, Musset, Comte, Oscar Wilde, Sarah Bernhardt, Proust, Modigliani, Apollinaire, Isadora Duncan, Anna de Noailles, Colette, Gertrude Stein, Edith Piaf, Jim Morrison, Simone Signoret, and Yves Montand.

Some of these graves are veritable pilgrimage sites, such as that of Chopin for Poles; Allan Kardec, founder of spiritualism, whose grave is always heaped with flowers; and Jim Morrison, for truly devout Doors fans. The tomb of murdered journalist Victor Noir has attracted hordes of women who believe the odd superstition that if they rub a certain part of his statue they will conceive a child. The tragic love story of Abélard and Héloïse has faded from our consciousness but in the 19th century their tombs were a magnet for disappointed lovers. "Go when you will, you find somebody snuffling over that tomb," wrote Mark Twain in *Innocents Abroad.*

Also at Père-Lachaise are moving memorials to the Holocaust, and the **Mur des Fédéres,** a wall against which the last insurgents of the Paris Commune were shot in 1871. You can't miss the elaborate **Monument aux Morts** by Bartholomé. Inside the locked doors are underground chambers filled with containers of bones from abandoned mausoleums. Curiously, the doors are outfitted with heavy brass knockers. I have banged many times but no one, as yet, has answered the door.

Note: You can pick up a free map in the office at the main entrance, but the map sold for 10F ($1.75) by the newsstand across the street is more detailed and easier to follow.

✪ **Jardin du Luxembourg.** 6e. ☎ **01-42-34-23-62.** Métro: Odéon. RER: Luxembourg.

The French love of order and harmony is perfectly expressed in these formal gardens that were commissioned by King Henri IV's queen, Marie de Medici, in the 17th century. Long gravel walks shaded by tall trees lead to a central pond and fountain. Along the way flower beds and classical statues create a calm, inviting space.

With the first breath of spring, Parisians flock to the park, grab a metal chair, and settle in for a serious bout of reading, sunbathing or people-watching. Sunday afternoon band concerts draw a crowd in the summer and The Medici Fountain at the end of a long pool is a cool, shady spot on a hot day. Children love the park, too, especially for the *parc à jeux* (playground) and the *théâtre des marionettes* (puppet theater). Besides pools and fountains and statues there are tennis courts and spaces for playing *boules.* In the southwest corner of the garden there is an orchard where several hundred species of apple and pear trees blossom each spring.

The **Palais du Luxembourg,** at the northern edge of the park, was also built for Marie de Medici. Upon the queen's banishment in 1630, the palace was abandoned until the Revolution, when it was used as a prison. The American writer Thomas Paine was imprisoned in the palace in 1793 when he fell out of favor with Robespierre. He only narrowly escaped execution. The palace is now the seat of the French Senate.

"And the view! Ethyl, you should've seen it . . ."
Great Spots for Getting That Panoramic Shot

Everyone who goes to Paris dreams of seeing the rooftops, either by day or by night. The highest look-out spot is the 276-meter-high platform on the **Eiffel Tower.** The second-highest perch is the outdoor terrace on the 56th floor of the 209-meter-high **Tour Montparnasse.** From the **Grande Arche de la Défense** you have a magnificent view of the triumphal way designed by Le Nôtre in the 17th century, with its series of landmark points—the Arc de Triomphe, the place de la Concorde, the Tuileries, and the Cour Napoléon at the Louvre. Great views can also be had from **Sacré-Coeur** and the **Arc de Triomphe.** Other less obvious viewpoints include **La Samaritaine,** which provides exceptional views of the Conciergerie, Notre-Dame, Pont Neuf and the Institut de France; and **Le Printemps,** which looks out over the Opéra and La Madeleine. There's also a good view of the islands from the **Institut du Monde Arabe.**

✪ **Sainte-Chapelle.** 4 bd. du Palais, Palais de Justice, Ile de la Cité, 4e. ☎ **01-53-73-78-50.** Admission 32F ($5.50) adults, 21F ($3.65) ages 12–25, free for children under 12. Combined ticket Sainte-Chapelle–Conciergerie 50F ($8.70). Apr–Sept, daily 9:30am–6:30pm; Oct–Mar, daily 10am–5pm. Closed major holidays. Métro: Cité or St-Michel. RER: St-Michel.

After the austerity of Notre-Dame, Sainte-Chapelle is an explosion of color. True, the columns were painted in the 19th century renovation, but two-thirds of the stained-glass windows are original, most of them from the 13th century. The sun streaming through the brilliant red and blue windows is one of the most unforgettable sights in Paris.

Sainte-Chapelle really consists of two chapels, one on top of the other. The *chapelle basse,* or lower chapel, was used by palace servants; it is ornamented with fleur-de-lis designs. The *chapelle haute,* or upper chapel, is one of the highest achievements of Gothic art. Here, Old and New Testament scenes are emblazoned in 15 perfect stained-glass windows covering 612 square meters. They should be read from bottom to top and from left to right. The 1134 scenes trace the Christian story from the Garden of Eden to the Apocalypse. The first window to the right represents the story of the Crown of Thorns; St. Louis is shown several times.

Louis IX, the only French king to become a saint, had the "Holy Chapel" built as a shrine to house the relics of the crucifixion, including Christ's Crown of Thorns (now in Notre-Dame). Building Sainte-Chapelle cost less than the immensely expensive Crown of Thorns, which he bought from the emperor of Constantinople. More valued in medieval times than any saint's femur or martyr's skull, the Crown of Thorns was said to have been acquired at Christ's crucifixion.

Built with unusual speed between 1246 and 1248, Sainte-Chapelle was a notable engineering feat. Supporting the roof with pillars and buttresses allowed the architect, Pierre de Montreuil, to brighten the interior with 50-foot high windows. Amazingly, the Sainte-Chapelle survived a fire in the 17th century as well as plans for its destruction during the French Revolution. The 247-foot spire soars above the law courts that encircle this remarkable chapel.

✪ **Musée Rodin.** Hôtel Biron, 77 rue de Varenne, 7e. ☎ **01-47-05-01-34.** Admission 28F ($4.85) adults, 18F ($3.15) ages 18–24 and adults on Sun; 5F for the garden only; free for ages 17 and under. Apr–Sept Tues–Sun 9:30am–5:45pm; Oct–Mar Tues–Sun 9:30am–4:45pm. Métro: Varenne.

Père-Lachaise Cemetery

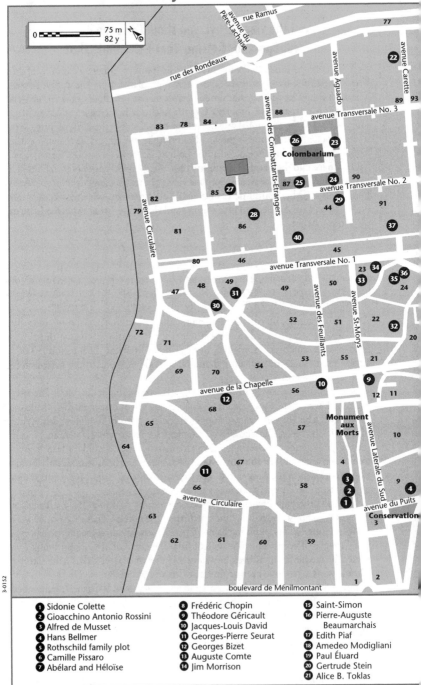

Sidonie Colette
Gioacchino Antonio Rossini
Alfred de Musset
Hans Bellmer
Rothschild family plot
Camille Pissaro
Abélard and Héloïse
Frédéric Chopin
Théodore Géricault
Jacques-Louis David
Georges-Pierre Seurat
Georges Bizet
Auguste Comte
Jim Morrison
Saint-Simon
Pierre-Auguste Beaumarchais
Edith Piaf
Amedeo Modigliani
Paul Éluard
Gertrude Stein
Alice B. Toklas

3-0152

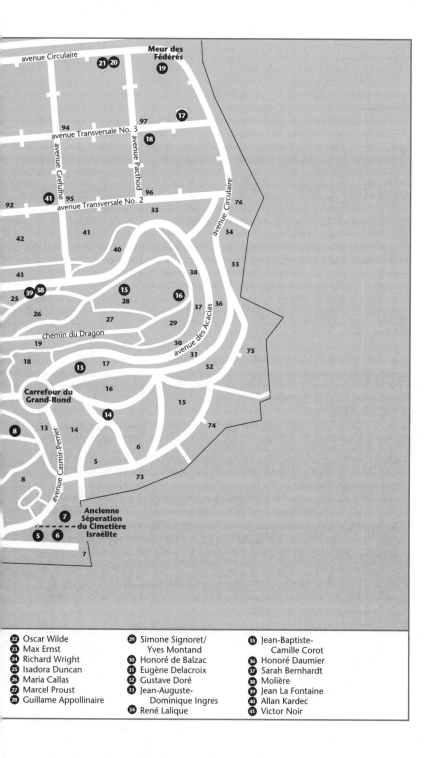

avenue Circulaire

Meur des Fédérés

21 20

19

17

94   97

18

avenue Transversale No. 3

avenue Grefulhe

avenue Pathod

96

92   41   95

avenue Transversale No. 2

35

avenue Circulaire

76

41

42

40

34

43

38

33

39 38

15   16

36

25   28

37

26   27   29

avenue des Acacias

chemin du Dragon

30

19

18   17   31   75

13   16   32

Carrefour du Grand-Rond

15

8   13   14

74

avenue Casmir-Perrier

14

5   6

8   73

7

Ancienne Séperation du Cimetière Israélite

5   6

7

22	Oscar Wilde	29	Simone Signoret/ Yves Montand	35	Jean-Baptiste-Camille Corot
23	Max Ernst	30	Honoré de Balzac	36	Honoré Daumier
24	Richard Wright	31	Eugène Delacroix	37	Sarah Bernhardt
25	Isadora Duncan	32	Gustave Doré	38	Molière
26	Maria Callas	33	Jean-Auguste-Dominique Ingres	39	Jean La Fontaine
27	Marcel Proust	34	René Lalique	40	Allan Kardec
28	Guillame Appollinaire			41	Victor Noir

The extraordinary ability of Rodin to breathe life into marble and bronze makes this museum a stand-out in a city full of great art. Rodin's own legendary sensuality outraged 19th-century critics and was expressed in his sculpted nudes. This wide-ranging collection offers a superlative insight into Rodin's genius and includes all of his greatest works.

The Kiss immortalizes in a sensuous curve of white marble the passion of doomed 13th-century lovers Paolo Malatesta and Francesca da Rimini. In the courtyard, *Burghers of Calais* is a harrowing commemoration of the siege of Calais in 1347, after which the triumphant Edward III of England kept the town's six richest burghers as servants. Also in the courtyard is *The Thinker,* "primal, tense, his chin resting on a toil worn hand," wrote Helen Keller. "In every limb I felt the throes of emerging mind." The *Gates of Hell* is a portrayal of Dante's *Inferno.* Intended for the *Musée des Arts Decoratifs,* these massive bronze doors were not completed until seven years after the artist's death.

Some of the 16 rooms are taken up by studies done by Rodin before executing the sculptures. Particularly interesting is the evolution of his controversial nude of Balzac, which was his last major work. Don't miss the portrait heads of his many women friends, as well as the work of his mistress, Camille Claudel.

The museum is housed in the 18th century Hôtel Biron, which had been a convent before it became a residence for artists and writers. Matisse, Jean Cocteau, and the poet Rainer Maria Rilke lived and worked in the mansion before Rodin moved there in 1910 at the height of his popularity. In 1911 the government bought the studio and transformed it into a museum devoted to France's greatest sculptor.

3 Ile de la Cité & Ile St-Louis

ILE DE LA CITÉ

Little is known about the Parisii, the Celtic tribe of fishermen who built their huts on Ile de la Cité around 250 B.C. Living on an easily defensible island allowed the tribe to fish in peace, at least until the Romans came along in 52 B.C. and conquered them. Later on, the island provided a safe haven from barbarian invasions and withstood an assault and siege by the Normans in the 9th century.

The Merovingian kings and later the Capetians also felt secure within the arms of the Seine and made the island their royal residence and administrative headquarters. The Ile de la Cité blossomed in the 13th century as **Notre-Dame** (see page 146) arose, followed by **Sainte-Chapelle** (see page 151) and the royal palace of the **Conciergerie** (see below). At the end of the 14th century the royal residence moved to the right bank but the island remains a judicial and administrative center. While tourists admire the splendid Gothic art of Notre-Dame and Sainte-Chapelle, Parisians are likely to be found either in the law courts of the Palais de Justice or tangling with French bureaucracy in the Prefecture.

Conciergerie. Palais de Justice, Ile de la Cité, 1er. ☎ **01-53-73-78-50.** Admission 32F ($5.50) adults, 21F ($3.65) ages 12–25, free for children under 12. Combined ticket Sainte-Chapelle–Conciergerie 50F ($8.70). Open Apr–Sept daily 9:30am–6:30pm; Oct–Mar daily 10am–5pm. Métro: Cité, Châtelet-les-Halles, or St-Michel. RER: St-Michel.

Every French schoolchild must shudder on passing the Conciergerie. This building dates from the Middle Ages, when it was an administrative office of the Crown; tortures were frequent at the Tour Bonbec. Ravaillac, Henri IV's murderer, was a prisoner here before he was literally torn apart by an angry crowd. But the Conciergerie is most famous for its days as a prison during the French Revolution, when 4,164 "enemies of the people" passed through here, more than half of them

Bridge Over the River Seine

The city of Paris has embarked on a program to illuminate all 35 bridges crossing the Seine before the year 2000, and those already lit make an after-dark stroll along the river particularly lovely. Each of the spans has its own rich and unique history. Among the most distinctive are the ironically named Pont Neuf (New Bridge), which, completed in 1604 and inaugurated by Henri IV, is the oldest bridge in town; the pont Royal (1685–89), where Parisians celebrated festivities for centuries; the pont des Arts (1804), an iron footbridge built in 1804, which crosses from the Institut on the Left Bank to the Louvre on the Right; the pont Mirabeau (1895–97) adorned by four bronze statues and immortalized by Apollinaire; and the elegantly sculptured single-span Pont Alexandre III (1896–1900).

headed for the guillotine on the place de la Révolution, now the place de la Concord. Besides revolutionary ringleaders Danton and Robespierre, Charlotte Corday and the poet André Chenier were imprisoned here. Marie Antoinette was kept in a fetid 11-foot-square cell to await her fate. When she was taken to her execution the despised queen was forced to ride backward in the cart so she would have to face a jeering, taunting crowd. (By the way, historians now consider it extremely unlikely that Marie Antoinette ever said "Let them eat cake" in response to the peasants' demand for bread.)

Marie Antoinette's cell is now a chapel and the dank cells have been transformed with exhibits and mementos designed to convey a sense of prison life in a brutal era. The Gothic halls built by Philip the Fair in the 14th century are impressive examples of medieval secular architecture.

Place Dauphine.

Laid out by Henri IV in 1607, this triangular square followed the place des Vosges in the Marais and was supposed to be surrounded by brick and stone houses. Unfortunately most of the houses were later destroyed, but it remains a quiet square between the quays of the Seine.

Pont Neuf.

After leaving the Conciergerie, turn left and stroll along the Seine past medievalesque towers till you reach the Pont Neuf or "New Bridge." The span isn't new, of course; actually it's the oldest bridge in Paris, erected in 1604. In its day the bridge had two unique features: It was not flanked with houses and shops, and it was paved.

At the Hôtel Carnavalet, a museum in the Marais section (see below), is a painting called *Spectacle of Buffons,* showing what the bridge was like between 1665 and 1669. Duels were fought on the structure; great coaches belonging to the nobility crossed it; peddlers sold their wares; and as there were no public facilities, men defecated right on the bridge. With all those crowds, it attracted entertainers, such as Tabarin, who sought a few coins from the gawkers. The Pont Neuf is decorated with corbels, a mélange of grotesquerie.

Vert-Galant Square.

Take the steps from behind the statue of Henri IV to this peaceful square along the Seine, dedicated to France's most beloved king. Upon Henri IV's birth it is said that his mother sprinkled wine on his tongue to give him the right spirit. He went on to lead a boisterous life of wine, women, and more women but along the way managed to end France's ruinous religious wars by issuing the Edict of Nantes, which

Attractions—Ile de la Cité & Ile St-Louis

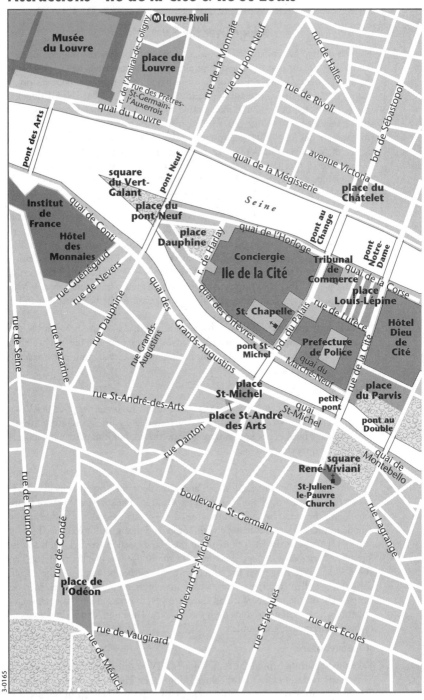

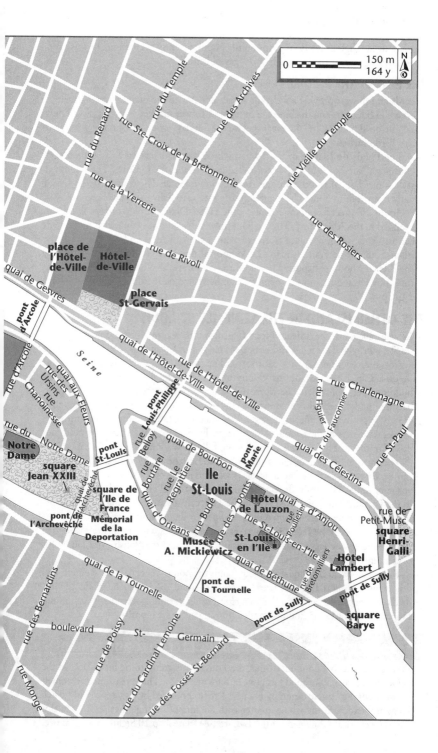

157

guaranteed religious freedom. Enormously popular during his lifetime, he was affectionately known as the Vert Galant or "gay old spark."

THE REST OF THE PICTURE

Birds and flowers provide a welcome splash of color to the island, even if the flowers are in bouquets and the birds are in cages. A **flower market** is held at place Louis-Lépine on Ile de la Cité, 4e, every day except Sunday, when the space is given over to a **bird market.**

The **Palais de Justice** or law courts, which Balzac described as a "cathedral of chicanery," are bustling with black-robed lawyers and their clients. The building's style is neoclassical and the proportions are monumental. The courts may be visited daily from 9am to 6pm. The main entrance is next to Sainte-Chapelle.

Across the street from Notre-Dame is the **Hôtel-Dieu,** the oldest hospital in Paris, founded in the 7th century. The spacious inner courtyard was remodeled in the 19th century and is a quiet place to relax. Behind the cathedral and on the tip of the island is the Ile de France square. **Le Memorial de la Déportation** commemorates the French who were deported to concentration camps in World War II. The sculpture is by Desserprit and the memorial can be visited daily from 10am to noon and 2 to 7pm.

THE OTHER ISLAND IN THE SEINE: ILE ST-LOUIS

As you walk across the little iron footbridge from the rear of Notre-Dame toward the Ile St-Louis, you'll enter a world of tree-shaded quays, restaurants, antique shops, and aristocratic town houses with courtyards. The special appeal of this sister island of Ile de la Cité is the extraordinary unity of its architectural design. Nearly all of its buildings were constructed between 1627 and 1674, when two islets were joined to become the Ile St-Louis. In contrast to the grandeur of Ile de la Cité, this island is as cozy as aristocratic housing can get. Plaques on the facades of houses identify the former residences of the famous—Marie Curie lived at 36 quai de Béthune, near Pont de la Tournelle. The island is covered more fully in Walking Tour 3 in chapter 7.

The most exciting mansion is the **Hôtel de Lauzun,** at 17 quai d'Anjou, which can be viewed only from the outside. It was the home of the duc de Lauzun, a favorite of Louis XIV until his secret marriage angered the king and the duc was sent to the Bastille. Baudelaire lived here in the 19th century, squandering his family fortune and penning poetry that would be banned in France until 1949.

Voltaire lived in the **Hôtel Lambert,** at 2 quai d'Anjou, with his mistress, and their quarrels here were legendary. The mansion also housed the Polish royal family for over a century.

Farther along, at no. 9 quai d'Anjou, stands the house where painter, sculptor, and lithographer Honoré Daumier lived between 1846 and 1863. Here he produced hundreds of lithographs satirizing the bourgeoisie and attacking government corruption. His caricature of Louis-Philippe landed him in jail for six months.

4 Louvre, Tuileries & Les Halles (1er Arrondissement)

In 1527, François I announced that the Louvre was going to be his palace on the Seine and the neighborhood hasn't been the same since. The extensions and embellishments of the Louvre begun by François I were continued by a succession of French kings and endowed the whole quarter with an aura of prestige that remains to this day. The classical refinement of the **Louvre** (see "The Top 10 Sights to See," above)

Attractions—Louvre, Tuileries & Les Halles

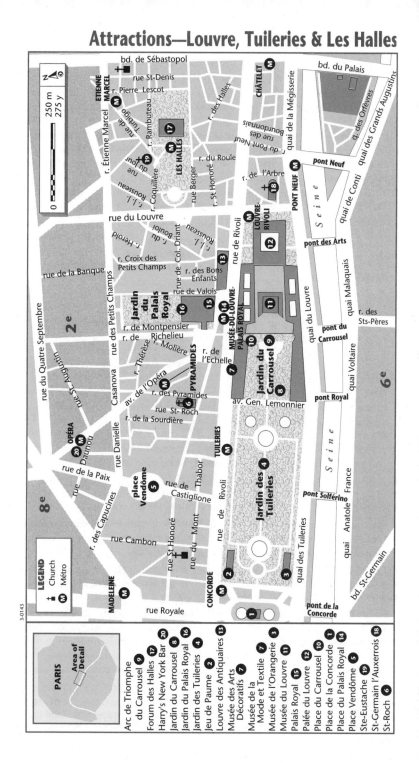

bd. de Sébastopol

rue St-Denis

r. Pierre Lescot

ÉTIENNE MARCEL

r. Étienne Marcel

rue de Turbigo

r. Rambuteau

LES HALLES

r. du Jour

rue Coquillère

r. J.-J. Rousseau

bd. du Palais

CHÂTELET

r. des Halles

rue des Bourdonnais

quai de la Mégisserie

quai des Grands Augustins

r. du Pont Neuf

pont Neuf

PONT NEUF

quai de Conti

r. de l'Arbre

Seine

rue du Louvre

rue de Rivoli

LOUVRE RIVOLI

r. Croix des Petits Champs

r. Hérold

r. du Bouloi

r. J.-J. Rousseau

r. de Col. Driant

rue de la Banque

r. des Bons Enfants

pont des Arts

quai Malaquais

r. des Sts-Pères

Jardin du Palais Royal

rue de Valois

MUSÉE-DU-LOUVRE-PALAIS ROYAL

quai du Louvre

2e

rue des Petits Champs

r. de Montpensier

r. de Richelieu

r. de Molière

r. Thérèse

r. de l'Echelle

Jardin du Carrousel

pont du Carrousel

quai Voltaire

6e

rue du Quatre Septembre

rue St-Augustin

Casanova

PYRAMIDES

av. de l'Opéra

r. des Pyramides

rue St-Roch

r. de la Sourdière

rue Danielle

av. Gen. Lemonnier

pont Royal

Seine

quai Anatole France

OPÉRA

rue Daunou

rue de la Paix

place Vendôme

rue de Castiglione

TUILERIES

Jardin des Tuileries

8e

rue de la Paix

r. des Capucines

Thabor

rue de Rivoli

rue du Mont

pont Solférino

quai des Tuileries

bd. St-Germain

rue Cambon

rue St-Honoré

MADELEINE

CONCORDE

rue Royale

pont de la Concorde

PARIS

Area of Detail

LÉGENDE
+ Church
M Métro

250 m
275 y

0

3-0143

159

Arc de Triomphe du Carrousel 9
Forum des Halles 17
Harry's New York Bar 20
Jardin du Carrousel 8
Jardin du Palais Royal 16
Jardin des Tuileries 4
Jeu de Paume 2
Louvre des Antiquaires 13
Musée des Arts Décoratifs 7
Musée de la Mode et Textile 7
Musée de l'Orangerie 7
Musée du Louvre 11
Palais Royal 15
Palée du Louvre 12
Place du Carrousel 10
Place de la Concorde 3
Place du Palais Royal 14
Place Vendôme 5
Ste-Eustache 19
St-Germain l'Auxerrois 18
St-Roch 6

is echoed in the formal **Jardins Des Tuileries,** which once adjoined a palace, Cardinal Richelieu's stately **Palais Royale,** the ritzy **Place Vendôme,** and the long stretch of arcades making up the Rue de Rivoli. Even the repertoire of the **Comédie-Française** is classical; Corneille, Molière, and Racine are performed in a style that is, what else?, classical.

The decorous facades and promenades are offset by a thriving commercialism. Shopping runs the gamut from Cartier on Place Vendôme to Eiffel Tower key rings along the Rue de Rivoli, with the underground shopping mall of Les Halles focusing on the middle range. Although the shopping center itself is somewhat creepy at night, the streets around Les Halles are often going strong long after the rest of Paris has gone to sleep. Connected to Les Halles by a vast Métro station is **Châtelet,** the geographical center of Paris and a hub for Paris's lively theater, music, and jazz scene.

Musée de l'Orangerie des Tuileries. Place de la Concorde, 1er. ☎ **01-42-97-48-16.** Admission 30F ($5.20) adults (20F [$3.50] on Sun), 20F ($3.50) ages 18–25, free for ages 17 and under. Wed–Mon 9:45am–5:15pm. Métro: Concorde.

A pavilion built during the Second Empire, the Orangerie has housed the renowned Jean Walter and Paul Guillaume art collection since 1984. The collection was sold to the French state by Domenica Walter, who was married to both men (not at the same time, of course). Although the collection has fewer than 150 paintings, it is a truly remarkable group of impressionist and early 20th-century painters. Among the artists represented are Cézanne, Renoir, Rousseau, Matisse, Derain, Picasso, Laurencin (whose portrait of Coco Chanel is marvelous), and Soutine. The lower floor contains the most incredible display of Monet's *Nymphéas* anywhere, two oval rooms that are wrapped around with almost 360° of water lilies that Monet painted especially for the Orangerie. The effect is like being in the gardens at the artists' home in Giverny yourself. After the vastness of the Louvre, the Orangerie's intimate rooms are refreshing. The nudes by Aristide Maillol are outstanding and plans are afoot to add modern works by Picasso, Miro, Rodin, and Giacometti.

Galerie Nationale du Jeu de Paume. Place de la Concorde, Jardin des Tuileries, 1er. ☎ **01-47-03-12-50.** Admission 38F ($6.60) adults, 28F ($4.85) for students and seniors. Wed–Fri noon–7pm, Sat–Sun 10am–7pm, Tues noon–9:30pm. Métro: Concorde or Tuileries.

This former tennis court once housed the famous impressionist collection now at the Orsay. The gallery now features changing exhibitions of contemporary paintings, sculpture, photographs, and videos.

Musée des Arts Decoratifs. Palais du Louvre, 107 rue de Rivoli, 1er. ☎ **01-44-55-57-50.** Admission 25F ($4.35) adults, 16F ($2.75) ages 5–25 and over 60. Wed–Sat 12:30–6pm; Sun noon–6pm. Métro: Palais-Royal-Tuileries or Pyramides.

Located in the north wing of the Palais du Louvre, the Musée des Arts Décoratifs has a vast collection of about 180,000 items. All forms of decoration, including furniture and objets d'art, are represented, as are all periods from the Middle Ages to the present. As of this writing, the permanent exhibition is closed for renovation and is scheduled to re-open sometime in 1998. Meanwhile, the museum is scheduled to present a series of temporary exhibitions.

Musée de La Mode et Textile. Palais du Louvre, 107 rue de Rivoli, 1er. ☎ **01-44-55-57-50.** Admission 25F ($4.35) adults, 16F ($2.75) ages 18–25; free for ages 17 and under. Tues 11am–6pm; Wed 11am–10pm; Thurs–Fri 11am–6pm; Sat–Sun 10am–6pm. Métro: Tuileries or Palais-Royal.

In the same wing as the Musée des Arts Decoratifs, this sleek new museum is devoted to the history of fashion. Only a portion of the 16,000 costumes and 35,000 accessories in the collection will be presented in changing thematic exhibitions. Beautifully restored clothing from France's finest couturiers—Chanel, Dior, Shiaparelli, Lanvin, Balenciaga, Gaultier, Lacroix—are as much a social commentary as an esthetic pleasure.

St-Eustache. 2 rue du Jour, 1er. ☎ **01-42-36-31-05.** 9am–8pm daily. Closed Sundays 12:30pm–2:30pm. Métro: Les Halles.

A massive church at the heart of Les Halles and the rue St-Denis district, St-Eustache has been famous for its music ever since Franz Liszt played the organ here. It has very rich historical associations. Molière and Madame de Pompadour were baptized here and Molière's funeral was held here in 1673. Colbert, Louis XIV's finance minister, is buried in a black marble tomb embellished with a sculpture of Abundance by Coysevox.

St-Germain-L'Auxerrois. 2 place du Louvre, 1er. Daily 9am–8pm. Métro: Tuileries.

Begun on the site of an 8th-century church, St-Germain-L'Auxerrois is a melange of architectural styles. The Romanesque tower was built in the 12th century, the chancel is 13th-century Gothic, the porch is 15th-century flamboyant Gothic, the rose windows are from the Renaissance, and it was all restored in the 19th century. The interior contains excellent carved church-wardens' pews from the 17th century.

The church's history is as eventful as its architecture. When the monarchy moved to the Louvre in the 14th century, St-Germain became the royal church and welcomed Henri III, Henri IV, Marie de Médici, and Louis XIV. On August 24, 1572, the infamous St. Bartholomew Massacre was signaled by the bells of St-Germain. The scheming Catherine de Médici had persuaded her son, Charles IX, to sign the order for the massacre of Protestant Huguenots, some 50,000 of whom were slaughtered in Paris and the provinces.

St-Roch. 296 rue St-Honoré, 1er. 8am–7pm daily. Métro: Tuileries or Palais-Royal.

A battle around this church is what secured Bonaparte's ascent to power on October 5, 1795. The 17th-century church contains several important sculptures, including a bust of the gardener Le Nôtre by Coysevox, the Monument to Mignard (a painter) by Girardon, and works by Coustou and Delorme. Among the famous French buried here are Corneille and Diderot.

Palais-Royal. Rue St-Honoré, 1er. 8am–7pm daily. Métro: Palais-Royal–Musée-du-Louvre.

The Palais-Royal was originally known as the Palais-Cardinal, for it was the residence of Cardinal Richelieu, Louis XIII's prime minister. Richelieu had it built, and after his death it was inherited by the king, who died soon afterward. Louis XIV spent part of his childhood here with his mother, Anne of Austria, but later resided at the Louvre and Versailles. The palace was later owned by the duc de Chartres et Orléans (see "Parc Monceau," below), who encouraged the opening of cafes, gambling dens, and other public entertainments.

Although government offices presently occupy the Palais-Royal and visits are not allowed, do visit the **Jardin du Palais-Royal,** an enclosure bordered by arcades. Don't miss the main courtyard either, with the controversial 1986 sculpture by Buren: 280 prison-striped columns oddly placed here.

Jardins des Tuileries. Quai des Tuileries, 1er. ☎ **01-42-96-01-20.** May–Sept, daily 7am–9pm; Oct–Apr, daily 7am–7:30pm. Métro: Tuileries or Concorde.

Spread out over 63 acres, these formal gardens provide a history of French sculpture from the 17th century to the present within elegantly designed paths and promenades. Although some of the sculptures are of indifferent quality, the classical motif blends well with the design of the gardens. Plans are afoot to add modern works by Picasso, Miro, Rodin, and Giacometti.

Place Vendôme. Rue de Castiglione, 1er. Métro: Tuileries, Concorde, or Madeleine.

The patrician grandeur of the 17th-century place Vendôme epitomizes the age of Louis XIV, when grace and harmony were the dominant architectural values. The instantly recognizable names installed on the square—Hotel Ritz, Cartier, Van Cleef & Arpels, Boucheron—create an aura of opulence that seems designed to make only excessively wealthy people feel comfortable here. Among the famous residents of place Vendôme was Chopin, who died at no. 12 in 1849.

The **column** in the center, modeled on Trajan's column in Rome, was commissioned by Napoléon to honor those who fought and won the battle of Austerlitz. Austrian cannons were used in its construction. Napoléon's statue has graced the top of the column at different periods; royalists in 1815 substituted a fleur-de-lis, symbol of France's monarchy. A statue of Henri IV was also placed here. During the months of the Paris Commune, this changing condition was temporarily resolved when the column was destroyed (it was re-erected during the Third Republic).

THE REST OF THE PICTURE

Until the revolution, the quai de la Mégisserie was a slaughterhouse. Now, there's a daily **market** where you'll find a veritable menagerie of birds, dogs, cats, fishes, chickens, rabbits, and geese. The **Samaritaine** department store terrace at building 2 provides an exceptional view of the Conciergerie, Notre-Dame, pont Neuf and the Institut de France. The **pont des Arts** (1804), the city's only footbridge, is perhaps the most romantic bridge in Paris, especially at sunset. Tucked away between rue Bouloi and rue J. J. Rousseau is the **galerie Véro-Dodat,** a covered arcade built in 1826 and noted for its black and white paved floors.

5 The Opéra, Bourse & the Grand Boulevards (2e, 9e & 10e Arrondissements)

From the ornate Opéra to the sprawling boulevards that radiate out from it, lined with major department stores, the operative word is *big*. Although the fast food outlets and international chain stores may make it the least "Parisian" part of Paris, the area around the Opéra is a magnet for tourists. Banks and change places are abundant on boulevard des Italiens and many airlines, travel agencies, and government tourist offices have outlets on the Avenue de l'Opéra. I find the boulevards most appealing at night, when the crowds thin out and the illuminated streets reveal the grandeur Baron Haussmann must have intended. Best of all is Christmas along the Boulevard Haussmann, when Galeries Lafayette and Printemps try to outdo each other in staging elaborate window displays.

The boulevards run east into the rather workaday 10e arrondissement and the sex shops of rue Faubourg St-Denis. Unique 19th-century **arcades** zigzag through the 2e arrondissement from the boulevards south to the classically proportioned **place des Victoires.**

Opéra Garnier. Place de l'Opéra, 9e. ☎ **01-40-01-23-34.** 10am–5:30pm daily. Métro: Opéra.

In 1860 the city planners held a competition to choose the best design for a new opera house. The contest was won by a young unknown named Charles Garnier, whose design mixed elements of 17th-century Spanish style with an Italian Renaissance

Attractions–The Opéra, Bourse & the Grand Boulevards

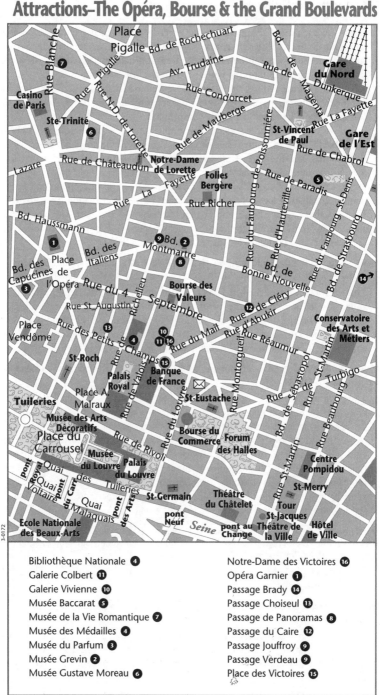

Bibliothèque Nationale ④

Galerie Colbert ⑪

Galerie Vivienne ⑩

Musée Baccarat ⑤

Musée de la Vie Romantique ⑦

Musée des Médailles ④

Musée du Parfum ③

Musée Grevin ②

Musée Gustave Moreau ⑥

Notre-Dame des Victoires ⑯

Opéra Garnier ①

Passage Brady ⑭

Passage Choiseul ⑬

Passage de Panoramas ⑧

Passage du Caire ⑫

Passage Jouffroy ⑨

Passage Verdeau ⑨

Place des Victoires ⑮

facade. "What a mess!" Empress Eugenie allegedly complained. "The style is neither Greek nor Roman." "It is the style of Napoléon III, Madame," replied Mr. Garnier, and indeed, the Opéra epitomizes the extravagant ornamentation of Second Empire style. The Chagall ceiling is the perfect top for the lush auditorium.

You can visit the auditorium for 30F ($5.20) unless there's a rehearsal in progress, but for the same price you might find a ticket for the evening ballet. And it doesn't cost anything to admire the majestic entrance hall.

Is there a "phantom of the opera"? The inspiration for Gaston Leroux's 1911 novel undoubtedly came from the vast subterranean caverns of the opera house, which enclose an underground lake. Although Leroux's tragic hero has not yet materialized from his mysterious palace on the lake, the building's nether regions do contain phantom voices. In 1907, a certain Alfred Clark buried two lead urns containing gramophone recordings of some of the greatest singers of the time, including Adelina Patti, Nellie Melba, Enrico Caruso, and Feodor Chaliapin. Opera lovers will have to wait another few years, however, to hear these gems, since Mr. Clark's instructions specified that the urns are not to be opened until the year 2007.

Musée Grevin. 10 bd. Montmartre, 9e. ☎ **01-47-70-85-05.** admission 50F ($8.70) adults; 36F ($6.25) children. Daily 1–7pm. Métro: Rue Montmartre or Richelieu-Drouot.

This waxworks, established in 1882, contains more than 500 figures arranged in animated tableaux that tell the history of France. Besides historical figures such as Charles VII being crowned at Reims in 1427 or Napoléon on the island of St. Helena, contemporary sports and political figures are represented, as well as stars of stage and screen. If you like waxworks, you'll love it; otherwise, avoid it.

Musée du Parfum. 39 Bd. des Capucines. ☎ **01-42-60-37-14**. Free admission. Open Mon– Sat 9am–6pm. Métro: Opéra.

The perfume museum is housed in a completely overhauled 19th-century theater on one of Paris' busiest thoroughfares. As you enter the lobby through a quiet courtyard, the lightly scented air reminds you why you're there—to appreciate perfume enough to buy a bottle in the ground floor shop. But first, a short visit upstairs introduces you to the rudiments of perfume history. The copper containers with spouts and tubes were used in the distillation of perfume oils and the exquisite collection of perfume bottles from the 17th to the 20th century is impressive. Even if perfume bores you, the air-conditioning is a welcome relief in the summer and the restrooms are spotless and free.

Musée des Médailles. Bibliothèque Nationale de France, 58 rue de Richelieu, 2e. ☎ **01-47-03-83-30.** Admission 22F ($3.80) adults, 15F ($2.60) students. Mon–Sat 1–5pm, Sun noon–6pm. Métro: Palais-Royal or Bourse.

The archaeological objects, cameos, bronzes, medals, and money displayed here were assembled originally by French kings.

Musée Baccarat. 30 bis, rue de Paradis, 10e. ☎ **01-47-70-64-30.** Admission 15F ($2.60). Mon–Sat 10am–6pm. Métro: Poissonnière.

Located on Paris' best street for china and glass shopping, this spectacular display shows the evolution of the famous glass manufacturer's style from the early 19th century to today. It's housed in one of the few remaining 19th-century warehouses in Paris.

Musée Gustave Moreau. 14 rue de la Rochefoucault, 9e. ☎ **01-48-74-38-50.** Admission 22F ($3.80); 15F ($2.60) students, ages 18–25; free under age 18. Thurs–Sun 10–12:45pm and 2–5:15pm; Mon and Wed 11am–5:15pm. Closed Tuesday. Métro: St-Georges.

Baron Haussmann: The Man Who Transformed Paris

Haussmann created so much of the Paris we see today that it's impossible to ignore him. He transformed the city in the 1850s and 1860s from a medieval town to a 19th-century metropolis. He razed old Paris, widened the streets, and laid out a series of broad boulevards leading from the then new railroad stations on the city's periphery into its heart. Along their routes he created dramatic open spaces like the place de l'Opéra and the place de l'Etoile (now the place Charles-de-Gaulle).

Haussmann was born in Paris in 1809 and went to the provinces, where he gained a reputation as a tough administrator capable of crushing socialism and republicanism wherever it was found. In 1853, Napoléon III appointed him prefect of the Seine, and he began his work of revising Paris. His lack of tact and his obstinate conviction that he was absolutely right were notorious, and he was widely hated for the destruction he caused. Despite the fact that his actions swept away most of the densest old neighborhoods, filled with mansions and private gardens, the straight, broad avenues he created have proven adaptable to different periods and fashions. That is more than can be said for some urban designs today.

This house and studio displays the works of the symbolist painter Gustave Moreau (1826–98), who embraced the bizarre and painted mythological subjects and scenes in a very sensuous romantic style. Among the works displayed are *Orpheus by the Tomb of Eurydice* and *Jupiter and Semele.* He taught at the Ecole des Beaux Arts and his influence can be seen in the works of Rouault, who became the first curator of this museum. Matisse was also a student of his.

Musée de la Vie Romantique. 16 rue Chaptal, 9e. ☎ **01-48-74-95-38.** Admission 17.50F ($3) adults; 9F ($1.55) students. Tues–Sun 10am–5:40pm. Closed holidays. Métro: St-Georges.

This small museum is located in a quarter that was called New Athens in the 19th century, when it was the center of literary and artistic life. Once the atelier of painter Ary Scheffer, the museum is now used to display the possessions and mementos of George Sand.

THE ARCADES

Far from the maddening crowds along the grand boulevards lie the iron and glass arcades that could be considered the Western world's first shopping malls. Most of them were built from the end of the 18th century to the middle of the 19th century. At the time, merchants were looking for innovative ways to display their wares to an increasingly numerous middle class. Streets were crowded, dirty, unpaved, and badly lit. Glass-topped markets spared their fashionable clientele the inconveniences of city life and launched a new pastime: window shopping. The covered arcades that remain today are still havens for strolling and shopping, and transport you to an era when Paris set the standard for urban style.

The arrondissement that has the greatest concentration of these charming galleries is the 2e. Each one has its own particular character. The **Passage du Caire,** 2 place du Caire (Métro: Sentier), was built in 1798 to commemorate Napoleon's triumphal entry into Cairo. The facade reflects the "Egyptomania" in vogue at the time. **Passage Choiseul,** at 44 rue des Petits-Champs (Métro: Quatre-Septembre), dates from 1827 and is the longest as well as the most animated arcade. Discount shoes and clothing are piled outside the renovated stores. **Passage des Panoramas,** at 11 bd. Montmartre and 10 rue Saint Marc (Métro: Montmartre), opened in 1800 and was enlarged with the addition of galleries Variétés, Saint-Marc, Montmartre, and Feydeau in 1834. This passage offers the largest choice of dining options—Korean food, a cafeteria, tea salons, bistros—as well as outlets for stamps, clothes, and knick-knacks. Across the street is **Passage Jouffroy,** at 10 bd. Montmartre or 9 rue de la Grange-Bateliére (Métro: Montmartre), built between 1845 and 1846. The richness of its decoration—as well as the fact that it was the first heated gallery in Paris—made Passage Jouffroy an immediate hit. The tile floors were restored in 1989 and the arcade now houses a wide variety of boutiques. The **Passage Verdeau,** at 31 bis, rue du Faubourg Montmartre (Métro: Le Peletier), was built at about the same time as the Passage Jouffroy and has always suffered in comparison to its more glamorous neighbor. Not much appears to have changed in the last 150 years, including the old postcards and books that are the specialties here. By far the most sumptuous interior is found at **Galerie Vivienne,** 4 place des Petits-Champs, 5 rue de la Banque, 6 rue Vivienne (Métro: Bourse), built in 1823. Now a national monument, the neoclassical style of this arcade has attracted upscale art galleries, hair salons, and fashionable boutiques. The classical friezes, mosaic floors, and graceful arches have been beautifully restored and linked to the adjoining **Galerie Colbert,** which was built in 1826 to capitalize on the success of the Vivienne gallery. For a complete change of pace, head north on the rue St-Denis to the **Passage Brady,** 46 rue faubourg St-Denis (Métro: Strasbourg St-Denis), which has become an exotic bazaar. Indian restaurants and spice shops scent the air of this unusual passage, which opened in 1828.

THE REST OF THE PICTURE

Flower vendors, cheese shops, butchers, and bakers crowd the pedestrian area of **rue Montorgueil** (Métro: Sentier). The refurbished outdoor market has been a gastronomic center since the 13th century and is now one of the liveliest and least touristy street markets in the city. Look inside Patisserie Stohrer (51 rue de Montorgueil) for the delicately painted ceiling done in 1864 by Paul Baudry, who also painted the interior of the Opéra.

6 Marais, Beaubourg & Bastille (3e, 4e & 11e Arrondissements)

Both the Marais and the Beaubourg neighborhoods began to flourish behind the fortified wall built by Philippe Auguste in the 12th century. When Charles V moved to the Right Bank in the 14th century, he extended the fortification east to the Bastille and built a palace next to **Village St-Paul.** Later kings abandoned the Right Bank until Henri IV swept in with his royal entourage in 1604 and transformed the Marais into a glittering center of royal power. Even before the razing of the Bastille in 1789 frightened the noble families into abandoning their mansions, the aristocracy was gravitating to Versailles. The Marais neighborhood fell into a lingering decay until a new law in 1962 provided for its restoration.

The mansions of the Marais are a reminder of the glorious 17th century but the lively bistros and bars have become the hub of young, *branché* (read: trendy) Parisians. The "look" is casual, the ambience is arty, and the boutiques lining the rue des Francs-Bourgeois are chic, and pricey. As you head north towards République the neighborhood loses some luster, but avant-garde art galleries are starting to crop up on the streets **rue Vieille-du-Temple, rue Debelleyme,** and **rue St-Gilles.**

Next to the Marais is the Beaubourg neighborhood, shaped by the **Centre Pompidou** and the many shops and businesses that have cropped up around the popular arts center. Beaubourg quiets down at night, however, just when the Marais and the streets around the Bastille begin to gear up for the night crawlers.

Attractions—Marais, Beaubourg & Bastille

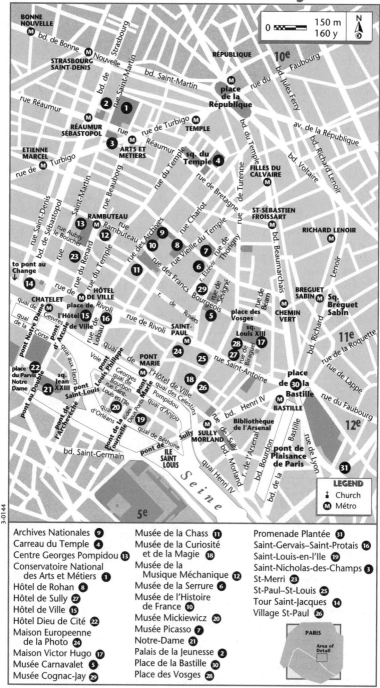

Archives Nationales ❾	Musée de la Chass ⓫	Promenade Plantée ㉛
Carreau du Temple ❹	Musée de la Curiosité	Saint-Gervais–Saint-Protais ⓰
Centre Georges Pompidou ⓭	et de la Magie ⓲	Saint-Louis-en-l'Ile ⓳
Conservatoire National	Musée de la	Saint-Nicholas-des-Champs ❸
des Arts et Métiers ❶	Musique Méchanique ⓬	St-Merri ㉓
Hôtel de Rohan ❽	Musée de la Serrure ❻	St-Paul–St-Louis ㉕
Hôtel de Sully ㉗	Musée de l'Histoire	Tour Saint-Jacques ⓮
Hôtel de Ville ⓯	de France ❿	Village St-Paul ㉖
Hôtel Dieu de Cité ㉒	Musée Mickiewicz ⓴	
Maison Europeenne	Musée Picasso ❼	
de la Photo ㉔	Notre-Dame ㉑	
Maison Victor Hugo ⓱	Palais de la Jeunesse ❷	
Musée Carnavalet ❺	Place de la Bastille ㉚	
Musée Cognac-Jay ㉙	Place des Vosges ㉘	

When Carl Ott's Opera House opened on the Bastille in 1989, the drab working-class neighborhood was reborn as the cutting edge of Parisian nightlife. Black-clad, intense 20-somethings smoke and pose in the refurbished bars that used to be famously seedy.

Musée Picasso. Hôtel Salé, 5 rue de Thorigny, 3e. ☎ **01-42-71-25-21.** Admission 30F ($5.20) adults (20F on Sun), 20F ($3.50) students, free for ages 17 and under. Apr 1–Sept 30 Mon and Wed–Sun 9:30am–6pm; Oct 1–Mar 31 Mon and Wed–Sun 9:30am–5:30pm. Métro: Chemin-Vert or St-Paul.

The Hôtel Salé is a renovated mansion in the Marais, built in the mid–17th century; it boasts a splendid staircase. Its name, the Salted Mansion, stems from the occupation of its original proprietor: Aubert de Fontenay, a salt tax collector.

The Hôtel Salé's present claim to glory belongs to Picasso. Here is housed the largest collection of the Spanish master's art in the world. In 1973, following the artist's death, his heirs donated his personal collection of art works to the state in lieu of inheritance taxes. It was from these holdings that the Musée Picasso was created. The spectacular collection includes more than 200 paintings, almost 160 sculptures, and 88 ceramics, as well as more than 3,000 prints and drawings (many of them too fragile for permanent display). Works can be viewed chronologically; budget at least a few hours here, if not more.

The museum also displays works by other artists collected by Picasso, including Corot, Cézanne, Braque, Rousseau, Matisse, and Renoir.

Musée Carnavalet. 23 rue de Sévigné, 3e. ☎ **01-42-72-21-13.** Admission 27F ($4.70) adults, 14.50F ($2.50) ages 18–24 and over 60, free for ages 17 and under. Tues–Sun 10am–5:40pm. Métro: St-Paul; then walk east on rue St-Antoine and turn left on rue de Sévigné.

Located in the Marais and recently renovated, the Musée Carnavalet (also known as the Musée Historique de la Ville de Paris) details the city's history and the daily lives of its inhabitants from prehistoric times to the present. On display are paintings, signs, splendid furniture, models of the Bastille, and Marie Antoinette's personal items.

The museum is housed in two splendid mansions: the 16th-century Hôtel Carnavalet and the Hôtel Le Peletier de St-Fargeau. The Hôtel Carnavalet was the home of Mme. de Sévigné, the 17th-century writer of masterful letters. She lived here from 1677 to 1694.

Musée Cognacq-Jay. 8 rue Elzévir, 3e. ☎ **01-40-27-07-21.** Admission 17.50F ($3) adults; 9F ($1.55) ages 18–25 and over 60, free for ages 17 and under. Tues–Sun 10am–5:40pm. Métro: St-Paul or Rambuteau.

This collection of 18th-century rococo art amassed by La Samaritaine department store founder Ernest Cognacq and his wife is a window into the lifestyles of the aristocracy that flourished before the revolution. Their exquisite cabinets, delicate porcelain, and fine furniture are displayed in the splendid 16th-century Hôtel Donon. Louis XV and Louis XVI paneled rooms are graced with works by Boucher, Fragonard, Watteau, and Tiepelo.

Maison Européenne de la Photo. 5–7 rue de Fourcy, 4e. ☎ **01-44-78-75-00.** Admission 30F ($5.20), 15F ($2.60) ages 8–25. Wed–Sun 11am–8pm. Métro: St-Paul.

This new museum, created from two magnificent 18th-century town houses in the Marais, is entirely devoted to photography. In addition to changing exhibits, there's an excellent video library that allows you to look up thousands of different photos as well as permanent collections of Polaroid art and the works of Irving Penn.

Musée de la Chasse et la Nature. 60 rue des Archives, 3e. ☎ **01-42-72-86-43.** Admission 25F ($4.35) adults, 12.50F ($2.15) students, 5F children. Wed–Mon 10am–12:30pm and 1:30–5:30pm. Closed Tues and holidays. Métro: Rambuteau or Hôtel-de-Ville.

Housed in a beautiful private mansion designed by Mansart that features a dramatic staircase, the museum displays a variety of weapons including crossbows and arquebuses; hunting theme paintings by Rubens, Bruegel, and Chardin, among others; and many animal trophies. Not for the animal lover unless you agree with the argument that there's a connection between hunting and conservation.

Musée d'Histoire de France. Hôtel de Soubise, 60 rue des Francs-Bourgeois, 3e. ☎ **01-40-27-62-18.** Admission 15F ($2.60) adults, 10F ($1.75) ages 18–24 and over 60, free for ages 17 and under. Wed–Mon 1:45–5:45pm. Métro: St-Paul.

The elegant Hôtel de Soubise, remodeled in the early 18th century, houses France's **Archives Nationales** as well as the Museum of French History. Here you will see some of the most important documents pertaining to the history of France, as well as personal papers related to famous French men and women. Exhibits include Henry IV's Edict of Nantes, which guaranteed religious liberties; Louis XIV's will; Louis XVI's diary and will; the Declaration of Human Rights; Marie Antoinette's last letter; Napoléon's will; and the French constitution. Rooms are devoted to the Middle Ages, the French Revolution, and other themes.

Maison de Victor Hugo. 6 place des Vosges, 3e. ☎ **01-42-72-10-16.** Admission 27F ($4.70), 19F ($3.30) children 8–17. Tues–Sun 10am–7:40pm. Métro: St-Paul.

Victor Hugo occupied this sprawling apartment on the place des Vosges from 1832 to 1848. Here you will see some of the writer's furniture, his drawings, samples of his handwriting, his inkwell, first editions of his works, and a painting of his funeral procession at the Arc de Triomphe in 1885. There are also portraits of his family, including Adèle, the subject of François Truffaut's excellent film, *L'Histoire d'Adèle H.* The Chinese salon from Hugo's house on Guernsey has also been reassembled here.

Musée de la Curiosité et de la Magie. 11 rue St-Paul, 4e. ☎ **01-42-72-13-26.** Admission 45F ($8) adults, 30F ($5.20) children under 13. Wed, Sat, Sun 2–7pm. Métro: St-Paul.

Although the Museum of Magic and Curiosity doesn't exactly explain how illusionists make buildings disappear, you do discover how cleverly arranged mirrors play tricks with your eyes. Kids will enjoy the interactive displays as well as the magicians that are on hand for live performances throughout the afternoon.

St-Paul–St-Louis. 99 rue St-Antoine, 4e. ☎ **01-42-72-30-32.** Métro: St-Paul.

Built by the Jesuit order in the first half of the 17th century, St-Paul–St-Louis, with its dome and ornate facade, is a fine example of the baroque art of the Counter-Reformation. It is one of the most interesting buildings of the Marais, an area where secular architecture otherwise prevails. The church contains some fine Delacroix paintings. Among its parishioners were Madame de Sévigné and Victor Hugo, residents of the Marais.

St-Gervais–St-Protais. Place St-Gervais, 4e. Métro: Hôtel-de-Ville.

This Flamboyant Gothic church was completed in 1657 and stands on the site of a 6th-century basilica dedicated to the saints Protais and Gervais. The organ was built in 1601 and is the largest in Paris. Note the paintings in the "Golden Chapel" and the 16th-century stained-glass windows.

St-Merri. 78 rue St-Martin, 3e. ☎ **01-42-71-40-75.** Métro: Châtelet-Les Halles.

This flamboyant Gothic church is famous for its Chasseriau murals, Renaissance stained-glass windows, and the organ loft built by Germain Pilon. Camille Saint-Saëns used to play the organ and the church frequently hosts concerts.

Hôtel de Sully. 62 rue St-Antoine, 3e. ☎ **01-44-61-20-00.** Free admission. Tours some Sat and Sun; call for information. Daily 9am–7pm. Métro: St-Paul or Bastille.

The Hôtel de Sully is one of the most impressive mansions in the Marais, a district filled with stately mansions. It was built in 1624 by the architect Robert Vassas and occupied by Maximilien de Béthune-Sully, a minister under Henry IV. The Sully family resided in the mansion well into the 18th century. The Caisse Nationale des Monuments Historiques is presently housed here, a most appropriate location for an agency in charge of watching over France's architectural heritage. Come and see the inner courtyard, with its honey-colored facade decorated by figures representing the seasons and the elements. The Orangerie, in the back, leads to the place des Vosges.

Hôtel de Ville. Place de l'Hôtel de Ville, 4e. ☎ **01-42-76-43-43.** Métro: Hôtel-de-Ville.

The Hôtel de Ville is Paris's City Hall. The current handsome neo-Renaissance building was built between 1874 and 1882. The earlier buildings that stood here have witnessed many great and dire French historic moments. It was here in July 1789 that Louis XVI was forced to kiss the new French flag: The blue and the red stood for Paris and the white represented the monarchy. In subsequent revolutions, in 1848 and 1870, the building was occupied by mobs, and indeed in 1870 the building that had been constructed by François I was burnt down. The place in front was also used for executions from 1313 to 1830 when witches, Huguenots, and criminals such as Ravaillac (the assassin of Henry IV) were dispatched.

As befits Paris's municipal building, the facade is adorned with 146 statues representing famous Parisians. (*Note:* Hotel de Ville is not open to the public except during the Journees Portes Ouvertes in September—see "Paris Calendar of Events," chapter 2.)

Centre Georges Pompidou. Place Georges-Pompidou, 4e. ☎ **01-44-78-12-33** for information. Web site: http://www.cnac-gp.fr. Mon and Wed–Fri noon–1pm, Sat–Sun 10am–10pm. Métro: Rambuteau, Hôtel-de-Ville, or Châtelet-Les-Halles.

The full name of this gigantic, futuristic arts center is Centre National d'Art et de Culture Georges Pompidou. In the late 1960s, President Pompidou proposed the construction of this building as part of a redevelopment plan for Beaubourg. The building was designed by Richard Rogers, a British architect, and Renzo Piano, an Italian. You'll recognize the center when you see it. It's very 1970s. Its bold "exo-skeletal" architecture and bright colors were seen as out of place in the traditional old Beaubourg neighborhood.

Like the Eiffel Tower and the Louvre pyramid, the Centre Pompidou was despised by many when it was built. Since then, many detractors have become grudging admirers. Many have not, but there's no arguing with the success of the center. Since its opening in 1977, more than 160 million people have visited the Centre Pompidou—far more than was anticipated. Unfortunately, the building began to crumble under the weight of its popularity and is undergoing a $100 million overhaul that is expected to last until the end of 1999. Meanwhile, the library, **Bibliothèque Publique Information,** will be housed in temporary quarters and the **Musée National d'Art Moderne** will be closed. The center expects to keep part of the building open for temporary exhibitions and you can still take an escalator to the top floor for a marvelous view of Paris. Don't miss the nearby Stravinsky fountain, containing mobile sculptures by Tinguely and Niki de Saint Phalle.

Place des Vosges. 3e. Métro: St-Paul.

In the early 17th century Henri IV transformed the Marais into the most prestigious neighborhood in France. On the site of the demolished Hôtel des Tournelles, where Henri II died after being wounded in a tournament, Henri IV put his Place Royale, deciding that the surrounding buildings should be "built to a like symmetry." The royal association was evident in the white fleurs-de-lis crowning each row of rose-colored brick houses and the new square quickly became the center of courtly parades and festivities. After the revolution, it became place de l'Indivisibilité and later place des Vosges, in honor of the first *département* that completely paid its taxes. Among the famous figures connected with the square are Mme. de Sévigné, who was born at no. 1 bis, and Victor Hugo, who lived at no. 6 for 16 years (his house presently contains a museum; see "Marais, Beaubourg & Bastille," above).

The fashionable promenades and romantic duels of the 17th century have long ceased and now the arcades are occupied by antique dealers, galleries, booksellers, tea rooms, and cafes. Children play and older residents chat—all in all, an evocative slice of Parisian life.

Place de la Bastille. 11e. Métro: Bastille.

Ignore the traffic and try to imagine it just over 200 years ago when it contained eight towers rising 100 feet. It was here, on July 14, 1789, that a Paris mob attacked the old prison, launching the French Revolution. Although the Bastille had long since fallen into disuse, it symbolized the arbitrary power of a king who could imprison anyone for any reason simply by issuing a *lettre de cachet.* Prisoners of means could buy a spacious cell and even host dinner parties. The less fortunate disappeared within its recesses or sometimes drowned when the Seine overflowed its banks. Even though only seven prisoners were discovered by the revolutionary mob, attacking the prison was a direct assault on royal power. "Is it a revolt?", Louis XVI allegedly asked after learning of the Bastille's fall. "No, sire," came the reply. "It is a revolution."

The Bastille was completely razed in 1792. In its place stands the **Colonne de Juillet,** a bronze column 171 feet high, built between 1830 and 1849.

THE REST OF THE PICTURE

The heart of the old Jewish quarter of the Marais is the **rue des Rosiers.** Although many of the ground floor shops have metamorphosed into fancy designer salons, the old delicatessens, felafel stands, and kosher goods stores still display signs in Hebrew as well as French. The street is quiet on Saturday afternoons except for black-coated men heading to the synagogue designed by Guimard on **rue Pavée.** (Métro: St-Paul.)

My favorite find in the Marais is the Village St-Paul, a secluded 17th-century village that has been turned into an outdoor arts fair. It's easy to walk right past the entrances to this town-within-a-town tucked between rue St-Paul, rue Jardins St-Paul, and rue Charlemagne, but look for the signs just inside the narrow passageways between the houses. You'll find yourself in a cluster of interlocking courtyards lined with shops displaying antiques, paintings, and bric-a-brac. The haphazard arrangement of courtyards dates from the 14th century when they were the walled gardens of King Charles V. When the palace was abandoned, common folk built houses along the walls and the gardens became their village squares. Special flea markets are usually held each spring and fall, drawing vendors from the Paris region. The stores are open daily except Tuesday and Wednesday from 11am to 7pm. The high stone wall you see on rue Jardins St-Paul is the only remaining part of Philippe-August's 13th-century fortification. (Métro: St-Paul.)

Carl Ott's futuristic **Opéra Bastille** may not be everyone's idea of an opera house, but it certainly did a lot for the Bastille neighborhood. Soon after its opening in 1989, the narrow side-streets around the opera house began to pulsate with a new beat—and it's not opera. Rue de la Roquette, rue de Charonne, and rue de Lappe are a strange blend of neon, cobblestones, fast food, old bistros, art galleries, and tapas bars. The scene starts after sundown and peaks on weekend nights. (Métro: Bastille.)

Daytime activity centers on the Promenade Plantée, which begins at the Opéra Bastille and runs for 4½ kilometers through the 12e arrondissement, along the line of an old railroad track. Although the promenade cuts through a somewhat drab neighborhood, a changing landscape of gardens, woods, tunnels, and cleverly designed rest areas makes a surprisingly pleasant stroll. The area underneath the elevated promenade has become a shopping street showcasing crafts, furnishings, and handiwork. (Métro: Bastille, Bel Air, or Dugommier.)

7 Champs-Elysées & Environs (8e & 17e Arrondissements)

A sense of moneyed splendor is found everywhere in this neighborhood from the grand couturier houses (Lacroix, Dior, Valentino) on the **avenue Montaigne** to the presidential residence, **Palais de l'Elysée,** on the Faubourg St-Honoré. Unlike other Parisian neighborhoods whose charms are hidden in a haphazard arrangement of old streets and narrow passages, the avenues from the **Champs-Elysées** to the **Parc Monceau** were designed to flaunt the wealth of their inhabitants. In the 19th century, city planners and real estate developers capitalized on the aristocracy's slow movement west by building the spacious avenues that still characterize this neighborhood. New money replaced old money as bankers and industrialists built ornate residences in the stylish district.

The "elysian fields" was originally a pathway bordered by trees, until the Second Empire and the urbanization of the surrounding neighborhood. Cafes, restaurants, and theaters sprang up to entertain a new clientele. The Champs-Elysées is still in the entertainment business even if the audience is mostly tourists and out-of-towners and the show is the nervy, jazzed-up multiplexes, megastores, and McFood that have taken over the boulevard. Parisians claim they wouldn't be caught dead there (except for the Bastille Day parade of course), but the grand promenade still has a certain glamour, especially at night.

Musée Nissim de Camondo. 63 rue de Monceau, 8e. ☎ **01-45-63-26-32.** Admission 27F ($4.70) adults, 18F ($3.15) for ages 17 and under. Wed–Sun 10am–5pm. Métro: Villiers-Monceau.

This private mansion near the Parc Monceau contains a fine collection gathered by the Camondo banking family while they lived here. The 18th-century interior is filled with exceptional furnishings, boiserie, Savonnerie carpets, Beauvais tapestries (including one depicting La Fontaine's "Fables"), and Sevres china, including a set known as the Buffon service, in which every piece is decorated with a different species of bird.

Musée Cernuschi. 7 av. Vélasquez, 8e. ☎ **01-45-63-50-75.** Admission 19F ($3.30) adults; 9.50F ($1.65) students and children under 18. Tues–Sun 10am–5:40pm. Closed holidays. Métro: Villiers or Monceau.

Banker Henri Cernuschi's mansion displays a major Chinese collection. Ceramics, bronzes, funerary statues, Buddhist sculptures, and contemporary paintings are among the objects to be found here. Two exquisite pieces alone are worth seeking out, a 5th-century bodhisattva and an 8th-century Tang silk painting, *Horses and Their Grooms.*

Attractions—Champs-Elysées & Environs

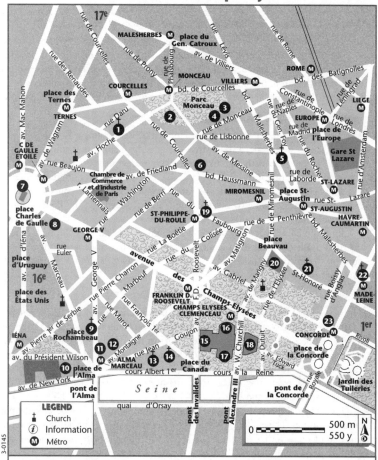

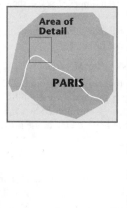

LEGEND
- ✝ Church
- ⓘ Information
- Ⓜ Métro

0 ━━━━ 500 m / 550 y

Area of Detail

PARIS

American Cathedral
  in Paris **9**
Arc de Triomphe **7**
Crazy Horse Saloon **11**
Grand Palais **16**
Hôtel de Crillon **23**
La Madeleine **22**
Musée Cernuschi **3**
Musée d'Art Moderne **10**
Musée Jacquemart
  André **6**
Musée Nissim de
  Camondo **4**
Notre-Dame de
  la Consolation **13**
Office de Tourisme **8**

Palais de la
  Découverte **15**
Palais de l'Elysée **20**
Parc Monceau **2**
Petit Palais **18**
St-Alexandre-Nevsky **1**
St-Augustin **5**
St-Jean-Baptiste **14**
St. Michael's
  English Church **21**
St-Philippe-
  du-Roule **9**
Théâtres des
  Champs-Elysées **12**
Université Paris IV **17**

Musée Jacquemart-Andre. 158 bd. Haussmann, 8e. ☎ **01-42-89-04-91.** Admission 45F ($7.80), 30F ($5.20) students under age 25. Daily 10am–6pm. Métro: St-Augustin.

After being closed for 5 years for a complete renovation, this charming museum reopened in the spring of 1996. It contains the fantastic collection of paintings, 172 drawings, and sculpture acquired by a wealthy couple, now shown to stunning advantage. Highlights of this intimate gallery include Italian Renaissance works by Bellini, Carpaccio, Mantegna, and Della Robbia, along with Dutch and Flemish old masters.

La Madeleine. Place de la Madeleine, 8e. Métro: Madeleine.

The Madeleine is one of Paris's minor landmarks. Resembling a Roman temple, it dominates the rue Royale, a short street designed by Gabriel that culminates in the place de la Concorde. Although its construction started in 1806, the Madeleine was consecrated as a church much later, in 1842. The building was originally intended as a temple to the glory of the Grande Armée (Napoléon's idea, of course). Later, several alternatives uses were considered: the National Assembly, the Bourse, and the National Library.

Climb the 28 steps leading to the facade and look back: You will be able to see the rue Royale, the place de la Concorde and the obelisk, and, across the Seine, the dome of the Invalides. Inside, don't miss Rude's *Le Baptême du Christ,* to the left as you enter.

Place de la Concorde. 8e. Métro: Concorde.

The place de la Concorde at the end of the Champs-Elysées may not be a restful place to sit during the day, but it looks quite bewitching when the sun begins to set and the obelisk becomes a piercing silhouette against the Parisian sky, its lines mirrored by the Eiffel Tower in the distance. This is one of the centers of Paris. On its perimeter stands the **Hôtel Crillon,** occupying the building where the Treaty of Friendship and Trade recognizing the United States of America was signed in February 1778 by Benjamin Franklin and Louis XVI.

This octagonal space, designed by Gabriel under Louis XV, soon became the place de la Révolution. The guillotine was installed here, and among the heads severed there was that of Louis XVI. From 1793 to 1795, 1,343 people were guillotined—Marie Antoinette, Mme du Barry, Charlotte Corday, Danton, Robespierre, and Alexandre de Beauharnais among them. After the Reign of Terror, in hopes of peace, the square was renamed place de la Concorde.

The **Egyptian obelisk** comes from the temple of Ramses II in Thebes, and it is more than three millennia old. It was offered to France in 1829.

Parc Monceau. Bd. de Coucelles, 8e. ☎ **01-42-27-39-56.** Métro: Monceau.

Located in a very affluent residential district, Parc Monceau boasts a number of odd features: a pyramid, ancient columns, a naumachia basin, and several tombs of an unknown origin. This green space, which children love, is surrounded by a majestic black-and-gold fence and magnificent Second Empire houses. One house is the setting for Carlos Fuentes's *Distant Relations.*

THE REST OF THE PICTURE

If you visit the Parc Monceau, you might want to pick up picnic supplies at the pedestrian shopping street of **rue de Levis** (daily except Monday; Métro: Villiers). There are also **flower markets** every day except Monday at the place de la Madeleine, 8e, alongside the church (Métro: Madeleine), and at place des Ternes in the 17e arrondissement (Métro: Ternes).

8 Montmartre (18e Arrondissement)

The Butte, as the top of Montmartre is called, sometimes seems almost too pictur-esque to be real. The meandering roads follow the paths medieval villagers used when the hilltop village was covered with vineyards and supplied wine to the city of Paris. The lamps, the steep stairs, the tiny whitewashed houses half hidden in foliage are a world away from the city beneath it.

Despite its bucolic image, Montmartre has had a turbulent history, beginning with its name. Historians are unsure whether the village was named after an ancient Roman Temple to Mars or refers to the martyrdom of St. Denis, who was allegedly decapitated on the hill. The strategically located village was occupied by Henri IV in the 16th century and by the Russians and the English in the 19th century before becoming a part of Paris in 1860.

In the end of the 19th century, Montmartre was reborn as a center of painting, poetry, and music. Composers Berlioz and Offenbach, writers Henri Murger and Tristan Tzara, and painters Henri Toulouse-Lautrec and Maurice Utrillo were among the more notable artists who gathered in the Lapin Agile and Moulin Rouge at the turn of the century. Later, Picasso painted *Les Demoiselles d'Avignon* in Bateau-Lavoir.

Artists have long since fled Montmartre, but the sense of an artists' village remains. You won't find it on the tourist-clogged place de Tertre, but among the web of streets on the hill you'll surely find one that seems to be waiting for an artist's easel. (See "Walking Tour 2" in chapter 7.)

Musée de Vieux Montmartre. 12 rue Cortot, 18e. ☎ **01-46-06-61-11.** Admission 25F ($4.35). Children under 8 free. Tues–Sun 11am–6pm. Métro: Lamarck-Caulaincourt.

This small, interesting museum that relates the history and folklore of Montmartre is housed in the home of the famous actor Florimond, who was a member of Molière's theater group. Displays include a reconstruction of the Café de l'Abreuvoir, frequented by Utrillo and his mother, Susan Valadon.

Musée d'Art Juif. 42 rue des Saules, 18e. ☎ **01-42-57-84-15.** Admission 30F ($5.20) adults, 20F ($3.50) students, 10F ($1.75) children. Sun–Thurs 3–6pm. Closed Fri, Sat, Aug, and Jew-ish holidays. Métro: Lamarck-Caulaincourt.

This museum displays religious and popular objects as well as models of synagogues. Most visitors, though, will be primarily interested in the lithographs by Chagall, Pissaro, and others.

Cimetière de Montmartre. Rue Caulincourt, 18e. Métro: place de Clichy.

Many of the artists that lived and worked in Montmartre are buried here. You'll find the graves of such notables as artist Edgar Degas; composers Hector Berlioz, Léo Delibes, and Jacques Offenbach; writers Théophile Gautier, Stendhal, and Emile Zola; cartoonist Francisque Poulbot; and filmmaker François Truffaut.

THE REST OF THE PICTURE

The residents of Montmartre surely aren't gawking at mimes or having their portraits sketched on the place de Tertre. Where do they go to escape the carnival? On a sunny day they might be found at the **parc de la Terlure,** a tranquil hideaway on rue de la Bonne, north of Sacré-Coeur. While browsing the market on **rue Lepic** (daily ex-cept Monday; Métro: Abbesses) walk up to no. 54, where Vincent van Gogh and his brother once lived.

Attractions—Montmartre

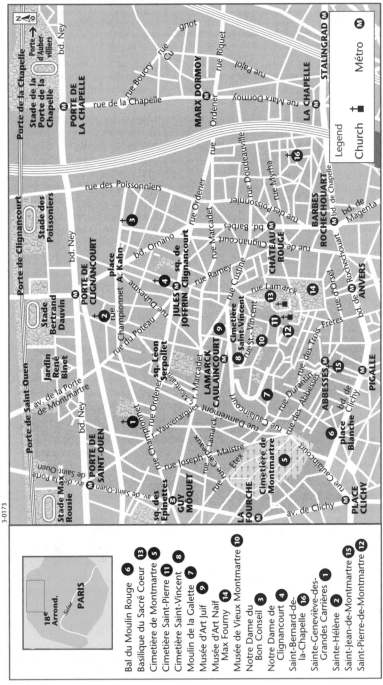

Legend

✝ Church

Ⓜ Métro

Bal du Moulin Rouge **6**
Basilique du Sacré Coeur **13**
Cimetière de Montmartre **5**
Cimetière Saint-Pierre **11**
Cimetière Saint-Vincent **8**
Moulin de la Galette **7**
Musée d'Art Juif **9**
Musée d'Art Naïf
  Max Fourny **14**
Musée de Vieux Montmartre **10**
Notre Dame du
  Bon Conseil **3**
Notre Dame de
  Clignancourt **4**
Saint-Bernard-de-
  la-Chapelle **16**
Sainte-Geneviève-des-
  Grandes Carrières **1**
Sainte-Hélène **2**
Saint-Jean-de-Montmartre **15**
Saint-Pierre-de-Montmartre **12**

176

9 Trocadéro & La Seizieme (16e Arrondissement)

"Paris is the capital of France and the 16e arrondissement the capital of Paris," wrote Victor Hugo. The 16e is one of the largest and most residential of Parisian arrondissements as well as the most prestigious. It has been the address of choice for the rich and powerful since the 17th century, when aristocrats and wealthy merchants built country houses in the villages of Chaillot, Passy, and Auteuil. They were attracted by the beauty of the stretch of land between the Seine and the **Bois de Boulogne,** as well as by its convenient location on the road to Versailles. Most of those country houses didn't survive the real estate boom that began in the 19th century and has turned the 16e into a repository for some of the best and worst architecture of the last hundred years. Angular buildings with balconies of smoked glass locked behind elaborate gates are not exactly charming, but the old villages of Passy and Auteuil at the Métro stops of the same names make a pleasant stroll. The art nouveau master Hector Guimard left some superb examples of his architecture on rue La Fontaine, especially the Castel Béranger at no. 14. In addition to sampling the fine museums in the 16e and taking in the view of the Eiffel Tower from **Trocadéro,** you can also play the horses at the racetracks of Longchamps and Auteil in the **Bois de Boulogne.**

Musée d'Art Moderne de la Ville de Paris. Palais d'Art Moderne, 11–13 av. du Président-Wilson, 16e. ☎ **01-53-67-40-00.** Admission 27.50F ($4.80) adults, 14.50F ($2.50) ages 7–24 and over 60. Open Tues–Fri 10am–5:30pm, Thurs and Sat–Sun 10am–8pm. Métro: Iéna.

Built in 1937, the Palais d'Art Moderne is composed of two wings: the Palais de New-York and the Palais de Tokyo. The former is occupied by the **Centre National de la Photographie,** the latter by the **Musée d'Art Moderne de la Ville de Paris.** One of two modern art museums in Paris—the other being the Musée National d'Art Moderne at the Centre Pompidou—this collection includes works from all major movements in 20th-century art and by most of the major artists. The collection of art deco furniture is impressive.

You won't miss Dufy's *La fée electricité* (The Good Fairy Electricity): With 250 panels, it's the largest picture in the world.

Musée des Arts et Traditions Populaires. 6 av. du Mahatma Gandhi, Bois de Boulogne, 16e. ☎ **01-44-17-60-00.** Admission 22F ($3.80) adults; 15F ($2.60) Sundays, students, ages 18–25; free for ages 17 and under. Wed–Mon 9:30am–5:15pm. Métro: Les Sablons.

If you're interested in the customs of the country, this museum examines the French way of life in serious ethnological manner. Customs, beliefs, and rural daily life are featured through the ages.

Maison de Balzac. 47 rue Raynouard, 16e. ☎ **01-42-24-56-38.** Admission 27F ($4.70) adults; 19F ($3.30) students ages 8–24 and ages over 60; children under 8 free. Tues–Sun 10am–5:40pm. Closed holidays. Métro: Passy or La Muette.

Balzac lived in this rustic cabin with its romantic garden from 1840 to 1847. Portraits, books, letters, and manuscripts are on display.

Musée du Vin. 5 rue des Eaux, 16e. ☎ **01-45-25-63-26.** Admission (including glass of wine) 35F ($6) adults, 30F ($5.20) students and ages over 60. Tues–Sun 10am–6pm. Métro: Passy.

The museum is housed in an ancient stone and clay quarry that was used by 15th century monks as a wine cellar. The visit is a good introduction to the art of winemaking, displaying various tools, beakers, cauldrons, and bottles in a series of exhibits. The quarry is right below Balzac's house (see above) and the ceiling contains a trap door he used to escape from his creditors.

Musée d'Ennery. 59 av. Foch, 16e. ☎ **01-45-53-57-96.** Free admission. Thurs and Sun afternoons only. Métro: Porte Dauphine.

A personal collection of Oriental art amassed by Madame d'Ennery and her author husband. The collection includes masks, ceramics, netsukes, paintings, and furniture, all displayed in their Napoléon III–style mansion.

Guimet-Musée du Pantheon Bouddhique. 19 av. d'Iéna, 16e. ☎ **01-47-23-61-65.** Admission 16F ($2.80) adults, 12F ($2) ages 18–24, free for ages 17 and under. Wed–Mon 9:45am–6pm. Métro: Iéna.

Like the nearby Musée National des Arts Asiatiques (currently closed for restoration and scheduled to reopen in 1999), this collection of Asian art was assembled by the collector Emile Guimet. The evolution of Buddhism in China and Japan is illustrated in works from the 4th to the 19th century, including some remarkably idiosyncratic Buddhas. A back door opens onto a lush Japanese garden shaded by bamboo trees and designed as a meditation space. The museum is housed in a neoclassical mansion built in 1906.

Musée Marmottan. 2 rue Louis-Boilly, 16e. ☎ **01-42-24-07-02.** Admission 40F ($7) adults, 25F ($4.35) students ages 18–25, free for ages 17 and under. Tues–Sun 10am–5:30pm. Métro: La-Muette.

Located between the Ranelagh garden and the Bois de Boulogne, the Musée Marmottan celebrates the painter Claude Monet and includes an outstanding collection of his water lily paintings. The problem of painting the delicate flowers floating on a reflective pool obsessed the artist during his years at Giverny. In addition to the water lilies, the Marmottan museum displays his more abstract representations of the Japanese Bridge at Giverny, as well as *Impression-Sunrise,* the painting from which the term *impressionist* was coined. Monet's personal collection is also presented, including works by his contemporaries Pissarro, Manet, Morisot, and Renoir.

The museum is in a 19th-century mansion that belonged to the art historian Paul Marmottan. When Marmottan died in 1932, he donated the mansion and his collection of Empire furniture and Napoleanic art to the Académie des Beaux Arts. After Claude Monet's son and heir bequeathed his father's collection to the Marmottan, the museum became an homage to the unique vision of this artist. Subsequent donations have expanded the collection to include more impressionist paintings and late medieval illuminated manuscripts.

Musée de la Mode et du Costume. Palais Galliera, 10 av. Pierre-Premier-de-Serbie, 16e. ☎ **01-47-20-85-23.** Admission 45F ($7.80) adults, 32F ($5.50) children under 25. Tues–Sun 10am–5:40pm. Métro: Iéna or Alma-Marceau.

Frequently changing exhibitions illustrate the history of French urban fashion from the 18th century to the present. Guided tours are given Thursday and Saturday at 2:30pm.

PALAIS DE CHAILLOT

This large-scale project, located on the place du Trocadéro, 16e (Métro: Trocadéro), was conceived for the Paris Exhibition of 1937. Today it shelters four museums: the Museum of Mankind, the Maritime Museum, the Museum of French Monuments, and the Museum of Cinema. From its terraces there are great views across to the Eiffel Tower, Champs de Mars, and Ecole Militaire.

Musée de l'Homme. Palais de Chaillot, place du Trocadéro, 16e. ☎ **01-44-05-72-72.** Admission 25F ($4.35) adults, 15F ($2.60) ages 18–24 and over 60, free for ages 17 and under. Wed–Mon 9:45am–5:15pm. Métro: Trocadéro.

Attractions—Trocadéro & La Seizieme

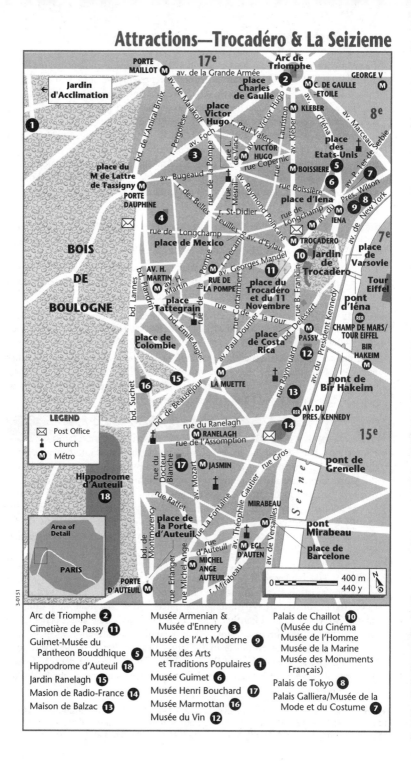

Arc de Triomphe 2
Cimetière de Passy 11
Guimet-Musée du
 Pantheon Bouddhique 5
Hippodrome d'Auteuil 18
Jardin Ranelagh 15
Masion de Radio-France 14
Maison de Balzac 13

Musée Armenian &
 Musée d'Ennery 3
Musée de l'Art Moderne 9
Musée des Arts
 et Traditions Populaires 1
Musée Guimet 6
Musée Henri Bouchard 17
Musée Marmottan 16
Musée du Vin 12

Palais de Chaillot 10
 (Musée du Cinéma
 Musée de l'Homme
 Musée de la Marine
 Musée des Monuments
 Français)
Palais de Tokyo 8
Palais Galliera/Musée de la
 Mode et du Costume 7

The Museum of Mankind is housed in the 1937 Palais de Chaillot, across the Seine from the Eiffel Tower. The collection contains representative objects from all over the world: Africa, Europe, the Arctic, Asia, Oceania, and the Americas. Many of the displays were designed several decades ago, so the museum's interest is double: Not only do you observe the timeless material behind the glass, but also the way in which Europeans viewed themselves and the rest of the world at a specific period of the 20th century. Many of the objects are extremely beautiful and quite rare, such as a stone seat built by native peoples in the Caribbean. And there are some poignant exhibits as well—for instance, those related to the native people of Tierra del Fuego, who have since been wiped out. The museum will help you understand the marvelous richness of our planet.

Musée de la Marine. Palais de Chaillot, place du Trocadéro, 16e. ☎ **01-45-53-31-70.** Admission 39F ($6.80) adults; 20F ($3.50) for ages under 18 or over 65, free for children under 6. Wed–Mon 10am–6pm. Closed May 1. Métro: Trocadéro.

The galleries that trace the history of navigation and sailing from the 17th century are arranged thematically, covering such topics as ship building, navigational instruments, explorers' routes, steamships, fishing, sea rescue, and deep-sea diving.

Musée du Cinéma Henri Langlois. Palais de Chaillot, 1 place du Trocadéro, 16e. ☎ **01-45-53-74-39.** Admission 30F ($5.20) adults, free for children under 6. Closed Mon–Tues. Guided tours at 10 and 11am and 2, 3, 4, and 5pm. Métro: Trocadéro.

Film buffs will appreciate the photographs, sets, costumes, soundtracks, and other mementos associated with the magic of cinema, which of course originated in France. On view are Reynaud's Théâtre Optique (1888), the Lumière Brothers Cinematograph and photorama, and Edison's cinetoscope (1894).

10 The Latin Quarter (5e & 6e Arrondissements)

Excavations indicate that the ancient Romans made the Left Bank their residential district while the Ile de la Cité was their administrative headquarters. The Baths at the **Musée de Cluny** and the remnants of an amphitheater at the **Arènes de Lutéce** recall the Roman city of Lutéce, which counted about 8,000 inhabitants.

The scholarly tradition that began with the opening of the Sorbonne in the 13th century is alive today in the Latin Quarter, a district that contains not only the famous Sorbonne but other extensions of the University of Paris, as well as large high schools and specialized graduate schools.

Nevertheless, you won't find much student life in the noisy snarl of crowds and traffic along the boulevard St-Michel. The pedestrian streets from the quai St-Michel to the boulevard St-Germain provide only a hint of bohemia amidst the rows of Greek restaurants. Take a walk through the quieter streets that head south from the quai de Montebello to the **Panthéon** and **rue Mouffetard** and you'll experience the true character of this historic district. At once studious and carefree, medieval and modern, with monumental university buildings and cobblestoned alleys, the Latin Quarter is a pleasant confusion of Parisian styles. For greenery, gardens, and playgrounds you can either head east to the **Jardin des Plantes** or west to the **Jardin du Luxembourg.**

Musée de Cluny. 6 place Paul Painlevé, 5e. ☎ **01-43-25-62-00.** Admission 28F ($4.85) adults, 18F ($3.15) ages 18–24 and over 60, free for ages 17 and under. Reduced admission 18F ($3.15) on Sun, Wed–Mon 9:15am–5:15pm. Métro: Cluny-Sorbonne.

AT&T Direct℠ Service

How to call internationally from overseas:

1. Just dial the AT&T Access Number for the country you are calling from.
2. Dial the phone number you're calling.
3. Dial the calling card number listed above your name.

AT&T Access Numbers

Argentina ✖	001-800-200-1111	Costa Rica ●■	0-800-0-114-114
Australia	1800-881-011	Czech Rep. ▲	00-42-000-101
Austria ●○	022-903-011	Ecuador ●▲	999-119
Bahamas	1-800-872-2881	Egypt●(Cairo)†	510-0200
Belgium●	0-800-100-10	France	0-800-99-0011
Brazil	000-8010	Germany	0130-0010
Canada ■	1-800-225-5288	Greece●	00-800-1311
China, PRC▲	10811	Guam	018-872
Colombia	980-11-0010	Guatemala ○	190

AT&T Direct℠ Service

How to call internationally from overseas:

1. Just dial the AT&T Access Number for the country you are calling from.
2. Dial the phone number you're calling.
3. Dial the calling card number listed above your name.

AT&T Access Numbers

Argentina ✖	001-800-200-1111	Costa Rica ●■	0-800-0-114-114
Australia	1800-881-011	Czech Rep. ▲	00-42-000-101
Austria ●○	022-903-011	Ecuador ●▲	999-119
Bahamas	1-800-872-2881	Egypt●(Cairo)†	510-0200
Belgium●	0-800-100-10	France	0-800-99-0011
Brazil	000-8010	Germany	0130-0010
Canada ■	1-800-225-5288	Greece●	00-800-1311
China, PRC▲	10811	Guam	018-872
Colombia	980-11-0010	Guatemala ○	190

AT&T Access Numbers

Country	Number	Country	Number
Honduras ■	123	Panama ●■	109
Hong Kong	800-1111	Philippines ●	105-11
Ireland ●	1-800-550-000	Saudi Arabia ◇	1-800-10
Israel	177-100-2727	Singapore	800-0111-111
Italy ●	172-1011	Spain ◇	900-99-00-11
Jamaica □	872	Sweden	020-795-611
Japan ●	0039-111	Switzerland ●	0-800-550011
Japan ▲	0066-55-111	Taiwan ●	0080-10288-0
Korea, Republic ●	00-911	Thailand ✕	0019-991-1111
Mexico ▽ ■	95-800-462-4240	U.K. ▲	0800-89-0011
Netherlands ●	06-022-9111	U. Arab Emirates ● ■	800-121
New Zealand	000-911	Venezuela ●■	800-11-120

For a wallet card listing over 140 AT&T Access Numbers, dial the number for the country you're calling from, and ask the operator for customer service. In the U.S., call 1 800-331-1140, ext 704.

- ■ Bold-faced countries permit country-to-country calling outside the U.S.
- ● Public phones require coin or card deposit
- ◇ Country-to-country calls can only be placed to this country.
- ✕ Calling available to most countries
- ✦ Not available from public phones
- ＋ Dial "02" first, outside of Cairo
- □ May not be available from every phone/pay phone
- ○ Public phones require local coin payment through the call duration.
- ▽ When calling from public phones, use phones marked "Ladatel."
- ☐ Calling card calls available from select hotels

©1996 AT&T

AT&T Access Numbers

Country	Number	Country	Number
Honduras ■	123	Panama ●■	109
Hong Kong	800-1111	Philippines ●	105-11
Ireland ●	1-800-550-000	Saudi Arabia ◇	1-800-10
Israel	177-100-2727	Singapore	800-0111-111
Italy ●	172-1011	Spain ◇	900-99-00-11
Jamaica □	872	Sweden	020-795-611
Japan ●	0039-111	Switzerland ●	0-800-550011
Japan ▲	0066-55-111	Taiwan ●	0080-10288-0
Korea, Republic ●	00-911	Thailand ✕	0019-991-1111
Mexico ▽ ■	95-800-462-4240	U.K. ▲	0800-89-0011
Netherlands ●	06-022-9111	U. Arab Emirates ● ■	800-121
New Zealand	000-911	Venezuela ●■	800-11-120

For a wallet card listing over 140 AT&T Access Numbers, dial the number for the country you're calling from, and ask the operator for customer service. In the U.S., call 1 800-331-1140, ext 704.

- ■ Bold-faced countries permit country-to-country calling outside the U.S.
- ● Public phones require coin or card deposit
- ◇ Country-to-country calls can only be placed to this country.
- ✕ Calling available to most countries
- ✦ Not available from public phones
- ＋ Dial "02" first, outside of Cairo
- □ May not be available from every phone/pay phone
- ○ Public phones require local coin payment through the call duration.
- ▽ When calling from public phones, use phones marked "Ladatel."
- ☐ Calling card calls available from select hotels

©1996 AT&T

I love 0-800-99-0011
in the springtime.

Every country has its own AT&T Access Number which makes calling from France and other countries really easy. Just dial the AT&T Access Number for the country you're calling from and we'll take it from there. And be sure to charge your calls on your AT&T Calling Card. It'll help you avoid outrageous phone charges on your hotel bill and save you up to 60%.* 0-800-99-0011 is a great place to visit any time of year, especially if you've got these two cards. So please take the attached wallet card of worldwide AT&T Access Numbers.

**All you need for the
fastest, clearest connections home.**

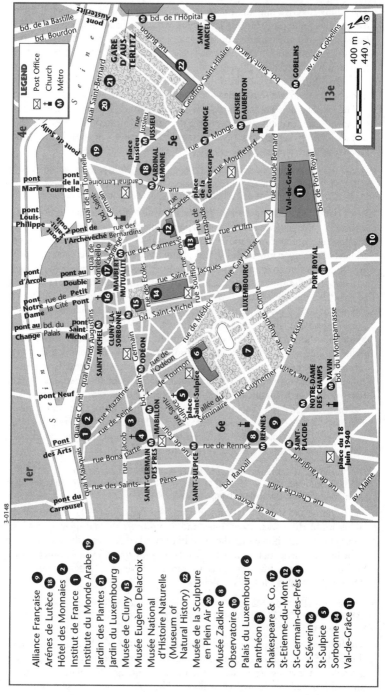

LEGEND

⊠ Post Office
╋ Church
Ⓜ Métro

Alliance Française ⑨
Arènes de Lutèce ⑱
Hôtel des Monnaies ②
Institut de France ①
Institut du Monde Arabe ⑲
Jardin des Plantes ㉑
Jardin du Luxembourg ⑦
Musée de Cluny ⑮
Musée Eugène Delacroix ③
Musée National
  d'Histoire Naturelle
  (Museum of
  Natural History) ㉒
Musée de la Sculpture
  en Plein Air ⑳
Musée Zadkine ⑧
Observatoire ⑩
Palais du Luxembourg ⑥
Panthéon ⑬
Shakespeare & Co. ⑰
St-Etienne-du-Mont ⑫
St-Germain-des-Prés ④
St-Séverin ⑯
St-Sulpice ⑤
Sorbonne ⑭
Val-de-Grâce ⑪

181

The Cluny is Paris's museum of medieval art. Its location in the Hôtel de Cluny is completely appropriate, for this 15th-century building is no doubt Paris's foremost example of civil architecture from the Middle Ages. Some parts date from Roman times, and you can see the ruins of late 2nd- and early 3rd-century baths (the frigidarium is especially well preserved).

In the 19th century, the Hôtel de Cluny belonged to a collector of medieval art; upon his death in the 1840s, the government acquired the house and its contents.

The exhibits here contain wood and stone sculpture, brilliant stained glass and metalwork, and rich tapestries, including the famous 15th-century series of *The Lady and the Unicorn,* an allegory representing the five senses (the meaning of the sixth tapestry remains a mystery).

Musée National D'Histoire Naturelle. 57 rue Cuvier, 5e. ☎ **01-40-79-30-00.** Admission Grande Gallerie 40F ($7) adults, 30F ($5.20) before 1pm, students, senior citizens, ages 4–16. Mon, Wed, Fri, Sat–Sun 10am–6pm; Thurs 10am–10pm. Métro: Jussieu or Austerlitz.

Bugs, bones, minerals, meteorites, dinosaurs, fossils, and endangered species are represented in the galleries of this wide-ranging collection. Located in the Jardin des Plantes, the natural history museum was established in 1793 as an extension of the schools of botany, natural history, and pharmacy founded in the botanical gardens. The museum flowered during the 19th century, becoming a prestigious center of research and education, a role it maintains today. Although your kids may tug you to the Paleontological Gallery, you'll find that the rows of dinosaur skeletons and cabinets of bottled organs are unimaginatively displayed in a dilapidated building. Far more impressive is the new Grande Gallery of Evolution, recently treated to a $90 million restoration. The subtle lighting and eerie sound effects of this vast hall induce a kind of trance, the better to absorb the museum's ecological theme. The exhibits trace the evolution of life and man's relationship to nature. Don't miss the endangered and extinct species room, which displays Gabonese monkeys, Sumatran tigers, lemurs of Madagascar, and a mock-up of the dodo bird. Some exhibits have explanations available in English. Also part of the natural history museum is the Mineralogical Gallery (1,800 minerals, meteorites, and precious stones), the Entomological Gallery (1,500 insect specimens of astonishing variety), and the Paleobotanical Gallery (plant evolution and specimens of fossil plants).

Musée Zadkine. 100 bis rue d'Assas, 6e. ☎ **01-43-26-91-90.** Admission adults 27F ($4.70), 19F ($3.30) students, ages 7–25, and seniors, free for children under 7. Tues–Sun 10am–5:30pm. Métro: Notre-Dame-des-Champs or Vavin.

In this house and studio, Russian sculptor Ossip Zadkine (1890–1967) worked until his death. His works, books, tools, and furniture are all on display, recreating the atmosphere of the home that the artist himself called Assas's folly. His works tend to be melodramatic, but his bronze *To a Destroyed City* (1953) is considered a 20th-century masterpiece (the original is in Rotterdam; there's a model on display here). The sculpture-filled gardens are pleasant.

Musée de l'Institut du Monde Arabe. 1 rue des Fosses-St-Bernard, 5e. ☎ **01-40-51-38-38.** Admission 25F ($4.35); 20F ($3.50) students and ages 12–25. Tues–Sun 10am–6pm. Métro: Jussieu or Cardinal-Lemoine.

The building, which opened in 1987, is remarkable in itself. The architects combined the modern materials of glass and aluminum with traditional Arab designs to create a serene and inviting structure. The south side contains 240 geometric panels that automatically adjust themselves to allow in the right amount of light. Inside, there are three floors of galleries displaying the riches of Arab-Islamic culture from the

7th to the 19th century. The ninth-floor tea salon and restaurant serves Moroccan food and provides a panoramic view across the Seine.

Musée de l'Assistance Publique Hôpitaux de Paris. 47 quai de la Tournelle, 5e. ☎ 01-46-33-01-43. Admission 20F ($3.50) adults; 10F ($1.75) children 13–18, students; free for ages 12 and under. Tues–Sat 10am–5pm; closed holidays and Aug. Métro: Maubert-Mutualité or St-Michel.

Not for the faint of heart, this museum features more than 3,000 objects that reflect the history of Paris's hospitals from the Middle Ages. After a visit here, you'll never take anesthesia for granted again.

Musée de la Sculpture en Plein Air. Quai St-Bernard, 5e. Free admission. Métro: Sully-Morland or Austerlitz.

In 1985, the banks of the Seine near the port Saint-Bernard were transformed into a promenade and showcase for the works of 29 contemporary sculptors. More a sculpture garden than a museum, this graceful waterside park displays the sculptures of César, Zadkine, Stahly, and others.

St-Séverin. Rue des Prêtres St-Séverin, 5e. Métro: St-Michel.

An oratory or similar religious building has stood here since the 6th century. The current building was begun in the 13th century and is in flamboyant Gothic style, featuring a double ambulatory. The brilliant stained-glass windows behind the altar depicting the Seven Sacraments were created by Jean Bazaine in 1966. The chapel to the right of the altar designed by Mansart is also notable and contains an intensely moving series of etchings by Georges Rouault and an extraordinary rendition of the crucifixion by G. Schneider (1989). Note also the dramatic palm tree–shaped vaulting.

St-Sulpice. Place St-Sulpice, 6e. 8am–7pm daily. Métro: St-Sulpice.

This massive church, founded by the abbey of St-Germain-des-Prés, houses three paintings by Delacroix in the Chapelle des Anges (1853–61) including *Jacob and the Angel* and *Heliodorus Expelled from the Temple,* which are both considered mature masterpieces demonstrating his brilliant use of color and dramatic sense of structure. The church was begun in 1646, with work continuing throughout the 17th and 18th centuries. The centerpiece of the square is a fountain built by Visconti in 1844.

Panthéon. Place du Panthéon, 5e. ☎ 01-43-54-34-51. Admission 32F ($5.50) adults, 21F ($3.65) ages 12–25 , free for children under 12. Apr–Sept, daily 9:30am–6:30pm; Oct–Mar, daily 10am–6:15pm. Métro: Cardinal-Lemoine or Maubert-Mutualité.

Few other monuments in Paris have had as versatile a career as the Panthéon. This neoclassical building with a huge dome—one of the landmarks of the Left Bank—was originally a church. It was ordered by Louis XV in thanksgiving for his having recovered from a serious illness. Construction started in 1755; the architect Soufflot chose a Greek cross design. It was first called the church of Ste-Geneviève, in honor of Paris's patron saint. A series of paintings by Puvis de Chavannes represents different scenes from the saint's life.

After the French Revolution, the church was renamed the Panthéon—in remembrance of pagan Rome's ancient Pantheon—and it was rededicated as a necropolis for France's secular heroes. Voltaire and Jean-Jacques Rousseau, clear representatives of the Enlightenment, were buried here, as was Victor Hugo in 1885. Also here are the remains of Louis Braille, inventor of the reading system for the blind, and novelist Emile Zola. Most recently, French writer/politician/adventurer André Malraux was honored by a tomb in the Panthéon. There is a pendulum suspended from the central dome which recreates Jean Bernard Foucault's 1851 demonstration proving the rotation of the earth.

Sorbonne. 47 rue des Ecoles, 5e. Métro: Cluny-Sorbonne.

Founded in 1253 by Robert de Sorbon, this theological college became the principal center of French higher education. Its inspiration cannot be grasped in its buildings, which are neither distinguished nor harmonious. Rather, the remarkable character of the Sorbonne lies in its intellectual vigor and the dedicated scholarship of the individuals who have taught and studied there—a tradition that began with such formidable early teachers as Abélard, St. Thomas Aquinas, Roger Bacon, and, later, Renan. The list of its great students includes Taine, Michelet, Baudelaire, Musset, Sainte-Beuve, and Bergson, and they are joined by such distinguished outsiders as Dante, Erasmus, John Calvin, and Henry Wadsworth Longfellow. In 1469, France's first printing press was set up here; during the German Occupation, the Sorbonne became one of the headquarters of the Resistance. Most of the present buildings were erected between 1885 and 1901. The courtyard and galleries are open to the public and in the Cour d'Honneur stand statues of Victor Hugo and Louis Pasteur.

Jardin des Plantes. 5e. ☎ **01-43-36-54-26.** 7:30am–7:45pm daily Apr 15–Oct 6; 7:30am–5:30pm Oct 7–Apr 14. Métro: Jussieu or Austerlitz.

More than just a lovely park for strolling, the immense selection of plants here serves as a valuable educational tool. The Alpine Garden has 2,000 mountain plants from the Alps and the Himalayas; a Winter Garden contains tropical plants and a Mexican Garden is planted with cacti.

THE REST OF THE PICTURE

If you've always yearned for the simple village life, try the market on **rue Mouffetard** (Tuesday, Thursday, and Saturday; Métro: Monge). Although hardly unnoticed by tourists, the area around rue Mouffetard reflects its origins as a 16th-century village, even if some of the local color is beginning to seem self-conscious. After strolling through the passages Postes and Patriarches and the rues Pot-de-Fer and Arbolete, take a break on the **place de la Contrescarpe,** one of the prettiest squares in Paris.

11 St-Germain-des-Prés (6e & 7e Arrondissements)

No other neighborhood better expresses the quintessential Parisian character—intellectual, argumentative, pleasure-seeking, cosmopolitan. St-Germain has remained the cultural and intellectual heart of Paris for centuries. Voltaire exercised his rapier wit at the restaurant (then a cafe) **Le Procope;** Jean-Paul Sartre expounded his existentialist philosophy at the cafes **Aux Deux-Magots** and **Café de Flore.** Today, newspeople and photogenic philosopher Bernard-Henri Lévy (known simply as BHL) still gather downstairs at **Brasserie Lipp.**

The scores of small bookstores in the neighborhood create an inviting atmosphere for both native and expatriate writers. When Sylvia Beach's circle of literary heavyweights moved on, the Beat generation moved in. Allen Ginsburg, Gregory Corso, and William Burroughs found a personal freedom and tolerance here that had eluded them in the United States, as did many African American writers and jazz musicians.

Artists have also made a home in the neighborhood. The Ecole des Beaux-Arts continues to influence young artists long after the days when Monet and Matisse studied there. You can visit **Delacroix's studio** and then get an overview of the contemporary scene in the galleries along the **rue de Seine** and **rue Bonaparte.**

Unfortunately, St-Germain is falling prey to a creeping commercialism totally at odds with its bohemian past. As the neighborhood has steadily moved upscale, slick new stores selling luxury products have begun driving out businesses that have been local fixtures for decades. In the process, St-Germain is losing its quirky individuality and beginning to resemble any tony Right Bank enclave. The old Left Bank is there, though—you just have to look harder to find it.

Musée Nationale Eugène Delacroix. 6 rue de Fürstenberg, 6e. ☎ **01-44-41-86-50.** Admission 22F ($3.80) adults; 18F ($3.15) for ages 18–25; free ages 17 and under. Wed–Mon 9:30am–noon and 1:30pm–5pm. Métro: St-Germain-des-Prés.

Delacroix (1798–1863) is considered the greatest painter of the Romantic movement. After his *Scenes of the Massacres of Scios* was purchased by the state, his success was assured. (The painting now hangs in the Louvre.) He painted an enormous number of works. At his death, more than 9,000 paintings, drawings, and pastels were found in his studio, along with the journals that he had kept for almost two decades. He inspired van Gogh, who said simply that only Rembrandt and Delacroix could paint the face of Christ, while Baudelaire dubbed him the "painter poet." The museum occupies Delacroix's old studio, which you enter through a small courtyard. The paintings, sketches, drawings, and mementos displayed in this homey atmosphere give a more intimate understanding of the artist than the enormous canvases at the Louvre. The most notable work is the *Seated Turk,* painted after a trip to North Africa.

St-Germain-des-Prés. 3 place St-Germain-des-Prés, 6e. ☎ **01-43-25-41-71.** 7:45am–8pm daily. Métro: St-Germain-des-Prés.

The most famous church of the 6e arrondissement is also one of the most important Romanesque monuments in France. Built in the 11th century, St-Germain-des-Prés was an important abbey and center of learning during the Middle Ages. At the time of the French Revolution, the monks were expelled and the church was vandalized. But much still remains. The large tower is the oldest in Paris. John Casimir, King of Poland, is among those buried at the church, as is the heart of René Descartes. A small square at the corner of place St-Germain-des-Prés and the rue de l'Abbaye contains Picasso's *Homage to Apollinaire.*

Institut de France. 23 quai de Conti, 6e. ☎ **01-44-41-44-41.** Métro: Pont-Neuf or Odéon.

Designed by Louis Le Vau, this dramatic baroque building with its enormous cupola is the seat of all five Academies—Academie Francaise, Academie des Sciences, des Inscriptions et Belles Lettres, des Beaux Arts, and des Sciences Morales et Politiques—which dominate the intellectual life of the country. Here gather the members of the Academy (limited to 40), the guardians of the French language who are referred to as "the immortals." Many of them are unfamiliar figures and indeed the Academy is remarkable for the great writers and philosophers who have *not* been invited to join—Balzac, Baudelaire, Diderot, Flaubert, Descartes, Proust, Molière, Pascal, Rousseau, and Zola, to name only a few. The cenotaph was designed by Coysevox for Mazarin.

THE REST OF THE PICTURE

Everyone has their own favorite hideaways in Paris, but I find the **place de Fürstemberg** (Métro: St-Germain-des-Prés) and the surrounding streets—rue Cardinale, rue de l'Echaudé and rue de Fürstembourg—simply enchanting. At the center of the place de Fürstemberg are the four trees described by Henry Miller in *Tropic of Cancer.* The market at **rue de Buci,** 6e (daily, except Monday; Métro: Odéon), is as colorful and animated as a neighborhood market should be.

Attractions—St-Germain-des-Prés

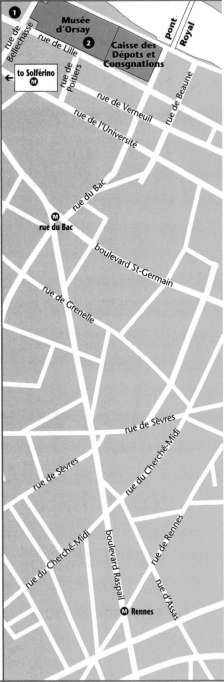

3-0149

186

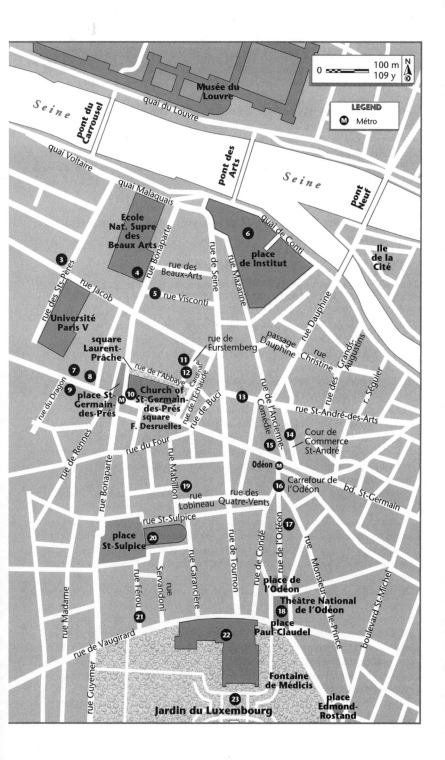

Seine

quai du Louvre

Musée du
Louvre

0 ⬛⬛⬛ 100 m
109 y

N

LEGEND

Ⓜ Métro

quai Voltaire

pont du
Carrousel

pont des
Arts

Seine

Pont
Neuf

quai Malaquais

Ecole
Nat. Supre
des
Beaux Arts

rue Bonaparte

rue des
Beaux-Arts

rue de Seine

rue Mazarine

quai de Conti

6

place
de Institut

Ile
de la
Cité

3

rue des Sts-Pères

rue Jacob

4

5 rue Visconti

Université
Paris V

square
Laurent-
Prâche

rue de
Furstemberg

passage
Dauphine

rue Dauphine

rue
Christine

rue des
Grands-
Augustins

r.-Séguier

rue de l'Abbaye

11

12

7 **8**

rue du Dragon

9

10 Ⓜ

place St-
Germain-
des-Prés

Church of
St-Germain-
des-Prés
square
F. Desruelles

rue Cardinal

rue de l'Echaudé

rue de Buci

13

rue de l'Ancienne-
Comédie

rue St-André-des-Arts

rue de Rennes

rue Bonaparte

rue du Four

rue Mabillon

14

15

Cour de
Commerce
St-André

Odéon Ⓜ

19

rue
Lobineau

rue des
Quatre-Vents

16

Carrefour de
l'Odéon

bd. St-Germain

rue St-Sulpice

20

place
St-Sulpice

rue Garancière

rue de Tournon

rue de Condé

rue de l'Odéon

17

rue Monsieur

boulevard St-Michel

rue Madame

rue Férou

rue
Servandoni

rue de Vaugirard

21

22

place de
l'Odéon

Théâtre National
de l'Odéon

18

place
Paul-Claudel

rue le-Prince

rue Guynemer

23

Jardin du Luxembourg

Fontaine
de Médicis

place
Edmond-
Rostand

12 Eiffel Tower & Invalides (7e Arrondissement)

It's not surprising that a neighborhood containing the **Eiffel Tower** (see "The Top 10 Sights to See," above), **Ecole Militaire, Musée d'Orsay,** and **Musée Rodin** is calm, dignified, and ever-so-respectable. East of the **Hôtel des Invalides** is the faubourg St-Germain with its splendid 18th-century mansions. French political life revolves around the **Assemblée Nationale, Ministère des Affaires Etrangéres,** and the **Hôtel Matignon** (residence of the prime minister), as well as the government offices and embassies that have addresses in this prestigious district (see "Walking Tour 4" in chapter 7). The construction of the Ecole Militaire and Invalides encouraged artisans and shopkeepers to populate the area between the Champ-des-Mars and Invalides, especially along rues St-Dominique, Champ-des-Mars, and the pedestrian rue Cler. Several flamboyant art nouveau buildings by Jules Lavirotte provide a dramatic contrast from the generally staid architecture. See 151 rue Cler, 3 square Rapp, and 29 av. Rapp for examples of his work.

Hôtel des Invalides. Place des Invalides, 7e. ☎ **01-44-42-37-72.** Admission 37F ($6.40) adults, 27F ($4.70) students age 12–25; free for children under 12. Oct 1–Mar 31 daily 10am–5pm; Apr 1–Sept 30 10am–6pm. The tomb of Napoléon is open until 7pm June 1–Aug 31. Closed major holidays. Métro: Latour-Maubourg, Invalides, or Varenne.

The majestic Hôtel des Invalides was built by Louis XIV as a hospital and home for veteran soldiers, many of whom had been reduced to the condition of beggars upon their return from foreign wars. It still functions as such and also houses a number of offices for numerous departments of the French armed forces.

But the value of the Invalides goes far beyond the symbolic qualities it may hold for the French military. The Invalides is one of Europe's architectural masterpieces. The building's facade, as you approach from the direction of the Seine, is truly majestic. The **Eglise du Dôme,** designed by Hardouin-Mansart, is one of the high points of classical art. Also part of the Invalides is the **Eglise de St-Louis,** also known as the Church of the Soldiers; Berlioz's *Requiem* was played here for the first time. Interestingly enough, during the French Revolution both churches were transformed into a Temple to Mars.

But most visitors come to see the **Tomb of Napoléon,** a great porphyry sarcophagus lying under the golden dome of the Invalides. In fact, the emperor is buried in six coffins, one inside the other. The first is iron, the second mahogany, the third and fourth are lead, the fifth is ebony, and the outermost coffin is oak. The emperor's remains were transferred to this monumental resting place in 1840, almost two decades after his death on the remote South Atlantic island of St. Helena, where he was sent in exile following his defeat at Waterloo. Paris was enveloped in a blizzard on December 15, the day the emperor's cortege made its way from the Arc de Triomphe, down the Champs-Elysées to the Esplanade. In the ten days following the funeral, 846,000 people came to pay their respects to Napoléon. The emperor's popularity has dipped since then. A recent poll placed him just ahead of Robespierre and behind six others, including Charlemagne, Jeanne d'Arc, and Clemenceau, on a list of historical figures the French people admire. Also buried here are Napoléon's brothers: Joseph, king of Spain, and Jérôme, king of Westphalia. His son, the king of Rome, was transferred here in 1940.

If you like military lore, you will want to visit the **Musée de l'Armée,** one of the greatest army museums in the world. It features thousands of weapons from

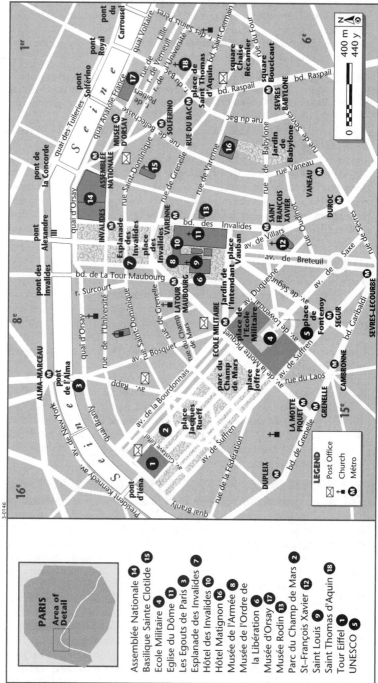

PARIS
Area of Detail

Attraction	No.
Assemblée Nationale	14
Basilique Sainte Clotilde	15
Ecole Militaire	4
Eglise du Dôme	11
Les Egouts de Paris	3
Esplanade des Invalides	7
Hôtel des Invalides	10
Hôtel Matignon	16
Musée de l'Armée	8
Musée de l'Ordre de la Libération	6
Musée d'Orsay	17
Musée Rodin	13
Parc du Champ de Mars	2
St-François Xavier	12
Saint Louis	9
Saint Thomas d'Aquin	18
Tour Eiffel	1
UNESCO	5

LEGEND

⊠ Post Office
✝ Church
Ⓜ Métro

0   400 m
      440 y

3-0146

189

different periods, from prehistory to World War II. You'll see spearheads and arrowheads, suits of armor, cannons, battle flags, booty, and all sorts of military paraphernalia. In honor of the 50th anniversary of the liberation, rooms 39 to 45 are devoted to the occupation and liberation of France.

Les Egouts. Face au 93 quai d'Orsay/Pont-de-l'Alma, 7e. ☎ **01-47-05-10-29.** Admission 25F ($4.35) adults, 20F ($3.50) ages 6–24 and over 60. May 1–Oct 30 Sat–Wed 11am–5pm; Nov 1–Apr 30 Sat–Wed 11am–4pm. Closed Thurs, Fri, and 3 weeks in Jan. Métro: Alma-Marceau. RER: Pont-de-l'Alma.

If you have followed Jean Valjean's adventures in Hugo's *Les Misérables* or seen old movies of World War II Resistance fighters, you will want to visit the sewers of Paris. Granted, this subterranean labyrinth is not as beautiful as the city above the ground, but the sewers are enormously interesting as well as being an engineering marvel. They were laid out by Eugène Belgrand during the reign of Napoléon III, at the same time that Haussmann was designing his *grands boulevards* across the city. If this kind of thing interests you, get in line for a visit on one of the afternoons when a glimpse is offered. Tours are conducted by an *égoutier* (sewer worker). Don't expect the aroma of Chanel No. 5.

Ecole Militaire and Champ-de-Mars. 1 place Joffre, 7e. Métro: Ecole-Militaire.

The idea for a military academy to train young gentlemen without means originated in 1751 with Madame Pompadour, Louis XV's long-time mistress. The project was entrusted to Jacques-Ange Gabriel, the architect of the place de la Concorde, who produced the magnificent Ecole Militaire, the vast building at the other end of the Champ-de-Mars from the Eiffel Tower. Their first illustrious student was Napoléon Bonaparte, who graduated in 1785. His excellent record in mathematics, geography, and fencing made up for his abysmal skills in drawing and dancing.

The Ecole Militaire presently houses the Institut des Hautes Etudes de Défenses Nationales and the Ecole Supérieure de Guerre. Tours of the interior are not allowed.

The Champ-de-Mars was originally used as a parade ground for the Ecole Militaire, but after the revolution it began to host fairs and exhibitions, most memorably for the Exposition of 1889, which saw the construction of the Eiffel Tower. Beginning in 1928, the esplanade was transformed into a vast park of shaded walks, flowers, statues, and plane trees.

13 Montparnasse (6e, 14e & 15e Arrondissements)

Even before the Lost Generation found themselves in the cafes of Montparnasse, the neighborhood had become a haunt of artists and intellectuals. In the 17th century, students began gathering here to read poetry and named the area Mount Parnassus after the Greek mountain consecrated to Apollo and the Muses. Where students go, fun follows; cafes, dance halls and theaters sprang up in 19th-century Montparnasse, eventually luring artists from the increasingly touristy Montmartre. Before World War I interrupted the party, you could sip absinthe and discuss art with the likes of Chagall, Matisse, Picasso, Modigliani, and Max Jacob in La Rotonde and La Dôme. You might even have noticed a small group of Russian exiles that included Lenin and Trotsky. The scene picked up again in the twenties with the opening of La Coupole and the addition of the American literary crowd—Hemingway, Dos Passos, Fitzgerald, and Miller. They liked the wine, they liked the conversation, and they especially liked the prices—the American dollar went a long, long way in those days.

The famous old cafes still draw a mix of Left Bank old-timers and tourists, but the rest of Montparnasse has changed dramatically. The Tour Montparnasse looms over

Attractions—Montparnasse

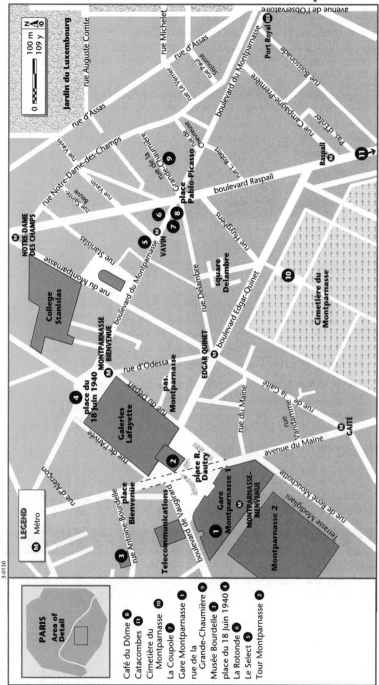

LEGEND

Ⓜ Métro

Jardin du Luxembourg

NOTRE-DAME DES CHAMPS

Collège Stanislas

place du 18 Juin 1940 ❹

Galeries Lafayette

place Bienvenüe

Telecommunications

place R. Dautry

Gare Montparnasse ❶

MONTPARNASSE-BIENVENUE Ⓜ

Montparnasse 2

Terrasse Modigliani

rue de René Mouchotte

avenue du Maine

GAITÉ Ⓜ

EDGAR QUINET Ⓜ

square Delambre

Cimetière du Montparnasse ❿

boulevard Edgar-Quinet

VAVIN Ⓜ ❺ ❻ ❼ ❽

❾

place Pablo-Picasso

boulevard Raspail

Raspail Ⓜ

❿⤳

Port Royal RER

avenue de l'Observatoire

PARIS Area of Detail

Café du Dôme ❽
Catacombes ⓫
Cimetière du Montparnasse ❿
La Coupole ❼
Gare Montparnasse ❶
rue de la Grande-Chaumière ❾
Musée Bourdelle ❸
place du 18 Juin 1940 ❹
La Rotonde ❻
Le Select ❺
Tour Montparnasse ❷

3-0150

191

an increasingly garish neighborhood. The 688-foot-high tower was despised as soon as it opened in 1967; unlike some other modern architectural ventures, time has only underlined its remarkable incongruity with the Parisian landscape. The tower contains an extensive commercial center, a train station, and an observatory on the 56th floor.

Fondation Cartier. 261 bd. Raspail, 14e. ☎ **01-42-18-56-51.** Admission 30F ($5.20), 20F ($3.50) ages 17 and under. Tues, Wed, Fri–Sun noon–8pm, Thurs noon–10pm. Métro: Raspail.

One of the most striking modern buildings in Paris, this almost completely transparent structure by architect Jean Nouvel hosts a changing array of first-rate contemporary art exhibits.

Musée Bourdelle. 18 rue Antoine Bourdelle, 15e. ☎ **01-49-54-73-73.** Admission 27F ($4.70) adults, 19F ($3.30) students with ID. Tues–Sun 10am–5:40pm. Métro: Montparnasse-Bienvenue.

The home and workshop of the sculptor Emile-Antoine Bourdelle, where he lived and worked from 1884 to 1929. He had served as Rodin's assistant and has largely been overshadowed by him. On display are studies and drawings as well as rooms filled with large bronzes and marbles.

Catacombes. 1 place Denfert-Rochereau, 14e. ☎ **01-43-22-47-63.** Admission 27F ($4.70) adults, 19F ($3.30) students, free under 6. Tues–Fri 2–4pm; Sat–Sun 9–11am and 2–4pm. Closed holidays. Métro: Denfert-Rochereau.

These ancient quarries were converted into ossuaries in 1785 because the existing burial grounds were a health hazard. About 1,000 yards long, the tunnels contain about 6 million skeletons arranged in skull-and-crossbones fashion. During much of the 19th century they were closed to the public. During the second world war they were one of the headquarters of the Resistance.

Cimetière de Montparnasse. 14e. Métro: Edgar Quinet or Raspail.

Although not as otherworldly as Pére-Lachaise, this cemetery is where you'll find the graves of Bartholdi, Baudelaire, Simone de Beauvoir, Samuel Beckett, Guy de Maupassant, Jean-Paul Sartre, and Maurice Zadkine, among others.

THE REST OF THE PICTURE

Any other city would put Rodin's **statue of Balzac** in a museum, but you can see this fine work for free at the corner of boulevard Montparnasse and boulevard Raspail (Métro: Raspail). There is a market on **rue Daguerre,** south of the cemetery, every day except Monday (Métro: Denfert-Rochereau).

14 Farther Afield

MUSEUMS

Musée des Arts d'Afrique et d'Océanie. 293 av. Daumesnil, 12e. ☎ **01-44-74-84-80.** Admission 30F ($5.20) adults, 20F ($3.50) ages 18 to 25, free for ages 17 and under. Wed–Mon 10am–noon and 1:30–5:20pm. Métro: Porte-Dorée.

The Musée des Arts d'Afrique et d'Océanie is divided into four main sections: the art of Oceania, including New Guinea and Australia; African art; North African art; and a tropical aquarium.

Manufacture Nationale des Gobelins. 42 av. des Gobelins, 13e. ☎ **01-43-37-12-60.** Admission 37F ($6.40) adults, 27F ($4.70) children for the tour. Guided tours are obligatory and are offered in French only on Tues, Wed, and Thurs at 2 and 2:45pm. Métro: Gobelins.

Visit the workshops of this famous 17th-century factory and view the great looms on which these glorious art objects are still woven. Gobelins is named after the 15th-century scarlet-dyers Jean and Philibert Gobelin, who established their workshop in Paris on a small stream called the Bievre. Here, Flemish weavers summoned to Paris by Henry IV set up their looms and here too in 1662 Louis XIV reorganized the weavers. Originally the factory made all kinds of fabrics for the royal household. In 1694 it was forced to close because of the king's financial problems and after it reopened in 1699 it confined itself to the weaving of tapestries.

Musée de la Musique. 221 av. Jean Jaurès, 19e. ☎ **01-44-84-44-84.** Web site: http://www.cite-music.fr. Admission 35F ($6) adults, 24F ($4.10) students. Tues–Thurs, Sat noon–6pm; Fri noon–9:30pm; Sun 10am–6pm. Métro: Porte de Pantin.

This ultramodern museum is in the heart of the new Cité de la Musique, which includes a conservatory, a concert hall, a documentation center, and several auxiliary buildings. The permanent exhibition displays 900 instruments and music-inspired paintings and sculptures from the Renaissance to today. A portable headset plays extracts from major works and offers commentaries that place the instruments in historical context as you examine the exhibits. Temporary exhibitions focus on non-Western musical traditions.

CHURCHES

Basilique St-Denis. Place de l'Hôtel de Ville. Apr–Sept, Mon–Sat 10am–7pm, Sun noon–7pm; Oct–Mar Mon–Sat 10am–5pm, Sun noon–5pm. Métro: St-Denis-Basilique.

Almost every French king from Dagobert I (639) to Louis XVIII (1824) was buried here. The present structure is one of the earliest examples of Gothic architecture. The cathedral of St-Denis was begun by Abbot Suger in 1136. All that remains today of the original is the apse and the narthex (west porch), which features a combination of rounded and pointed arches. The rest of the cathedral dates from the 13th century. From here, the Gothic style spread throughout France and the rest of Europe, culminating in such cathedrals as Chartres. The hallmarks of the style were the pointed arch, rib vaults, and flying buttresses. The last in particular enabled the walls of cathedrals to be converted virtually into curtains of stained glass, as can be seen here.

MONUMENTS

La Grande Arche de la Défense. 1 Parvis de la Défense. ☎ **01-49-07-27-57.** Admission 40F ($7) adults, 30F ($5.20) under 18, free for children under 6. Daily 10am–6pm. Métro: Grande-Arche-de-la-Défense. RER: La Défense.

From the huge 35-story arch—actually a colossal cube—you have a spectacular vista down the avenue Charles-de-Gaulle to the Arc de Triomphe, the Champs-Elysée, and the Louvre. Built in 1989 and designed by Danish architect Johan Otto von Spreckelsen as the centerpiece of La Défense suburb, it has caused a great deal of controversy.

Bibliothèque Nationale de France. Quai François Mauriac, 13e. ☎ **01-53-79-59-59.** Web site: http://www.bnf.fr. Admission 20F ($3.50); Tues–Sat 10am–9pm, Sun noon–6pm. Métro: Quai de la Gare.

With its four looming glass towers shaped like open books, this new national library is the grandest of the *Grand Projects* bestowed (or inflicted) upon Paris by former president François Mitterrand. Whatever one might say about the futuristic design, at least no one can accuse architect Dominique Perrault of having ruined a

charming Parisian neighborhood. In fact, the sprawling 17-acre library is expected
to pump new life into one of the drabbest residential areas in the city. The reading
rooms are austere but comfortable and include a state-of-the-art audiovisual room
devoted to films, photos, recordings, and videos. A gallery section showcases rotat-
ing exhibits of rare books and manuscripts from the national library collection.

FLEA MARKETS

Les Puces de Paris Saint Ouen, 18e, is the most famous of Paris flea markets. It's
vast, consisting of thousands of stalls selling everything from fine antiques to plain
junk. It's tough to find any bargains or unsung gems today, but it's still worth
going for the experience. (Between the Porte de St-Ouen and Porte de Clignancourt;
open Saturday to Monday 7:30am to 7pm. Métro: Porte de Clignancourt.)

Les Puces de la Porte de Montreuil, avenue de la Porte de Montreuil, sells domestic appliances, tools, old furniture, secondhand clothes and crockery. (Open Saturday to Monday 7am to 6pm. Métro: Porte de Montreuil.) **Les Puces de la Porte
de Vanves,** Porte de Vanves, Porte Didot, Avenue Georges Lafenestre, avenue Marc
Saugnier, features furniture, paintings, and old junk. (Open Saturday and Sunday
7am to 7:30pm. Métro: Porte de Vanves.)

15 Parks & Gardens

Most large Parisian parks are not green like, for instance, London's parks. Rather,
they're laid out in a formal manner with gravel pathways and avenues of chestnuts
and other trees, and decorated with monumental statues and fountains. They also
offer many benches where visitors can sit quietly and contemplate the life that passes
by. In addition to the historic parks noted here, you'll find numerous fenced-in
squares hidden in every arrondissement, often with a small playground, a boules
court, a few flower beds, well-trimmed shrubs, and large shady trees.

The **Bois de Boulogne** in western Paris, 16e (☎ 01-40-67-97-02), is the city's
most legendary and largest park. Formerly a royal forest and hunting ground, it was
donated to the city by Napoléon III but it was Baron Haussmann who transformed
it, using London's Hyde Park as his model. He also laid out the avenue de
l'Impératrice (now the avenue Foch), which led from the Arc de Triomphe to the
Bois. The park soon became a very fashionable place.

Today the Bois is a vast reserve of more than 2,200 acres. There's jogging, horseback riding, bicycling (you can rent a bike here), and boating on the two lakes. Also
here are the famous **Longchamps** and **Auteuil racecourses** and the beautiful **Jardin
Shakespeare** in the Pré Catelan, a garden containing many of the plants and herbs
mentioned in Shakespeare's plays. The **Jardin d'Acclimatation** is Paris children's
favorite amusement park. (Métro: Les Sablons, Porte-Maillot, or Porte-Dauphine.)

The **Jardin du Palais Royal** in the 1er is a fine spot in which to sit and imagine
what it was like here in the late 18th and early 19th centuries, when it was filled with
gamblers and others seeking more lascivious pleasures or when Camille Desmoulins
challenged the crowds at the Café de Foy to choose the cockade of the revolution.
Today, surrounded by the elegant covered arcades of the Palais Royal, you can contemplate the past as well as the present when you see the steel ball sculptures by Pol
Bury that decorate the fountains, and Daniel Buren's controversial prison-striped
columns built in 1986. (Métro: Palais-Royal.)

The 6e arrondissement's **Jardin du Luxembourg** (☎ 01-43-29-12-78) was commissioned by King Henri IV's queen, Marie de Medici, and is one of Paris's most
beloved parks. Large and located not far from the Sorbonne, just south of the Latin
Quarter, it is quite popular with students. Children love it too, especially for the *parc*

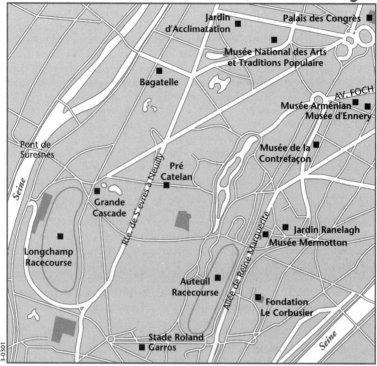

Jardin d'Acclimatation

Palais des Congrès

Musée National des Arts et Traditions Populaire

Bagatelle

AV. FOCH

Musée Arménian
Musée d'Ennery

Pont de Suresnes

Seine

Pré Catelan

Musée de la Contrefaçon

Grande Cascade

Rte de Sèvres à Neuilly

Longchamp Racecourse

Jardin Ranelagh
Musée Mermotton

Allée de Reine Marguerite

Auteuil Racecourse

Fondation Le Corbusier

Seine

Stade Roland Garros

3-0301

à jeux (playground) and the *théâtre des marionettes* (puppet theater). Besides pools, fountains, and statues of queens and poets—including Heredia, Baudelaire, and Verlaine—there are tennis courts and spaces for playing *boules.*

The **Palais du Luxembourg,** at the northern edge of the park, was also built for Marie de Medici. An Italian, she very much missed the Palazzo Pitti in Florence, where she had spent her childhood. The architect Salomon de Brosse combined the styles of France and Tuscany in the palace. It was for the Palais du Luxembourg that Rubens created the cycle of 24 paintings depicting Marie de Medici's life that now hang in the Louvre. (Métro: Odéon.)

Another historic garden can be found in the 5e arrondissement: the **Jardin des Plantes** (☎ 01-43-36-54-26). Louis XIII approved the foundation of the Jardin Royal des Plantes Médicinales in 1626, but the real builders of these botanical gardens were the king's physicians, who needed their own arsenal of medicinal herbs to cure the royal indispositions. The naturalist Buffon was director of the Jardin des Plantes from 1739 to 1788. The garden was also a favorite place of Jean-Jacques Rousseau. After the French Revolution, the **Musée National d'Histoire Naturelle** was created here, and exotic animals were brought in; elephants arrived in 1795, giraffes in the 1820s. Many of these, however, were eaten by hungry Parisians during the siege of the city in the Franco-Prussian War.

What you'll see today are straight rows of trees, neat beds of herbs and flowers, a 17th-century maze, a menagerie, and various specialized plantings, greenhouses, and displays of minerals and assorted insects. (Métro: Gare-d'Austerlitz or Jussieu.)

Everyone knows of the **Jardin des Tuileries,** between the Louvre and the place de la Concorde in the 1er arrondissement (☎ 01-42-60-38-01). After a recent substantial renovation and redesign, it's sunnier and prettier than it's been in many years.

It's still the city's most formal garden, with pathways laid out in a rational, precise manner. The name derives from *tuiles* (tiles)—the clay earth of the land here was once used to make roof tiles. The gardens were originally laid out in the 1560s for Queen Mother Catherine de Medici in front of the Tuileries Palace. A century later, Le Nôtre, creator of French landscaping, redesigned a large section of it in the classical style. He is responsible for the octagonal pools surrounded by statues and terraces that include *The Seasons* by Nicolas Coustou and Van Cleve, *The Seine and The Marne* by Coustou, *The Loire and Loiret* by Van Cleve, and *Fame* and *Mercury* by Coysevox (these last two are reproductions, though; the originals are in the Louvre).

Originally a fashionable carriageway, the Jardin des Tuileries today is a restful space in the center of Paris. The **Orangerie** and the **Jeu de Paume** (see "Louvre, Tuileries & Les Halles," above) are located at its western edge, and to the east you'll find 40 extraordinarily beautiful Maillol bronzes scattered among the trees. (Métro: Tuileries or Concorde.)

The **Parc Monceau,** boulevard de Coucelles, 8e (☎ 01-42-27-39-56), is the city's most English-style park and has some whimsical history attached to it. The park was commissioned by Louis Philippe Joseph, duc de Chartres et Orléans, an aristocrat whose democratic ideals led him to renounce his nobility and adopt the name Philippe-Egalité after the Revolution (he was later guillotined). The painter Carmontelle designed several things for this park, including a Dutch windmill, a Roman temple, a farm, medieval ruins, and a pagoda. The place became known as "Chartres's folly." Appropriately enough, it was here that Garnerin, the world's first parachutist, landed. In the mid–19th century, the park was redesigned in the English style. It was a favorite place for Marcel Proust to stroll.

At the **Parc de Bagatelle** in the 16e, the rose gardens in particular are sublime, while the thematic gardens reveal the art of gardening through the centuries. The château was built by the Comte d'Artois in 66 days, after he made a bet with his sister-in-law Marie Antoinette. Under Napoléon it was used as a hunting lodge and in the late 19th century it was added to by Richard Wallace. (Métro: Porte Maillot.)

The **Parc Montsouris** (14e) was laid out in 1868 by Haussmann on his return from exile in England and it does in fact resemble an English garden with its copses and winding paths. Swans and ducks gather on the pond and the bandstand is still in use. (RER: Cité Universitaire.)

The **Promenade Plantée** in the 12e begins at the Opéra Bastille and runs for 4½ kilometers along the length of Avenue Daumesnil, the Reuilly Garden, and the Porte Dorée, ending at the Bois de Vincennes. Stroll past the avenue viaducts, embankments, and other landmarks of the 11e and 12e arrondissements. (Métro: Bel Air or Dugommier.)

Among the city's most modern parks is the 19e arrondissement's **Parc de La Villette,** designed by Bernard Tschumi, who laid out a series of theme gardens including an exotic bamboo garden and a garden featuring steam and water jets. Scattered throughout the park are playgrounds and other attractions. (Located between the Porte de la Villette and Porte de Pantin. Métro: Porte de la Villette.)

16 Especially for Kids

Children can enjoy Paris as much as adults. Both you and your children will have a great time climbing to the top of the **Eiffel Tower, Notre-Dame,** or the **Arc de Triomphe.**

Puppet shows are a great Paris tradition. They're held at the Jardin du Luxembourg, the Champ-de-Mars, and the Jardin des Tuileries.

All Parisian parks, in fact, are wonderful for children, even if there happen to be no puppet shows there; one of the best is Parc Monceau, with its assorted ruins and other eccentric features around which children love to play. At the Bois de Boulogne, the Jardin d'Acclimatation (☎ 01-40-67-90-82; Métro: Les Sablons) is a wonderful amusement park; it's open daily from 10am to 6:30pm, Saturday until 7pm.

Children will also have great fun sailing along the Seine in the bateaux-mouches (see "Organized Tours," below).

Finally, there are the museums. Besides the Musée de l'Homme and the Musée National d'Histoire Naturelle (at the Jardin des Plantes, described above), try the following:

Cité des Sciences et de l'Industrie. 30 av. Corentin-Cariou, 19e. ☎ **01-40-05-81-00.** Web site: http://www.cite-sciences.fr. Admission to the exhibitions, including the Argonaut, 50F ($8.70), 35F ($6) after 4pm, children under 7 free; to the Geode, 57F ($9.90); cinéaxe, 34F ($5.90). A three-in-one ticket costs 124F ($21.50). Entrance to the Cité des Enfants is 25F ($4.35). Tues–Sat 10am–6pm, Sun 10am–7pm. Métro: Porte-de-la-Villette.

This complex in the Parc de la Villette was originally built as an abattoir but has been converted into a major museum and display showcase. There is a planetarium, which all children will love, and an adventure playground designed specifically for 3- to 12-year-olds. At Explora, exhibits, models, and interactive games demonstrate scientific techniques and present subjects including the universe, the earth, the environment, space, computer science, and health. The gigantic Géode sphere is a wonder, with its huge hemispheric screen that seems to immerse the audience in the spectacle of action provided by the six or so films shown daily.

Palais de la Découverte. Grand Palais, av. Franklin-D-Roosevelt, 8e. ☎ **01-40-74-80-00.** Admission 15F ($2.60) adults, 10F ($1.75) students and children under age 11. Supplement for the planetarium: 15F ($2.60) adults, 10F ($1.75) students and young adults under age 18. Tues–Sat 9:30am–6pm, Sun 10am–7pm. Métro: Franklin-D-Roosevelt.

Sheltered within the metal and art nouveau glass confines of the Grand Palais is the wonderful Palais de la Découverte, where your hair will stand on end in the electrostatics room and where your children will enjoy the other scientific exhibits. This is a full funhouse of things to do: displays to light up, machines to test your muscular reactions, live experiments to watch.

Paristoric. 11 bis rue Scribe, 9e. ☎ **01-42-66-62-06.** Admission 50F ($8.70) adults, 40F ($7) students, free for children 5 and under. Daily hourly shows from 9am–9pm.

This multiscreen presentation of the history of Paris runs 45 minutes and includes more than 2,000 different images. Commentary is available in English and offers an easy and interesting overview of the French capital, especially for children.

17 Organized Tours

BUS TOURS

Paris is the perfect city to explore on your own, but if time or leg muscles do not permit, consider taking an introductory tour. The most prominent company is **Cityrama,** 4 place des Pyramides, 1er (☎ **01-44-55-61-00;** Métro: Palais-Royal/ Musée-du-Louvre). The 2-hour "orientation tour" of Paris costs 150F ($26); there are also half- and full-day tours for 260F ($45.20) and 450F ($78.25), respectively. Tours to Versailles and Chartres are a better bargain, but the popular nighttime tours of Paris are expensive.

BOAT TOURS

Among the most favored ways to see Paris is by the **Bateaux-Mouches,** sightseeing boats that cruise up and down the Seine. They sail from the pont de l'Alma on the Right Bank (☎ **01-42-25-96-10** or 01-48-59-30-30 for reservations, 01-40-76-99-99 for schedules; Métro: Alma-Marceau). From March through mid-November, departures are usually on the hour and the half hour, while in winter there are 4 to 16 cruises per day, depending on demand. The voyage includes a taped commentary in six languages, lasts 1 1/4 hours, and costs 45F ($7.80) during the day and 50F ($8.70) at night. Similar tours at the same prices are offered by **Bateaux Parisiens,** which sail from the pont d'Iéna on the Left Bank (☎ **01-44-11-33-44**) and **Vedettes du Pont Neuf,** which sail from the riverside where the Pont Neuf crosses the Ile de la Cité. Their boats are smaller but not all of them are covered. Call ☎ **01-46-33-98-38** for information.

Longer and more unusual tours of Parisian waterways are offered by **Paris Canal** (☎ **01-42-40-96-97**). They leave at 9:30am from the Musée d'Orsay for a 3-hour cruise that ends at Parc de la Villette. The boat passes under the Bastille and enters the Canal St-Martin for a lazy journey along the tree-lined quai Jemmapes. An English-speaking guide is on hand to regale you with local lore as you cruise under bridges and through many locks. The boat leaves the Parc de la Villette at 2:30pm for the same voyage in reverse. Reservations are essential. The trip costs 95F ($16.50)adults, 70F ($12.20) ages 12 to 24, 5F ($9.35) children 4 to 11. Similar tours are offered by **Canauxrama** (☎ **01-42-39-15-00**).

18 Sports & Outdoor Activities

If you want to play your favorite sport, call **Allo Sport** at ☎ **01-42-76-54-54.** This service, provided by the Mairie de Paris, will answer your questions Monday to Thursday from 10:30am to 5pm, Friday until 4:30pm. The staff can give you the addresses of public **swimming pools** and **tennis courts.** It's also a good idea to check with your hotel or the tourist office. The **Pontoise Quartier Latin,** 19 rue de Pontoise, 5e (☎ **01-43-54-82-45;** Métro: Maubert-Mutualité), is one conveniently located municipal swimming pool. Another is the **Piscine des Halles** at 10 place Rotonde, 1er (☎ **01-42-36-98-44**).

For cyclists, there's a company that offers half-day tours of Paris for 150F ($26). Reservations are required. Contact **Paris a Vélo C'est Sympa** (☎ **01-48-87-60-01;** Métro: Bastille).

Otherwise, try the following sports federations and clubs: **Fédération Française de Base-Ball,** 73 rue Curial, 19e (☎ **01-40-36-83-01;** Métro: Riquet); **Fédération Française de Cyclisme,** 43 rue de Dunkerque, 10e (☎ **01-42-85-41-20;** Métro: Anvers); **Fédération Française de Cyclotourisme,** 8 rue Jean-Marie-Jégo, 13e (☎ **01-44-16-88-86;** Métro: Corvisart); **Fédération Française d'Equitation,** 64 rue St-Honoré, 1er (☎ **01-42-25-11-22;** Métro: Louvre-Rivoli); and the **Fédération Française de Football Américain,** 8 rue du Faubourg-Montmartre, 9e (☎ **01-40-22-03-60;** Métro: Rue-Montmartre).

City Strolls

7

Montaigne said that he could think only when he was walking. Think about this: Paris is a walker's paradise. Then start walking. The best way to discover the city's rich texture is on foot.

This chapter is devoted to seven walking tours covering some of the famous districts and sights of the city. As with all walking tours, don't be afraid to improvise. You'll doubtless be tempted by a shop window, a winding lane, or an especially animated cafe, which is why the time for each tour is, of course, an approximation. It will really depend on you: how many museums you visit and how thorough you want to be in your explorations.

Descriptions of the major attractions are, for the most part, brief. For complete details, see chapter 6, "Seeing the Sights."

WALKING TOUR 1
The Marais

Start: St-Paul Métro station.
Finish: Musée Picasso.
Time: 5 to 6 hours.
Best Times: On a sunny day Monday to Friday, when more buildings, not only their courtyards, are open. Because the stores along rue des Francs-Bourgeois are open on Sunday, any sightseeing is limited by mobs of shoppers.

On the Right Bank, the Marais is one of Paris's most interesting neighborhoods, filled with 17th-century mansions and cutting-edge boutiques and galleries, which will provide interesting detours along the way. After climbing the steps from the Métro station, walk to your right (eastward) along rue St-Antoine. You will soon see, also on your right, the unusual baroque facade of the:

1. **Eglise St-Paul et St-Louis.** Founded by the Jesuits, this church is a representative example of architecture at the time of the Counter-Reformation.

   Across rue St-Antoine is the:

2. **Hôtel de Sully.** This 17th-century mansion presently houses the Caisse Nationale des Monuments Historiques. The inner courtyard is astoundingly beautiful.

   At the end of rue St-Antoine is one of Paris's most historical squares:

Walking Tour—The Marais

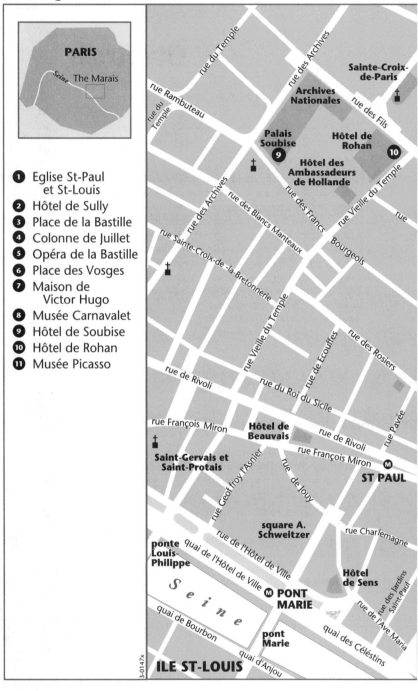

PARIS

The Marais

Seine

1. Eglise St-Paul et St-Louis
2. Hôtel de Sully
3. Place de la Bastille
4. Colonne de Juillet
5. Opéra de la Bastille
6. Place des Vosges
7. Maison de Victor Hugo
8. Musée Carnavalet
9. Hôtel de Soubise
10. Hôtel de Rohan
11. Musée Picasso

rue du Temple
rue des Archives
Sainte-Croix-de-Paris
Archives Nationales
rue des Fils
rue Rambuteau
rue du Temple
Palais Soubise 9
Hôtel de Rohan 10
Hôtel des Ambassadeurs de Hollande
rue Vieille du Temple
rue
rue des Archives
rue des Blancs Manteaux
rue des Francs Bourgeois
rue Sainte-Croix-de-la-Bretonnerie
rue Vieille du Temple
rue des Ecouffes
rue des Rosiers
rue de Rivoli
rue du Roi du Sicile
rue Pavée
rue François Miron
Hôtel de Beauvais
rue de Rivoli
Saint-Gervais et Saint-Protais
rue François Miron
ST PAUL
rue Geoffroy l'Asnier
rue de Jouy
square A. Schweitzer
rue Charlemagne
ponte Louis-Philippe
quai de l'Hôtel de Ville
Hôtel de Sens
rue des Jardins Saint-Paul
Seine
PONT MARIE
rue de l'Ave Maria
quai de Bourbon
pont Marie
quai des Céléstins
quai d'Anjou
ILE ST-LOUIS

3-0147x

200

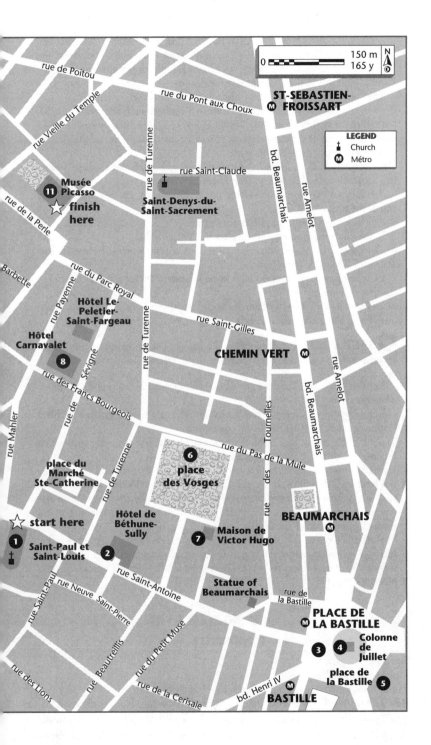

rue de Poitou

rue du Pont aux Choux

rue Vieille du Temple

rue de Turenne

bd. Beaumarchais

rue Amelot

0   150 m
     165 y

N

rue Saint-Claude

LEGEND

✝ Church
Ⓜ Métro

11 **Musée
Picasso**

☆ **finish
here**

rue de la Perle

✝
**Saint-Denys-du-
Saint-Sacrement**

Barbette

rue du Parc Royal

rue Payenne

**Hôtel Le-
Peletier-
Saint-Fargeau**

rue de Turenne

rue Saint-Gilles

CHEMIN VERT Ⓜ

rue Amelot

**Hôtel
Carnavalet**

8

rue de Sévigné

rue des Francs Bourgeois

rue de

bd. Beaumarchais

rue Mahler

rue de Turenne

6

**place
des Vosges**

rue du Pas de la Mule

rue des Tournelles

**place du
Marché
Ste-Catherine**

BEAUMARCHAIS
Ⓜ

☆ **start here**

**Hôtel de
Béthune-
Sully**

rue des

7 **Maison de
Victor Hugo**

1

✝ **Saint-Paul et
Saint-Louis**

2

rue Saint-Antoine

**Statue of
Beaumarchais**

rue de
la Bastille

rue Saint-Paul

rue Neuve Saint-Pierre

**PLACE DE
Ⓜ LA BASTILLE**

rue des Lions

rue Beautreillis

rue du Petit Muse

3 **4**

**Colonne
de
Juillet**

**place de
la Bastille** **5**

rue de la Cerisaie

bd. Henri IV

Ⓜ

BASTILLE

3. Place de la Bastille. Ignore the traffic and try to imagine it just over 200 years ago. It was here on July 14, 1789, that a Paris mob attacked the old prison, launching the French Revolution. Admittedly, it's hard to imagine the scene today, since the Bastille, built in 1369, was completely razed.

The column at the center of the place de la Bastille is the:

4. Colonne de Juillet (July Column). It does not commemorate the events of 1789, but rather the victims of the July Revolution of 1830. A subterranean vault contains the remains of the victims whose names are inscribed on the column.

Across the place de la Bastille is the:

5. Opéra de la Bastille. Carlos Ott's futuristic design has conferred a sense of beauty to a square that, frankly, was quite unremarkable before.

Retrace your steps along rue St-Antoine and turn right at rue de Birague. At the end of the street you'll see:

6. Place des Vosges, Paris's most beautiful square.

In the southeastern corner of the place des Vosges is the:

7. Maison de Victor Hugo. France's prolific 19th-century writer lived here for several years. You can visit his house.

Exit the place des Vosges through its northwestern corner and walk along rue des Francs Bourgeois to the:

8. Musée Carnavalet. The Museum of the City of Paris is housed in two mansions, one of which was Mme de Sévigné's.

☕ TAKE A BREAK   Marais Plus, 20 rue des Francs Bourgeois (for details, see chapter 6), a small cafe-cum-bookstore that is trés sympa.

Keep walking along rue des Francs Bourgeois to the corner of rue des Archives, where you'll find the:

9. Hôtel de Soubise. Another striking mansion, this one houses France's Archives Nationales and the Musée d'Histoire de France.

Walk north on rue des Archives to rue des Quatre Fils, the next right, which becomes rue de la Perle; at this intersection is the:

10. Hôtel de Rohan. This early 17th-century mansion at 87 rue Vieille du Temple was built by Delamair, who was also the architect of the Hôtel de Soubise. Actually, the house was built for the son of the Soubise family (the young man was reputed to be the son of Louis XIV). He later became bishop of Strasbourg, as did three other members of his family.

Walk along rue de la Perle to the next corner, rue de Thorigny. At no. 5 is the:

11. Musée Picasso. It houses the largest collection of the master's paintings in the world. Visit it now if you still have some energy left. Its pleasant cafe will make a nice refueling stop.

WALKING TOUR 2
Montmartre

Start: Place Pigalle.
Finish: Place Pigalle.
Time: 5 hours, more if you break for lunch; it's a 3-mile trek.
Best Times: Any day it isn't raining. Set out in the morning, 10am at the latest.

The traditional way to explore Montmartre is on foot. It's the highest point in the city, and visitors who find it too much of a climb will want to take the funicular to

Walking Tour—Montmartre

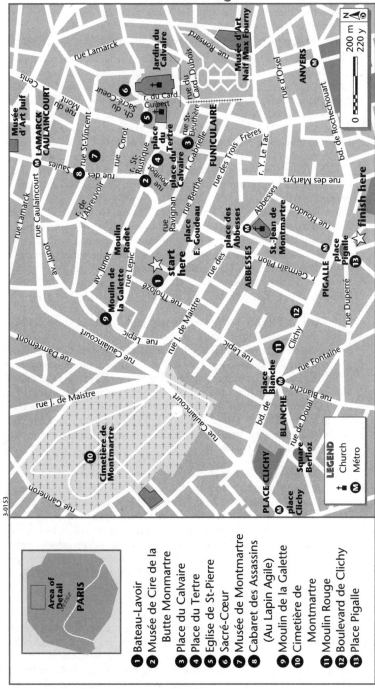

1. Bateau-Lavoir
2. Musée de Cire de la Butte Monmartre
3. Place du Calvaire
4. Place du Tertre
5. Eglise de St-Pierre
6. Sacré-Cœur
7. Musée de Montmartre
8. Cabaret des Assassins (Au Lapin Agile)
9. Moulin de la Galette
10. Cimetière de Montmartre
11. Moulin Rouge
12. Boulevard de Clichy
13. Place Pigalle

Area of Detail

PARIS

LEGEND
† Church
Ⓜ Métro

3-0153

Sacré-Coeur rather than walk (take the Métro to Anvers first and walk up rue Steinkerque) to reach the funicular, which operates from 6am to 11pm.

FROM PLACE PIGALLE TO MONT CENIS   Those who prefer to walk can take the Métro to Place Pigalle. Turn right after leaving the station and proceed down boulevard de Clichy, turn left at the Cirque Médrano, and begin the climb up rue des Martyrs. Upon reaching rue des Abbesses, turn left onto rue Ravignan, then right, and eventually you'll come to place Emile-Goudeau, a tree-studded square in the middle of rue Ravignan. At no. 13, across from the Timhôtel, stood the:

1. **Bateau-Lavoir (Boat Washhouse),** called the cradle of cubism. Fire gutted it in 1970, but it has been reconstructed by the city of Paris. Picasso once lived here and, in the winter of 1905–06, painted one of the world's most famous portraits, *The Third Rose* (Gertrude Stein). Other residents have included Kees van Dongen and Juan Gris. Modigliani had his studio nearby, as did Henri Rousseau and Braque.

   Rue Ravignan ends at place Jean-Baptiste-Clément. Go to the end of the street and cross it onto rue Norvins (which will be on your right). This intersection, one of the most famous street scenes of Montmartre (and painted by Utrillo), is the meeting point of rues Norvins, St-Rustique, and des Saules. Turn left and head down rue Poulbot. At no. 11, you will come to the:

2. **Musée de Cire de la Butte Montmartre,** the waxworks of the history of Montmartre (see "Especially for Kids" in chapter 6 for details).

   ☕ **TAKE A BREAK**   Many restaurants, especially those around place du Tertre, are unabashed tourist traps. You'll be asked eight times if you want your portrait sketched in charcoal. However, **La Maison-Rose,** 2 rue de'Abreuvoir, 18e, is a good bargain. This was once the atelier of Utrillo, and the famous French singer Charles Aznavour used to sing here. The little pink house is about 300 yards from place du Tertre. But if you want better food, then leave the place du Tertre area and take a 10-minute walk down rue Utrillo to **L'Eté en Pente Douce,** 23 rue Muller, 18e (☎ **01-42-64-02-67**). The picturesque terrace is vintage Montmartre and the moderately priced menu is strongly influenced by the owner's origins in the south of France.

   Rue Poulbot crosses the tiny:

3. **Place du Calvaire,** which offers a panoramic view of Paris. On this square (a plaque marks the house) lived artist, painter, and lithographer Maurice Neumont (1868–1930). From here, follow the sounds of an oompah band to:

4. **Place du Tertre,** the old town square of Montmartre. Its cafés are overflowing, its art galleries (in and out of doors) always overcrowded. Some of the artists still wear berets, and the cafes bear such names as La Bohéme—you get the point. Everything is so loaded with local color, applied as heavily as on a Seurat canvas, that it gets a little redundant.

   Right off the square fronting rue du Mont-Cenis is the:

5. **Eglise de St-Pierre.** Originally a Benedictine abbey, it has played many roles— Temple of Reason during the revolution, food depot, clothing store, even a munitions factory. Nowadays it's back to being a church. In 1147, the present church was consecrated; it's one of the oldest in Paris. Two of the columns in the choir stall are remnants of a Roman temple. Note among the sculptured works a nun with the head of a pig, a symbol of sensual vice. At the entrance of the church are three bronze doors sculpted by Gismondi in 1980. The middle door depicts the

life of St. Peter. The left door is dedicated to St. Denis, patron saint of Paris, and the right door to the Holy Virgin.

After visiting St-Pierre's, veer left around the huge reservoir of Montmartre and go through the Jardin du Calvaire until you arrive at the terrace of:

6. **Sacré-Coeur,** overlooking Square Willette. After a visit to Sacré-Coeur, walk between the basilica and the St-Pierre cemetery, turning left (west) and heading along rue Chevalier-de-la-Barre, taking a right turn onto rue du Mont-Cenis.

FROM MONT CENIS TO PLACE PIGALLE   Continue on this street until you reach rue Corot, then turn left. At no. 12 is the:

7. **Musée de Montmartre** (☎ **01-46-06-61-11**), with a wide collection of mementos of *vieux Montmartre.* This famous 17th-century house was formerly occupied by Dufy, van Gogh, and Renoir. Suzanne Valadon and her son, Utrillo, also lived here. It's open Tuesday through Sunday from 11am to 6pm; admission is 25F ($4.35).

From the museum, turn right, heading up rue des Saules past a winery, a reminder of the days when Montmartre was a farming village on the outskirts of Paris. A grape-harvesting festival is held here every October.

The intersection of rue des Saules and rue St-Vincent is one of the most visited and photographed corners of the Butte. Here, on one corner, sits the famous old:

8. **Cabaret des Assassins,** which was long ago renamed **Au Lapin Agile.**

Continue along rue St-Vincent, passing the Cimetiére St-Vincent on your right. Utrillo is just one of the many famous artists buried here. Take a left turn onto rue Girardon and climb the stairs. In a minute or two, you'll spot on your right two of the many windmills (*moulins*) that used to dot the Butte. One of these,

9. **Moulin de la Galette** (entrance at 1 av. Junot), was immortalized by Renoir.

Turn right onto rue Lepic and walk past no. 54. In 1886, van Gogh lived here with Guillaumin. Take a right turn onto rue Joseph-de-Maistre, then left again on rue Caulaincourt until you reach the:

10. **Cimetiére de Montmartre,** second in fame only to Pére-Lachaise, and the resting place of many famous personages. The burial ground (Métro: Clichy) lies west of the Butte, north of boulevard de Clichy. Opened in 1795, the cemetery shelters such composers as Berlioz and Offenbach, and such writers as Heinrich Heine, Stendhal, the Goncourt brothers, and poets Alfred de Vigny and Théophile Gautier. I like to pay my respects at the tomb of Alphonsine Plessis, the heroine of *La dame aux camélias,* and Mme Récamier, who taught the world how to lounge.

From the cemetery, take avenue Rachel, turn left onto boulevard de Clichy, and go to place Blanche, where an even better known windmill than the one in Renoir's painting stands, the:

11. **Moulin Rouge,** one of the most talked-about nightclubs in the world. It was immortalized by Toulouse-Lautrec.

From place Blanche, you can begin a descent down:

12. **Boulevard de Clichy,** fighting off the pornographers and hustlers trying to lure you into tawdry sex joints. With some rare exceptions—notably the citadels of the *chansonniers*—boulevard de Clichy is one gigantic tourist trap. Still, as Times Square is to New York, boulevard de Clichy is to Paris: Everyone who comes to Paris invariably winds up here. The boulevard strips and peels its way down to:

13. **Place Pigalle,** center of nudity in Paris. The square is named after a French sculptor, Pigalle, whose closest association with nudity was a depiction of Voltaire in the buff. Place Pigalle, of course, was the notorious "Pig Alley" of World War II.

In those days, when she was lonely and hungry, Edith Piaf (the "little sparrow") sang in the alleyways of Pigalle, hoping to earn a few francs for the night. Toulouse-Lautrec had his studio right off Pigalle at 5 av. Frochot.

WALKING TOUR 3
The Ile de la Cité & St-Germain-des-Prés

Start: Pont Neuf.
Finish: Pont des Arts.
Time: 4 to 5 hours.
Best Times: Any morning or afternoon Monday through Saturday.
Worst Times: Sunday, when Mass may prevent you from seeing the churches at your leisure.

The Ile de la Cité is the heart of Paris. The neighborhood of St-Germain, so linked to the lives and loves of Sartre, Beauvoir, and other existentialists, is just across the river on the Left Bank.

This walking tour starts and ends at two different bridges over the Seine. The bridge marking the beginning is:

1. **Pont Neuf.** Despite its name, pont Neuf is Paris's oldest bridge. Its construction was completed in the early 17th century. If you look closely at a good map, you'll notice that the half linking the Ile de la Cité to the Left Bank and the half linking the Cité to the Right Bank are not in a straight line. The equestrian statue here represents Henri IV, under whose reign the bridge was completed. Down below, at the tip of the island, is the Square du Vert-Galant.

Also on the Cité are three historic buildings that you may want to visit now:

2. **Sainte-Chapelle,** built by Louis IX as a repository for the Crown of Thorns and with stained glass virtually in lieu of walls, it is one of the foremost examples of Gothic architecture; the:

3. **Conciergerie,** where Marie Antoinette and other prisoners were held before being guillotined at the place de la Révolution; and

4. **Notre-Dame,** Paris's cathedral.

After visiting these sites, take pont St-Michel to place St-Michel on the Left Bank.

Walk south on boulevard St-Michel—better known simply as "Boul-Mich"—and turn right onto:

5. **Boulevard St-Germain.** One of the city's best-loved boulevards, traversing from west to east the northern parts of the 7e, 6e, and 5e arrondissements. Its name is now virtually synonymous with the existentialism that its denizens subscribed to in the 1940s and 1950s. Bookstores abound in this area.

☕ **TAKE A BREAK** For a rest and a snack go to **Café de Cluny,** 102 bd. St-Germain, 6e (☎ **01-43-26-98-40**), a great spot for people-watching.

Just before the St-Germain-des-Prés church, turn right on the small passage de la Petite-Boucherie, turn left on rue Cardinal, and then right to:

6. **Rue de Fürstemberg.** Perhaps the prettiest square on the Left Bank, it is small and intimate, with trees and atmospheric lampposts. It was named after Cardinal Egon de Furstenberg, who built it in 1699. Here, at no. 6, is the Musée Eugéne Delacroix, the great Romantic painter's house.

Walking Tour–Ile de la Cité & St-Germain-des-Prés

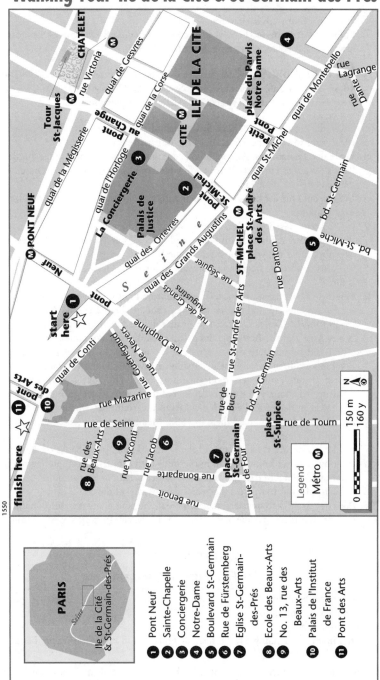

Legend
Métro

0   150 m
    160 y

PARIS

Ile de la Cité
& St-Germain-des-Prés

1 Pont Neuf
2 Sainte-Chapelle
3 Conciergerie
4 Notre-Dame
5 Boulevard St-Germain
6 Rue de Fürstemberg
7 Eglise St-Germain-
  des-Prés
8 Ecole des Beaux-Arts
9 No. 13, rue des
  Beaux-Arts
10 Palais de l'Institut
   de France
11 Pont des Arts

Retrace your steps back to the:

7. Eglise St-Germain-des-Prés. One of France's foremost Romanesque monuments, it was a major center of learning in the Middle Ages.

🎯 **TAKE A BREAK**　**Café des Deux–Magots,** 170 bd. St-Germain (☎ 01-45-48-55-25), and **Café de Flore,** 173 bd. St-Germain (☎ 01-45-48-55-26), were the favorites of the existentialist writers. See "Cafes" in chapter 5 for details.

On the northern side of place St-Germain-des-Prés is the start of rue Bonaparte, which runs towards the Seine. At 14 rue Bonaparte is the:

8. Ecole des Beaux-Arts. Although you can't go in, you can look at the facade of Paris's School of Fine Arts. The building used to be a convent, and its church was the first one to have a dome in Paris.

Turn onto rue des Beaux-Arts, which starts right in front of the Ecole des Beaux-Arts. Look for:

9. No. 13, rue des Beaux-Arts. Oscar Wilde died here in 1900 when it was the flea-bag Hôtel d'Alsace. Now it is the luxury l'Hôtel. Jorge Luis Borges, the Argentinean writer, was a more recent guest.

Turn back to rue Bonaparte and walk to the river. Here, at 23 quai de Conti, is the:

10. Palais de l'Institut de France. The Institut de France incorporates the nation's five prestigious cultural academies: the Académie Française; the Académie des Inscriptions et Belles Lettres; the Académie des Sciences; the Académie des Beaux-Arts; and the Académie des Sciences Morales et Politiques. Of these, the oldest and most interesting—as well as the most exclusive—is the Académie Française. Its 40 members, not all of whom are writers, wear green robes and carry swords (though not every day) and meet every Thursday to talk about the Academy's dictionary, the official lexicon of the French language. Not until 1980 was a woman elected to the Academy: Marguerite Yourcenar, who lived on Maine's Mt. Desert Island and died there in 1987. Members of the French Academy are known as "immortals."

The Institut de France is one of the landmarks along the banks of the Seine. Built by architect Louis Le Vau in the mid–17th century with funds from a bequest by Cardinal Mazarin, this classical edifice is famous for its dome.

To finish your tour, cross the Seine again by way of the:

11. Pont des Arts. Directly facing the pont Neuf, the pont des Arts is one of only four pedestrian bridges over the Seine. The view of the city from here is wonderful.

WALKING TOUR 4
The Faubourg St-Germain

Start: Palais-Bourbon.
Finish: Palais-Bourbon.
Time: 4 to 6 hours.
Best Times: On a sunny day Monday to Friday; as in the Marais, more buildings are open on weekdays.

The Faubourg St-Germain is located in the eastern part of the 7e arrondissement between the Seine and rue Babylone to the south. It owes its name to its origin as a *faubourg,* or suburb, of the old town of St-Germain, which had grown around the church of St-Germain-des-Prés. In the 18th century, Parisian nobility left the Marais for the Faubourg St-Germain and created quite a collection of *hôtels particuliers* there.

Walking Tour—The Fauborg St-Germain

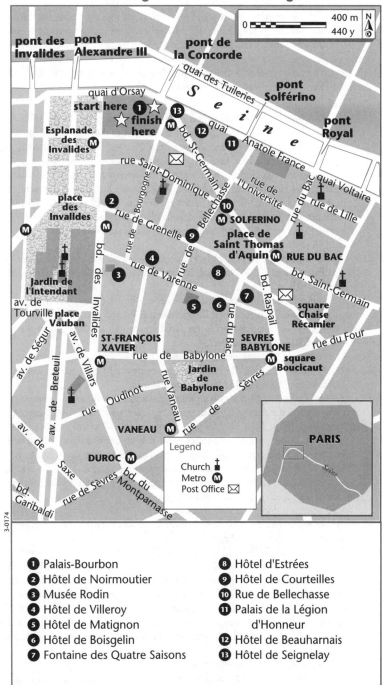

1 Palais-Bourbon
2 Hôtel de Noirmoutier
3 Musée Rodin
4 Hôtel de Villeroy
5 Hôtel de Matignon
6 Hôtel de Boisgelin
7 Fontaine des Quatre Saisons
8 Hôtel d'Estrées
9 Hôtel de Courteilles
10 Rue de Bellechasse
11 Palais de la Légion
   d'Honneur
12 Hôtel de Beauharnais
13 Hôtel de Seignelay

Many of these are now government ministries and foreign embassies. In fact, the 7e arrondissement is known for its "official" character. It has even been called "Washington-sur-Seine." Yet, sharing the space with all the sober architecture are many smaller enterprises: stores selling antiques, clothing, books, and gourmet food. This is also a prime residential district. Rodin lived here, as well as André Gide and, on rue du Bac, philosopher Michel Foucault.

Start your tour at the:

1. **Palais-Bourbon.** The Palais-Bourbon should be approached from the Seine. Located right on the quai d'Orsay, just across the river from the place de la Concorde, the Palais-Bourbon houses the French Assemblée Nationale. This was the residence of the duchesse de Bourbon, Louis XIV's illegitimate daughter, but it was confiscated during the Revolution. Ever since, it has served one official purpose or another. It was Napoléon who insisted that the facade be changed to resemble a Roman temple like the Madeleine. Visits are limited; call ☎ **01-42-97-60-00.**

   Walk around the building to the elegant place du Palais-Bourbon, where the offices of *Vogue* are fashionably located; walk southward along rue de Bourgogne to no. 138–140:

2. **Hôtel de Noirmoutier.** This early 17th-century building is the headquarters of the Institut Géographique National. Marshall Foch, of World War I fame, lived here from 1919 to 1929.

   Keep on rue de Bourgogne until it ends at rue de Varenne, and turn right on that street. At no. 77 is the Hôtel Biron, housing the:

3. **Musée Rodin.** All the major sculptures are here, as well as a fine café in the garden, a good place to rest your feet.

   Also on rue de Varenne, at no. 78, is the:

4. **Hôtel de Villeroy.** This 1724 building is presently the Ministry of Agriculture.

   A few doors down and across the street is the:

5. **Hôtel de Matignon.** *Matignon* is a meaningful and powerful word in France, for it is often used interchangeably with prime minister, whose official residence this has been since 1958. The 1721 building was owned by Talleyrand in the early 19th century; his dinner parties were so splendid that an entire new wing had to be added to serve as the dining hall. The Austro-Hungarian embassy was here from 1884 to 1914. When Lionel Jospin became prime minister in 1997, he also became the occupant of the house with the largest private garden in Paris, extending all the way south to rue de Babylone.

   Almost next door, at no. 47, is the:

6. **Hôtel de Boisgelin.** Built by Jean-Sylvain Cartaud in the 1730s, the Hôtel de Boisgelin houses the Italian Embassy.

   Turn left on rue du Bac and right on rue de Grenelle to the:

7. **Fontaine des Quatre Saisons.** Between rue du Bac and boulevard Raspail, this monumental fountain was sculpted by Bouchardon from 1739 to 1745. Like other parts of Paris in the 18th century, the Faubourg St-Germain lacked an adequate water supply. When somebody complained, the answer was the construction of this fountain. Voltaire commented, "So much stone for so little water." The statues represent Paris, the Seine, the Marne, and the seasons; there are several cherubs as well.

   Walk back on rue de Grenelle to no. 79, the:

8. **Hôtel d'Estrées.** This 1711 mansion is the residence of the Russian ambassador. Nicholas II and Alexandra stayed here in 1896. (Incidentally, the Russian embassy is located in the 16e arrondissement, near the Bois de Boulogne.)

Also on rue de Grenelle, at no. 110, is the:

9. **Hôtel de Courteilles.** The Ministry of National Education is in this 1778 building; as early as 1820 the Ministry of Public Instruction had been housed here.

In the direction of the river, turn right on:

10. **Rue de Bellechasse.** The name of this street can be roughly translated as "good hunting." When it was laid out in 1805, it halved the convent of the Dames de Bellechasse, who had adopted the name when they established themselves here at an ancient hunting lodge.

☕ **TAKE A BREAK**   At the end of rue de Bellechasse, to the left, is the **Musée d'Orsay,** Paris's museum of 19th-century art. If you're up for a visit, drop by the pleasant cafe, before roaming the exhibits.

Right in front of the museum is the:

11. **Palais de la Légion d'Honneur.** This large building houses the Musée de la Légion d'Honneur, with exhibits related to that prestigious decoration created by Napoléon and still awarded today.

Parallel to the Seine and quai Anatole-France, rue de Lille will take you to the:

12. **Hôtel de Beauharnais.** At no. 78, the Hôtel de Beauharnais is the residence of the German ambassador. Also known as the Hôtel de Torcy, this building was constructed in 1713 by Germain Boffrand; it has some neo-Egyptian details, and John Russell has called it "the noblest of houses." Eugéne de Beauharnais bought it in 1803. He was Napoléon's stepson, the son of Josephine and Alexandre de Beauharnais, a nobleman from Martinique who fought in the American Revolution and embraced the French Revolution, only to die later by the guillotine. Eugéne was named Viceroy of Italy, and his sister Hortense, who also lived here, was married to Louis Bonaparte, king of Holland, who was Napoléon's brother. In other words, Hortense was both Napoléon's stepdaughter and sister-in-law. She was also the mother of Napoléon III.

Next door, at no. 80, is the:

13. **Hôtel de Seignelay.** Built in 1716, also by Germain Boffrand, the Hôtel de Seignelay presently houses the Ministry of Foreign Trade.

The Palais-Bourbon is just to the west, and so is the Assemblée Nationale Métro station.

WALKING TOUR 5
The Quays of the Seine

Start: The Louvre.

Finish: The Louvre.

Time: At least 3 hours, not including stops; it's a 3-mile walk.

Best Times: Any time of the day or night. You'll see more during the day, but you'll miss the nighttime illuminations. Consider doing part of this tour during the day, the rest at night.

Worst Time: A sunny Saturday afternoon, when it's crowded with strollers.

A stroll along the banks and quays of the noble Seine is for many visitors the most memorable walk in Paris. Some of the city's most important monuments, such as Notre-Dame on the Ile de la Cité, are best viewed from the riverbank. Many attractions, such as the mighty facade of the Louvre, take on even more interest at night, when they are floodlit.

Walking Tour—The Quays of the Seine

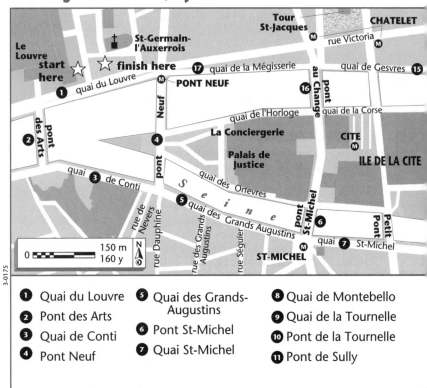

- ❶ Quai du Louvre
- ❷ Pont des Arts
- ❸ Quai de Conti
- ❹ Pont Neuf
- ❺ Quai des Grands-Augustins
- ❻ Pont St-Michel
- ❼ Quai St-Michel
- ❽ Quai de Montebello
- ❾ Quai de la Tournelle
- ❿ Pont de la Tournelle
- ⓫ Pont de Sully

The Seine is called the loveliest avenue in Paris. You'll walk past flower vendors, seed merchants, pet shops, and sellers of caged birds, and perhaps stop at one of the *bouquinistes* (booksellers) who line the parapets. If you should fall in love with the Seine, you can always moor your houseboat here, as did the writer Anaïs Nin, recording her experience in a memorable short story, "Houseboat."

With your back to place du Louvre, facing the Seine, turn right and walk along the:

1. **Quai du Louvre** until you come to the bridge on the quay. Cross the:

2. **Pont des Arts,** dating from 1803, one of only four pedestrian bridges in Paris. The oldest iron bridge in the city, it gives you a spectacular view of the Louvre and Sainte-Chapelle, and, in the distance, the spires of Notre-Dame Cathedral. You emerge onto the:

3. **Quai de Conti,** on the Left Bank. Bypassing the Institut de France, head left along the river. Pause for a look at the:

4. **Pont Neuf,** on your left, which is the most famous and the oldest bridge in Paris, recalling the Middle Ages. In those days you came to the bridge to have a tooth pulled. The Pont Neuf, begun in 1578, has never been enlarged in four centuries. From it, you can see the little Square du Vert Galant, jutting out like the prow of a ship from Ile de la Cité. You'll pass the Palais de Justice (the law courts) and Sainte-Chapelle on Cité. Here scientist Pierre Curie, husband of the famous Marie, was killed by a horse-drawn carriage in 1906.

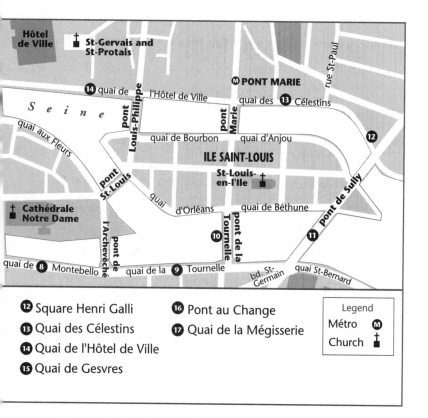

☕ **TAKE A BREAK** Drop in at **Taverne Henri IV,** 13 place du Pont-Neuf, 1er (☎ **01-43-54-27-90**), a 17th-century building opposite the statue of the *Vert Galant* at the pont Neuf. This is one of the most famous wine bars of Paris.

Continuing along the river, you'll come to the:

5. **Quai des Grands-Augustins,** constructed by Philip the Fair in 1313. It's named after an Augustine monastery that stood there. Rue des Grands-Augustins juts off to your right. Picasso had his studio at no. 7, and there he painted *Guernica.*

Continuing along the river, you'll reach the:

6. **Pont St-Michel,** with its fountain by Davioud. The scene of some of the most bitter fighting in 1944 against the Nazis, it again became a scene of turmoil during the student riots in the May Revolution of 1968.

At this point, the promenade becomes the:

7. **Quai St-Michel.** Lined with booksellers' stalls, it is intersected by two of the most charming old and narrow streets of Paris, rue du Chat-qui-Pêche and rue Xavier-Privas. Stroll along either or both of them.

☕ **TAKE A BREAK** Head for **Café le Départ,** 1 place St-Michel, 5e (☎ **01-43-54-24-55**), an art nouveau cafe long popular with students. It's open 24 hours a day.

The quai St-Michel leads to the:

8. Quai de Montebello. Pause here at the intersection with Square René-Viviani for a remarkable view—Notre-Dame on one side, the Left Bank church of St-Julien-le-Pauvre on the other.

Still strolling, you'll reach the:

9. Quai de la Tournelle, the setting for one of the world's most famous restaurants, Tour d'Argent. At the:

10. Pont de la Tournelle, you will be at one of the newest bridges of Paris, dating from 1928. From the bridge there's a magnificent panoramic view of Notre-Dame.

At the end of the quay, turn left onto the:

11. Pont de Sully, which cuts across Ile St-Louis and takes you back to the Right Bank. The bridge dates from 1876 and it, too, offers a splendid view of Notre-Dame and of Ile St-Louis itself. You'll arrive at:

12. Square Henri Galli, containing, in part, stones from the Bastille, destroyed by the revolutionary mob. Keeping left, you'll emerge onto the:

13. Quai des Célestins, enjoying yet another view of Ile St-Louis as you walk along. Pause to take in the pont Marie, which connects the Right Bank with Ile St-Louis.

You are now on the:

14. Quai de l'Hôtel de Ville. On your right you'll pass the Hôtel de Ville, or city hall. Passing it, you'll arrive at the:

15. Quai de Gesvres and its pont Notre-Dame, dating from 1913. The next bridge along the river is the:

16. Pont au Change (Money-Changer's Bridge). It leads to place du Châtelet, with an 1808 fountain commemorating the victories of Napoléon. The riverbank walk now becomes the:

17. Quai de la Mégisserie, once, long ago, the site of the public slaughterhouse of Paris. Seed merchants and pet shops line this quay, from which you can enjoy a good view of the Conciergerie and the Law Courts.

Now you're back at the pont Neuf, that famous landmark bridge. If you continue along, you'll return to the Louvre, where you began.

WALKING TOUR 6
Ile St-Louis

Start: Pont St-Louis.
Finish: Pont St-Louis.
Time: 2¹/₂ hours.
Best Times: 9am to noon and 2 to 5pm any day.

As you walk across the little iron footbridge, pont St-Louis, with Notre-Dame behind you, you'll be entering Ile St-Louis, a world of tree-shaded quays, aristocratic town houses, courtyards, restaurants, and antique shops.

Sibling island of Ile de la Cité, Ile St-Louis is primarily residential; its denizens fiercely guard their heritage, privileges, and special position. When asked where they live, residents don't answer "Paris"; they say instead "Ile St-Louis," or sometimes just "Ile."

St-Louis was originally two "islets," one named "Island of the Heifers." The two islands were joined by Louis XIII. Many famous people have occupied these patrician mansions, and they are identified by plaques on the facades.

On reaching the island, turn left and walk around the:

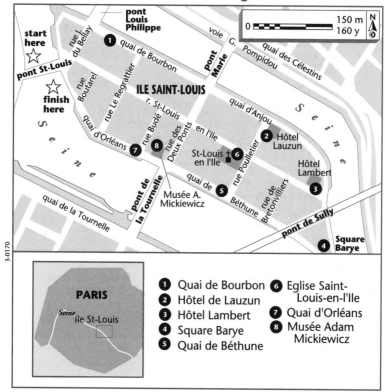

1. **Quai de Bourbon.** Two of the most splendid mansions on the island are found at no. 15 and no. 19, both former homes of parliamentarians that display much architectural adornment. At pont Marie, the quay changes its name to quai d'Anjou.

   Most people agree that the most elegant mansion is the:

2. **Hôtel de Lauzun,** located at 17 quai d'Anjou. It is owned by the city, and permission to visit is required. Built in 1657, it is named after the 17th-century rogue duc de Lauzun, famous lover and on-again, off-again favorite of Louis XIV. At the hôtel, the French courtier was secretly married to "La Grande Mademoiselle" (the duchesse de Montpensier), much to the displeasure of Louis XIV, who dealt with the matter by hustling him off to the Bastille.

   That "Flower of Evil," Charles Baudelaire, French poet of the 19th century, lived at Lauzun with his "Black Venus," Jeanne Duval. At the same time that he was squandering the family fortune, Baudelaire was working on poems that celebrated the erotic. Although he had high hopes for them, they were dismissed by many as "obscene, vulgar, perverse, and decadent." (It was only in 1949 that the French court lifted the ban on all his works.) Baudelaire attracted such artists as Delacroix and Courbet to his apartment, which was often filled with the aroma of hashish. Occupying another apartment was 19th-century novelist Théophile Gautier, who espoused the doctrine of "art for art's sake" in the preface to his novel *Mademoiselle de Maupin.*

Voltaire lived at 2 quai d'Anjou, in the:

3. **Hôtel Lambert,** with his mistress, Emilie de Breteuil, the marquise du Châteley, who had an "understanding" husband. The couple's quarrels at the Hôtel Lambert were known all over Europe. (Emilie did not believe in confining her charms, once described as "nutmeg-grater skin" and "bad teeth," to her husband or her lover.) But not even Frederick, king of Prussia, could permanently break up her liaison with Voltaire.

The mansion was built by Louis Le Vau in 1645 for Nicolas Lambert de Thorigny, the president of the Chambre des Comptes. For a century the hôtel was the home of the royal family of Poland, the Czartoryskis, who entertained Chopin, among others.

Continuing along quai d'Anjou, you'll reach the tip of the island, called:

4. **Square Barye,** which is all that remains from the terraced gardens that were built by the financier Bretonvilliers. With your back to the square, you can now proceed along:

5. **Quai de Béthune.** The duc de Richelieu (great-nephew of Cardinal Richelieu) lived at no. 16, and Madame Curie resided at 36 quai de Béthune, near pont de la Tournelle, from 1912 until her death in 1934.

Turn right onto rue de Bretonvilliers, which comes to an arcade. Turn left onto the principal street of the island, rue St-Louis-en-l'Ile, and pause at the:

6. **Eglise St-Louis-en-l'Ile,** dating from 1726. It was built according to plans devised by the architect Le Vau, who also designed portions of the Louvre and Versailles. Inside, look for a plaque presented by the city of St. Louis, Missouri, honoring its namesake. Badly attacked and damaged during the Revolution, the interior is elegantly decorated with much gilt, marble, and woodwork, all *grand siécle* style. It is open Tuesday through Saturday from 9:30am to noon and 3 to 7pm, and on Sunday from 9:30am to noon.

☕ **TAKE A BREAK** Try **Berthillon,** 31 rue St-Louis-en-l'Ile (☎ **01-43-54-31-61**), famous for the best ice cream and sorbet in Paris. Some 50 flavors are served to hordes of tourists in summer (except in August). Wednesday through Sunday from 10am to 8pm, they dispense their black-currant ice cream and their kumquat sorbet—you name it, they've got it, no matter how exotic. There's always a line.

Continue your stroll up rue St-Louis-en-l'Ile. Notable mansions include Hôtel Chenizot, 51 rue St-Louis-en-l'Ile, the archbishop's residence. Another resident of this mansion was the notorious noblewoman Térésia Cabarrus, nicknamed "Notre-Dame de Thermidor" after the sexual favors she offered to numerous revolutionaries. Cut left down rue Bude until you come to:

7. **Quai d'Orléans,** which overlooks the Cité and enjoys many famous associations. The main attraction of the quay is the:

8. **Musée Adam Mickiewicz,** 6 quai d'Orléans (☎ **01-46-34-05-44**), immediately to your right. It is dedicated to the exiled poet, who was known as "the Byron of Poland." The second-floor museum displays mementos and also contains a 20,000-volume library. The Chopin Room, dedicated to the composer, is on the ground floor. The museum has the only known daguerreotype of the young Chopin. The museum has very limited hours (2 to 6pm on Thursday only) and is closed for 2 weeks during Christmas and Easter.

Many expatriate Americans have lived on this quay, including columnist Walter Lippmann (no. 18–20) in 1938 and novelist James Jones, author of *From Here to*

Eternity, who lived at no. 10 from 1958 to 1975. Many literary greats, including Henry Miller and William Styron, came to visit Jones here.

Having traversed the island, you will now find yourself back where you started, with a glorious view of Notre-Dame.

WALKING TOUR 7
The Literary Left Bank

Start: Place St-Michel.
Finish: Rue de Seine.
Time: 3 hours, not counting stops.
Best Time: Any pleasant, sunny day. Try to begin at 9am and end by 4pm.
Worst Time: Morning or late-afternoon rush hour.

Paris is filled with streets, houses, monuments, and cafes where famous writers and artists lived, worked, and played. Many of these were Americans, such as Gertrude Stein and Ernest Hemingway. Other famous names include Henry Miller (*Tropic of Cancer*) and his friend and lover Anaïs Nin, famous for her controversial *Diaries.* Some of the places they patronized, although vastly changed, are still here to greet visitors. Many have gone, of course, but the streets remain.

Take the Métro to place St-Michel to begin your tour. From the square, with your back to the Seine, turn left and walk along:

1. **Rue de la Huchette,** one of the most typical and famous of Left Bank streets. This short street, not more than 300 yards long, was where Elliot Paul lived, and the story of this street—its shopkeepers, radicals, growing children, workers, hotel-keepers—was described in his memorable *The Last Time I Saw Paris.*

After exploring that street, perhaps looking for a modern-day "Robert the pimp" or "l'Hibou," cross rue St-Julien-le-Pauvre and Square René-Viviani onto:

2. **Rue de la Bûcherie,** heading for no. 27, Shakespeare and Company, still a literary gathering place for young English-speaking writers living in Paris.

Retrace your steps to place St-Michel (this time walk on the opposite side of the streets). Once you reach place St-Michel, head directly south to:

3. **Place St-André-des-Arts** and a street that begins here, rue Danton, named after the French revolutionary who was guillotined.

☕ **TAKE A BREAK**   If you want a short rest, go to **Café le Départ,** 1 place St-Michel, 5e (☎ **01-43-54-24-55**), which has views of both the spire of Sainte-Chapelle and the dragon statue of place St-Michel.

Walk along rue Danton, turn right onto rue Suger, one of the fine old Left Bank streets. At no. 11, J. K. Huysmans was born in 1848. This French novelist is best known for his morbid psychological studies such as *A rebours (Against the Grain).* At the end of the street, turn left onto rue de l'Eperon, which leads to boulevard St-Germain and:

4. **Carrefour de l'Odéon.** Danton ("we need audacity") lived here. Today, a pigeon-decorated statue stands where his house once did. From here, turn left onto:

5. **Rue Monsieur-le-Prince.** Practically everybody used to live on this street, including French philosopher Pascal, at no. 54. The street has been called a "Yankee alleyway." The street's roster of figures includes Richard Wright (no. 14), James McNeill Whistler (no. 22), Henry Wadsworth Longfellow (no. 49), and Oliver Wendell Holmes (no. 55).

Walking Tour—The Literary Left Bank

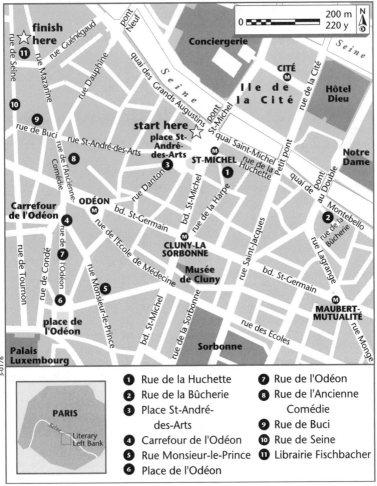

❶ Rue de la Huchette	❼ Rue de l'Odéon
❷ Rue de la Bûcherie	❽ Rue de l'Ancienne
❸ Place St-André-	Comédie
des-Arts	❾ Rue de Buci
❹ Carrefour de l'Odéon	❿ Rue de Seine
❺ Rue Monsieur-le-Prince	⓫ Librairie Fischbacher
❻ Place de l'Odéon	

☕ **TAKE A BREAK**   At 62 rue Monsieur-le-Prince, 6e, **Slice** (☎ **01-43-54-21-67**), is said to have the best pizza in town, and I'm talking Big Apple–style pizza here. Finish with a rich chocolate-banana cake. You can do so daily from 11am to 11pm.

At the intersection with rue Racine, cut right into the:

6. Place de l'Odéon, with its landmark Théâtre de l'Odéon, where the premiere of *The Marriage of Figaro* in 1794 landed Beaumarchais in jail. During the postwar era, this theater hosted the avant-garde, presenting plays by Ionesco, Edward Albee, and Samuel Beckett.

Place de l'Odéon is the site of the Institut Benjamin-Franklin, an American cultural institute on the square. The same location was once occupied by Café Voltaire, a celebrated gathering point for the *philosophes* and much frequented in the 1920s by American expatriates. From the square, take:

7. Rue de l'Odéon north. The original Shakespeare and Company stood at no. 12. Here Sylvia Beach entertained such writers as MacLeish, Pound, Fitzgerald, and Hemingway. She also published James Joyce's *Ulysses.*

Cross carrefour de l'Odéon again onto:

8. Rue de l'Ancienne Comédie, the setting of Procope at no. 13. A literary haunt since 1686, the restaurant was patronized by Balzac, Victor Hugo, Racine, and Moliére and such early American visitors as Jefferson and Franklin. At the intersection, turn onto:

9. Rue de Buci, site of the Buci Market, one of the most charming in Paris. It's open Tuesday through Saturday from 9am to 1pm and 4 to 7pm, Sunday from 9am to 1pm. Now turn right onto:

10. Rue de Seine. The house at no. 21 was once occupied by George Sand. The art gallery and craft center now there were founded by Isadora Duncan. Jean-Paul Sartre lived at Louisiane, 60 rue de Seine, one among many other famous names.

Finally, you might want to end this literary tour appropriately enough at:

11. Librairie Fischbacher, 33 rue de Seine, 6e (☎ **01-43-26-84-87**), a bookshop that sells many English titles and carries a superb array of fine art editions. It's open Monday through Friday from 9am to 7pm and Saturday from 10am to 7pm.

8 Shopping

Part of the timeless allure of Paris has always been its image as the capital of fashion and design. No other city has become so identified with style that its very name bespeaks elegance and good taste. Parisian style is evident in nearly every shop window. Gourmet food shops arrange their wares in mouth-watering displays, furniture shops make you want to take up residence in their showrooms, and clothes are so skillfully draped and accessorized that the most lackluster suit looks like haute couture.

The downside of the enticingly displayed products is their price. A value-added tax (VAT) of 20.6% is tacked onto most products, which means that bargains are few and far between (for details on getting a VAT refund, see below). Even goods that are made in France are not necessarily cheaper here than elsewhere. Appliances, housewares, computer supplies, CDs, and women's clothing are notoriously expensive in France. On the other hand, you can often get good deals on cosmetics such as **Bourjois,** skin care lines such as **Lierac, Galenic, Roc,** and **Vichy,** and some luxury goods. In order to recognize a bargain, it helps to check out the prices of French products before your trip.

The key word to look for on shop windows is *soldes;* it means "sales." Even when the rate of exchange doesn't favor the dollar, the *soldes* will help you find good values. The best times to find those magic "soldes" banners are the first 3 weeks of both January and July when all Paris goes on sale. If you can brave the bargain-hungry crowds, you just might find the perfect designer outfit at a fraction of the retail price.

Store hours are Monday through Saturday from 9 or 9:30am (sometimes 10am) to 6 or 7pm, without a break for lunch. Some of the smaller stores are closed on Monday or Monday mornings and break for lunch for 1 to 3 hours, beginning at 1pm. Small stores also may be closed all or part of August as well as some days around Christmas and Easter. Sunday shopping is gradually making inroads in Paris but is limited to tourist areas. Try **rue de Rivoli** across from the Louvre, **rue des Francs-Bourgeois** in the Marais, and the **Carrousel du Louvre.**

Remember, shopping is a much more formal activity in Paris than it is in other cities; always greet the salespeople with a "Bonjour, madame (or monsieur)" when you arrive and, whether you've bought anything or not, say, "Merci, au revoir," when you're leaving.

Visitors staying in France for less than 6 months are entitled to a **value-added tax (VAT) refund** on purchases made in the country, but only if you spend more than 2,000F ($347.80) in a single store. The discount, however, is not automatic. For U.K. residents and European Community members, the figure is almost 3,200F ($556.50). Food, wine, and tobacco don't count, and the refund is granted only on purchases you take with you out of the country—not on merchandise you ship home.

To apply, you must show the clerk your passport to prove your eligibility. You'll then be given an export sales document in triplicate (two pink sheets and a green one), which you must sign, as well as an envelope addressed to the store. Travelers departing Paris from Charles de Gaulle Airport may visit the Europe Tax-Free Shopping (ETS) refund point, operated by CCF Change, to receive an immediate VAT refund in cash. Otherwise, when you depart Paris, arrive at the airport as early as possible to avoid lines at the *détaxe* (refund) booth at French Customs. If you're traveling by train, go to the détaxe area in the station before boarding—you can't get your refund documents processed on the train. Give the three sheets to the customs official, who will countersign and hand you back the green copy. (Save it in case any problems arise.) Give the official the stamped envelope addressed to the store. One of the processed pink copies will be mailed to the store for you. Your reimbursement will either be mailed by check (in French francs) or credited to your credit card account. In some cases you may get your refund immediately, paid at an airport bank window. If you don't receive your tax refund in 4 months, write to the store, giving the date of purchase and the location where the forms were given to customs officials. Include a photocopy of your green refund sheet.

Here is a partial list of some of the best deals in town—from both the shopper's and the spectator's point of view.

ANTIQUES

Le Louvre des Antiquaires. 2 place du Palais-Royal, 1er. ☎ **01-42-97-27-00.** Métro: Palais-Royal.

After visiting the Musée du Louvre, cross the street to visit this establishment, which is almost as fine as a museum—and even better, in a way, since here you can take the loot home with you. The Louvre des Antiquaires is an enormous mall filled with an amazing diversity of antiques shops.

Village St-Paul. 23–27 rue St-Paul, 4e. No phone. Métro: St-Paul.

Even if you don't buy anything, admiring the antiques and objets d'art displayed in a 17th-century village makes a very Parisian Sunday afternoon. The stores are closed Tuesday and Wednesday.

ART PRINTS

Galerie Documents. 53 rue de Seine, 6e. ☎ **01-43-54-50-68.** Métro: Odéon.

If you're interested in old posters, this is the place for you. You'll find some wonderful things, in a wide price range.

Librarie Elbe. 213 bis, bd. St-Germain, 7e. ☎ **01-45-48-77-97.** Métro: Solferino.

One of the most memorable things you can buy in Paris is a poster, etching, or cartoon that you can frame when you get home. The souvenir stands are filled with copies of Toulouse-Lautrec posters, but if you want something original this shop sells turn-of-the-century advertising and railroad posters, as well as etchings and cartoons, at very reasonable prices. Note that everything is filed by category and that you should ask if you can browse before just opening up a portfolio.

BOOKS

A cosmopolitan city, Paris has a full range of bookstores specializing in foreign languages: Spanish, Italian, German, Polish, Arabic, and Armenian. All fields of knowledge are represented, too, in specialized bookstores: archaeology, film, music, hunting, and eroticism, to name a few. Books are expensive here, however, especially English-language books. You should also know that French law prohibits discounts of more than 5% on new books published in France, which makes bargain-hunting nearly futile.

Abbey Bookshop. 29 rue de la Parcheminerie, 5e. ☎ **01-46-33-16-24.** Métro: St-Michel or Cluny-Sorbonne.

This small two-floor store tucked away behind St. Severin is crammed with English-language books. It's an outpost of a store in Toronto, Canada, and many Canadians gather here. Their prices are better than at any other English-language bookstore in Paris.

Brentano's. 37 av. de l'Opéra, 2e. ☎ **01-42-61-52-50.** Métro: Opéra.

One of the leading English-language bookstores in the city, with a broad general fiction and nonfiction stock that includes guides and maps. They usually have a shelf of discounted books.

Institut Géographique National. 107 rue de la Boétie, 8e. ☎ **01-43-98-85-00** or 01-43-59-10-83. Métro: Franklin-D-Roosevelt.

Map lovers will be amazed by the selection available: Every corner of the globe is represented.

Gibert Joseph. 26, 30, 32, and 34 bd. St-Michel, 6e. ☎ **01-44-41-88-88.** Métro: Odéon or Cluny-Sorbonne.

The quintessential Parisian students' bookstore, selling new and secondhand books, records, videos, and stationery on several floors.

Jullien Cornic. 118 rue du Faubourg-St-Honoré, 8e. ☎ **01-43-59-10-50.** Métro: Miromesnil.

Jullien Cornic specializes in art books. You can find an amazing number of books on all the major artists, and much more.

Librarie La Hune. 170 bd. St-Germain. ☎ **01-45-48-35-85.** Métro: St-Germain.

Sandwiched between the famous literary cafes Les Deux Magots and Café Le Flore, La Hune has been a center for Left Bank intellectuals since 1945. The atmosphere is existential and the selection of books outstanding.

Shakespeare & Co. 37 rue de la Bûcherie, 5e. No phone. Métro or RER: St-Michel.

Today, English-speaking residents of Paris still gather in the cluttered store named after Sylvia Beach's legendary literary lair.

Tea and Tattered Pages. 24 rue Mayet, 6e. ☎ **01-40-65-94-35.** Métro: Falguière.

Most of the 15,000 English-language books here are used and sell for around 30F ($5.20), which is as cheap as you'll find in Paris.

Village Voice. 6 rue Princesse, 6e. ☎ **01-46-33-36-47.** Métro: Mabillon.

Quality fiction in English is highlighted here, along with an excellent selection of poetry, plays, and nonfiction.

W. H. Smith. 248 rue de Rivoli, 1er. ☎ **01-44-77-88-99.** Métro: Concorde.

Besides a full stock of English books, this store carries a broad selection of English and American newspapers and magazines.

Shakespeare & Co.

Born in Baltimore, Sylvia Beach (1887–1962) first came to Paris with her family as an adolescent. In 1917 she met Adrienne Monnier at her bookshop at 7 rue de l'Odéon, where they sat down and discussed literature for hours. Monnier encouraged and inspired Beach to open an American bookshop, which she did on November 19, 1919, at 8 rue Dupuytren. The shop was furnished with flea market gleanings and hand-me-downs, and the walls were bare except for two drawings by William Blake and, later on, some photographs supplied by Man Ray. In 1921, she transferred the shop to 12 rue de l'Odéon and moved in nearby with Monnier. Every American and English-speaking writer or artist, from James Joyce to Hemingway, Gertrude Stein, and Fitzgerald, visited her shop, and she became a great friend to many of them—going so far as to publish the first edition of Joyce's *Ulysses*, at great personal and financial cost, when no publisher would accept it.

CERAMICS, CHINA & GLASS

Au Père Fragile. 50 rue du Commerce, 15e. ☎ **01-45-75-20-84.** Métro: Commerce.

At Au Père Fragile you'll find china from all over Europe. There are some excellent prices, especially on discontinued pieces.

Baccarat. 30 bis, rue de Paradis, 10e. ☎ **01-47-70-64-30.** Métro: Château-d'Eau, Poissonnière, or Gare-de-l'Est.

Baccarat has produced its world-renowned crystal since the 18th century. This store is also a museum, so even if the prices make you faint, you can still enjoy browsing through the finest crystal in the world.

La Maison Ivre. 38 rue Jacob, 6e. ☎ **01-42-60-01-85.** Métro: St-Germain-des-Prés.

This charming table-top shop in the heart of the antiques and gallery district (on the Left Bank between St-Germain-des-Prés and the Seine) is a perfect place to shop for the country-style ceramics that add authenticity to any French Country decor. They carry an excellent selection of handmade pottery from all over France, with an emphasis on Provençal and southern French ceramics, including ovenware, bowls, platters, plates, pitchers, mugs, and vases.

La Tisanière. 25 and 35 rue de Paradis. ☎ **01-47-70-40-49.** Métro: Chateau d'Eau.

These two stores sell discontinued lines of prestigious china and glass makers. You can find some great bargains here.

Limoges Center. Usine Center, Paris Nord. ☎ **01-48-63-20-75.** RER: Palais des Expositions.

If you love Limoges, then this is the place to hurry to. It's discounted anywhere from 20% to 60%. Glassware and silverware are on sale, too.

Paradis Porcelaine. 56 rue de Paradis, 10e. ☎ **01-48-24-50-90.** Métro: Poissonnière.

This store contains a great selection of china and crystal at fantastic prices.

CRAFTS

107 Rue de Rivoli. 1er. ☎ **01-42-61-04-02.** Métro: Palais-Royal/Tuileries.

This boutique, connected with the Musée des Arts Décoratifs, offers a variety of attractive household goods, some of them museum replicas. Artisans have copied museum pieces in faïence and molded crystal, and they have crafted art nouveau jewelry and porcelain boxes, scarves, and other items. There is no charge for admission, and you can find merchandise in any price range.

Viaduc des Arts. 9–147 av. Daumensil, 12e. ☎ **01-43-40-80-80.** Métro: Bastille, Ledru-Rollin, Reuilly-Diderot, or Gare-de-Lyon.

When the elevated railroad track cutting across the 12e was transformed into the Promenade Plantée, the lower level was redesigned to accommodate a long stretch of shops. The galleries and crafts boutiques along the viaduct offer a fascinating overview of French design and you can take a breather in the gardens overhead.

DEPARTMENT STORES

Au Printemps. 64 bd. Haussmann, 9e. ☎ **01-42-82-50-00.** Métro: Havre-Caumartin.

Au Printemps is Paris's largest department store, but, in my view, it's not as good as Galeries Lafayette. There are fashion shows held under the 1920s glass dome every Tuesday throughout the year and every Tuesday and Friday at 10:15am from March through October.

Galeries Lafayette. 40 bd. Haussmann, 9e. ☎ **01-42-82-34-56.** Métro: Opéra or Chaussée-d'Antin.

Housed in a very attractive building with a wonderful dome from the belle epoque, Galeries Lafayette makes shopping an easy task for the foreign visitor. English is spoken at the information desks, and you can even exchange money (not at the best rates, though). But most important, the quality of the merchandise sold here is excellent, and the prices aren't bad. The January sales are famous. The bookstore in the basement is very good, and the self-service cafeteria on the sixth floor, though often crowded, has great close-up views of the Opéra roof and, in the distance, the Eiffel Tower.

La Samaritaine. 19 rue de la Monnaie, 1er. ☎ **01-40-41-20-20.** Métro: Pont-Neuf or Châtelet-Les-Halles.

Less expensive than Galeries Lafayette or Au Printemps is La Samaritaine, between the Louvre and Pont Neuf. It's housed in several buildings with art nouveau touches and has an art deco facade on quai du Louvre. The fifth floor of store no. 2 has a fine restaurant that's not expensive. Also, look for signs to the *panorama,* a free observation point with a wonderful view of Paris.

Marks and Spencer. 35 bd. Haussmann, 9e. ☎ **01-47-42-42-91.** Métro: Havre-Caumartin.

An outpost of the British stores known for good values. In addition to clothes and household items it has a well-priced supermarket. Great for picnic items or evening snacks.

Monoprix-Uniprix. ☎ **01-40-75-11-02.**

This is where average Parisians go to purchase their everyday casual clothes. Prices are reasonable, and you'll find the selection surprisingly stylish. Great for accessories and housewares as well. There are about 30 stores in the city, so you'll probably be able to spot one from wherever you stand. If you want, though, you can call the number above to find the nearest location.

Tati. 4 bd. Rochechouart, 18e. ☎ **01-42-55-13-09.** Métro: Anvers.

This madhouse of a store is very much a local legend, originally opened to cater to budget-conscious shoppers in this neighborhood heavily populated by immigrants. Be prepared for a near brawl over the huge bins of merchandise here, but odds are good that you'll come across a strikingly inexpensive treasure that shouts Paris once you get it home. There are branch stores at 140 rue de Rennes, 6e; and 13 place de la Republique, 3e; and a new Tati Or specializing in gold at 19 rue de la Paix, 2e (see "Jewelry," below).

FASHION

When you see the prices in Paris boutiques you may wonder how Parisian women can afford to look as put together as they do. The answer is in the words *soldes* (sales), *dégriffés* (labels cut out), *stock* (overstock), and *dêpot-vente* (resale). Paying retail is as much of a budget-buster for residents as it is for visitors. It's also unnecessary.

Some of the best fashion deals are found in resale shops that deal directly with designer showrooms and people in the fashion industry. Designer clothing that has been worn on a runway or for a fashion shoot is on sale for half-price, along with other gently used clothes and accessories. Most *depôts-vente* are on the right bank in the stylish 8e, 16e, and 17e arrondissements. A few favorites are listed below.

For overstock, end-of-series, and *dégriffé* clothes, bargain-hunters head to the south of Paris. Rue St-Placide (Métro: Sèvres-Babylone) has become a street of dreams for penny-wise shoppers looking for affordable sportswear and men's fashions. Rue d'Alesia in the 14e (Métro: Alésia) offers last season's Cacherel, Chantal Thomas, Daniel Hechter, Diapositive, Régina Rubens, and Sonia Rykiel, among other mid-priced lines. Many of these stores are closed Monday or Monday morning. Call first.

DISCOUNT

Reciproque. 89–123 rue de la Pompe, 16e. ☎ **01-47-04-30-28.** Métro: Pompe.

The largest *depôt-vente* in Paris fills its racks with lightly used clothing for men, women, and children, as well as jewelry, furs, and accessories. If you've always dreamed of owning a designer outfit, you might find one here that fits your budget. Midrange labels are also well represented.

Nip Shop. 6 rue Edmond-About, 16e. ☎ **01-45-04-66-19.** Métro: La Pompe.

In the same neighborhood as *Reciproque* but much smaller, this *depôt-vente* has good connections with Yves Saint-Laurent, Sonia Rykiel, and Guy Laroche, as well as lesser known designers.

Anna Lowe. 104 rue Faubourg St-Honoré, 8e. ☎ **01-42-66-11-32.** Métro: Miromesnil or St-Phillippe-de-Roule.

Right next to the ritzy Hotel Bristol, this shop is a find for those that want the very best designers—Yves Saint-Laurent, Chanel, Giorgio Armani—at a steep discount. Shopping is genteel and substantially less uptight than at the same designers retail shops.

Le Mouton a Cinq Pattes. 8, 10, 14–18, and 48 rue St-Placide, 6e. ☎ **01-45-48-86-26** for all stores. Métro: Sèvres-Babylone.

This is a local chain of discount fashion shops where you'll often come across extremely well-known designer names—Jean-Paul Gaultier, for example—in their jam-packed racks. They sell women's, men's, and children's clothing, along with shoes and accessories, and the stock turns over constantly.

FOR CHILDREN

Bonpoint. 82 rue de Grenelle, 7e. ☎ **01-45-48-05-45.** Métro: Rue-du-Bac.

Bonpoint is part of a well-known haute couture chain for children. Their clothing is very well tailored and very expensive at the boutique near Maxim's, on the Right

Bank. At this store, on the Left Bank, you can often find the same merchandise at reduced prices, especially after the yearly sales in February and July.

Le Mouton à Cinq Pattes. 10 rue St-Placide, 6e. ☎ **01-45-48-50-77.** Métro: Sèvres-Babylone.

An excellent selection of children's clothing can be found here, at excellent prices, too. The sales here can be unbelievably good.

FOR MEN

Dépôt de Grandes Marques. 15 rue de la Banque, 2e. ☎ **01-42-96-99-04.** Métro: Bourse.

Near the Banque de France, on the fourth floor of no. 15, you'll find very proper, very chic men's suits at reduced prices.

Mi-prix. 27 bd. Victor, 15e. ☎ **01-48-28-42-48.** Métro: Balard.

A great place to sift through the racks of men's designer clothes at a steep discount. Karl Lagerfeld, Alaia, Missoni, Gianfranco Ferre—you'll find them all.

FOR WOMEN

King's. 24 rue St-Placide, 6e. ☎ **01-42-22-39-40.** Métro: St-Placide.

On the same street as Le Mouton à Cinq Pattes (see below), King's also has a vast range of women's fashions at very good prices.

Le Mouton à Cinq Pattes. 8 and 18 rue St-Placide, 6e. ☎ **01-45-48-86-26.** Métro: Sèvres-Babylone.

Here you'll find a great selection of fashions from all parts of Europe at reduced prices.

FOOD

Chocolaterie de Puyricard. 27 av. Rapp, 7e. ☎ **01-47-05-59-47.** Métro: Alma-Marceau.

Chocolate lovers beware. Not far from the Eiffel Tower and the art nouveau creations of architect Jules Lavirotte is another masterpiece: Puyricard's chocolate—almost 90 types of it. The confections are not cheap, but they're worth it.

Fauchon. 26 place de la Madeleine, 8e. ☎ **01-47-42-60-11.** Métro: Madeleine.

Fauchon is one of the world's great food stores. Its fruits, for instance, are as beautiful as the most beautiful of still lifes. Two buildings and several impeccable rooms feature delicacies from every corner of France and the globe: delicate pastries, fresh meats, perfect fruits from far-away places, and much more. Prices are not low, but the quality and the presentation are outstanding. Even if you don't buy anything, a visit is well worth it.

Foie Gras Import. 34 rue Montmartre, 1er. ☎ **01-42-33-31-32.** Métro: Etienne Marcel.

Located just on the northern edge of Les Halles, this boutique sells all kinds of canned foie gras (duck or goose liver) at very reasonable prices. They also sell various types of pâté, canned snails, dried wild mushrooms, and truffles. These gourmet treats are considerably cheaper in France than they are in North America, and are easy to pack.

La Grande Epicerie. Bon Marché, 38 rue de Sèvres, 7e. ☎ **01-44-39-81-00.** Métro: Sèvres-Babylone.

The food hall of this venerable Left Bank department store is one of the most intriguing luxury supermarkets in Paris. A great place to look for gourmet gifts like hazelnut oil or bouquet garni packaged in cheesecloth, like tea bags. It makes for perfect one-stop picnic shopping, too, since they offer a large range of prepared foods, cheeses, breads, and pastries.

La Maison du Miel. 24 rue Vignon, 9e. ☎ **01-47-42-26-70.** Métro: Madeleine.

This delightful boutique specializes in honey and honey products, a fact emphasized by the charming decor of old-fashioned tiles featuring buzzing bees and their hives. The French are great connoisseurs of honey, and this shop offers honeys that are identified according to the primary plant or flower the bees were exposed to. Lemon-flower, Linden, and Pine Tree all have distinct flavors, make fine gifts, and are fun to experiment with in the kitchen.

Lafayette Gourmet. 52 bd. Haussmann, 9e. ☎ **01-48-74-46-06.** Métro: Chaussée d'Antin.

Conveniently located in the heart of Paris, this attractive and well-stocked supermarket is a fine spot to browse for gifts or your own pantry. Note that their own brand's merchandise, often cheaper than other labels, is of very good quality. They also have counters selling prepared foods—ideal for picnics or train meals—and several eat-on-the-premises areas for quick meals or snacks.

L'Epicerie. 51 rue St-Louis-en-l'Ile, 4e. ☎ **01-43-25-20-14.** Métro: St-Paul.

Everything is artfully designed and packaged here—mustards, oils, vinegars, jams and jellies, teas, and chocolates. It's not cheap, but everything, right down to the smallest jar of mustard, is beautiful to the eye.

L'Epicerie du Monde. 30 rue François-Miron, 4e. ☎ **01-42-72-66-23.** Métro: Hôtel-de-Ville.

There is no doubt that Paris is an international metropolis, but if you need any proof, go to L'Epicerie du Monde, where you can buy products from all over the world: coffees, teas, chutney, tortillas, honey.

Léonidas. 31 rue Coquillière, 1er. ☎ **01-42-33-09-65.** Métro: Châtelet-Les-Halles.

Great Belgian chocolates. There are about a dozen stores in the city.

La Maison du Chocolat. 225 rue du Faubourg-St-Honoré, 8e. ☎ **01-42-27-39-44.** Métro: Ternes.

La Maison du Chocolat is the best place in Paris to buy chocolate. The subtle decor contains racks and racks of the stuff, priced individually or by the kilo. Each is made from a blend of as many as six different kinds of South American and African chocolate, flavored with just about everything imaginable. All the merchandise, including the chocolate pastries, is made in the store's supermodern cellar facilities.

J. Papin. Prestige et Tradition, 8 rue de Buci, 6e. ☎ **01-43-26-86-09.** Métro: Odéon.

In the heart of the rue de Buci market, this store has some of the most ravishingly displayed foodstuffs you'll ever see, including trout in aspic, exquisite pâtés and salads, lobsters, and smoked salmon.

Sacha Finkelsztajn. 27 rue des Rosiers, 4e. ☎ **01-42-72-78-91.** Métro: St-Paul.

Right in the center of the Jewish Marais, Sacha Finkelsztajn specializes in products from Central Europe. The store carries everything from sacher torte to eggplant caviar.

GIFTS

Axis. 14 rue Lobineau, Marché de St-Germain, 6e. ☎ **01-43-29-66-23.** Métro: Mabillon.

If you're looking for a set of dinner plates imprinted with the cartoon character Rin-Tin-Tin or a Philippe Stark chrome spider lemon press, this is the place to come, since they carry a wonderful and very offbeat assortment of contemporary gifts. Actually, this is an ideal place to come when you have no idea what you're looking for, since the stock is generally both cheap and very original. A branch store is located at 11 rue de Charonne, 11e.

La Boutique Tibétaine. 4 rue Burq, 18e. ☎ **01-42-59-14-86.** Métro: Abesses.

This store stocks a wonderful array of Tibetan goods—silver and coral jewelry, silk and cotton blouses, ritual objects, incense, bags, scarves, and many other appealing items.

Galerie Afghane. 31 rue Descartes, 5e. ☎ **01-44-07-01-53.** Métro: Cardinal-Lemoine or Monge.

This store has a great selection of arts and crafts from India, Nepal, Afghanistan, Iran, China, and Tibet, including clothing, decorative and ritual objects, jewelry, and more at decent prices—for Paris, anyway.

HOUSEWARES

Déhillerin. 18–20 rue Coquillière, 1er. ☎ **01-42-36-53-13.** Métro: Les Halles.

Any cook will love this store filled with copper cookware, glasses, dishes, china, gadgets, utensils, ramekins, pots, and kitchen appliances. Prices are discounted.

Verrerie des Halles. 15 rue du Louvre, 1er. ☎ **01-42-36-86-02.** Métro: Louvre.

A cook's dream. All the accoutrements of the kitchen are here at discount prices usually reserved for professionals.

JEWELRY

Burma. 72 rue du Faubourg-St-Honoré, 8e. ☎ **01-42-65-44-90.** Métro: Miromesnil.

If you're feeling crestfallen because you can't afford any of the spectacular and spectacularly expensive bijoux you see in the windows of the city's world-famous jewelers, come here to console yourself with some of the very best fakes to be found anywhere. This quality costume jewelry is the secret weapon of many a Parisian woman.

Monic. 5 rue des Francs-Bourgeois, 4e. ☎ **01-42-72-39-15.** Métro: St-Paul.

At this store in the Marais you'll find very affordable custom jewelry as well as designer creations at a discount. A wide range of merchandise. And they're open Sunday afternoon, too.

Tati Or. 19 rue de la Paix, 2e. ☎ **01-40-07-06-76.** Métro: Opéra.

Gold and nothing but gold are on sale at Tati's new outlet here, which sells 18-carat gold jewelry up to 40% cheaper than traditional jewelers. More than 3,000 bracelets, earrings, necklaces, rings, and pins are offered with about 500 items selling for less than 400F ($70).

MALLS & SHOPPING ARCADES

Forum des Halles. 1–7 rue Pierre-Lescot, 1er. ☎ **01-42-96-68-74.** Métro: Etienne-Marcel.

Once the great old market of the city—which Emile Zola called *le ventre de Paris* ("Paris's stomach")—Les Halles is now a vast subterranean mall in the middle of Paris, selling, among other things, clothing, accessories, food, and gifts.

Galerie Vivienne. Entrance at 6 rue Vivienne and 4 rue des Petits-Champs, 2e. Métro: Rue Montmartre.

Boutiques here are very pretty; you can buy shoes, sweaters, and rare books, or simply have afternoon tea at A Priori Thé (see "Tea Salons" in chapter 5). For more on arcades see "The Arcades" in chapter 6.

Marché St-Germain. 14 rue Lobineau, 6e. Métro: Odéon.

This modern shopping mall seems out of place in a neighborhood known for its bookstores and publishing houses, and its presence is not greatly appreciated by Left Bank residents. No matter. The Gap and other international chain stores have eagerly taken up residence here.

MARKETS

For a real shopping adventure, come to the vast **Marché aux Puces de la Porte de St-Ouen,** 18e (Métro: Porte-de-Clignancourt). The Clignancourt flea market features several thousand stalls, carts, shops, and vendors selling everything from used blue jeans to antique paintings and furniture. The best times for bargains are right at opening time and just before closing time. Watch out for pickpockets. It is open Saturday through Monday from 9am to 8pm.

More comprehensible, and certainly prettier, is the **Marché aux Fleurs** (Métro: Cité), the flower market on place Louis-Lépine on the Ile de la Cité. Come Monday through Saturday to enjoy the flowers, even if you don't buy anything. On Sunday it becomes the **Marché aux Oiseaux,** an equally colorful bird market.

Of course, you shouldn't miss the food markets, including the **Mouffetard Market** on rue Mouffetard, the **Buci Market** on rue de Buci, and the **Montorguiel market** on rue Montorguiel. All three sell the freshest fruits, vegetables, meats, and cheeses.

PERFUMES

Cambray. 9 rue Pasquier, 8e. ☎ **01-42-65-27-51.** Métro: Madeleine.

Here you'll receive excellent discounts on perfumes and cosmetics, as well as on articles like luggage, watches, and pens.

Freddy of Paris. 3 rue Scribe, 9e. ☎ **01-47-42-63-41.** Métro: Auber or Opéra.

Discounts here are fabulous: up to 40% on perfumes, handbags, cosmetics, silk scarves, and neckties. Freddy of Paris is located near American Express and the Opera.

Michel Swiss. 16 rue de la Paix, 2e. ☎ **01-42-61-61-11.** Métro: Opéra.

In a very chic location not far from place Vendôme, Michel Swiss offers all the famous French perfume brands at excellent prices. House discount is 25%, and there's an additional 15% tax discount for non–European Union residents purchasing over a certain amount. Michel Swiss also sells watches, neckties, leather goods, silk scarves, pens, and fashion accessories from top designers.

RECORDS

Virgin Megastore. Galerie du Carrousel du Louvre, 99 rue de Rivoli, 1er. ☎ **01-49-53-50-00.** Métro: Palais-Royal or Musée-du-Louvre.

A blockbuster store of the British chain, filled with CDs, videos, books, and stereos. Get ready for sticker-shock when you see the prices, but if you must bring back a sample of French music, this is the place to find it. There is another branch at 52–60 av. des Champs-Elysées, 8e. Métro: Franklin-D-Roosevelt (☎ 01-49-53-50-00).

STATIONERY

Cassegrain. 422 rue St-Honoré, 8e. ☎ **01-42-60-20-08.** Métro: Concorde.

Cassegrain opened right after World War I and is considered the premier stationery shop in the city. The store offers beautifully engraved traditional stationery, as well as business cards and gift items. *Note:* there's another store at 81 rue des Saints-Perès, 6e (☎ 01-42-22-04-76).

TOYS

Au Nain Bleu. 406 rue St-Honoré, 8e. ☎ **01-42-60-39-01.** Métro: Concorde.

In business for over 150 years, Au Nain Bleu is filled with toy soldiers, stuffed animals, games, model airplanes, model cars, and puppets.

Jeux Descartes. 40 rue des Ecoles, 5e. ☎ **01-43-26-79-83.** Métro: Cluny.

Can toys be approached scientifically? Some of the salespeople here seem to have received advanced degrees in engineering when they were five. So much fun!

WINE

Le Jardin des Vignes. 91 rue de Turenne, 3e. ☎ **01-42-77-05-00.** Métro: St-Sébastien-Froissart.

The owners of Le Jardin des Vignes really know their wine and will even offer enological lessons. Here you'll find very interesting bottles of rare wine, champagne, and cognac, at reasonable prices.

Lescene-Dura. 63 rue de la Verrerie, 4e. ☎ **01-42-72-08-74.** Métro: Hôtel-de-Ville.

As perhaps the ultimate shop for enophiles, this crowded, friendly place is a good bet for gifts. They sell an amazing array of corkscrews, glassware, and pocket knives, and everything you might need to make wine at home.

Nicholas. 31 place de la Madeleine, 8e. ☎ **01-42-68-00-16.** Métro: Madeleine.

The flagship store of this boutique chain with over 110 branches in and around Paris offers very fair prices for bottles you might not be able to find in the United States. Aside from the usual Bordeaux and Burgundies, take a look at some of the rarer regional wines like Gewürztraminer from Alsace, Collioure from the Languedoc-Rousillon, or the pricey but sublime Cote Rotie from the Cotes du Rhone outside of Lyon.

Paris After Dark 9

Nightlife in Paris is incredibly diverse. Whatever you want to see or do is here. Opera, ballet, classical music, and theater performances are world-class. Movie listings are varied, including everything from the old classics to the avant-garde and foreign films from the Middle East, Latin America, Africa, and Australia. The bars and dance clubs are as trendy or as sophisticated or as wild as you want them to be. And there are many free diversions as well. Walking along the Seine, catching the latest fire-eating performance outside the Centre Pompidou, or hanging around the Latin Quarter are romantic and exciting ways of spending an evening in Paris.

In the last few years, a certain retrenchment has been observed; they say that Parisians don't go out as much as they did in the past, that France is too intent on competing economically with Germany, that the streets are empty and the nightlife is not what it used to be. All of this may be true, but the signs of a diminishing nightlife are not evident in too many places.

WHERE TO FIND OUT WHAT'S ON

Several local **publications** provide up-to-the-minute listings of performances and other evening entertainment. Foremost among these is *Pariscope: Une Semaine de Paris,* a weekly guide with very thorough listings of movies, plays, ballet, art exhibits, clubs, and more. It contains an English-language insert with selected listings and can be purchased at any newsstand for 3F (50¢). *L'Officiel des Spectacles* is another weekly guide, and *Paris Nuit* is a monthly for 30F ($5.20); the latter contains good articles as well as listings, and it's very popular with young in-the-know Parisians. The *Paris Free Voice* is a free monthly that spotlights events of interest to English-speakers, including poetry readings, plays, and literary evenings at English-language bookstores and libraries.

SAVING MONEY

For **half-price theater tickets,** go to the Kiosque-Théâtre at the northwest corner of the Madeleine church (Métro: Madeleine). You can buy tickets only for that same day's performance. The little panels all around the kiosk indicate whether the performance is sold out (little red man) or whether tickets are still available (little green man). The Kiosque-Théâtre is open Tuesday through Saturday from 12:30 to 8pm. A second ticket counter selling discount tickets is located in the basement of the Châtelet-Les-Halles Métro station, and a third is located in front of the Gare Montparnasse.

Students can often get last-minute tickets by applying at the box office an hour before curtain time. Have your International Student Identity Card (ISIC) with you.

In the following listings, ticket prices are an approximation; costs will go up or down depending on who exactly is performing what on which day of the week. Call the theaters for information or consult *Pariscope* and the other entertainment listings.

1 The Performing Arts

OPERA/BALLET

Opéra Paris Garnier. Place de l'Opéra, 9e. ☎ **01-47-42-53-71.** Métro: Opéra. RER: Auber.

The interior is a positive symphony of marble—red, blue, pink, green, and white, and the ceiling in the auditorium is brilliantly decorated by Chagall. Although the total area covers more than 118,000 square feet, the backstage offices and rehearsal rooms are so extensive that the auditorium only seats 2,200 people. Recent renovations have restored the opera house to its full glory and the auditorium has been modernized.

The Ballet de l'Opéra de Paris and the Opéra National de Paris schedule some performances here and some at the Opéra de la Bastille. In both venues, reduced price tickets may be available at the box office 15 minutes before performance time for students and people under 25 or over 65.

Opéra de la Bastille. Place de la Bastille, 12e. ☎ **01-44-73-13-00,** or 01-43-43-96-96 for recorded information. Métro: Bastille.

After more than 100 years at Garnier's grand Théâtre de l'Opéra, the Opéra National moved to the new Opéra de la Bastille in 1989. Opened to commemorate the bi-centennial of the French Revolution, this state of the art performance center was designed by Uruguayan-Canadian architect Carlos Ott, with curtains by Japanese designer Issey Miyake. Initially the project was vehemently opposed on social grounds because so many low-cost apartment buildings were razed, or on aesthetic grounds because the architecture was considered too avant-garde. The controversy continued even after the Opera opened. There were technical problems maneuvering the elaborate sets. Conductors came and left. Opera fans couldn't get used to the "surtitles" on a screen over the stage. But now the National Opera has settled into its new home and, under the baton of conductor James Conlon, the productions are both popular and critically acclaimed.

Opéra-Comique/Salle Favart. 5 rue Favart, 2e. ☎ **01-42-44-45-40.** Tickets 50–490F ($8.70–$85.20). Box office open daily 11am–7pm. Métro: Richelieu Drout.

The other major venue for opera in Paris is the Opéra-Comique, located in a turn-of-the-century building that's also known as Salle Favart. The decoration is full of belle epoque ornaments. As its name implies, the Opéra-Comique features the lighter operas and operettas for which the French are so well known.

CONCERT HALLS & CLASSICAL MUSIC

There are many classical music concerts throughout the year, and many of them are quite affordable. More than a dozen Parisian **churches** regularly schedule free or in-expensive (tickets around $20) organ recitals and concerts, among them **Notre-Dame** (☎ **01-44-41-49-99;** Métro: Cité); **St-Eustache,** 1 rue Montmartre, 1er (☎ **01-42-49-26-79;** Métro: Châtelet); **St-Sulpice,** place St-Sulpice (☎ **01-46-33-21-78;**

Métro: St-Sulpice), which has the largest organ; **St-Germain-des-Prés,** place St-Germain-des-Prés (☎ **01-44-62-70-90;** Métro: St-Germain-des-Prés); the **Madeleine,** place de la Madeleine (☎ **01-42-77-65-65;** Métro: Madeleine); and **Saint Louis en l'Ile,** 19 bis rue Saint-Louis-en-l'Ile (☎ **01-46-34-11-60;** Métro: Pont-Marie). In a less magnificent setting, the Sunday concerts at 6pm at the **American Church,** 65 quai d'Orsay (☎ **01-47-05-07-99;** Métro: Invalides) are friendly and inviting.

Free concerts are staged occasionally in the parks and gardens. Call ☎ **01-40-71-76-47** for information. **Maison de la Radio,** 116 av. du President Kennedy, 16e (☎ **01-42-30-15-16**), offers free tickets to the recordings of some concerts. Tickets are available on the spot one hour before the recording starts. The **Conservatoire National de Musique** at the Cité de la Musique, 209 av. Jean Jaurès, 19e (☎ **01-40-40-46-46**), also stages free concerts and ballets performed by students at the conservatory.

Salle Pleyel. 252 rue du Faubourg-St-Honoré, 8e. ☎ **01-45-61-53-00.** 75–360F ($13–$62.60). Métro: Ternes.

Under Semyon Bychkov, the Orchestre de Paris plays at the Salle Pleyel, their official concert hall, from September to Easter. The Salle Pleyel is located a few blocks northeast of the Arc de Triomphe.

THEATERS

Most theatrical performances in Paris are, of course, in French. With luck, though, you may be able to catch something in English, especially in summer.

The first three theaters listed here are "national theaters," supported by the government, but there are also many private ones. For full listings, consult *Pariscope.*

Comédie Française. 2 rue de Richelieu, 1er. ☎ **01-40-15-00-15.** Tickets 50–200F ($8.70–$34.80), last-minute seats even cheaper. Métro: Palais-Royal–Musée-du-Louvre.

The classic tragedies and comedies of Corneille, Racine, Molière, and other French playwrights are staged in marvelous performances at the more than 300-year-old Comédie Française. Created in 1680 by Louis XIV, the troupe moved to its present location in 1799. Not until much later were foreign authors such as Shakespeare admitted into the Comédie's repertoire. Nowadays, schedules are varied with the addition of more modern works and plays translated from other languages. Even if you don't understand French, you'll probably enjoy the outstanding performances.

Théâtre National de l'Odéon. Place de l'Odéon, 6e. ☎ **01-44-41-36-36.** Tickets 30–170F ($5.20–$29.55); tickets usually sold 2 weeks before performance. Métro: Odéon.

Home of the Comédie Française until the revolution, the Odéon is now very much a European stage, not a narrowly nationalistic one. The theater is a beautiful early 19th-century building, and its row of columns overlooks a pretty semicircular square. Beaumarchais's *Le Mariage de Figaro* was performed for the first time here.

Théâtre des Champs-Elysées. 15 av. Montaigne, 8e. ☎ **01-49-52-50-50.** Tickets 50–690F ($8.70–$120). Métro: Alma-Marceau.

This theater features visiting international orchestras and opera and ballet companies.

Théâtre National de Chaillot. Place du Trocadéro, 16e. ☎ **01-47-27-81-15.** Tickets 160F ($27.80); 120F ($20.85) for people 25 or younger; 80F ($13.90) students. Métro: Trocadéro.

Part of the art deco Palais de Chaillot, directly across the Seine from the Eiffel Tower, the Théâtre National de Chaillot used to be the Théâtre National Populaire. Plays as well as musical events are staged here.

Jardin Shakespeare. Pré Catelan, Bois de Boulogne. ☎ **01-42-72-00-33.** Bus: No. 244 from Porte-Maillot Métro station.

At this garden in the Bois de Boulogne, where plants mentioned by Shakespeare are grown, the Bard's plays are performed during the summer, in English.

MUSIC VENUES

Olympia. 28 bd. des Capucines, 9e. ☎ **01-47-42-82-45.** Métro: Opéra.

At press time, the Olympia was undergoing extensive renovation. This historic pop venue is due to reopen by 1998. Call for details of concerts and prices.

2 The Club & Music Scene

NIGHTCLUBS & CABARETS

The nightclubs of Paris have been famous for decades, and the performances associated with the names Lido, Folies Bergère, Crazy Horse Saloon, and Moulin Rouge are mimicked in dozens of other big cities and small towns. Though the heyday of the great supper-club revues was before World War II, tourists still flock to the city looking for music, spectacular costumes, variety acts, comedians, and a lot of nudity.

If you've ever seen a nightclub act in Las Vegas or Atlantic City, however, you may go away feeling not only poorer but rather let down, since many of the famous Paris clubs exist in a pre-'70s time warp. Remember, too, that a lot of what originally made these clubs popular was their naughtiness; today, of course, you can find more daringly erotic images on the Internet.

If you must see a Paris spectacle, be prepared to spend at least $110 per person, and perhaps as much as $200 (drinks can cost as much as $35 apiece). Then choose among these places:

Crazy Horse Saloon. 12 av. Georges-V, 8e. ☎ **01-47-23-32-32.** Métro: Georges-V.

Considered by many aficionados to be the best nude show in the city. Variety acts go on in between the femmes fatales, who appear on swing seats or in cages or . . . you get the picture. Sultry entertainment to some, an expensive bore to others. Cover and one drink minimum from 220F ($38.25). Additional drinks from 60F ($10.45).

Lido Cabaret Normandie. 116 bis, av. des Champs-Elysées, 8e. ☎ **01-40-76-56-10** for reservations. Métro: Georges-V.

Be Warned: The show alone with half a bottle of champagne will cost you 540F ($93.90). If you have dinner with half a bottle of champagne the price soars to 770F ($133.90). There are usually two shows a night.

Moulin Rouge. Place Blanche, Montmartre, 18e. ☎ **01-46-06-00-19.** Métro: Place-Blanche.

Here you'll see a variety of acts—comedy, animal, and magic—with major fantasy spectacles in-between, featuring a bevy of nudes. Revue only is 510F ($88.70) with champagne; dinner from 750F ($130.45). For 350F ($60.85) you can sit at the bar and have two drinks. If you're in the right frame of mind, this place offers a good measure of hokey fun.

Paradis Latin. 28 rue Cardinal-Lemoine, 5e. ☎ **01-43-25-28-28.** Métro: Cardinal-Lemoine.

Perhaps the most French of them all. In the heart of the Latin Quarter, the building was designed by Gustave Eiffel. The revue is a typical mix of risqué badinage by the master of ceremonies (in French and English) and revue acts and nudity. Revue only with half a bottle of champagne 465F ($80.85); dinner 680F ($118.25).

MUSIC HALLS & BOÎTES

Paris is famous for its chansonniers, who write the songs of the day that have been sung by such artists as Piaf and Aznavour and Jacques Brel, to name only a few. The tradition continues today and an evening spent at a boîte listening to French songs is still one of the most intimate and timeless experiences that one can enjoy in Paris.

Au Lapin Agile. 22 rue des Saules, 18e. ☎ **01-46-06-85-87.** Métro: Lamarck.

On the Butte of Montmartre, this was once the haunt of Utrillo, Toulouse-Lautrec, and many other artists, though then it was called the Café des Assassins. Go for an evening of nostalgia—love songs and ballads sung in a bohemian atmosphere—and sing along to the traditional French songs. Cover is 110F ($19.15), including one drink.

Caveau des Oubliettes. 11 rue St-Julien-le-Pauvre, 5e. ☎ **01-43-54-94-07.** Métro: St-Michel.

Tucked away by St-Julien-le-Pauvre is an atmospheric candlelit cellar that originally served as a prison. Here you can enjoy an evening of traditional French songs and love ballads performed by costumed artists. Good clean tourist fun.

Café Concert Ailleurs. 13 rue Jean de Beausire, 11e. ☎ **01-44-59-82-82.** Métro: Bastille.

Forget about Piaf and Brel in this funky cabaret and listen to what a new generation of songsmiths are singing about. This relaxed space is run by an artists' collective and attracts bohemians of all ages who are interested in up-and-coming artists. Admission is based on what you can afford—30F, 50F, 80F ($5.20, $8.70, $13.90)—but reservations are absolutely essential for the nightly 9:30pm show. Dinner is served at 8:30pm.

ROCK

Bus Palladium. 6 rue Fontaine, 9e. ☎ **01-53-21-07-33.** No cover Wed, Thurs; Tues, Fri, Sat 100F ($17.40). Métro: Pigalle.

This club is the best bet in Paris for people who still love guitar rock. What might be a surprise is the crowd—well-dressed young French yuppies. They like to party, though, and everyone gets down as the night grows long. This place is usually a reliably good time.

Le Gibus. 18 rue du Faubourg du Temple, 10e. ☎ **01-47-00-78-88.** Cover 20–80F ($3.45–$13.90), depending upon who's playing. Métro: Republique.

Though it remains one of the most famous rock dance clubs in Paris, this place has recently started a series of very popular techno nights. So if you have your heart set on rock, call ahead or check the listings in *Pariscope* to see what's on. Regardless of the music, an easygoing young crowd gives this old dance hall a slightly divey feel.

La Locomotive. 90 bd. de Clichy, 18e. ☎ **01-42-57-37-37.** Cover Fri–Sat 100F ($17.40), including 1 drink; Sun–Thurs 65F ($11.30), including 1 drink; women admitted free on Sun. Métro: Place-Clichy.

At La Locomotive, a generally clean-cut crowd wears jeans and sits on Indian cushions on the floor. There are many American students, especially on Sunday, and people dance a lot. Most of the time people are climbing up and down the stairs, from which pretty bodies lean. Graffiti art and psychedelic flowers decorate the walls. This is a very big place; there are three levels, and in the lower level you can see an old railway line.

DANCE CLUBS

The clubs of Paris must be among the hippest and most chic in the world. At present, many Parisian circles seem to favor salsa, rap, reggae, house, and techno disco, and they fastidiously extol the virtues of going out on weeknights, to avoid the suburban crowds who come into the city Friday and Saturday nights. The later one goes, the better. And what does one wear? Black plus leather, plastic, vinyl, and/ or metal. But everything can change overnight. What will it be like next season? Who knows, although *Paris Nuit* or the very hip *Nova* magazine can probably give you some idea. Most clubs don't open until 11pm, and the music doesn't stop pumping until dawn.

Les Bains. 7 rue du Bourg-l'Abbe, 3e. ☎ **01-48-87-01-80.** Mon–Thurs and Sun, cover 100F ($17.40); Fri–Sat, 150F ($26) with 1 drink. Métro: Etienne-Marcel.

The doorman here will decide whether or not you'll be allowed in to play with the supermodels, designers, and movie people who frequent this *tres chic* Paris clubs. If this doesn't put you off, dress as chicly as you can and show up around 1am. Inside, this is one of the best parties in town. The DJ spins mostly house music and soul, and the crowd's very mixed in terms of nationality, age, outlook, and sexual preference.

Le Balajo. 9 rue de Lappe, 11e. ☎ **01-47-00-07-87.** Cover 50–100F ($8.70–$17.40), including 1 drink. Métro: Bastille.

Edith Piaf used to perform here, but now the music is rap, reggae, and salsa combined with the musette of yesteryear. The crowd is racially mixed, fun, hip, and wild. Sometimes there are live bands. Everybody dances together, and there's very little posing. It really gets going around 3am, and the best nights/mornings are Monday/ Tuesday and Thursday/Friday. Sunday afternoons are given over to *bal musette* or ballroom dancing to traditional French tunes.

La Chapelle des Lombards. 19 rue de Lappe, 11e. ☎ **01-43-57-24-24.** Cover Thurs 100F ($17.40), Fri, Sat 120F ($20.85). Métro: Bastille.

A festive tropical ambience and diverse music—everything from salsa to reggae— attract a lively mixed crowd to this hip club near the Bastille. To really enjoy this place, you have to dress the part, which means no sneakers or jeans, but rather your sophisticated best.

La Coupole. 102 bd. du Montparnasse, 14e. ☎ **01-43-20-14-21.** Cover Sun afternoon 80F ($13.90); Sat afternoon and weekend nights 95F ($16.50). Métro: Montparnasse-Bienvenue.

In addition to the famous cafe upstairs, La Coupole has a basement dance hall—a nostalgic retro venue with plush banquettes and old-fashioned sounds.

La Java. 105 rue du Faubourg-du-Temple, 10e. ☎ **01-42-02-20-52.** Cover 100F ($17.40). Métro: Belleville.

If you have a taste for something fun, funky, and very authentic, and if you like Latin music, this charming old dance hall might be your great night out. A very mixed crowd comes to dance without restraint to mostly Cuban and Brazilian music.

Rex Club. 5 bd. Poissonnière, 2e. ☎ **01-42-36-83-98.** Cover 60F ($10.45) Mon and Thurs; 70F ($12.15) Fri; 80F ($13.90) Sat, including 1 drink. Drinks 60F ($10.45), beer 35F ($6). Métro: Bonne-Nouvelle.

Follow a stairway that seems to lead to the middle of the earth. Everything is gray and high-tech. It's big. There are mirrors. There is smoke that smells like strawberries. One customer is young. Another wears clothes like silver. Still another dances by herself. Tuesday is a big rap party, Wednesday is hard rock, Friday is oldies,

Saturday is funk and salsa. The big lure here these days, though, is Paris's most famous DJ, Laurent Garnier, who spins house music on those wildly well-attended nights when he's present.

La Scala. 188 bis, rue de Rivoli, 1er. ☎ **01-42-60-45-64.** Cover 100F ($17.40) including 1 drink (free for women Mon–Thurs). Drinks 45F ($7.80). Métro: Palais-Royal–Musée-du-Louvre.

The Scala is flamboyant, with an exquisite sound-and-light system and impressive decoration. The laser show creates designs that bounce all through the three-story-high space and the surrounding balconies. American Top 40, rap, disco, and reggae predominate. There's plenty of comfortable seating and at least five bars. Few locals; mostly tourists and suburbanites. The ultimate meat factory.

JAZZ

Parisians still have an insatiable craving for American music, especially jazz, and the scene is vibrant as a new generation develops a taste for the blues. Look through the current *Pariscope* for the artists you admire. If you don't care who's playing, and you're just out for a night of good music, try the following.

Le Baiser Sale. 56 rue des Lombards, 1er. ☎ **01-42-33-37-71.** Cover 40–90F ($7–$15.65). Drinks from 30F ($5.20). Métro: Châtelet-Les-Halles.

A small club where the jazz sounds are fusion. A cool spot and good value too.

Caveau de la Hûchette. 5 rue de la Hûchette, 5e. ☎ **01-43-26-65-05.** Cover Sun–Thurs 70F ($12.15), Fri–Sat 80F ($13.90). Sodas from 22F ($3.80), alcohol from 30F ($5.20), but note there's a minimum. Métro: St-Michel. RER: St-Michel.

This Paris jazz club has been on the scene for 50 years. It's popular with both foreigners and locals of all ages who want to listen and dance to good music. Reached by a winding staircase, the *caveau* was used as a tribunal and prison during the French Revolution. Art Blakey, Lionel Hampton, and Memphis Slim are just a few of the big names who have performed here.

Le Duc des Lombards. 42 rue des Lombards, 1er. ☎ **01-42-33-22-88.** Cover varies. Métro: Châtelet-Les-Halles.

A great jazz spot with a casual, down-to-earth crowd. Every night there's a different band performing.

Hot Brass. 221 av. Jean-Jaures, 19e. ☎ **01-42-00-54-44.** Cover varies. Métro: Porte de Pantin.

Though it's a bit of a nuisance to get to (it's located in the Parc de la Villette complex on the city's northern edge), this is probably the hottest jazz club right now. A hip younger crowd comes to hear artists like Steve Coleman.

New Morning. 7–9 rue des Petites-Ecuries, 10e. ☎ **01-45-23-51-41.** Cover 120F ($20.85). Métro: Château-d'Eau.

When the Lounge Lizards played here, the audience withheld their approval until they were totally seduced by the music. But once the crowd was convinced, the concert lasted until 4am. New Morning is one of Paris's best jazz clubs, and the audience one of the toughest in the world to win over. The best perform here, from Archie Shepp, Bill Evans, and Elvin Jones to Kevin Coyne and Koko Ateba from the Cameroons.

Le Petit Journal Saint-Michel. 71 bd. St-Michel, 5e. ☎ **01-43-26-28-59.** Cover 100F ($17.40), including 1 drink. Métro: Cluny-La-Sorbonne. RER: Luxembourg.

This is a small club with a more French atmosphere. The Claude Bolling Trio is a regular visitor, as are the Claude Luter Sextet and the Benny Bailey Quartet. You can dine as well as drink here in a warm relaxed atmosphere.

Slow Club. 130 rue de Rivoli, 1er. ☎ **01-42-33-84-30.** Cover Tues–Thurs 70F ($12.15), Fri–Sat 85F ($14.80). Sodas 25F ($4.35), alcohol from 40F ($7). Métro: Châtelet-Les-Halles.

Slow Club is across the street from the La Samaritaine department store. Look for the neon sign, enter the big unmarked double door, and follow the signs inside and down the stairs to the club. This self-styled "jazz cellar" is a favorite with big American and European artists swing, Dixieland, and classic jazz.

Le Sunset. 60 rue des Lombards, 1er. ☎ **01-40-26-46-60.** Cover from 80–100F ($13.90–$17.40), including 1 drink. Métro: Châtelet.

A small cavelike spot that features contemporary jazz and fusion. If you're interested in French jazz, this is the spot to head for.

GAY PAREE

The Marais, Les Halles, and the Bastille are the main gay and lesbian neighborhoods in Paris. Gay male bars are concentrated in the Marais, while the hottest lesbian bar, El Scandalo, is near the Bastille.

Le Bar Central. 33 rue Vieille-du-Temple, 4e. ☎ **01-48-87-99-33.** Drinks about 20F ($3.50). Métro: Hôtel-de-Ville.

Le Central is one of Paris's best-known bars for men. It's small and usually very crowded.

Café Cox. 15 rue des Archives, 4e. ☎ **01-42-72-08-00.** Drinks about 35F ($6). Métro: Hôtel-de-Ville.

This lively new bar is perhaps the most popular in the Marais and attracts an interesting cross-section of Parisian men, although women are welcome. A nice change from the dingy neoleather bars that prevail in the neighborhood.

La Champmeslé. 4 rue Chabanais, 2e. ☎ **01-42-96-85-20.** Drinks about 35F ($6). Métro: Bourse, Pyramides, 4-Septembre, or Opéra.

A few blocks east of the avenue de l'Opéra, La Champmeslé is a comfortable bar for women. Thursday night is cabaret night and draws a large crowd.

Le Piano Zinc. 49 rue des Blancs-Manteaux, 4e. ☎ **01-42-74-32-42.** Drinks from 25F ($4.35). Métro: Hôtel-de-Ville or Rambuteau.

A popular, comfortable bar with fine chansons playing in the background early in the evening. Later the patrons provide the chansons themselves at the cabaret downstairs. Fun, friendly, and comfortable even for straight friends.

Queen. 102 av. des Champs-Elysées, 8e. ☎ **01-53-89-08-90.** Cover varies, but usually runs about 80F ($13.90). Daily midnight–dawn. Métro: Georges-V.

Not only the busiest gay disco in Paris but the hottest club in town, this place attracts the wildest of Paris's night people. The door policy is unofficially selective, so look hip if you want to give this a go. Women usually only get in with male friends.

El Scandalo. 21 rue Keller, 11e. ☎ **01-47-00-24-59.** Drinks from 20F ($3.50). Métro: Bastille.

Lots of women like this tiny little bar near the Bastille for its diverse, friendly young crowd. More lipstick than flannel shirt, but both are welcome.

3 The Bar Scene

In Paris, bars are different. They are not places reserved solely for drinking, but nor are they reserved for nighttime entertainment. People are as likely to drop into a cafe or wine bar for a brandy at breakfast as they are to hang out there at night. Parisians frequent cafes and bars at all hours of the day. For this reason, the bars listed below are classic American-style cocktail bars. Although some open at noon and others not until after dinner, most bars stay open until 2am. For a fuller listing of the more traditional cafes and wine bars, see chapter 5, "Great Deals on Dining."

Buddha Bar. 8 rue Boissy d'Anglas, 8e. ☎ **01-53-05-90-09.** Drinks from 35F ($6). Métro: Concorde.

A giant, impassive Buddha presides over the very un-Zenlike doings in this cavernous bar/restaurant. From the upstairs balcony you can observe the fashionable diners below or mix with the swanky international crowd at the balcony bar. The music is spacey but the atmosphere is electric, and you'll see the prettiest people in Paris. For the trendiest spot in town, the food is surprisingly mediocre, but food is not really the point here. The point is to see and be seen and then say you saw it.

Café de L'Industrie. 16 rue St-Sabin, 11e. ☎ **01-47-00-13-53.** Drinks from 16F ($2.80). Métro: Bastille.

The mood is young, friendly, and casual in this immensely popular bar/cafe. Plants, wood floors, and wood Venetian blinds lend the two spacious rooms a vaguely colonial flavor. Hip Bastille denizens drift in and out all day, grazing on inexpensive salads, pastas, and *plats,* but after 9:30pm the place is mobbed. Strangely, it's closed Saturdays.

China Club. 50 rue de Charenton, 12e. ☎ **01-43-43-82-02.** Drinks from 40F ($7). Métro: Bastille.

Everyone seems to enjoy the sleek colonial decor at this chic and very atmospheric place just a few steps from the Bastille. This is the type of bar where you wouldn't be surprised to spot someone like Faye Dunaway, especially since the mood evokes her film *Chinatown.* Take a place either at the downstairs bar or the busier upstairs one and take in the scene, which is about as high-voltage glamour as Paris produces. Cigar smokers will rejoice in the trendy upstairs fumoir, or smoking room. All cocktails are well made, but the Chinese food served is not worth the money.

La Closerie des Lilas. 171 bd. du Montparnasse, 6e. ☎ **01-40-51-34-50.** Drinks from 34F ($5.90). Métro: Port-Royal.

La Closerie des Lilas is a Montparnasse institution, favored in the 1920s by writers and artists such as Hemingway and Picasso. If you find the drinks too expensive and the service too brusque—a distinct possibility—try the Café Select nearby.

Coolin. Marche St-Germain, 15 rue Clement, 6e. ☎ **01-44-07-00-92.** Drinks from 20F ($3.50). Métro: Mabillon.

Irish pubs are popular in Paris, and this new one in the renovated market in Saint Germain is a great place to relax over a pint of Guinness. They also do light meals—smoked salmon and salads—and the decor and staff are amusing.

Harry's New York Bar. 5 rue Daunou, 2e. ☎ **01-42-61-71-14.** Drinks from 45F ($7.80). Métro: Opéra or Pyramides.

Founded in 1911, Harry's is one of Europe's famous bars and as popular with Americans today as it was in the time of F. Scott Fitzgerald and Gertrude Stein. The Bloody Marys are legendary and there's an amazing selection of whiskeys. There's also a cabaret-cellar bar downstairs. It's not cheap, of course, but you may want to splurge just so you can lift a glass to the ghost of Hemingway.

The Lizard Lounge. 18 rue du Bourg-Tibourg, 4e. ☎ **01-42-72-81-34.** Drinks from 25F ($4.35). Métro: Hôtel-de-Ville.

Stylish but easygoing, this bar is a pleasant place to hang out with an arty, international crowd after dinner. You could also come early in the evening for a light meal prepared in their open kitchen. The heavy-gauge steel balcony overlooking the main bar offers a chance for a quiet conversation, while a livelier crew gathers around the pool table in the basement bar.

O'Sheas. 10 rue des Capucines, 2e. ☎ **01-40-15-00-30.** Drinks from 25F ($4.35). Métro: Opéra.

If you're weary of the language barrier or find the French frosty, this attractive Irish pub offers the perfect refuge. Popular with Anglophone expatriates, it's busy every night with a mixed crowd that runs from stockbrokers to au pairs on their night off. Note that in addition to fine Irish and foreign brews, they also serve excellent food in the first-floor restaurant.

La Perla. 26 rue Francois-Miron, 4e. ☎ **01-42-77-59-40.** Drinks from 20F ($3.45) but half-price during happy hour Mon–Fri 6–8pm. Métro: St-Paul.

Even in Paris, the yearning for a Margarita might overtake you. If so, come here to this pleasant bar in the Marais. They pride themselves on having the largest collection of Tequilas in Europe and also stock seven different Mexican beers. Friendly service and decent nachos make this an engaging place to sip away under the ceiling fans. On Tuesday nights, Margaritas are reduced from 52F ($9) to 38F ($6.60).

Le Piano Vache. 8 rue Laplace, 5e. ☎ **01-46-33-75-03.** Drinks from 25F ($4.35). Métro: Maubert Mutualité.

A classic student's dive with a lot of charm, this is one of the rare examples of the genus surviving in the gentrifying Latin Quarter, and almost as close as you'll be able to get these days to the type of bar made famous by films like *Funny Face*. The animated young crowd ignores the smoke-stained walls and old wood beams, happily throwing back their beers and occasionally glancing at the only concession to the nineties here: the MTV-playing video monitor.

Pub 64 WE. 64 rue de Charenton, 12e. ☎ **01-44-75-39-55.** Drinks from 20F ($3.50). Métro: Ledru-Rollin.

A great place to hang out if you don't want a high-voltage scene, this neighborhood place, located not far from the Bastille, draws a friendly, often multilingual international crowd. They've got two pool tables and a good selection of Belgian, Irish, British, and other beers. The bartender would have it that the glass-paneled staircase leading downstairs is as effective a sobriety test as any Breathalyzer.

Sanz Sans. 49 rue du Faubourg St-Antoine, 12e. ☎ **01-44-75-78-78.** Drinks from 30F ($5.20). Métro: Bastille.

Sanz Sans is a very popular Bastille bar done up with big gilt mirrors, red velvet chairs, and ersatz Old Masters on the walls. A trendy young crowd surrounds the U-shaped bar and listens to acid jazz and funk music. Those seated in the back of the bar get a high-tech view of the action in the front via a closed circuit camera that projects onto a screen on the back wall. It's very crowded on weekends.

Le Satellit Café. 44 rue de la Folie Mericourt, 11e. ☎ **01-47-00-48-87.** Drinks from 15F ($2.60). Métro: Oberkampf.

With an intriguing and constantly changing array of world music—one night there's a singer from Madagascar, the next a Cuban funk band—this is one of the livelier and most original nocturnal options in Paris. Sort of a cross between a cafe and a disco—there's a live DJ spinning danceable exotica when there's not live music—this place attracts a young, cool crowd. It's very friendly, though, so almost everyone feels comfortable here, even if they sometimes need a selection from the joint's very good wine list (itself a rarity in Paris bars) to get that way.

4 Yet More Entertainment

CITY SPECTACLES

Paris residents often say that showing their out-of-town friends around the city is not hard at all, because no matter where you look there seems to be something worth seeing. At night the city is spellbinding when all the major monuments loom floodlit out of the night.

Don't underestimate the pleasure of walking around after sunset. Approaching the illuminated Eiffel Tower from either the Palais de Chaillot and the place du Trocadéro, across the Seine, or the Ecole-Militaire and the Champs-de-Mars is a memorable experience. Notre-Dame acquires a wonderful golden hue and so does the Louvre, when the pyramids take on an outlandish appearance. The Marais and the place des Vosges somehow anchor themselves more strongly in the 17th century after the sun sets. Crowds mill around the place de la Bastille and wander through the Latin Quarter. The Champs-Elysées glitters as it never does during the day, and the Arc de Triomphe becomes truly triumphant as yellow streams of automobile lights careen around it. At this hour, rambling about the streets or the waterways of Paris without any particular destination is just fabulously romantic. If your legs have given out after a long day of sightseeing, though, you can take a nighttime bus tour (see "Organized Tours" in chapter 6).

FILMS

The diversity of films being shown at any given time in Paris is fantastic. The glitzy theaters along the Champs-Elysées show new blockbuster films, both French and foreign. Smaller cinemas located on both banks of the Seine show the classics, as well as lesser known titles from all over the world. *Pariscope* has the most complete listings, organized both by area and alphabetically.

There are some things you should know when going to the movies in France. "V.O." next to a listing stands for *version originale,* which means the soundtrack will be in the original language of the film; "V.F." (*version française*) means that the film has been dubbed in French; *sous-titres* are subtitles. Movie tickets cost anywhere from 32F to 50F ($5.55 to $8.70), depending on the cinema and the film that's playing. Students can sometimes get reductions on ticket prices; other discounts are offered during the daytime and on Mondays. Theater ushers are normally tipped 2F (35¢).

Two cinemas deserve special attention:

Cinémathèque Française. Musée de Cinéma Henri-Langlois, Palais de Chaillot, place du Trocadéro, 16e. ☎ **01-47-04-24-24.** Tickets 30F ($5.20). Métro: Trocadéro.

Supported by the French government and associated with the Musée de Cinéma, the Cinémathèque Française shows up to five films Tuesday through Sunday. The selections are usually very interesting, and there are films from different periods and from all parts of the world. There are often long lines.

Le Grand Rex. 1 bd. Poissonnière, 2e. ☎ **01-42-36-83-93.** Tickets 46F ($8); student tickets 36F ($6.25). Métro: Bonne-Nouvelle.

With 2,800 seats, this is the largest theater in Paris. As you can imagine, watching a movie here is different from watching a movie elsewhere.

10 Side Trips from Paris

Versailles, Fontainebleau, the Cathedral of Chartres, and Disneyland Paris are the most frequently visited attractions in the Ile de France—the verdant region surrounding Paris. All four attractions are easy day trips from the city, conveniently reached by rail.

If you're going to be in Paris for a longer period of time, you might also want to visit the magical gardens of the painter Claude Monet in Giverny, which can easily be visited as day trips from Paris.

1 Versailles

13 miles SW of Paris, 44 miles NE of Chartres

Louis XIV, who reigned from 1643 to 1715, commissioned the **Château de Versailles** (☎ **01-30-84-74-00**) and its vast grounds and gardens. Construction took nearly 50 years, but the effort was worth it. More than three million visitors come every year, and one glance will tell you why: Versailles is simply astounding.

Louis XIII was the first to build a château at Versailles. Constructed between 1631 and 1634, it was a very small affair compared with what was to follow. The Sun King set out to create a palace that would be the awe of Europe. By 1684, 22,000 men and 6,000 horses were at work on the château and gardens, draining the marshes, often at the cost of their lives, and demolishing the forests. Two architects worked on this dream: Louis Le Vau and Jules Hardouin-Mansart. André Le Nôtre, who designed the Jardin des Tuileries in Paris, supervised the design of the gardens and the park. Le Brun decorated the interior.

In 1682, Louis XIV transferred the court to Versailles, and here all French monarchs resided until the Revolution. To keep an eye on the aristocrats, Louis XIV summoned them to live here, where he amused them with constant entertainment and lavish banquets. He bestowed on them such duties and privileges as holding his ermine-lined robe. About 3,000 people, including the servants, lived at Versailles.

When Louis XIV died in 1715, he was succeeded by his great-grandson, Louis XV, who continued the outrageous pomp and ceremony and made interior renovations until stopped by lack of funds. His son, Louis XVI, and his queen, Marie Antoinette, had simpler

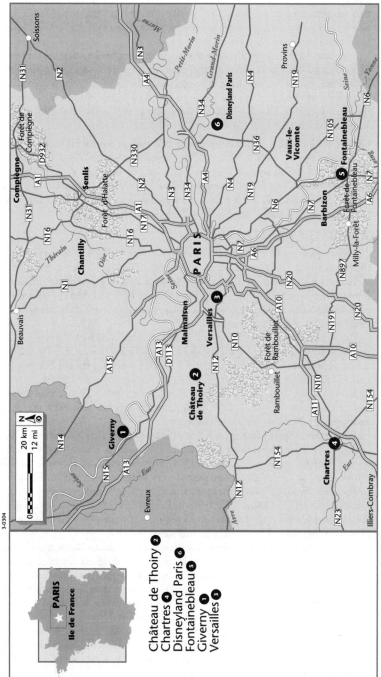

Château de Thoiry **2**
Chartres **4**
Disneyland Paris **6**
Fontainebleau **5**
Giverny **1**
Versailles **3**

tastes and made no major changes at Versailles. When, on October 6, 1789, a mob marched on the palace and forced the royal couple to return to Paris, Versailles ceased to be a royal residence.

Napoléon made some limited renovations to Versailles, but he was never very fond of the château. Perhaps the image of the Sun King burned too strongly in his mind. Louis-Philippe, the Citizen King, who reigned from 1830 to 1848, prevented its destruction by donating his own money to convert it into a museum dedicated to the glory of France. John D. Rockefeller later also contributed to the restoration of Versailles, which continues to this day.

GETTING THERE   To get to the palace at Versailles, catch RER Line C5 at the Gare d'Austerlitz, St-Michel, Musée d'Orsay, Invalides, Pont de l'Alma, Champs-de-Mars, or Javel station and take it to the Versailles Rive Gauche station. From there you can walk or take a shuttle bus to the château. Holders of a Eurailpass can use it for the trip. The 13F ($2.25) trip takes about half an hour. A regular train also leaves from the Gare St-Lazare to the Versailles Rive Gauche RER station.

TOURING THE PALACE

The six magnificent **Grands Appartements** are in the Louis XIV style, and they take their names from the allegorical ceiling paintings. The best known is the Salon of Hercules, which depicts the club-carrying strongman riding in a chariot; the artist François Lemoyne painted the ceiling from 1733 to 1736 and then committed suicide. In the Salon of Mercury, Louis XIV lay in state for eight days following his death in 1715, ending a 72-year reign.

You will pass through the Salon of War and see a bas-relief by Coysevox that depicts the triumphant Sun King on horseback, trampling his enemies. Finally, you will arrive at the most famous room at Versailles, the 236-foot-long **Hall of Mirrors.** Begun by Mansart in 1678 in Louis XIV style, it was decorated by Le Brun with 17 large windows matched with corresponding reflecting mirrors. The German Empire was proclaimed here in 1871. Forty-eight years later, on June 28, 1919, the treaty ending World War I was signed in this room.

The Grands Appartements were for ceremonial events; Louis XV and Louis XVI retired to the **Petits Appartements** to escape the demands of court life. Louis XV died of smallpox in his bedchamber in 1774. In the second-floor apartment, which can be visited only with a guide, he stashed away Mme du Barry and, earlier, Mme de Pompadour. Also shown is the apartment of Mme de Maintenon, who was first mistress, later wife, of Louis XIV. Attempts have been made to restore the original decor of the Queen's Apartments—as in the days of Marie Antoinette, when she played her harpsichord for specially invited guests.

Louis XVI had an impressive **library,** designed by Gabriel; but library or no library, the monarch remained dim-witted. The library's panels are delicately carved, and the room has been restored and refurnished. The Clock Room contains Passement's famous astronomical clock, which is encased in gilded bronze and is supposed to keep time until the year 9999; it took 20 years to make and was completed in 1753. At the age of 7, Mozart played in this room for the court.

Gabriel designed the **Royal Opéra** for Louis XV in 1748, although it wasn't completed until 1770. The bas-reliefs are by Pajou, and bearskin rugs once covered the floor. At one time, 3,000 powerful candles were needed to light the place. The final restoration of the theater was finished in 1957.

With gold-and-white harmony, Hardouin-Mansart built the **Royal Chapel** between 1699 and 1710. Louis XVI, still the dauphin, married Marie Antoinette here when they were just teenagers.

Versailles

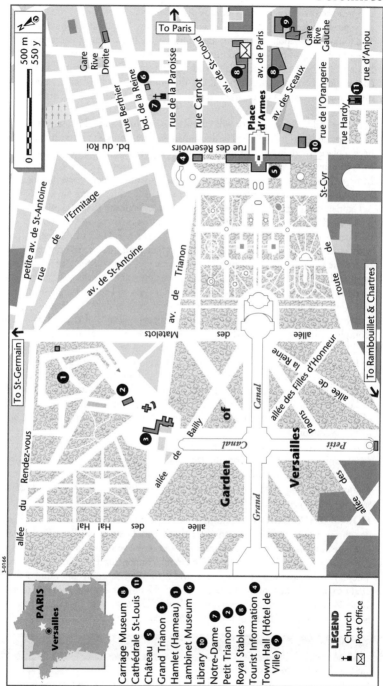

To Paris

Gare Rive Droite

rue Berthier
bd. de la Reine
rue de la Paroisse
rue Carnot
av. de St-Cloud
av. de Paris
av. des Sceaux

Gare Rive Gauche
rue d'Anjou

Place d'Armes
rue des Réservoirs
rue de l'Orangerie
rue Hardy

St-Cyr

To St-Germain

Rendez-vous
allée du Hal
Hal
allée des

petite av. de St-Antoine
rue de l'Ermitage
av. de St-Antoine

av. de Trianon
allée des Matelots

Bailly
allée de

Garden of Versailles

Grand Canal
Canal
Petit Canal

allée de la Reine
allée des Filles d'Honneur
allée de Fleurs

route de

To Rambouillet & Chartres

500 m
550 y

PARIS
Versailles

- Carriage Museum ⑧
- Cathédrale St-Louis ⑤
- Château ⑤
- Grand Trianon ③
- Hamlet (Hameau) ①
- Lambinet Museum ⑥
- Library ⑩
- Notre-Dame ⑦
- Petit Trianon ②
- Royal Stables ⑧
- Tourist Information ④
- Town Hall (Hôtel de Ville) ⑨
- ⑪

LEGEND
+ Church
⊠ Post Office

245

Spread across 250 acres, the **Gardens of Versailles** were laid out by the great land-scape artist André Le Nôtre. At the peak of their glory, 1,400 water fountains played. The fountains of Apollo, Neptune, and Latona—the latter with its statues of people being turned into frogs—are exceptional. Le Nôtre created a Garden of Eden in the Ile de France, using ornamental lakes and canals, geometrically designed flower beds, and avenues bordered with statuary. On the mile-long "Grand Canal," Louis XV, imagining he was in Venice, used to take gondola rides with his "favorite" of the moment.

A long walk across the park will take you to the pink-and-white marble **Grand Trianon,** designed in 1687 by Hardouin-Mansart for Louis XIV. Traditionally, it's been a place where France has lodged important guests, although de Gaulle wanted to turn it into a weekend retreat for himself. Nixon slept here in the room where Mme de Pompadour died, and Napoléon I also spent the night here. The original furnishings are gone, of course; today it's filled mostly with Empire pieces.

Gabriel, the designer of the place de la Concorde, built the **Petit Trianon** in 1768 for Louis XV. Actually, its construction was inspired by Mme de Pompadour, who died before it was complete. Not one to waste a good space, Louis used it for his trysts with Mme du Barry. In time, Marie Antoinette adopted it as her favorite residence, where she could escape the constraints of palace life. Many of the current furnishings, including a few in her modest bedroom, belonged to the ill-fated queen. Napoléon I once presented the Petit Trianon to his sister, Pauline Borghese, but the emperor ungallantly took it back and gave it to his new bride, Marie-Louise.

Behind the Petit Trianon is the **Hamlet,** a collection of small thatched farmhouses (complete with a water mill) where Marie Antoinette could stroll through the farm-yard and be enchanted by the simple tasks of farm life—milking cows, milling grain, and fishing in the lake. It was on October 6, 1789, in a grotto nearby, that she first heard the news that a mob from Paris was marching on Versailles. She quickly fled to the château, never to return to her bucolic retreat. Near the Hamlet is the **Temple of Love,** built in 1775 by Richard Mique, the queen's favorite architect. In the center of its Corinthian colonnade is a reproduction of Bouchardon's *Cupid* shaping a bow from the club of Hercules.

Between the Grand and the Petit Trianons is the entrance to the **Carriage Museum,** which houses coaches from the 18th and 19th centuries, among them one used at the coronation of Charles X and another used at the wedding of Napoléon I and Marie-Louise. One sleigh rests on tortoise runners. (Your ticket to the Petit Trianon will also admit you to see this museum.)

HOURS & ADMISSION   From May 2 to September 30, the palace is open Tuesday through Sunday from 9am to 6pm; the Grand Trianon and Petit Trianon are open the same days from 10am to 6pm. The rest of the year, the palace is open Tuesday to Sunday from 9am to 5:30pm; the Grand Trianon and Petit Trianon are open Tuesday to Friday from 10am to noon and 2 to 5pm, Saturday and Sunday from 10am to 5pm. Admission to the palace is 45F ($7.80) for adults; 35F ($6) for ages 18 to 24 and over 60, and for everyone on Sunday. Admission to the Grand Trianon is 25F ($4.35) and 15F ($2.60) for the Petit Trianon.

2 Fontainebleau

37 miles S of Paris, 46 miles NE of Orléans

Napoléon called the **Palais de Fontainebleau** (☎ 01-60-71-50-70) the house of the centuries, and indeed rightly so, for this château contains more than 700 years of royal history, from the enthronement of Louis VII in 1137 to the fall of the

Fontainebleau

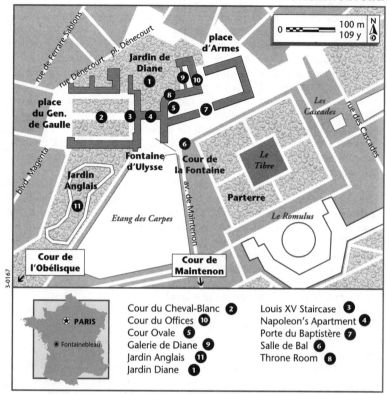

Cour du Cheval-Blanc ②
Cour du Offices ⑩
Cour Ovale ⑤
Galerie de Diane ⑨
Jardin Anglais ⑪
Jardin Diane ①
Louis XV Staircase ③
Napoleon's Apartment ④
Porte du Baptistère ⑦
Salle de Bal ⑥
Throne Room ⑧

Second Empire. It has witnessed many great and poignant moments in French history, few more moving than Napoléon's farewell to his Imperial Guard, which he delivered from the horseshoe-shaped stairway before leaving for Elba and exile. That scene has been the subject of numerous paintings, including Vernet's *Les adieux*.

GETTING THERE   Trains to Fontainebleau depart from the Gare de Lyon in Paris and take from 35 minutes to an hour. Fontainebleau station is just outside the town in Avon, a suburb of Paris; the town bus makes the 2-mile trip to the château every 10 to 15 minutes on weekdays, every 30 minutes on Sundays.

TOURING THE PALACE

Napoléon's affection for Fontainebleau was understandable: He was emulating many earlier French kings, who used Fontainebleau as a retreat and hunted in its magnificent forests. François I rebuilt part of the château in the Renaissance style, importing Italian artisans to design and craft the interiors. Their work—fresco, stucco, and boiserie—can be seen in the Gallery François I, the ballroom, and on the Duchesse d'Etampes staircase. Painters Rosso Fiorentino and Primaticcio adorned the 210-foot-long **Gallery of François I.** Stucco-framed paintings depict mythological and allegorical scenes related to the life of François I. The salamander, symbol of the Chevalier King, is everywhere.

If it is true that François I built Fontainebleau for his mistress, then his successor, Henri II, left a fitting memorial to the woman he loved, Diane de Poitiers. Sometimes called the Gallery of Henri II, the **Ballroom** is in the mannerist style, and the monograms H & D are interlaced in the decoration. At one end of the room is a monumental fireplace supported by two bronze satyrs, made in 1966 (the originals were melted down in the Revolution). At the other side is the salon of the musicians, with sculptured garlands. The coffered ceiling is adorned with rosettes. Above the wainscoting is a series of frescoes, painted between 1550 and 1558, which depict such mythological subjects as *The Feast of Bacchus.*

An architectural curiosity is the richly and elegantly adorned **Louis XV Staircase.** The ceiling above it was originally decorated by Primaticcio for the bedroom of the duchesse d'Etampes; but when an architect was designing the stairway, he simply ripped out her floor and used the bedroom ceiling to cover the stairway. Of the Italian frescoes that were preserved, one depicts the Queen of the Amazons climbing into Alexander's bed.

When Louis XIV ascended to the throne, Fontainebleau was largely neglected because of his preoccupation with Versailles. However, he wasn't opposed to using the palace for house guests—specifically such unwanted ones as Queen Christina, who had abdicated the throne of Sweden. Apparently thinking she still had "divine right," she ordered one of the most brutal royal murders on record—that of her lover, Monaldeschi, who had ceased to please her.

Although neglected by Louis XIV and his heirs, Fontainebleau found renewed glory under Napoléon I. You can walk around much of the palace on your own, but most of the **Napoleonic Rooms** are accessible by guided tour only. His throne room and bedroom (look for his symbol, a bee) are equally impressive. You can also see where the emperor signed his abdication—the document exhibited is a copy. The furnishings in Empress Joséphine's apartments and the grand apartments of Napoléon evoke the imperial heyday.

Minor apartments include those once occupied by Mme de Maintenon, the second wife of Louis XIV. Another was occupied by Pope Pius VII, who was kept a virtual prisoner by Napoléon; still another was occupied by Marie Antoinette.

The Chinese collections of Empress Eugénie are on display in the Napoléon III salons.

After a visit to the palace, wander through the **gardens** and see especially the carp pond; the gardens, however, are only a prelude to the forest of Fontainebleau.

HOURS & ADMISSION   Château de Fontainebleau: 35F ($6) for adults; 23F ($4) for ages 18 to 24 and over 60, and for everyone else on Sunday. Open Wednesday to Monday from 9:30am to 12:30pm and 2 to 5pm November to May; 9:30am to 5pm June; 9:30am to 6pm July and August; 9:30am to 5pm September.

3 Chartres

60 miles SW of Paris, 47 miles NW of Orléans

"For a visit to Chartres, choose some pleasant morning when the lights are soft, for one wants to be welcome, and the Cathedral has moods, at times severe." Thus wrote Henry Adams in *Mont-Saint-Michel and Chartres,* and, yes, the cathedral may at times have severe moods—as gray and cold as the winter weather in the Ile de France— but it's always astonishingly beautiful, with its harmonious architecture and lofty stained-glass windows.

GETTING THERE   Trains run frequently from Paris's Gare Montparnasse to the town of Chartres. A round-trip ticket costs about 140F ($24.35); the trip takes about an hour each way.

SEEING THE CATHEDRAL

The **Cathédrale de Notre-Dame-de-Chartres** (☎ 01-37-21-32-33) is one of the greatest Gothic cathedrals and one of the finest creations of the Middle Ages. It survived the French Revolution (when it was scheduled for demolition) and two world wars. Take one of the excellent **guided tours** (30F/$5.20)of the cathedral—especially those by Englishman Malcolm Miller (☎ 02-37-28-15-58). Mr. Miller gives tours daily except Sunday at noon and 2:45pm from Easter to November and is sometimes available in winter as well. Save some time to stroll around the graceful, tranquil town of Chartres.

Before entering the cathedral, contemplate the awesome royal portal. Reportedly, Rodin sat for hours on the edge of the sidewalk, spellbound by the sculptures. To him, Chartres was the French Acropolis.

The origins of the cathedral are uncertain; some have suggested that it was built on the site of an ancient Druid shrine and, later, a Roman temple. There was a Christian basilica here as early as the 4th century. A fire in 1194 destroyed most of what had then become a Romanesque cathedral, but it spared the western facade and the crypt. The cathedral that you see today dates principally from the 13th century, when it was built with the combined efforts and contributions of kings, princes, church officials, and pilgrims from all over Europe.

One of the greatest of the world's high Gothic cathedrals, it was one of the first to use flying buttresses.

The **Clocher Vieux (Old Tower)** has a 350-foot-high steeple and dates from the 12th century. The so-called **Clocher Neuf (New Tower)** is from 1134, although the elaborate ornamental tower was added between 1507 and 1513 by Jehan de Beauce, following one of the many fires that swept over the cathedral.

French sculpture in the 12th century came into bloom with the construction of the **Royal Portal** on the west front. A landmark in Romanesque art, the sculptured bodies are elongated and draped in long, flowing robes; the faces are amazingly lifelike. In the central tympanum, Christ is shown in all his majesty at the Second Coming, while his nativity is depicted on the right, his ascent on the left. Before entering, walk around to both the north and south portals, each dating from the 13th century. The bays depict such biblical scenes as the expulsion of Adam and Eve from the Garden of Eden and scenes from the life of the Virgin.

Inside is a celebrated **choir screen;** work on it began in the 16th century and lasted until 1714. The niches, 40 in all, contain statues illustrating scenes from the life of Mary.

But few of the rushed visitors ever notice the screen; they're too transfixed by the light from the **stained-glass windows.** Covering more than 3,000 square yards, the glass is unequaled anywhere in the world and is truly mystical. It was spared in both world wars because of a decision to remove it—piece by piece. Most of the stained glass dates from the 12th and 13th centuries.

It is difficult to single out one panel or window of special merit; however, an exceptional one is the 12th-century *Notre Dame de la belle verrière* (Our Lady of the Beautiful Window) on the south side. And of course, the three fiery rose windows are spectacular.

The nave—the widest in France—still contains its ancient labyrinth. The wooden **Virgin of the Pillar,** to the left of the choir, dates from the 14th century. The crypt was built over a period of 200 years, beginning in the 9th century. Enshrined is **Our Lady of the Crypt,** a 1976 Madonna that replaces one destroyed during the French Revolution.

HOURS & ADMISSION   Entrance to the **cathedral** is free. It's open daily April through September 7:30am to 7:30pm; October through March, it's open 7:30am to 7pm. French-language tours of the cathedral are given in summer Tuesday through Saturday at 10:30am and daily at 3pm; in winter, they are given daily at 2:30pm. Ask at the Chartres tourist office (☎ **02-37-21-50-00**) outside the cathedral about tours in English.

Tours of the crypt are given at 11am and 2:15, 3:30, and 4:30pm (also at 5:15pm in summer). The crypt tour costs 10F ($1.75) for adults, 7F ($1.20) for ages 18 to 24 and over 60.

From April to September, the **tower** is open Monday to Saturday from 9:30 to 11:30am and daily from 2 to 5:30pm; October to March, hours are Monday to Saturday 10 to 11:30am and daily from 2 to 4pm. Admission to the tower is 20F ($3.45) for adults, 10F ($1.75) for young people and seniors.

4 Disneyland Paris

20 miles E of Paris

After evoking some of the most enthusiastic and most controversial reactions in recent French history, **Disneyland Paris** opened its doors in 1992 as one of the most lavish theme parks in the world. Set on a 5,000-acre site (about one-fifth the size of Paris) in the suburb of Marne-la-Vallée, the park incorporates the elements of its Disney predecessors but gives them a European flair.

The Disneyland Paris resort is conceived as a total vacation destination, clustering together five different "lands" of entertainment, six massive and well-designed hotels, a campground, and dozens of restaurants, shows, and shops. Visitors from virtually every country in Europe stroll amid an abundance of flower beds, trees, reflecting ponds, fountains, and a very large artificial lake flanked with hotels. An army of smiling and largely multilingual employees and Disney characters—including Buffalo Bill, Mickey and Minnie Mouse, and Caribbean pirate Jean Laffitte—are on hand to greet and delight the thousands of children in attendance.

GETTING THERE   **By Train**   Take the RER Line A from the center of Paris (Invalides, Nation, or Châtelet-Les Halles) to Marne-la-Vallée/Chessy, a 45-minute ride. The round-trip fare is 38F ($6.60). Trains run every 10 to 20 minutes, depending on the time of day.

By Bus   Each of the hotels within the resort is connected by shuttle bus to and from Orly Airport (departing every 45 minutes daily between 9am and 7pm) and Roissy-Charles-de-Gaulle (departing every 45 minutes daily between 8am and 8pm). One-way transport to the park from either airport costs 80F ($13.90). Within the park, a free shuttle bus connects the various hotels with the theme park, stopping every 6 to 15 minutes, depending on the time of year. They begin their runs an hour before the opening of the park and stop an hour after its closing.

By Car   Take the A-4 highway east. Exit where it's marked "Park Euro Disney." Guest parking at any of the thousands of parking spaces costs 40F ($7). An interconnected series of moving sidewalks speeds up pedestrian transit from the parking areas to the entrance of the theme park.

For more information, contact the **Disneyland Paris Guest Relations** office, located within City Hall on Main Street, U.S.A. (☎ **01-64-74-30-00**).

THINGS TO SEE & DO

Of the attractions, Main Street, U.S.A., is replete with horse-drawn carriages and street-corner barbershop quartets. From there, steam-powered railway cars embark from Main Street Station for a trip through a Grand Canyon Diorama to Frontier-land, with its paddle-wheel steamers, "The Critter Corral at the Cottonwood Creek Ranch" petting zoo, and "The Lucky Nugget Saloon," straight from the gold-rush era. There, visitors find an array of cancan shows (which, ironically enough, origi-nated in the cabarets of turn-of-the-century Paris).

The resort's steam trains chug past Adventureland—with its swashbuckling 18th-century pirates, its Swiss family Robinson tree house, and its reenacted legends from the *Arabian Nights*—and then on to Fantasyland. There lies the sym-bol of the theme park: the Sleeping Beauty Castle ("Le Château de la Belle au Bois Dormant"), the soaring pinnacles and turrets of which are an idealized interpretation of the châteaux of France. Parading within its shadow are time-tested though Euro-peanized versions of Snow White and the Seven Dwarfs, Peter Pan, Dumbo the Flying Elephant, Alice in Wonderland's Mad Tea Party, and Sir Lancelot's magic carousel.

Visions of the future are exhibited at Discoveryland, whose tributes to human invention and imagination are drawn from the works of Leonardo da Vinci. . .Jules Verne, H. G. Wells, the modern masters of science fiction. . .and the *Star Wars* trilogy.

The latest attraction is Space Mountain, which sends riders on a virtual journey from the earth to the moon via the Milky Way.

In addition to the theme park, Disney maintains an entertainment center, **Le Festival Disney,** the layout of which might remind visitors of a mall in California. Illuminated inside by a spectacular gridwork of lights suspended 60 feet above the ground, the complex contains dance clubs, shops, restaurants, bars, a French govern-ment tourist office, post office, baby-sitting service, and a marina. Outside the park is a 27-hole golf course, swimming pools, and tennis courts.

HOURS & ADMISSION   Admission for one day costs 195F ($34) for adults (ages 12 and over) and 150F ($26) for children ages 3 to 11. Off-season (early Novem-ber to late March) prices are 150F ($26) and 120F ($20.85) respectively. Open Mon-day to Friday from 9am to 6pm, Saturday and Sunday 10am to 7pm.

TOURS   Guided tours can be arranged for 45F ($7.80) for adults and 35F ($6) for children ages 3 to 11. Tours last 3^1/2 hours and group size is generally 20 or more. The tours offer one of the best opportunities for a complete visit.

FOR FAMILIES   Children's **strollers** and **wheelchairs** can be rented for 30F ($5.20) per day, with a 50F ($8.70) deposit.

5 Giverny—Following in the Footsteps of Claude Monet

50 miles NW of Paris

Even before you arrive at Giverny, it's very likely that you'll already have some idea of what you're going to see, since Claude Monet's paintings of his garden are known and loved throughout the world.

Monet moved to Giverny in 1883, and the water lilies beneath the Japanese bridge in the garden, as well as the flower garden, became his regular subjects until his death in 1926. In 1966, the Monet family donated Giverny to the Academie des Beaux-Arts in Paris, perhaps the most prestigious fine-arts school in France, and they sub-sequently decided to open the site to the public. It has since become one of the most popular attractions in France, but even the crowds can't completely overwhelm the magic of this place.

Though the gardens are lovely year-round, they're usually at their best in May and June and again in September and October. Should you yearn to have them almost to yourself, you should plan to be at the gates some morning when they first open. For more information, call ☎ **02-32-51-28-21.**

GETTING THERE   By Train   Trains leaves the Gare Saint Lazare in Paris approximately every 45 minutes for Vernon, the town nearest the Monet gardens. The fare is roughly 132F ($23). From the station, buses make the 3-mile trip to the museum for 11F ($1.90) or you can go on foot—the route along the Seine makes for a nice walk.

By Car   Take autoroute A13 from the Porte d'Auteuil to Bonnieres, and then D201 to Giverny.

HOURS & ADMISSION   The gardens are open from April to October from 10am to 6pm Tuesday through Sunday. Admission to the house and gardens is 35F ($6) adults, 25F ($4.35) students, 20F ($3.45) ages 7 to 12; gardens only 25F ($4.35).

Appendix

A Menu Terms

Aiguillettes Long thin slivers, usually of duck
Aïolli Garlic-laced mayonnaise
A l'ancienne Old-fashioned, "in the style of grandmother"
Alsacien/à l'alasacienne Alsace-style (usually with sauerkraut, foie gras, or sausage)
Amuse-gueule A preappetizer
Andouillette Chitterling or tripe sausage
A point Medium rare
Assiette du pêcheur Mixed seafood plate
Ballottine Deboned, stuffed, and rolled poultry
Basquais/à la basquaise Basque-style, usually with tomatoes, red peppers, and ham
Béarnaise Sauce made with egg yolks, shallots, white wine, vinegar, butter, and tarragon
Béchamel Buttery white-flour sauce flavored with onion and herbs
Beurre blanc "White butter" sauce with white wine, butter, and shallots
Bigarade Bitter orange sauce, often served with duck
Blanc de volaille Breast of hen
Blanquette Stewed meat with white sauce, cream, and eggs
Boeuf à la mode Marinated beef braised with red wine and served with vegetables
Boeuf en Daube Beef stew with red wine
Bordelais/à la bordelaise Bordeaux-style; usually accompanied with a wine-laced brown sauce flavored with shallots, tarragon, and bone marrow
Boudin noir blood sausage
Bouillabaisse Mediterranean fish soup, made with tomatoes, garlic, saffron, and olive oil
Bourguignon/à la bourguignonne Burgundy-style, usually with red wine, mushrooms, bacon, and onions
Bourride Mediterranean fish soup with aïoli, served over slices of bread
Breton/à la bretonne Brittany-style, often with white beans
Brunoise Tiny cut-up vegetables

Canard à la presse   Duck killed by suffocation, then pressed to extract the blood and juices, which are simmered with cognac and red wine

Canard sauvage   Wild duck

Carbonnade   Beef stew, originally from Flandres, often cooked with beer

Carré d'agneau   Crown roast or loin of lamb

Cassolette   Dish served in a small casserole

Cassoulet   Toulousien specialty of white beans cooked with preserved goose or duck, pig's trotters, sausages, carrots, and onions

Céleri rémoulade   Shredded celery root with a tangy mayonnaise

Cèpes à la bordelaise   Large, meaty wild boletus mushrooms cooked with oil, shallots, and herbs

Choucrôute garni   Alsatian sauerkraut garnished with pork products and boiled potatoes

Cochon de lait   Roast suckling pig

Confit   Meat (usually duck or goose) cooked and preserved in its own fat

Coq au vin   Chicken stewed with mushrooms and red wine

Côte d'agneau   Lamb chop

Côte de boeuf   Rib steak

Court-bouillon   A broth with white wine, herbs, carrots, and soup greens in which poultry, fish, or meat is cooked

Crème brûlée   Thick custard dessert with a caramelized topping

Crème Chantilly   Sugared whipped cream

Crème fraîche   Sour heavy cream

Crème pâtissière   Custard filling for cakes

Croque-monsieur   Toasted sandwich containing cheese and ham; if prepared with a fried egg on top, it's called a *croque-madame*

Darne   A slice of fish steak, usually salmon

Daurade   Prized sea bream (similar to porgy)

Desmoiselles de Cherbourg   Small Norman lobsters in court-bouillon

Diable   Deviled and peppery

Digestif   Any after-dinner liqueur (such as Armagnac) that is presumed to aid the digestive processes

Dijonnais/à la dijonnaise   Denotes the presence of mustard in a dish, usually Dijon

Duxelles   Chopped shallots and mushrooms sautéed and mixed with rich cream

Eau-de-vie   "Water of life"—brandy distilled from fruit or herbs; usually has a very high alcohol percentage and is consumed at the end of a meal

Ecrevisse   Freshwater crayfish

Escabèche   Provençale dish of small fish (often sardines) browned in olive oil, marinated, and served cold

Escargot de Bourgogne   Land snail prepared with garlic, parsley, and butter

Estoficado   Purée of dried codfish, tomatoes, olive oil, onions, and herbs; a specialty of Nice

Faisan   Pheasant

Farci   Stuffed

Feu de bois, au   Cooked over a wood fire

Fraise des bois   Wild strawberry

Française, à la   Garnish of peas with lettuce, pearl onions, and herbs

Fricassée   Braised meat or poultry stew; any medley of meat, even fish, that is stewed or sautéed

Friture   Fried food

Fromage Blanc   White cheese (like cottage cheese)

Fumet   Fish-based stock

Galantine   Classic dish of cooked meat or fowl, served cold in jelly aspic

Galette   Flat round cake or pastry; in Brittany, a crêpe of buckwheat flour

Garni   Garnished

Gâteau   Cake

Gelée   Jelly or aspic

Gibelotte   Rabbit fricassee in wine sauce

Gigot   Haunch (or leg) of an animal, almost always that of lamb or mutton

Glace   Ice in general; ice cream in particular

Gratin   Brown crust that forms on top of a dish when it's oven-browned; a dish that is covered with bread crumbs and melted cheese

Grenouilles   Frogs' legs

Grillé   Grilled

Herbes de Provence   A medley of rosemary, summer savory, bay leaf, and thyme

Hollandaise   Yellow sauce of egg yolk, butter, and lemon juice whipped into a smooth blend

Homard à l'armoricaine   Lobster browned and simmered with shallots, cognac, white wine, and onions

Huile d'olive   Olive oil

Ile flottante   "Floating Island," a rich dessert of a kirsch-soaked biscuit dressed with maraschino cherries and whipped cream

Jambon de Bayonne   Salt-cured ham from the Basque region

Jardinière   Garnish of freshly cooked vegetables

Jus   Juice; *Au jus* means with natural, unthickened gravy

Landais/à la landaise   Landes-style—a garnish of goose fat, pine nuts, and garlic

Langouste   Clawless spiny lobster or rock lobster

Langoustine   Clawed crustacean (in Britain, a prawn)

Lardons   Cubes of bacon, often served with soups and salads

Léger/légère   Light in texture, flavor, and calories

Limande   Lemon sole

Lotte   Monkfish or angler fish

Lou margret   Breast of fattened duck

Loup de mer   Wolf-fish, a Mediterranean sea bass

Lyonnais/à la lyonnaise   White-wine sauce with shredded and sautéed onions

Macédoins   Medley of diced vegetables or fruits

Marchand de vins   Wine merchant; it also implies a rich sauce made from shallots and red wine

Marmite   A thick soup made from beef and vegetables, simmered for hours on a low fire; also, the pot in which the soup is cooked. A *marmite des pêcheurs* refers to a fish soup, or stew, prepared in a marmite

Ménagère, à la   "Housewife style"—accompanied by potatoes, onions, and carrots

Meunière, à la   "In the style of the Miller's wife"—rolled in flour and sautéed in butter

Meurette   A red-wine sauce, often served with poached eggs and freshwater fish; any wine sauce

Mignonette   A substance (usually beef) cut into small cubes

Mille-feuille   A napoleon

Mirepoix   Minced onions, ham, and carrots sautéed in butter and flavored with herbs

Mornay   Béchamel sauce flavored with cheese

Moules à la marinière   Mussels in herb-flavored white wine with shallots

Nage, à la   An aromatic court-bouillon used for poaching

Nantua   Pink sauce made of white wine, crayfish, and tomatoes

Navarin   Mutton prepared with potatoes and turnips

Normande   Sauce of eggs, cream, and mushrooms, Norman-style; meat or fish flavored with Calvados

Oeufs à la neige   "Eggs in snow"—beaten egg whites poached in milk and served with a vanilla-flavored custard

Omelette norvégienne   Baked Alaska à la française

Pain   Bread

Palourde   Clamlike mollusk, most often stuffed

Pamplemousse   Grapefruit

Panaché   Any mixture

Papillote, en   Cooked in parchment paper

Parfait   Layered ice cream dessert

Parisienne, à la   With leeks and potatoes

Parmentier   A dish with potatoes

Pâté feuilletée   Puff pastry

Paysanne   Chicken or meat braised and garnished with vegetables

Périgourdine, à la   Sauce usually made with foie gras and truffles

Pipérade   Classic Basque dish of scrambled eggs with onions, tomatoes, peppers, and ham

Piquante   Tangy sauce made with shallots, vinegar, herbs, small pickles, and white wine

Pistou   Sauce of garlic, fresh basil, and olive oil, from Provence

Plat du jour   The daily special

Poêlé   Panfried

Poisson   Fish—*de mer* is from the ocean; *de lac* from the lake; *de rivière* from the river

Poivrade   Peppery brown sauce made with wine and vinegar

Pomme   Apple

Pommes de terre   Potatoes; *pommes de terre* is frequently shortened to *pommes,* as in *pommes frites* (french fries)

Porc   Pork; *porc salé* is salt pork

Pot-au-feu   "Pot on the fire"—meat stew cooked in an earthenware pot

Poulet, poularde   Chicken—*poulet fermier* is free-range; *poussin* is a chick

Pré salé   Seaside meadow whose grasses are said to be beneficial for the pasturing of lambs or sheep; flesh from lambs raised in these meadows is especially succulent

Pressé   Pressed or squeezed, as in fresh orange juice

Prix fixe   A set meal with a fixed price

Profiteroles   Small cream puffs of chou pastry with a filling of whipped cream or custard

Provençal/à la provençale   In the style of Provence, most often with garlic, tomatoes, onion

Purée   Mashed or forced through a sieve

Quenelles   Rolls of pounded and baked fish, often pike, usually served warm; can also be made from chicken or veal

Ragoût   Stew, usually made from beef

Rascasse   A scorpion fish in Mediterranean bouillabaisse

Ratatouille   A Mediterranean medley of peppers, tomato, eggplant, garlic, and onions

Ravigote   Sauce made with vinegar, lemon sauce, white wine, shallot butter, and herbs

Rémoulade   Cold mayonnaise flavored with mustard

Rillettes   Minced pork spread, popular in Tours

Ris de veau   Veal sweetbreads

Rognons   Kidneys, usually veal

Rosé   Meat or poultry cooked rare

Rôti   Roasted

Rouennaise, canard à la   Duck stuffed with its liver in a blood-thickened sauce

Rouille   Olive-oil based mayonnaise, with peppers, garlic, and fish broth, served with bouillabaisse in Provence

Roulade   Meat or fish roll, most often stuffed

Sabayon   Egg custard flavored with marsala wine

Saignant/saignante   "Bleeding"; rare

Salade Lyonnaise   Green salad flavored with cubed bacon and soft-boiled eggs

Salade Niçoise   Made with tomatoes, green beans, tuna, black olives, potatoes, artichokes, and capers

Salade verte   Green salad

Sandre   Pickerel; a perchlike river fish

Saucisse   French pork sausage

Sole cardinal   Poached filet of sole with a crayfish-flavored cream sauce

Sommelier   Wine steward

Soubise   A béchamel sauce with onion

Soufflé   A "blown up" fluffy baked egg dish flavored with almost anything, from cream cheese to Grand Marnier

Steak au poivre   Pepper steak, covered with fresh peppercorns, with a cognac flambé

Suprême   White sauce made with heavy cream

Table d'hôte   A fixed-price preselected meal, usually offering a limited (if any) choice of the specific dishes that comprise it

Tartare   Any preparation of cold chopped raw meat flavored with piquant sauces and spices (including capers and onions)

Tartare (sauce)   Cold mayonnaise spiced with herbs, vinegar, and mustard

Tarte tatin   Caramelized upside-down apple pie

Tartine   Open-faced sandwich slathered with jam and butter

Terrine   Potted meat or fish in a crock

Timbale   Fish or meat dishes cooked in a casserole

Tournedos Rossini   Beef fillet sautéed in butter with pan juices, served with a foie gras garnish

Tripes à la mode de Caen   Beef tripe cooked in Calvados, with carrots, leeks, onions, herbs, and spices

Truite au bleu   Fish that is gutted moments before being plunged into a mixture of boiling vinegar and water, which turns the flesh blue

Vacherin   Ice cream in a meringue shell; also, a rich cheese from eastern France

Velouté   Classic, velvety sauce, thickened with a *roux* of flour and butter

Véronique, à la   Garnished with peeled white grapes; usually applies to filet of sole

Vichy   With glazed carrots

Vichyssoise   Cold creamy potato-and-leek soup

Vol-au-vent   Puff pastry shell

Xérès, vinaigre de   Sherry flavored vinegar

Index

See also separate Accommodations, Restaurants, and Cafes and Tea Salons indexes, below.

ACCOMMODATIONS

RESTAURANTS

CAFES AND TEA SALONS

Welcome to Paris!
Besides the wonderful discounts we give you,
we will be glad to hand you a surprise gift.
See you soon.

40% DISCOUNT
PERFUMES • HANDBAGS • SILK SCARVES • NECK TIES

3 rue Scribe - 75009 Paris
Tel: 47 42 63 41 - Fax: 40 06 03 14

PARIS
14 Boulevard Montmartre
Metro: Richelieu-Drouot or Rue Montmartre
Tel: 01 53 24 60 00

Present this voucher for complimentary souvenir with any purchase.
One gift per coupon. Expires 12/31/98.

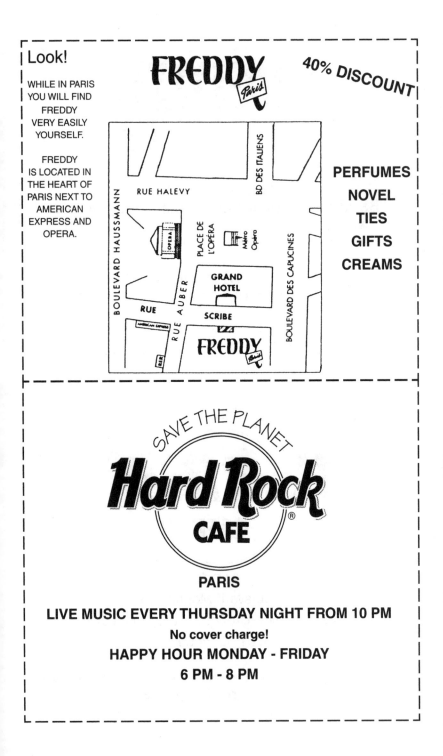

kemwel holiday autos, llc
106 calvert street
harrison, ny 10528-3199

FOR RESERVATIONS CALL:

	1-800-62-SLEEP
	1-800-228-5150
	1-800-228-5151
	1-800-CLARION
	1-800-55-ECONO
	1-800-228-2000

Advance reservations are required through 1-800-4-CHOICE. Discounts are
based on availability at participating hotels and cannot be used in conjunction
with other discounts or promotions.

COMMONWEALTH EXPRESS®

Commonwealth Express is a tour and travel company specializing in trips to **Europe, Eastern Europe, Russia and the CIS.**
For more information call: **800-995-9934**

Coupon Validity

- n Valid January 1 through December 31, 1998.
- n Valid only for purchases in the United States.
- n Valid only for packages purchased directly from Commonwealth Express.
- n Limit one coupon per order.
- n Not valid in conjunction with any other discounts, promotions or packages.

Commonwealth Express, Florida Seller of Travel #ST-16541.

WHEREVER YOU TRAVEL, *H*ELP IS NEVER FAR AWAY.

From planning your trip to providing travel assistance along the way, American Express® Travel Service Offices are always there to help you do more.

Paris

American Express Bureau de Change
14 Bd. de la Madeleine
1/53 30 50 94

American Express Bureau de Change
26 Avenue de L'Opéra
1/53 29 40 39

American Express TFS Bureau de Change
5 rue St. Eleuthère
1/42 23 93 52

American Express Travel Service
11 rue Scribe
1/47 77 77 07

do more

Travel

http://www.americanexpress.com/travel

American Express Travel Service Offices are found in central locations throughout France.